Wireless History

Manuscript 2nd Version

Title: Ubiquity

Subtitle: A Conversational Approach To Understanding: What, When, Who, Where, How and Why of Wireless Telecommunications

Author: Patriot Galt

Copyright: 2019

All rights reserved.

No portion of this work may be reproduced in any way without written permission by the author.

Author Contact US Mail Only:
Equest Publications
5973 Eagle Hill Hts., 105
Colorado Springs, CO 80919

Author Note: The title of the finished work for publication will be *Ubiquity*; subtitled: *A Conversational Approach to Understanding What, When, Who, Where, How and Why of Wireless Telecommunications*. Until the final touches have all been applied and the manuscript is ready for publication, all pre-publications manuscript titles will be some form of Wireless History; subtitled: Manuscript.

Patriot Galt is the pseudonym for Lee Horsman, author of the work.

ACKNOWLEDGMENT

The author thanks the following contributors without whose generous investment of their time, enthusiastic participation in many meetings, telephone conversations and unprecedented expertise this work could not have been accomplished:

    Baroch, Steve
    Bowie, Al
    Deford, William
    Dreese, Greg
    Feige, Larry
    Humphries, Bob
    Mason, Charlie
    Mathis, Carl
    Nelms, Emily
    Nenni, Daniel
    Peterson, Donn
    Reubenstein, Stan
    White, Bob

Table of Contents

Chapter	Title	Page
	Title Page	i
	Acknowledgments	ii
	Nikola Tesla Quote	iii
	Dedication	iv
	Author's Letter To The Student	v
1	In The Beginning	1
2	Early Critical Discoveries	13
3	Vacuum Tubes (Valves – British synonym)	15
4	Transistors & Semiconductors	17
5	Crystal Oscillators	30
6	Telegraphy & Telephony	33
7	AT&T	39
8	Electromagnetism – Electromagnetic Spectrum	43
9	General Electric Research Lab & Charles Proteus Steinmetz	46
10	Electromechanical Telephone Swtiching	49
11	Pre-cellular Mobile Telephones & Paging	57
12	Radio Frequency (RF) Modulation	70
13	2 Cellular Licensees Per Market	95
14	Antennas (not antennae)	113
15	Let's Talk Radio	118
16	Paging	131
17	The Invention Of Voice Mail	144
18	Big RF (cellular/PCS) Systems Manufacturers	149
19	Major Carriers	162
20	What Is PCS? (aka: PCN – Personal Communications Networks)	183
21	History Of Numbering	187
22	Circuit Switching & Packet Switching	190
23	Cellular Fundamentals	198
24	Cellular/PCS: AMPS-5G	204
25	Iridium	221
	Appendix A	225
	Appendix B	227
	Appendix C	240

"When wireless is perfectly applied, the whole earth will be converted into a huge brain, which in fact it is, all things being particles of a real and rhythmic whole.

We shall be able to communicate with one another instantly, irrespective of distance.

Not only this but, through television and telephony, we shall see and hear one another as perfectly as though we were face to face, despite intervening distances of thousands of miles and the instruments through which we shall be able to accomplish our will, will be amazingly simple compared with our present telephone.

A man will be able to carry one in his vest pocket."

Nikola Tesla, 1926

Dedication

This book is dedicated to Jonah.

Jonah is the author's model for the young, fearless engineering student to whom this text is directed. He is determined to make a positive difference in the world around him.

With so many different engineering disciplines from which to pursue a career, Jonah is faced with daunting choices and challenges. His academic record places him well above average as a high school graduate and early college entrant. His future is bright regardless of the engineering field he chooses to enter

Considering the wide variety of engineering disciplines to pursue, the Jonahs of today are often left to their own devices to make lifetime altering decisions without benefit of practical experience embodied in men and women who have devoted years to careers who are also treasure troves of information that could assist in the decision-making process.

To Jonah and all of his counterparts, in Tesla's breathtaking visionary style, the world is counting on you to catapult it onto the stage of the future.

This book is intended to assist you in your contemplations of opportunities you may otherwise miss.

Author's letter to the student...

My career, spanning thirty-seven years (1973-2010) in wireless communications, encourages me to deliver a textbook I hope will motivate you to study rigorously as you prepare for your career regardless of the discipline you choose.

If you are a high school or college age student not yet aware of possible career opportunities in telecommunications, studying this text may provide encouragement to consider one of many different disciplines that may appeal to you in this field.

My efforts are devoted to producing a reliable, credible and verifiable resource you may keep readily at hand to dispel myths as well as equipping you to understand and appreciate the history, evolution, technologies, products, notable contributors, applications and future implications of technologies, devices, networks and services discovered, invented, produced and distributed during the evolution of telecommunications from its beginning to today's and tomorrow's universe of wireless telecommunications.

Before we delve into the historical and technological areas, it is important to be aware of a few basic concepts and terms.

While it may be hard to believe, there was a lengthy history of analog telecommunications before digital. Fundamentally, all of today's communications were spawned by early analog experiments with electromagnetic energy resulting in telegraphy (technically a form of digital) spawning telephony and wireless (radio) communications.

Let's start by defining: 1) electromagnetism, 2) electricity, 3) electromagnetic spectrum (we will deal with this specific term in much deeper detail), 4) oscillation/frequency, 5) radio, 6) analog, 7) digital, 8) telegraphy, 9) telephony, 10) telemetry, 11) Morse Code.

[1]Definition of Electromagnetism

Phenomena associated with electric and magnetic fields and their interactions with each other and with electric charges and currents

Also electromagnetics: the science that deals with these phenomena

[2]Definition of Electricity

One of the basic properties of the elementary particles of matter giving rise to all electric and magnetic forces and interactions. The two kinds of charge are given negative and positive algebraic signs.

Electric Charge: A form of energy, designated positive, negative, or zero, found on the elementary particles that make up all known matter. Particles with electric charge interact with each other through the electromagnetic force, creating a repulsive force between particles with charges of the same sign, and an attractive force between charges of opposite sign. The electron is defined to have an electric charge of -1; the protons in an atomic nucleus have a charge of +1, and the neutrons have a charge of 0.

In an ordinary atom, the number of protons equals the number of electrons; so, the atom normally has no net electric charge. An atom becomes negatively charged if it gains extra electrons and it becomes positively charged if it loses electrons; atoms with net charge are called ions. Every charged particle is surrounded by an electric field, the area in which the charge exerts a force. Particles with non-zero electric charge interact with each other by exchanging photons, the carriers of the electromagnetic force. The strength and direction of the force charged particles exert on each other depends on the product of their charges: they attract each other if the product of their charges is negative and repel each other if the product is positive. Thus, two electrons, each with negative charge will repel each other since -1 x 1 = +1, a positive number.

Static electricity consists of charged particles at rest.

---

[1] https://www.dictionary.com/browse/electromagnetism
[2] Ibid

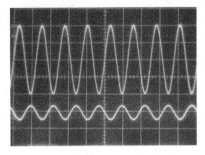

Electric current consists of moving charged particles, especially electrons or ions.

[3]Definition of Electromagnetic Spectrum

The entire spectrum is considered a continuum of all kinds of electric, magnetic and visible radiation from gamma rays with a wavelength of 0.001 angstrom to long waves having a wavelength of more than 1 million kilometers.

[4]Definition of Oscillation

1. Oscillation is going back and forth repeatedly between two positions or states. An oscillation can be a periodic motion that repeats itself in a regular cycle, such as a *sine wave,* the side-to-side swing of a pendulum, or the up-and-down motion of a spring with a weight. An oscillating movement is around an equilibrium point or mean value. It is also known as a periodic motion. One oscillation is a complete movement, whether up and down or side to side over a period of time.

Variables of Oscillation

Amplitude is the maximum displacement from the equilibrium point. If a pendulum swings one centimeter from the equilibrium point before beginning its return journey, the amplitude of oscillation is one centimeter.

Period is the time it takes for a complete round trip by the object, returning to its initial position. If a pendulum starts on the right and takes one second to travel all the way to the left and another second to return to right, its period is two seconds. Period is usually measured in seconds.

Frequency is the number of cycles per unit of time. Frequency equals one divided by the period. Frequency is measured in Hertz, or cycles per second.

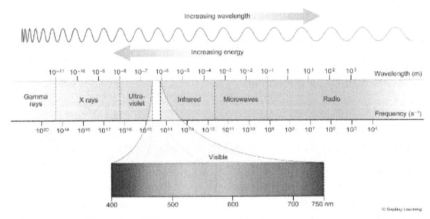

[5]Definition of Radio – 300Hz-300GHz (3THz, Tera-Hertz)

a: Of or relating to electric currents or phenomena of frequencies between about 300 hertz and 300 gigahertz. See spectrum graphic.

b: The wireless transmission and reception of electric impulses or signals by means of electromagnetic waves.

c: The use of these waves for the wireless transmission of electric impulses into which sound is converted.

[6]Definition of Analog

a: Of, relating to, or being a mechanism or device in which information is represented by continuously variable physical quantities. Your speakers are *analog* technology in all its nearly century-old glory. "As the speakers get their signals from the cables, the drivers vibrate in a continual state of flux as the changing *analog* signals are fed to them. The drivers are presenting an analogy of what came from the original source, even if the source started off digital, such as a CD." Ron Goldberg

b: Of, or relating to, an analog computer: In an *analog* machine each number is represented by a suitable physical quantity, whose value, measured in some pre-assigned unit, is equal to the number in question.

---

[3] Ibid
[4] Ibid
[5] Ibid
[6] Ibid

c: *Of a timepiece*: having both hour and minute hands on an *analog* watch.

d: Not digital: not computerized.

[7]Definition of Digital

a: Of, relating to, or using calculation by numerical methods or by discrete units

b: Composed of data in the form of binary digits—*digital* images/photos a *digital* read out, a *digital* broadcast [=a broadcast employing digital communications signals]— compare ANALOG.

c: Providing a readout in numerical digits: a *digital* voltmeter, a *digital* watch/clock.

d: Relating to an audio recording method in which sound waves are represented digitally (as on magnetic tape) so that in the recording, *wow* and *flutter* are eliminated and background noise is reduced.

e: ELECTRONIC *digital* devices/technology *also*: characterized by electronic and especially computerized technology in the *digital* age.

[8]Definition of Telegraphy

Telegraphy is the long-distance transmission of textual or symbolic (as opposed to verbal or audio) messages without the physical exchange of an object bearing the message. Thus semaphore is a method of telegraphy, whereas pigeon post is not.

Telegraphy requires that the method used for encoding the message be known to both sender and receiver. Many methods are designed according to the limits of the signaling medium used. The use of smoke signals, beacons, reflected light signals, and flag semaphore signals are early examples.

In the 19th century, the harnessing of electricity led to the invention of electrical telegraphy. The advent of radio in the early 20th century brought about radiotelegraphy and other forms of wireless telegraphy. In the Internet age, telegraphic means developed greatly in sophistication and ease of use, with natural language interfaces that hide the underlying code, allowing such technologies as electronic mail and instant messaging.

[9]Definition of Telephony

Telephony is the field of technology involving the development, application, and deployment of telecommunication services for the purpose of electronic transmission of voice, fax, or data between distant parties. The history of telephony is linked to the invention and development of the telephone.

Telephony is commonly referred to as the construction or operation of telephones and telephonic systems and as a system of telecommunications in which telephonic equipment is employed in the transmission of speech or other sound between points, with or without the use of wires. The term is also used frequently to refer to computer hardware, software, and computer network systems that perform functions traditionally performed by telephone equipment. In this context the technology includes references to it as Internet telephony, or voice over Internet Protocol (VoIP).

[10]Definition of Telemetry

Telemetry is an automated communications process by which measurements and other data are collected at remote or inaccessible points and transmitted to receiving equipment for monitoring. The word is derived from Greek roots: *tele* = remote, and *metron* = measure. Systems that need external instructions and data to operate require the counterpart of telemetry, telecommand.

Although the term commonly refers to wireless data transfer mechanisms (*e.g.*, radio, ultrasonic, or infrared systems), it also encompasses data transferred over other media such as telephone or computer networks,

---

[7] Ibid
[8] https://www.google.com/search?source=hp&ei=BV_fW4f0JOKcjgTwjbXwCA&q=define+telephony&btnK=Google+Search&oq=define+telephony&gs_l=psy-ab.3.2.0j0i22i30l9.1208.4463..4773...0.0..0.147.1747.5j12......0....1..gws-wiz.....0..35i39j0i67j0i10i67j0i20i263j0i10.ntn8JdozwbU
[9] Ibid
[10] Ibid

optical links or other wired communications like power line carriers. Many modern telemetry systems take advantage of the low cost and ubiquity of cellular networks by using SMS to receive and transmit telemetry data.

A telemeter is a device used to remotely measure any quantity. It consists of a sensor, a transmission path, and a display, recording, or control device. Telemeters are the physical devices used in telemetry. Electronic devices are widely used in telemetry and can be wireless or hard-wired, analog or digital. Other technologies are also possible, such as mechanical, hydraulic and optical.

Telemetry may be commutated to allow the transmission of multiple data streams in a fixed frame.

Author's note: "If it can be measured, it can be metered. If it can be metered, it can be telemetered."

[11]Definition of Morse Code

Morse code is a method of transmitting text information as a series of timed interruptions of steady electric current, on-off tones, lights, or clicks that can be directly understood by a skilled listener or observer without special equipment. It is named for Samuel F. B. Morse. The International Morse Code encodes the ISO basic Latin alphabet, some extra Latin letters, the Arabic numerals and a small set of punctuation and procedural signals (*prosigns*) as standardized sequences of short and long signals called "dots" and "dashes", or "dits" and "dahs", as in amateur radio practice. Because many non-English natural languages use more than 26 letters, extensions to the Morse alphabet exist for those languages.

Each Morse code symbol represents either a text character (letter or numeral) or a *prosign* and is represented by a unique sequence of dots and dashes. The dot duration is the basic unit of time measurement in code trans-mission. The duration of a dash is three times the duration of a dot. Each dot or dash is followed by a short silence equal to the dot duration. The letters of a word are separated by a space equal to three dots (one dash), and the words are separated by a space equal to seven dots. To increase the speed of the communication, the code was designed so that the length of each character in Morse is approximately inverse to its frequency of occurrence in English. Thus the most common letter in English, the letter "E", has the shortest code, a single dot.

SOS, the standard emergency signal, is a Morse code *prosign*.

In an emergency, Morse code can be sent by improvised methods that can be easily "keyed" on and off, making it one of the simplest and most versatile methods of telecommunication. The most common distress signal is SOS – three dots, three dashes, and three dots – internationally recognized by treaty.

[12]Definition of decibel

The **decibel** (symbol: dB) is a unit of measurement used to express the ratio of one value of a physical property to another on a logarithmic scale. It can be used to express a change in value (*e.g.*, +1 dB or −1 dB) or an absolute value. In the latter case, it expresses the ratio of a value to a reference value; when used in this way, the decibel symbol should be appended with a suffix that indicates the reference value, or some other property. For example, if the reference value is 1 volt, then the suffix is "V" (*e.g.*, "20 dBV"), and if the reference value is one milliwatt, then the suffix is "m" (*e.g.*, "20 dBm").

There are two different scales used when expressing a ratio in decibels depending on the nature of the quantities: field power, and root-power. When expressing *power* quantities, the number of decibels is ten times the logarithm to base 10 of the ratio of two power quantities. That is, a change in *power* by a factor of 10 corresponds to a 10 dB change in level. When expressing field quantities, a change in *amplitude* by a factor of 10 corresponds to a 20 dB change in level. The extra factor of two is due to the logarithm of the quadratic relation-ship between power and amplitude. The decibel scales differ so that direct comparisons can be made between related power and field quantities when they are expressed in decibels.

---

[11] Ibid
[12] https://en.wikipedia.org/wiki/Decibel

The definition of the decibel is based on the measurement of power in telephony of the early 20th century in the Bell System in the United States. One decibel is one tenth (deci-) of one **bel**, named in honor of Alexander Graham Bell; however, the *bel* is seldom used. Today, the decibel is used for a wide variety of measurements in science and engineering, most prominently in acoustics, electronics, and control theory. In electronics, the gains of amplifiers, attenuation of signals, and signal-to-noise ratios are often expressed in decibels.

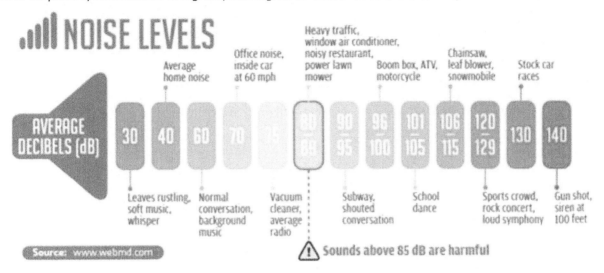

In the International System of Quantities, the decibel is defined as a unit of measurement for quantities of type level or level difference, which are defined as the logarithm of the ratio of power or field-type quantities.

While there will be many more terms, concepts and technical issues to learn, under-standing these listed above are critical to moving forward with this study. In this regard, it is in your best interest to research each one of them. If possible, find an engineer or telecommunications technician with whom you may discuss them. Visiting a radio shop (most cities have a radio communications department with an installation and maintenance shop) to witness technicians operating telecommunications test equipment will help you understand, remember and apply this new vocabulary to your continuing study and potential career. It will give you a real world look at what these terms mean when you see them demonstrated on an oscilloscope, spectrum analyzer or other piece of test equipment. To watch a technician run tests on fiber or coaxial cable, radio equipment, antennas and the RF envelope surrounding a site to locate and resolve interference issues (often called "inter-mod" [intermodulation]), might encourage you to pursue a career in wireless technology as an engineer or technician.

In the absence of technical assistance, searching the web for these terms, reading and deliberating on them, as well as expanding on them by visiting recommended sites will be of significant value. Researching telecommunications equipment, products and test equipment will produce a wealth of valuable information for your purposes. Here are a few suggestions: cellular antennas, coaxial cable, fiber optics, base stations, RF test equipment, spectrum analyzer, oscilloscope, microwave antennas.

In the third paragraph of this letter, I mention dispelling myths. In this regard, there is one particular myth I keep hearing that is so absurd I feel compelled to address it here.

"Cellular" was not invented at a Silicon Valley restaurant by two HP engineers who drew it up on a napkin. As you will learn, the wireless networks and devices associated with the term "cellular" are the culmination of decades of invention, investment, technological evolution and the lifetime dedication of many ingenious and committed scientists, inventors, entrepreneurs, engineers, regulatory controls, and myriad others. Within this text, you will read much of the history as well as many critical intersections of diverse technologies, inventions, and work of dedicated telephone, radio and computer industry giants upon whose shoulders today's telecommunications customers stand.

Just consider your "smart phone." How many components can you imagine require decades of ancestral versions to get to today's advanced designs and materials – CPUs, ICs, transistors, DSPs, miniaturized circuit boards, batteries, plastics, glass and the amazing software? There are so many, no single individual can understand all of them.

In our study, we will delve into these and many more issues to understand what, when, who, where, why and how much of this happened. My hope is that, by studying them in this text, you will appreciate your opportunities to advance the science, application, distribution and utility into the next century where cloud and q-bit computing, coupled with quantum physics and super-conductors will contribute to solutions required to save our habitable planet and you may be the one who, by utilizing all the power and resources at your fingertips, finds a key to reversing global warming, restoring clean air, water, soil and oceans as well as contributing to the possibilities of taking our civilization to the stars.

Wishing you all the best in your studies and career, I am yours sincerely,

Patriot Galt

Patriot Galt

Chapter One -- In The Beginning

UBIQUITY

Ubiquity – to the telephone company it means a physical "wireline" connection to every home and office in the world that will connect any other home or office in the world for the purposes of human-to-human or machine-to-machine or machine-to-human "telecommunications."

Ubiquity – to the radio industry, it means a wireless (non-wireline) network/system with compatible devices connecting anyone, anywhere, any time to anyone else anywhere, any time to facilitate the exchange of voice, data (text, e-mail, machine-to-machine [think telemetry], graphics, video, streaming) and internet connectivity.

Ubiquity – to the World Wide Web user, it means a virtual connection between devices serving humans for any number (perhaps this could qualify for an 'infinite' number) of applications, *e.g.*, voice related, text, e-mail, video, photo sharing, gaming, myriad business applications, social networking and oh, by the way, retention of connections to the 'Public Switched Telephone Network' (PSTN), for anyone, anywhere, any time.

I like to imagine the first early man out hunting, driven by an instinctive commitment to protect his family, too far from his female and family for voice communications, using his son as a communication device to run back and forth from the fire to wherever he was at the time, keeping the mother informed of the father's situation – this, to me, is likely the first out-of-voice-range application demanding a solution. From that to all other methods, *e.g.*, *bullae* - Sumerian dried clay cylinders containing specified numbers of pebbles delivered by traders, printed paper delivered in too many ways to list but pony express and the US Postal Service come to mind, mail packets carried by ships, smoke signals, sticks with marks carried by runners, drum beats, signal fires, flags and semaphores, mirrors, pigeons and likely others drove advancing society to invent everything required to produce today's telecommunications technologies delivering the myriad services we now enjoy in the ubiquitous environment we take for granted.

Figure 1: Marconi's antenna system at Poldhu, Cornwall, England, Dec.,1901. (John Belrose)

It is a mix. No single individual or organization may legitimately claim credit for it. At its base lies a foundation of four fundamental platforms: 1) global electric power grids; 2) telephony; 3) radio; 4) computerization. Within each of these lie myriad disciplines, sciences, inventions, *etc.*, demonstrating primary physics, chemistry, and mathematical principles without which none of what we enjoy today exists.

The pioneers of "anyone, anywhere, anytime" stood on the shoulders of giants who preceded them with the genius and perseverance responsible for emergence from the dark ages with the industrial revolution and political radicalism from which free thinking and new ideas could manage and mine natural resources making them available for inventions and conceptual considerations never before contemplated.

Here is a photo of Marconi's transmitting station when he demonstrated the first transatlantic radio transmission spawning a new age free of physical wiring connections. Take a few minutes to study the photo. How many disparate technologies can you list that are required for Mr. Marconi to construct this facility?

Steel in several different forms is a huge issue, not just for the towers but think of the many different steel products he needed—wires (who delivered the different 'standardized' gauges?), bolts (who devised and standardized different thread systems assuring compatible bolts and nuts?). How were the towers anchored to the earth to withstand the weather conditions common to Cornwall, England, and the wild weather common to Nova Scotia?

These and too many more to list should provide sufficient thought provoking fodder to ignite your imagination. However, the equipment to generate and regulate electromagnetic devices, regardless of their primitive nature, required hundreds of disparate components from suppliers that have long since been relegated to the dust bins of antiquity but were, nevertheless, critical.

Your undivided attention is required as you read, and hopefully thoroughly digest, the following information dispelling myths and delivering realities of wireless telecommunications' origins and fundamentals.

Who really was first to demonstrate wireless (RF) as a way to communicate? The answers delivered by Mr. Belrose in his extraordinarily well researched presentation below will surprise you.

Fessenden and Marconi: Their Differing Technologies and Transatlantic Experiments During the First Decade of this Century

by John S. Belrose[13]; International Conference on 100 Years of Radio -- 5-7 September 1995

1. Introduction

Many scientists and engineers have contributed to the early development of electromagnetic theory, the invention of wireless signaling by radio, and the development of antennas needed to transmit and receive the signals. These include, Henry, Edison, Thomson, Tesla, Dolbear, Stone-Stone, Fessenden, Alexanderson, de Forest and Armstrong in the United States; Hertz, Braun and Slaby in Germany; Faraday, Maxwell, Heaviside, Crookes, Fitzgerald, Lodge, Jackson, Marconi and Fleming in the UK; Branly in France; Popov in the USSR; Lorenz and Poulsen in Denmark; Lorentz in Holland; and Righi in Italy. The inventor of wireless telegraphy, that is messages as distinct from signals, is Italian-born Guglielmo Marconi, working in England; and the inventor of wireless telephony is Canadian-born Reginald Aubrey Fessenden, working in the United States.

According to Marconi, he (Marconi) was an amateur in radio: in fact this was far from the truth. He foresaw the business side of wireless telegraphy. He was aware, however, of his own limitations as a scientist and engineer, and so he enlisted (in 1900) the help of university professor John Ambrose Fleming, as scientific advisor to the Marconi Company; and he chose engineers of notably high caliber, R.N. Vyvyan and others, to form the team with which he surrounded himself. Marconi's systems were based on spark technology, and he persevered with spark until about 1912. He saw no need for voice transmission. He felt the Morse code was adequate for communication between ships and across oceans. He was a pragmatist and uninterested in scientific inquiry in a field where commercial viability was unknown. He, among others, did not foresee the development of the radio and broadcasting industry.

For these reasons Marconi left the early experimentation with wireless telephony to others, Reginald Fessenden and Lee de Forest.

Fessenden was a radio scientist and an engineer, but he did not confine his expertise to one discipline. He worked with equal facility in the chemical, electrical, radio, metallurgical and mechanical fields. He recognized that continuous wave (CW) transmission was required for speech and continued the work of Nikola Tesla, John Stone-Stone, and Elihu Thomson on this subject. Fessenden also felt that he could transmit and receive Morse code better by the continuous wave method than with the spark apparatus that Marconi was using.

This paper overviews the differing technologies of Fessenden and Marconi at the turn of the century, and their endeavours to achieve transatlantic wireless communications.

2. Transatlantic Wireless Communications Began at LF (Low Frequency)

Heinrich Hertz's classical experiments were conducted in his laboratory using a small end-loaded dipole driven by an induction coil and a spark gap for his transmitter. His receiver was a small loop, and detection was by induced sparking. Since the frequency generated by a spark transmitter is determined by the resonant mean

---

[13] **John S. (Jack) Belrose** (born 24 November 1926), is a Canadian radio scientist
#13 footnote continued: He was born in the small town of Warner, Alberta. He attended the University of Cambridge, where he was awarded a PhD in 1958. He has worked for the Defence Research Telecommunications Establishment (DRTE) for 33 years. He is a member of the Canadian Amateur Radio Hall of Fame and, along with Walter Cronkite, was awarded the Radio Club of America's Armstrong Medal on 16 November 2007.

frequency of the antenna system, his experiments in 1887 were conducted at VHF/UHF (60 to 500 MHz) -- the corresponding wavelengths (5.0 to 0.6 metre) being practical for indoor experiments.

Marconi started experimenting with Hertz's apparatus in 1894. He was fascinated by the idea that, by means of Hertzian waves, it might be possible to send telegraph signals, without wires, far enough for such a system to have commercial value. By 1896 he achieved a transmission distance of 2.5 kilometres, by using an earth and an elevated aerial at both transmitter and receiver (nowadays called a Marconi antenna). His first permanent station established a link between the Isle of Wight and Bournemouth, England, some 22 km away (in 1897). He established communications across the Channel in 1899. By now he must have been using frequencies in the low HF band, since his aerial systems were much larger.

In 1900 he decided to try and achieve transatlantic communications. The required aerial size, and so the signaling frequency, at best could only be projected by extrapolation from values successful over a range of much shorter distances. The aerial at Poldhu, Cornwall, in December 1901 (see Fig. 1), more by circumstance than design (to be discussed), radiated signals in the MF (Medium Frequency) band (about 850 kHz).

Marconi kept building larger antenna systems, larger since he was striving for greater transmission distance and improved signal reception, which lowered the operating frequency. At Poldhu the frequency of his station in October 1902 was 272 kHz. His initial station at Table Head, Glace Bay, Nova Scotia, in December 1902, was a massive structure comprising 400 wires suspended from four 61 metre wooden towers, with down leads brought together in an inverted cone at the point of entry into the building. The frequency was 182 kHz. By 1904 his English antenna had become a pyramidal monopole with umbrella wires, and the frequency was 70 kHz. In 1905 his Canadian antenna, moved to Marconi Towers, Glace Bay, was a capacitive top-loaded structure, with 200 horizontal radial wires each 305 metres long, at a height of 55 metres, and the frequency was 82 kHz. By late in 1907 he was using a frequency of 45 kHz.

Fessenden's early experiments using spark transmitters were probably conducted at a frequency in the lower part of the HF band, since initially he was testing over short links of a few kilometres using 50-metre masts to support wire aerials. His belief was that radio transmission should be by way of continuous waves (CW), not the damped-wave or whip-and-lash type of transmission provided by spark-gap transmitters. The only way he knew to generate true CW was by a high-frequency alternator, and in the period 1890-1905 10 kHz was the highest frequency achieved using an HF alternator. But the efficiency of practical aerial systems was very poor at such a low frequency. So he strove to increase the speed and frequency of his HF alternator. In the meantime he invented the synchronous rotary-spark-gap transmitter. His transatlantic experiments in 1906 were conducted using such a transmitter and 420-foot umbrella top loaded antennas at Brant Rock, MA, and Machrihanish, Scotland, tuned to a frequency of about 80 kHz.

3. Marconi and Fessenden – Their Differing Technologies

Marconi, those working with him, and most experimenters in the new field of wireless communications at the turn of the century, were unanimous in their view that a spark was essential for wireless, and he actively pursued this technology from the beginning (in 1895) until about 1912.

Fessenden was a proponent of the continuous wave (CW) method of wireless transmission. Somewhat alone in this direction in 1900-1906, his CW patents had little impact on the users of radio technology. The golden age for spark was from 1900 to 1915; dominated by Marconi, who fought to quell any divergence from that mode. The fact that the damped wave-coherer system could never be developed into a practical operative telegraph system and that the sustained oscillation method should be used was perceived by Fessenden in 1898 [see *Electrical World*, July 29, August 12, September 16, 1899 and *Proceedings American Institute of Electrical Engineers*, November, 1899, p. 635 and November 20, 1906, p. 7311.] In 1900-1902, only two methods were available for generating CW: 1) the HF alternator; and 2) the oscillating arc.

Plain Aerial Apparatus

Marconi's early experiments employed plain aerial apparatus, and placed the spark gap directly across the terminals of his vertical wire aerial-ground antenna. His receiver employed a similar set-up, with a coherer type of detector. The transmitter/receiver systems were untuned, excepting by the natural amplitude-frequency response of the aerials. Unbeknownst to him, his transmitter and receiver were in effect "tuned" to different frequencies. The oscillating damped wave on the transmitting aerial, which was in effect "connected" to ground through the low resistance of the conducting spark, was in effect "tuned" to the fundamental quarter wave resonant response of the aerial. His receiver however, awaiting reception of the spark signal, would in effect be tuned to the half-wave resonant frequency of the wire aerial -- since the coherer, prior to the reception of the RF impulse-like signal, would present a high impedance between the aerial and ground.

This problem was solved by using a closed tuned circuit for the receiver; and for the transmitter by using the circuit arrangement devised by Braun,

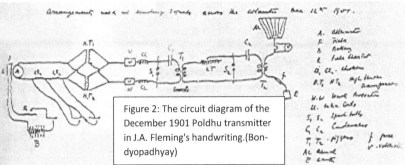

Figure 2: The circuit diagram of the December 1901 Poldhu transmitter in J.A. Fleming's handwriting.(Bondyopadhyay)

in which the oscillatory circuit (discharge capacitor and spark gap) was placed in a separate primary circuit transformer-coupled to the antenna system. This latter arrangement also lengthened the duration of the damped wave signal, since when the spark ceased, the oscillation in the antenna circuit continued, damped only by its natural L-C-R response.

Transmitter Technology

The Poldhu transmitter was a curious two-stage circuit, in which a first-stage spark at some attainable lower voltage provided the energy for the second stage in tandem (Fig. 2), to spark at a specified higher voltage. While this voltage multiplication system was innovative in the field of wireless at the time, it carried with it many problems, and the inefficiencies of two spark stages.

Marconi clearly realized that to achieve high power from a spark transmitter it was necessary to charge the condenser to a very high voltage (voltages of up to 150 kV were spoken about and may have been realized); and that a very large discharge capacitance was needed, since the stored energy in the condenser was understood (Energy equals $1/2\ CV^2$). But he carried the latter requirement to an extreme.

The power capability of the Poldhu AC generator (25 amperes at 1500 volts) in 1901 was insufficient to recharge the condenser every period. It seems like several periods of the supply generator (operating at 36 Hz) were required to bring the condenser voltage to gap break-down potential. Fleming's estimates of the spark rate lie between wide limits. Thackeray [1992] has estimated that the spark rate for the primary circuit was 7.5 to 12 sparks/sec at most; and the spark rate for the secondary circuit might have been as low as two or three sparks/sec. After that time there was clearly a redesign to a single-stage transmitter that sparked directly from the power transformer; and Fleming began to develop rotating dischargers in an attempt to achieve rapid quenching of the spark.

It is perhaps ironic that the low spark rate was compromised by Marconi himself, when in Newfoundland he put a telephone receiver to his ear to listen for the dot transmissions from Poldhu. At the low spark rate he employed, all he would hear would be a click, not distinguishable from an atmospheric. But recall that Marconi's early experience was with coherer-type detectors, which worked best when the spark rate was low.

Before leaving our discussion about Marconi's methodology, let me comment on some of the physical arrangements for his stations. The discharge capacitor for his Clifden and Marconi Towers, Glace Bay stations consisted of thousands of steel plates hanging from floor to ceiling (see photo), which filled the wings of the building, and this room was subsequently called the "condenser building." The power supply was a 15 kV DC generator (three 5 kV generators in series) driven by a steam engine. Note the power source was DC. Standby batteries (6000, 2 volt, 30 AH batteries in series) at both stations may well have been the largest battery the world has ever seen. The heart of his Clifden/Marconi Towers stations was a whirling five foot spark discharge disk, with studs on its perimeter. Each time a stud passed between two electrodes, a 15 kV spark jumped the gaps. The regular spark rate was about 350 sparks/sec. The awesome size of the station and the din of the transmitter must have been something to behold. The power consumed by these stations was in the range of 100 to 300 kW, and the spark was a display of raw power. It is said that the awesome din of the transmitter could be heard several kilometres away.

Fessenden's technology and circuit arrangements were very different. He tried all the various methods of generating wireless signals in the early days, by spark, by arc and by the high frequency alternator. It is likely that he would have used the HF alternator from the outset, see for example his patent No. 706,787 filed 29 May 1901; except that a suitable HF alternator, generating frequencies above about 10 kHz, was not available until 1906. There is no fundamental reason that long distance wireless communications could not have begun at VLF, except for the practical realization of efficient antenna systems for such a low frequency.

Fessenden's work was dominated by his interest in transmitting words without wires. By 1903 and 1904 fairly satisfactory speech had been transmitted by the arc method, but the news of Marconi's attempts to achieve transatlantic wireless telegraphy transmission had caught the attention of the world. Since the development of his HF alternator was taking longer than anticipated, Fessenden set his mind to make a more CW-like spark transmitter. This led to the development of the synchronous rotary-spark-gap transmitter. An AC generator was used, driven by a steam engine, which, as well as providing the energy for the spark transmitter, was directly coupled to a rotating spark gap so that sparks occurred at precise points on the input wave, *viz.* at waveform maximum for best efficiency. The spark was between fixed terminals on the stator and terminals on the rotor, which was in effect a spoked wheel, rotating in synchronism with the AC generator.

As the speed of the wheel and the AC frequency both depend on the speed of the generator, the number of times/sec at which the condenser voltage reaches a peak value and the number of opportunities it has for discharging can be made equal, and the positions of the stator terminals can be arranged so that these conditions occur simultaneously. Another advantage was realized, since in effect a rotary gap was a kind of mechanically quenched spark-gap transmitter. The oscillations in the primary circuit ceased after a few oscillations, when the rotating gap opened. The quenched gap was more efficient and certainly less noisy than the unquenched gap.

With a synchronous spark-discharger phased to fire on both positive and negative peaks of a 3-phase waveform, precisely at waveform peak, a 125 Hz generator could produce a spark rate of 750 times a second. These rotating gaps produced clear almost musical signals, very distinctive and easily distinguished from any other signal at the time. It was not true CW but it came as close as possible to that, and the musical tone could be easily read through noise and interference from other transmitters.

Fessenden's Brant Rock and Machrihanish stations employed a rotary gap 1.8 metres in diameter at the rotor. Its rotor had 50 electrodes (poles) and its stator had four. It was driven by a 35 kVA alternator, powered by a steam engine.

The synchronous rotary gap spark discharger should not be confused with the asynchronous rotary gap in more general use at the time (*e.g.* by Marconi ship-borne equipment, and radio amateurs in general used asynchronous rotary gaps). Here the speed of rotation of the wheel is entirely independent of the speed of the generator, and while it was possible to realize several sparks during one cycle of the generator, the sparks occur at different points on the cycle. The conditions are not exactly repeated each time as in the case of the synchron-ous spark, because the charging current from the generator is charging up the condenser during different parts of its own cycle of variation, and hence neither the voltage to which it is charged, nor the breakdown voltage is constant. Not only is it possible to miss a spark altogether, but the interval between sparks is not absolutely constant. In addition, the energy stored in the condenser and the proportion radiated in the separate wave trains is variable. The result is that the note heard at the receiving station is impure.

By the summer of 1906 many of the difficulties had been overcome and the Alexanderson HF alternator developed by GE for Fessenden giving 50 kHz was installed at Brant Rock. Various improvements were made by Fessenden and his assistants, and by the fall of 1906 the alternator was working regularly at 75 kHz with an output of one half a kilowatt. This was the beginning of pure CW transmission, c.f. Alexanderson [1919].

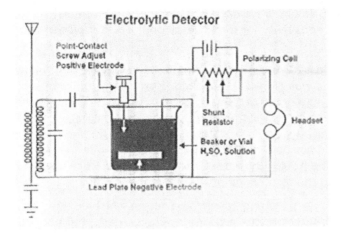

Continuous waves was the method of generation Fessenden had long sought, since he wanted to transmit words without wires. He inserted a carbon microphone in series with the lead from his alternator to the antenna, and he had an amplitude modulated transmitter. But more on that later.

Receiver Technology

The ability to receive wireless signals at the turn of the century was very poor, for several reasons: 1) Initially the receiver was un-tuned or, if tuned, the selectivity was poor; 2) there was no means to amplify the signal; and 3) a sensitive detector had yet to be invented.

The early experiments employed a device called a coherer. The coherer as we have noted was a device which normally exhibited a high resistance, but when subjected to a voltage above a given threshold, there was a marked decrease in this resistance. The change in resistance could be detected by means of a secondary relay circuit, or by listening to the current change with a telephone earpiece. The filings coherer was a bi-stable device. It needed an electrical voltage to effect one transition, and a physical shock (a tapper) to return it to its initial state. The sensitivity of the device was poor; the action of the receiver depended upon a voltage rise and so was independent of the energy of the signal; it did not discriminate between impulses of different character, *viz.* between signals and atmospherics; the selectivity of the receiver was a function of the state of the coherer; and it could not be used as a detector for continuous waves.

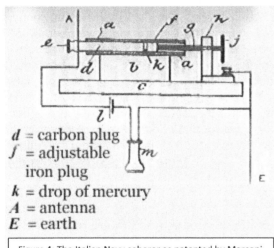

Figure 4: The Italian Navy coherer as patented by Marconi in September 1901 (Brit. Pat. 18 105). (Phillips)

For his transatlantic experiment in 1901, Marconi had two types of receivers and three types of coherers. One was a tuned receiver, which he referred to as a "syntonic receiver," that is a receiver tuned to the frequency of the transmitter. The second earlier receiver was untuned. The three types of coherers that he used were: one containing loose carbon filings; another designed by Marconi containing a mixture of carbon dust and cobalt dust; and thirdly the Italian Navy coherer (see Fig. 4) containing a globule of mercury between a carbon plug and a moveable iron plug. This latter device, when critically adjusted, or more or less by luck, acted like a crude form of a rectifier, but its performance was poor and unpredictable [Phillips, 1993]. Later, in 1902, he devised a form of current operated receiver, called a magnetic detector, which greatly enhanced his receiver sensitivity. This detector was used by Marconi until it was replaced by the vacuum tube in 1913.

When Marconi designed the receiver he intended to use for the first transatlantic HF experiment, he designed it so it could be tuned, and so respond selectively to signals of different frequencies -- his famous four sevens patent of 1900. This idea was however not his own, as was the case for many of Marconi's "inventions," but was devised by Oliver Lodge, who in 1897 had filed four patents. Two dealt with improvements to coherers, and two to "tuning" or "syntony" [Austin, 1994].

Fessenden was convinced that a successful detector for reception of wireless signals must be constantly receptive, instead of requiring resetting as was the characteristic of the coherer. Although his experiments with wireless receivers began when he was a Professor of Electrical Engineering in the Western University of Pennsylvania, in 1896/97; it was not until 1901/02 that he discovered the electrolytic detector. In 1902 and 1903 he patented the first practical detector [US Patents 706,744 and 727,331] -- which he called a *barretter*, a name coined from the French word for exchanger. This name implies the exchange of AC for DC, *i.e.*, the device behaved like a rectifier, c.f. [Pickworth, 1994]. In Fig. 5 we sketch one of Fessenden's early radio receivers using this detector; which was the standard of sensitivity for many years until it was replaced by the vacuum tube some ten years later.

Fessenden's *barretter* detector was, however, useless for reception of unmodulated CW. All that one would hear would be the clicks as the Morse telegraph key was closed and opened. However, very early, some 11 years ahead of its time, Fessenden's fertile mind had already devised a solution. He invented the methodology (and the word) for combining two frequencies to derive their sum and difference frequencies, *viz*. the heterodyne method of detecting continuous waves (US Pat. No. 706,740 dated 12 August 1902; and Nos. 1,050,441 and 1,050,728 dated 14 January, 1913). But it was not before 1912-1914, when the triode's versatility to be an oscillator, or RF source, was established, that the **heterodyne** receiver became a practical method for detecting CW. Today, heterodyning is fundamental to the technology of radio communications.

Fleming, in 1904, invented the valve diode (known as a Fleming valve). The patent which covered its use as a detector of Hertzian waves became the property of the Marconi Company, and eventually, but not until after WWI, Fleming valves were put into operation in Marconi stations.

Meanwhile de Forest, who was following in the footsteps of Fessenden, experimenting with the electric arc as a CW wireless transmitter for telephony, needed a good detector. The electrolytic detector that he had been using was judged by the courts in 1906 to be an infringement on Fessenden's patent. As a result he had to change all of his stations to use the silicon detector, which had been patented in 1906 by H.H. Dunwoody, an officer in his company. Because of this incident, de Forest resigned from the company in November 1906. De Forest started looking for a better valve detector. He made some Fleming valves, and, in a moment of inspiration, he added a third element, a control element shaped like a grid-iron, called a grid. De Forest patented his *audion*, the first three-element valve in 1907. Although the *audion* was more sensitive as a detector than the Fleming valve, he was prevented from using it for commercial purposes by a lawsuit launched by the Marconi Company (claiming infringement in spite of the fact that it was a different valve). De Forest did not understand how the valve operated, and it remained for Langmuir, Armstrong, and van der Pol to discover its full possibilities. The time interval between Fessenden's heterodyne receiver (1902) and Armstrong's "feedback" receiver or regenerative receiver (1913) is the 11 years mentioned above. **Armstrong's *superheterodyne*** receiver was not invented until 1918.

4. The First Transatlantic Experiment

On 12 December, 1901, signals from a high power spark transmitter located at Poldhu were reported to have been received by Marconi and his assistant George Kemp, at a receiving station on Signal Hill, near St. John's, Newfoundland. The signals had traveled a distance of 3500 kilometres. Even at the time of the experiment there were those who said, indeed there are some who still say, that he misled himself and the world into believing that atmospheric noise crackling was in fact the Morse code letter 'S'.

A little later, in February 1902, when Marconi returned to England on the SS Philadelphia, using a tuned shipborne antenna, he received signals using his filings coherer from the same sender up to distances of 1120 km by day and 2500 km by night. Even these distances are rather remarkable considering the receiving apparatus he used.

We discuss here in detail that first transatlantic experiment.

The Poldhu Station

Marconi's ambition at the turn of the century to demonstrate long-distance wireless communication and develop a profitable long-distance wireless telegraph service, led to his pragmatic proposal in 1900 to send a wireless signal across the Atlantic. He conceived a plan to erect two super-stations, one on each side of the Atlantic, for two-way wireless communications, to bridge the two continents together in direct opposition to the cable company (Anglo-American Telegraph Company). For the eastern terminal, he leased land overlooking Poldhu cove in southwestern Cornwall, England. For the western terminal, the sand dunes on the northern end of Cape Cod, MA, at South Wellfleet, was chosen.

The aerial systems comprised 20 masts, each 61 metres high, arranged in a circle 61m in diameter. The ring of masts supported a conical aerial system of 400 wires, each insulated at the top and connected at the bottom, thus forming an inverted cone. Vyvyan [1933], the Marconi engineer who worked on the 1901 experiment, when shown the plan, did not think the design sound. Each mast was stayed to the next one, and only to ground in a radial direction, to and away from the centre of the mast system. He was overruled, construction went ahead, and both aerial systems were completed in early 1901.

However, before testing could begin catastrophe struck. The Poldhu aerial collapsed in a storm on 17 September, and the South Wellfleet aerial suffered the same fate on 26 November, 1901.

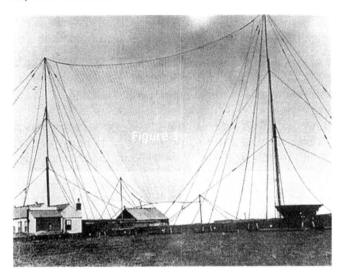

At Poldhu, Marconi quickly erected two masts and put up an aerial of 54 wires, spaced 1 metre apart, and suspended from a triadic stay stretched between these masts at a height of 45.7 m. The aerial wires were arranged fan shaped, presumably insulated at the top, as was his conical wire aerial, and connected together at the lower end, see Fig. 1. This photograph has been published and republished, and clearly one can see only 12 wires -- but the view generally held is that the aerial system as described above by Vyvyan [1933] is right; that is, there were 54 wires, and the photograph has been retouched.

The antenna was driven by the curious two stage spark transmitter previously discussed. There were many problems in getting it to work at the high power levels desired [see Thackeray, 1992]. Our principal concern here is the frequency generated by the Poldhu station. The oscillation frequency is determined by the natural resonant response of the antenna system, which includes the inductance of the secondary of the antenna transformer T_2, since, in effect, the antenna system is a base-loaded monopole.

The primary of this transformer consisted of 2 7/20 wires in parallel, the secondary consisted of 7 or 9 wires of 7/20 wire in series. Fleming's sketch indicates 9 wires; Entwisle [1922] said there were 7 wires. The inductance values for this transformer have long been debated. Since the original transformer is lost, there are no drawings, and reports about them differ [Thackeray, 1992]. G. Garratt made a copy of L_s (the secondary of this transformer) and measured its inductance to be 6×10^{-6} H [see Ratcliffe 1974].

While the inductance L_s changes the resonant frequency, the exact value does not change the conclusion reached in our study. For L_s equal to 6×10^{-6} H, we have modeled Marconi's Poldhu antenna, assuming the fan comprised 12 wires. According to the antenna analysis code MININEC, the resonant frequency of the antenna system was 850 kHz.

A number of scientists and engineers interested in the actual frequency or frequencies radiated by this first high power transmitter at Poldhu have discussed the possibility that the aerial transformer was over-coupled, resulting in a double-humped frequency/amplitude response. We do know that Fleming tuned the primary oscillatory circuit by varying the discharge capacitor C_2 to maximize the aerial current. Since our best estimate for the component values ($C_2 = 0.037$ muF and $L_p = 8 \times 10^{-7}$ H) would result in a resonant frequency of 925 kHz, it seems logical to conclude that the overall system response would result in a single peak centered on the resonant frequency of the aerial system, *viz.* about 850 kHz.

Historians have also speculated the transmitter might also have radiated a high-frequency signal as well, since an HF signal would have been more suitable for transatlantic communications (to be discussed), see for example Ratcliffe [1974]. If Marconi had used a thin wire transmitting antenna at Poldhu, this antenna would indeed have radiated efficiently at odd harmonics of the fundamental resonant frequency. But, for our model, the antenna is inductive for all frequencies greater than the fundamental resonant frequency response of the antenna system. One must conclude therefore, that the Poldhu spark-transmitter system radiated efficiently only on the fundamental oscillation frequency of the tuned antenna system -- about 850 kHz.

Marconi himself has been evasive concerning the frequency of his Poldhu transmitter. Fleming in a lecture he gave in 1903, said the wavelength was 1000 feet or more; say, one-fifth to one-quarter of a mile (820 kHz is the generally quoted frequency). Marconi remained silent on this wavelength, but, in 1908, in a lecture to the Royal Institution, he quotes the wavelength as 1200 feet, see Bondyopadhyay[14] [1993].

Reception on Signal Hill

For his transatlantic experiment, Marconi decided to set up receiving equipment in Newfoundland. In December, 1901, he set sail for St. John's with a small stock of kites and balloons to keep a single wire aloft in stormy weather.

A site was chosen on Signal Hill and apparatus was set up in an abandoned military hospital. A cable was sent to Poldhu, requesting that the Morse letter "S" be transmitted continuously from 3:00 to 7:00 PM local time.

On 12th December, 1901, under strong wind conditions, a kite was launched with a 155m long wire. The wind carried it away. A second kite was launched with a 152.4m wire attached. The kite bobbed and weaved in the sky, making it difficult for Marconi to adjust his new syntonic receiver which employed the Italian Navy coherer. "Difficult" I will accept, but how he determined the frequency of tuning for his receiver is a mystery to me. Whatever, because of this difficulty, Marconi decided to use his older un-tuned receiver. History has assumed that he substituted the metal filings coherer previously used with this receiver for the newly acquired Italian Navy coherer, but Marconi never really said he did [see Phillips, 1993]. He referred only to the use of three types of coherers.

Despite the crude equipment employed, and in our view the impossibility of hearing the signal, Marconi and his assistant George Kemp convinced themselves that they could hear on occasion the rhythm of three clicks more or less buried in the static, and clicks they would be if heard at all, because of the low spark rate. Marconi wrote in his laboratory notebook: Sigs at 12:30, 1:10 and 2:20 (local time). This notebook is in the Marconi Company archives and is the only proof [evidence – author] today that the signal was received.

The Enigma

Today we know that signals (depending on frequency used) can indeed travel across the Atlantic, and far beyond. But in 1901, anyone who believed that they could, and did, believed so as an act of faith based on the integrity of one man -- Marconi.

If 850 kHz was indeed the frequency used, the tests took place at the worst time of day, because the entire path would have been daylight, and the daytime sky wave would be heavily attenuated, even though it was a winter day, in sunspot minimum period; and there were no magnetic storms at the time, or for ten days before. The day-time absorption of an ionospherically-reflected signal is a maximum in the LF/MF band. Ratcliffe [1974] has deduced that, from a knowledge only of propagation conditions, reception on Signal Hill is consistent with the observed limiting ranges of reception on the ship only if the un-tuned land based receiver was 10-100 times more sensitive than the tuned receiver on the ship.

It is therefore difficult to believe that signals could have been heard on Signal Hill, since the receiving equipment after all consisted of a long-wire antenna coupled to an un-tuned receiver which had no means of amplification whatsoever, and the type of detector used was less sensitive and its performance unpredictable compared with Fessenden's *barretter* detector, or the

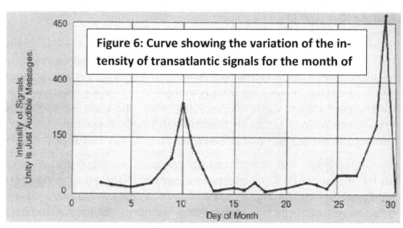

Figure 6: Curve showing the variation of the intensity of transatlantic signals for the month of

---

[14] https://onlinelibrary.wiley.com/doi/abs/10.1002/srin.199301032

galena crystal detector which evolved a few years later.

5. The First Radio Propagation Experiments

There is no evidence that Marconi made any serious attempt to systematically investigate the characteristics of the HF, MF and LF portions of the radio frequency spectrum when he began the downward frequency trend in his struggle to achieve transatlantic wireless communications. He did not do this until 20 years later, in the early 1920's, when attracted to the HF band by amateur radio operators. The radio amateurs had been banished to the then-believed useless frequencies higher than 1500 kHz.

The first record showing qualitatively the variation of the intensity of transatlantic messages transmitted between Brant Rock, MA, and Machrihanish, Scotland, at night, during the month of January, 1906, is reproduced in Fig. 6 [Fessenden, 1908]. Nothing at all was received that month during daytime.

It was found (measurements made during 1906) that absorption at a given instant was a function of direction as well as distance since, on a given night, the signals received by stations in one direction would be greatly weakened, while there would be less weakening of the signals received by stations lying in another direction; and a few hours or minutes later the reverse would be the case. It was also found that variations of absorption on transatlantic signals appeared to have a quite definite relation with variations of the geomagnetic field, *i.e.*, the greater the absorption, the greater the magnetic variation [Fessenden, 1908].

Experiments were made between Brant Rock and the West Indies, a distance of 2735 km, during the spring and summer of 1907. Frequencies in the band 50 kHz to 200 kHz were used. It was found that the absorption at 200 kHz was very much greater than at 80 kHz, and that messages could be successfully received over this path in daytime at the latter frequency. Antenna radiation efficiency was an important factor for frequencies less than 80 kHz. No messages were received in daytime with the higher frequency.

The fact that these experiments were made during summer, that the receiving station was in the tropics (high noise levels), and the fact that the distance, 2735 km, was practically the same as between Ireland and Newfoundland was reported by Fessenden [1907]. After publication of the above results, Marconi, in early October, 1907, abandoned his previously used frequencies and immediately succeeded in operating between Glace Bay and Clifden, a distance of more than 3000 km, the frequency being about 70 kHz. The same messages were received at Brant Rock, MA, a distance of nearly 4825 km. A little later Marconi moved to an even lower frequency, 45 kHz.

6. Verifiable Transatlantic Radio Communications

The first East-West transatlantic radio transmission was made during October, 1902, from Poldhu, Cornwall, to the Italian cruiser, Carlos Alberto, anchored in the harbour of Sydney, NS, with Marconi aboard. The frequency employed was about 272 kHz. This successful transmission was considered an experimental prerequisite to the start-up of the permanent land based wireless Marconi station under construction at Glace Bay, NS.

The first West-East transatlantic radio transmission was recorded on 5 December, 1902, between Glace Bay and Poldhu. The frequency was about 182 kHz.

The first Canada/UK transatlantic radio message (as opposed to hearing the signal) was sent from Glace Bay to Poldhu on 15 December, 1902. It was a press message from a London Times correspondent at Glace Bay to his home office.

The first USA/UK transatlantic radio message received at Poldhu from the Marconi station at South Wellfleet, MA, was from President Roosevelt to King Edward VII, on 18 January, 1903.

History has recorded that the above messages were successfully transmitted, but how well these messages were received is a matter of conjecture. In 1902-c.1912, both the Clifden and Glace Bay stations were using "disc discharger" transmitters and a form of current operated receiver (Marconi's magnetic detector). It is clear that Marconi was still struggling in 1908 to achieve reliable transatlantic radio communications. It is interesting to read a letter written on 19 March, 1909, to Hon. Chauncey M. Depew, US Senate, Washington, DC, signed by five members of The Junior Wireless Club (now The Radio Club of America). The thrust of the letter was to comment on a proposed bill before the Senate that would, in effect, restrict the use of the air waves by radio amateurs, because of presumed malicious interference caused by radio amateurs. I quote from a part of that letter, which can be found in the Seventy-Fifth Anniversary Diamond Jubilee Year Book of The Radio Club of America, 1984:

"At the Narragansett Bay there were certain Naval tests made about two years ago, and the various so-called Wireless Companies wanted to get the first news to the newspapers of these tests, so as to boom their companies' stocks, and to say the news was received first through their company, and when some of them found they were unable to cut out interference between themselves, in order to prevent other Wireless Companies from getting the news first they sent a lot of fake messages of confused dashes.

"Only a few of the so-called Wireless Companies have efficient methods of cutting out interference, and these are the companies that are now crying for the most protection.

"You probably have heard of the tests made last year between Glace Bay, NS, and Clifden, Ireland, when the National (Electric) Signaling Company (Fessenden's Brant Rock station) picked up the messages, which Marconi, on the test, was unable to deliver between his own stations, from both Glace Bay and Clifden, Ireland, in spite of the fact that the Marconi Company kept up a constant interference of dash, dash, dash from their Cape Cod Station for 48 hours without interruption, but the National (Electric) Signaling Company paid no attention to such interference and picked up all the messages, which Marconi was unable to exchange between their own stations, and all these messages were handed over to Lord Northcutt at the Hotel St. Regis."

Marconi himself, in his 1909 Nobel Prize address said: "What often happens in pioneer work repeated itself in the case of radiotelegraphy. The anticipated obstacles or difficulties were purely imaginary or else easily surmountable, but in their place unexpected barriers presented themselves, and recent work has been directed to the solutions of problems that were neither expected nor anticipated when long distances were first attempted."

Certainly after Marconi's first transatlantic radio experiment in 1901, he found that the realization of reliable transatlantic radio communications was more distant (for him) than he realized at the time.

The first two-way transatlantic radio telegraphy transmission took place on 10 January 1906, between Fessenden's stations at Brant Rock, MA, and Machrihanish, Scotland. Repeatedly regular exchange of messages across the Atlantic Ocean took place on most days during winter, spring and into early summer. The frequencies used were in the 80-100 kHz band. The reliability and the quality of signal reception (signal-to-noise ratio) for the Fessenden system must have been very much better than anything Marconi could achieve at this point in time. Fessenden was using his synchronous rotary-spark transmitters at both ends, and tuned receivers with his *barretter* detector. The signals were superior to other signals used at the time, which by comparison were rough and ragged. His antenna system was an umbrella top-loaded radiator 128 metres high. The Marconi antennas were multi-wire conical structures, or wire antennas with extensive top loading, 61 metres high. Since the radiation efficiency of electrically short antennas varies (approximately) as the height of the antenna, Fessenden's antenna systems were probably four times more efficient than Marconi's.

Radio Telephony

At the turn of the century Fessenden was using a spark transmitter, employing a Wehnelt interrupter operating a Ruhmkorff induction coil. In 1899 he noted, when the key was held down for a long dash, that the peculiar wailing sound of the Wehnelt interrupter could be clearly heard in the receiving telephone. He must have had a detector of some sort that was working for him, even at this early stage in the development of wireless. This suggested to him that by using a spark rate well above voice band (10,000 sparks/sec), wireless telephony could be achieved; and this he did transmitting speech over a distance of 1.5 km on 23 December 1900, between 15 metre masts on Cob Island, MD, [Belrose, 1994a; 1994b].

In autumn of 1906, Fessenden had his HF alternator working adequately on frequencies up to about 100 kHz. About midnight in November, 1906, Mr. Stein, at Fessenden's Brant Rock station, was telling the operator at a nearby test station at Plymouth, MA, how to run the HF alternator. It was usual for these two operators to use speech over this short distance. However his voice was heard by Mr. Armor at Machrihanish, Scotland, with such clarity that there was no doubt about the speaker, and the station log books confirmed the report.

Fessenden's equipment was working exceptionally well in the early hours of that morning, and (remarkable for that time) the echo of the telegraphy signals from the Scotland station could clearly be heard one fifth of a second later, having travelled the long way around the earth.

The Machrihanish tower crashed to the ground on 5 December, 1906, during a severe winter storm. The station was never rebuilt, and Fessenden's transatlantic experiments came to an abrupt end.

Fessenden's greatest success took place on Christmas Eve, 1906, when he and his colleagues presented the world's first wireless broadcast. The transmission included a speech by Fessenden and selected music for Christmas. Fessenden played Handel's *Largo* on the violin.

That first broadcast, from his transmitter at Brant Rock, MA, was heard by radio operators on board US Navy and United Fruit Company ships equipped with Fessenden's wireless receivers at various distances over the South and North Atlantic, and in the West Indies. The wireless broadcast was repeated on New Year's Eve. The transmitter was an HF alternator, in which one terminal was connected to ground, the other terminal to the tuned antenna, and a carbon microphone was inserted in the antenna lead.

Recall that Fleming, in the first edition of his book on Electromagnetic Waves, published in 1906, stated that an abrupt impulse was a necessary condition for wireless transmission, and that high frequency currents, even of sufficient frequency, could not produce radiation. The highest frequency of HF alternators prior to the summer of 1906 was about 10 kHz. This belief, and an earlier belief that the terminals of an antenna had to be bridged by a spark, show how wrong some of the early "experts" were.

Continuing in the same vein, Fessenden, in his 1908 paper, restated his long held view: "The coherer is well adapted for working with damped waves, but the coherer-damped wave method can never be developed into a practical telegraph system. It is a question whether the invention of the coherer has not been on the whole a misfortune as tending to lead development of the art astray into impracticable and futile lines, and thereby retarding the development of a really practical system."

7. Concluding Remarks

There are those who say that Marconi's greatest triumph (the mother of all experiments) was when he succeeded in 1901 in passing signals across the Atlantic. There are those who say that he misled himself and the world into believing that atmospheric noise crackling was in fact the Morse code letter 'S'. Whether Marconi heard the three faint dots or not is really unimportant. His claim "sparked" a controversy among contemporary scientists and engineers about the experiment that continues today.

Certainly engineers and scientists of the present day are unanimous in admiring the bold and imaginative way in which Marconi attempted to take one spectacular step forward, to extend the range of wireless communications from one or two hundred kilometres to the 3500 kilometre distance across the Atlantic Ocean.

The world has acclaimed Marconi as the "father of wireless," although some say that Alexander Popov and Oliver Lodge were first in the field. History has accredited Marconi with the invention of an early form of radio telegraphy. Tesla's patent precedes Marconi but Tesla did not produce a demonstrable application qualifying him to be labeled "father of wireless."

Fessenden's continuous waves, a new type of detector and his invention of the method, as well as the coining of the word heterodyne, did not, by any means, constitute a satisfactory wireless telegraphy or wireless telephony system judged by today's standards. They were, however, the first real departure from Marconi's damped-wave-coherer system for telegraphy which other experimenters were merely imitating or modifying. They were the first pioneering steps toward radio communications and radio broadcasting.

Today, heterodyning is fundamental to the technology of radio communications. Some historians consider that Fessenden's heterodyne principle is his greatest contribution to radio science. Edwin Howard Armstrong's super-heterodyne receiver is based on the heterodyne principle. Except for method improvement, Armstrong's super-heterodyne receiver remains the standard radio receiving method today.

Fessenden, a genius, and a mathematician was the inventor of radio as we know it today.[15] END

---

[15] https://www.ieee.ca/millennium/radio/radio_differences.html

Chapter Two -- Early Critical Discoveries

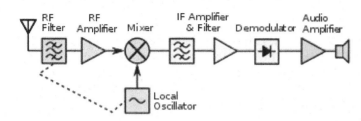

Heterodyne

Heterodyning is a signal processing technique invented by Canadian inventor-engineer Reginald Fessenden that creates new frequencies by combining or mixing two frequencies. Heterodyning is used to shift one frequency range into another, new one, and is also involved in the processes of *modulation* and *demodulation*. The two frequencies are combined in a nonlinear signal-processing device such as a vacuum tube transistor, or diode, usually called a *mixer*. In the most common application, two signals at frequencies f_1 and f_2 are mixed, creating two new signals, one at the sum $f_1 + f_2$ of the two frequencies, and the other at the difference $f_1 - f_2$. These new frequencies are called **heterodynes**. Typically only one of the new frequencies is desired, and the other signal is filtered out of the output of the mixer. Heterodynes are related to the phenomenon of "beats" in acoustics.

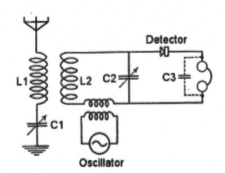

A major application of the heterodyne process is in the *superheterodyne* radio receiver circuit, which is used in virtually all modern radio receivers.

History

Fessenden's heterodyne radio receiver circuit

The incoming radio frequency and local oscillator frequency mix in the crystal diode detector.

In 1901, Reginald Fessenden demonstrated a direct-conversion heterodyne receiver or beat receiver as a method of making continuous wave radiotelegraphy signals audible. Fessenden's receiver did not see much application because of its local oscillator's stability problem. A stable yet inexpensive local oscillator was not available until Lee de Forest invented the triode vacuum tube oscillator. In a 1905 patent, Fessenden stated that the frequency stability of his local oscillator was one part per thousand.

In radio telegraphy, the characters of text messages are translated into the short duration dots and long duration dashes of Morse code that are broadcast as radio signals. Radio telegraphy was much like ordinary telegraphy. One of the problems was building high power transmitters with the technology of the day. Early transmitters were spark gap transmitters. A mechanical device would make sparks at a fixed, but audible rate; the sparks would put energy into a resonant circuit that would then ring at the desired transmission frequency (which might be 100kHz). This ringing would quickly decay, so the output of the transmitter would be a succession of damped waves. When these damped waves were received by a simple detector, the operator would hear an audible buzzing sound that he could transcribe back into alpha-numeric characters.

With the development of the arc converter radio transmitter in 1904, continuous wave (CW) modulation began to be used for radiotelegraphy. CW Morse code signals are not amplitude modulated, but rather consist of bursts of sinusoidal carrier frequency. When CW signals are received by an AM receiver, the operator does not hear a sound. The direct-conversion (heterodyne) detector was invented to make continuous wave radio-frequency signals audible.

The "heterodyne" or "beat" receiver has a local oscillator that produces a radio signal adjusted to be close in frequency to the incoming signal being received. When the two signals are mixed, a "beat" frequency equal to the difference between the two frequencies is created. By adjusting the local oscillator frequency correctly, the beat frequency is in the audio range, and can be heard as a tone in the receiver's earphones whenever the transmitter signal is present. Thus the Morse code "dots" and "dashes" are audible as beeping sounds. This technique is still used in radio telegraphy, the local oscillator now being called the beat frequency oscillator or BFO. Fessenden coined the word *heterodyne* from the Greek roots *hetero-*"different," and *dyn-*"power."

Superheterodyne receiver

In this block diagram of a typical superheterodyne receiver, from left to right, the incoming RF is received by the antenna and passed through an RF filter to an RF amplifier and on to the mixer. The signal is then passed to the IF (Intermediate Frequency) and on to the demodulator or audio amplifier to the speaker.

An important and widely used application of the heterodyne technique is in the superheterodyne receiver (superhet), which was invented by U.S. engineer Edwin Howard Armstrong in 1918. In the typical superhet, the incoming radio frequency signal from the antenna is mixed (heterodyned) with a signal from a local oscillator (LO) to produce a lower fixed frequency signal called the intermediate frequency (IF) signal. The IF signal is amplified and filtered and then applied to a detector that extracts the audio signal; the audio is ultimately sent to the receiver's loudspeaker.

The superheterodyne receiver has several advantages over previous receiver designs. One advantage is easier tuning; only the RF and LO are tuned by the operator; the fixed-frequency IF is tuned ("aligned") at the factory and is not adjusted. In older designs such as the tuned radio frequency receiver (TRF), all of the receiver stages had to be simultaneously tuned. In addition, since the IF filters are fixed-tuned, the receiver's selectivity is the same across the receiver's entire frequency band. Another advantage is that the IF signal can be at a much lower frequency than the incoming radio signal, and that allows each stage of the IF amplifier to provide more gain. To first order, an amplifying device has a fixed gain-bandwidth product. If the device has a gain-bandwidth product of 60MHz, then it can provide a voltage gain of 3 at an RF of 20MHz or a voltage gain of 30 at an IF of 2MHz. At a lower IF, it would take fewer gain devices to achieve the same gain. The regenerative radio receiver obtained more gain out of one gain device by using positive feedback, but it required careful adjustment by the operator; that adjustment also changed the selectivity of the regenerative receiver. The superheterodyne provides a large, stable gain and constant selectivity without troublesome adjustment.

The superior superheterodyne system replaced the earlier TRF and regenerative receiver designs, and since the 1930s, most commercial radio receivers have been superheterodynes.

Applications

Heterodyning, also called *frequency conversion*, is used very widely in communications engineering to generate new frequencies and move information from one frequency channel to another. Besides its use in the superheterodyne circuit found in almost all radio and television receivers, it is used in radio transmitters, modems, satellite communications and set-top boxes, radar, radio telescopes, telemetry systems, cell phones, cable television converter boxes and head-ends, microwave relays, metal detectors, atomic clocks, and military electronic countermeasures (jamming) systems.

Up and down converters

In large scale telecommunication networks such as telephone network trunks, microwave relay networks, cable television systems, and communication satellite links, large bandwidth capacity links are shared by many individual communication channels by using heterodyning to move the frequency of the individual signals up to different frequencies, which share the channel. This is called frequency division multiplexing (FDM).

For example, a coaxial cable used by a cable television system can carry 500 television channels at the same time because each one is given a different frequency, so they don't interfere with one another. At the cable source or headend, electronic up-converters convert each incoming television channel to a new, higher frequency. They do this by mixing the television signal frequency, f_{CH} with a local oscillator at a much higher frequency f_{LO}, creating a heterodyne at the sum $f_{CH} + f_{LO}$, which is added to the cable. At the consumer's home, the cable set top box has a downconverter that mixes the incoming signal at frequency $f_{CH} + f_{LO}$ with the same local oscillator frequency f_{LO} creating the difference heterodyne, converting the television channel back to its original frequency: $(f_{CH} + f_{LO}) - f_{LO} = f_{CH}$. Each channel is moved to a different higher frequency. The original lower basic frequency of the signal is called the baseband, while the higher channel to which it is moved is called the pass-band.

Chapter Three – Vacuum Tubes ("Valves" – British Synonym)

The impact vacuum tubes has had on the development of all forms of telecommunicating cannot be over-emphasized. These tubes ('valves' in Europe) performed the functions today's miniaturized transistors and circuits deliver; thus, we will devote time to these early devices and the entrepreneurial efforts capitalizing on them igniting the radio industry to which we owe so much.

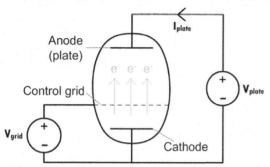

Thermionic Emission

The basic working principle of a vacuum tube is a phenomenon called thermionic emission. It works like this: you heat up a metal, and the thermal energy knocks some electrons loose. In 1904, English physicist John Ambrose Fleming took advantage of this effect to create the first vacuum tube device, which he called an oscillation valve.

Fleming's device consisted of two electrodes, a cathode and an anode, placed on either end of an encapsulated glass tube. When the cathode is heated, it gives off electrons *via* thermionic emission. Then, by applying a positive voltage to the anode (also called the plate), these electrons are attracted to the plate and can flow across the gap. By removing the air from the tube to create a vacuum, the electrons have a clear path from the cathode to the anode, and a current is created.

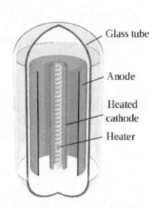

When the cathode is heated, and a positive voltage is applied to the anode, electrons can flow from the cathode to the anode. Note: A separate power source (not shown) is required to heat the cathode.

This type of vacuum tube, consisting of only two electrodes, is called a diode. The term diode is still used today to refer to an electrical component that only allows an electric current to flow in one direction, although today these devices are all semiconductor based. In the case of the vacuum tube diode, a current can only flow from the anode to the cathode (though the electrons flow from the cathode to the anode, recall that the direction of conventional current is opposite to the actual movement of electrons—an annoying holdover from electrical engineering history). Diodes are commonly used for rectification, that is, converting from an alternating current (AC) to a direct current (DC).

See diagram for a more realistic representation of a vacuum tube diode. The electrodes are arranged as concentric cylinders within the tube, maximizing the surface area for electrons. Here, the cathode is heated by a separate heating filament, labeled Heater. (Image courtesy of Wikipedia user Svjo.)

Third Electrode's the Charm

While diodes are quite a handy device to have around, they did not set the limit for vacuum tube functionality. In 1907, American inventor Lee de Forest added a third electrode to the mix, creating the first triode tube. This third electrode, called the control grid, enabled the vacuum tube to be used not just as a rectifier, but as an amplifier of electrical signals.

The control grid is placed between the cathode and anode, and is in the shape of a mesh (the holes allow electrons to pass through it). By adjusting the voltage applied to the grid, you can control the number of electrons flowing from the cathode to the anode. If the grid is given a strong negative voltage, it repels the electrons from the cathode and chokes the flow of current. The more you increase the grid voltage, the more electrons can pass through it, and the higher your current. In this way, the triode can serve as an on/off switch for an electrical current, as well as a signal amplifier.

A minute adjustment to the grid voltage has a comparatively large effect on the plate current, allowing the triode to be used for amplification.

The triode is useful for amplifying signals because a small change in the control grid voltage leads to a large change in the plate current. In this way, a small signal at the grid (like a radio wave) can be converted into a much larger signal, with the same exact waveform, at the plate. Note that you could also increase the plate current by increasing the plate voltage, but you'd have to change it by a greater amount than the grid voltage to achieve the same amplification of current.

The evolution of triode vacuum tubes from a 1916 model (left) to one from the 1960s. (Image courtesy of Wikipedia user RJB1.)

But why stop at three electrodes when you could have four? Or five, for that matter? Further enhancements of vacuum tubes placed an additional grid (called the screen grid) and yet another (called the suppressor grid) even closer to the anode, creating a type of vacuum tube called a tetrode and a pentode, respectively. These extra grids solve some stability problems and address other limitations with the triode design, but the function remains largely the same.

Chapter Four -- Transistors and Semiconductors

The Transistor Is Born, but the Tube Lives On

A replica of the first transistor created in 1947.

In 1947, the trio of physicists William Shockley, Walter Brattain and John Bardeen (Bell Labs) created the world's first transistor and marked the beginning of the end for the vacuum tube. The transistor could replicate all the functions of tubes, like switching and amplification, but was made out of semiconductor materials.

Once the transistor cat was let out of the bag, vacuum tubes were on their way to extinction in all but the most specific of applications. Transistors are much more durable (vacuum tubes, like light bulbs, will eventually need to be replaced), much smaller (imagine fitting 2 billion tubes inside an iPhone), and require much less voltage than tubes in order to function (for one thing, transistors don't have a filament that needs heating).

Despite the emergence of the transistor, vacuum tubes aren't completely extinct, and they remain useful in a handful of niche applications. For example, vacuum tubes are still used in high power RF transmitters, as they

can generate more power than modern semiconductor equivalents. For this reason, you'll find vacuum tubes in particle accelerators, MRI scanners, and even microwave ovens.

But perhaps the most charming modern application of vacuum tubes is in the musical community. Audiophiles swear by the quality of vacuum tube amplifiers, preferring their sound to semiconductor amps, and many professional musicians won't consider using anything in their place. Whether there's any merit to this preference is a matter of some debate. This is a photo of vacuum tubes being used in a modern guitar amplifier.

Vacuum tubes had their day, and now the world is powered by transistors. But what does the future hold for electronics? With Moore's Law reaching its limits, and quantum computing looming tantalizingly on the horizon, it's anybody's guess where the wave of technological advancement will bring us next.

Semiconductors

What are semiconductors?

A semiconductor material has an electrical conductivity value falling between that of a conductor, such as metallic copper, and an insulator, such as glass. Its resistance falls as its temperature rises; metals are the opposite. Its conducting properties may be altered in useful ways by introducing impurities ("doping") into the crystal structure. When two differently-doped regions exist in the same crystal, a semiconductor junction is created. The behavior of charge carriers, which include electrons, ions and electron holes, at these junctions is the basis of diodes, transistors and all modern electronics. Some examples of semiconductors are silicon, germanium, gallium arsenide, and elements near the so-called "metalloid staircase" on the periodic table. After silicon, gallium arsenide is the second most common semiconductor and is used in laser diodes, solar cells, microwave-frequency integrated circuits and others. Silicon is a critical element for fabricating most electronic circuits.

Semiconductor devices can display a range of useful properties, such as passing current more easily in one direction than the other, showing variable resistance, and sensitivity to light or heat. Because the electrical properties of a semiconductor material can be modified by doping, or by the application of electrical fields or light, devices made from semiconductors can be used for amplification, switching, and energy conversion.

The conductivity of silicon is increased by adding a small amount (of the order of 1 in 10^8) of pentavalent (antimony, phosphorus, or arsenic) or trivalent (boron, gallium, indium) atoms. This process is known as doping and resulting semiconductors are known as doped or extrinsic semiconductors. Apart from doping, the conductivity of a semiconductor can equally be improved by increasing its temperature. This is contrary to the behavior of a metal in which conductivity decreases with increase in temperature.

The modern understanding of the properties of a semiconductor relies on quantum physics to explain the movement of charge carriers in a crystal lattice. Doping greatly increases the number of charge carriers within the crystal. When a doped semiconductor contains mostly free holes it is called "p-type", and when it contains mostly free electrons it is known as "n-type". The semiconductor materials used in electronic devices are doped under precise conditions to control the concentration and regions of p- and n-type dopants. A single semiconductor crystal can have many p- and n-type regions; the p–n junctions between these regions are responsible for the useful electronic behavior.

Some of the properties of semiconductor materials were observed throughout the mid-19th and first decades of the 20th century. The first practical application of semiconductors in electronics was the 1904 development of the cat's-whisker detector, a primitive semiconductor diode used in early radio receivers. Developments in quantum physics in turn led to the development of the transistor in 1947, the integrated circuit in 1958, and the MOSFET (metal–oxide–semiconductor field-effect transistor) in 1959.

Transistors

A **transistor** is a semiconductor device with at least three terminals for connection to an electric circuit. The vacuum-tube triode, also called a (thermionic) valve, was the transistor's precursor, introduced in 1907. The principle of a field-effect transistor was proposed by Julius Edgar Lilienfeld in 1925.

John Bardeen, Walter Brattain and William Shockley invented the first working transistors at Bell Labs, the point-contact transistor in 1947 and the bipolar junction transistor in 1948. The MOSFET (metal-oxide-semiconductor field-effect transistor), also known as the MOS transistor, was later invented by Mohamed Atalla and Dawon Kahng at Bell Labs in 1959, which led to the mass-production of MOS transistors for a wide range of uses. The MOSFET has since become the most widely manufactured device in history.[16]

The first patent for the field-effect transistor principle was filed in Canada by Austrian-Hungarian physicist Julius Edgar Lilienfeld on October 22, 1925, but Lilienfeld published no research articles about his devices, and his work was ignored by industry. In 1934, German physicist Dr. Oskar Heil patented another field-effect transistor. There is no direct evidence that these devices were built, but later work in the 1990s shows that one of Lilienfeld's designs worked as described and gave substantial gain. Legal papers from the Bell Labs patent show that William Shockley and a co-worker at Bell Labs, Gerald Pearson, had built operational versions from Lilienfeld's patents, yet they never referenced this work in any of their later research papers or historical articles.[17]

The following excerpts, diagrams, and information are quoted from the Motorola Power Transistor Handbook: Theory – Design Characteristics – Applications; first edition, (fourth printing), Motorola Semiconductor Products, Inc.; 5005 E. McDowell Rd., Phoenix, AZ 85008; "This handbook has been compiled by the Applications Engineering Department of Motorola's Semiconductor Products Division. Edited by: Ralph Greenburg, Group Leader, Industrial Applications. This department is always available to help with application problems." ©Motorola, Inc., 1961. Circuit diagrams are included as a means of illustrating typical power transistor applications, and the complete information necessary for constructional purposes is not necessarily given. The information in this handbook has been carefully checked, and is believed to be entirely reliable, but no responsibility is assumed for inaccuracies. Furthermore, such information does not convey to the purchaser of the semiconductor devices described any license under the patent rights of Motorola, Inc. or others."[18]

---

[16] https://en.wikipedia.org/wiki/History_of_the_transistor
[17] Ibid
[18] Motorola Power Transistor Handbook: Theory – Design – Applications; Motorola, Inc., 1961

Introduction

This handbook is intended as a single source of much needed information covering the proper design of power transistor circuits, specific circuit applications, and areas of promise for future transistor circuit development. The information presented here will be helpful to the design engineer, development engineer, hobbyist and experimenter.

The power transistor is an extremely efficient and versatile device. Capable of handling large amounts of power, it is, nevertheless, very compact physically. Circuits have been designed to solve any practical combination of voltage, current, and power requirements. Usable transistor circuits have been designed for series operation at 300 volts and higher, and for parallel operation at current (1961) levels exceeding 1000 amperes. One of the first applications of the power transistor was as a replacement for the power output stage in automobile radios. Since the power transistor could work directly from the 12-volt vehicular battery, the vibrator power supply was eliminated. Other early applications for the power transistor were as a replacement for dynamotors or vibrators in DC-to-DC converters.

The power transistor was, in fact, one of the first semiconductor devices to achieve widespread application and production. The diamond-shaped germanium power transistor developed by Motorola in 1954 demonstrated excellent power handling characteristics as well as a new standard of high reliability. Today, power transistors are found in many types of power supplies, TV sweep circuits, electronic automobile ignition systems, audio amplifiers and industrial control applications. There are more than 10 million Motorola power transistors in field use and it is conservatively estimated that these units have registered more than 10 billion hours of operation under extreme environmental operating conditions. Failures have been negligible.

Refinements are continually being made in transistor design and application. For example, Motorola now specifies all of its industrial germanium power transistors for continuous operation at junction temperatures of 100°C. This is a conservative rating to assure the ultimate in transistor life and reliability. High temperature storage life tests have been conducted on Motorola units at 125°C without detrimental effects.

It is important that the circuit design engineer thoroughly understand the operating characteristics and ratings of power transistors. It is the purpose of this handbook to provide the background necessary to utilize the characteristics and ratings in designing circuits which will provided completely reliable operation and permit the benefits of transistorized circuits to be more widely utilized.[19]

Chapter 1

Semiconductor Electronics

The transistor has unique amplification characteristics resulting from the electrical properties of a class of elements and compounds known as semiconductors. Semiconductors are so called because they display conductive characteristics intermediate between metals (which are good electrical conductors) and insulators (which are very poor conductors).

At the present time (1961), the chemical elements most often used as the basic material in semiconductor devices are germanium and silicon. Both are in Group IV of the periodic table and have four valence electrons in the outer shell. In the crystalline space lattice these electrons join with the valence electrons of neighboring atoms to form a completely saturated system of covalent bonds. The structure is identical for both germanium and silicon.

Since all the electrons are locked in place in this structure, there are no free electrons to impart conductivity. These materials, when very pure, are poor electrical conductors, although thermal effects may give a few electrons enough energy to break their bonds and by drifting to conduct electricity in an applied field. The spaces vacated by such electrons – called "holes" in semiconductor terminology – leave a net positive charge on the associated atom. These atoms are not free to move; hence, the charge cannot drift with an applied field. However, the atoms may capture a free electron drifting by in a process known as *recombination*. The

---

[19] Ibid – page 1

captured electron may have originated from another nearby bond, in which case that hole may be said to have moved, thus imparting conductivity.

The conductivity is greatly enhanced by adding controlled amounts of certain impurities. For example, the addition of small amounts of antimony to the pure germanium imparts relatively high conductivity. In this case, extra or free electrons are introduced into the semiconductor since the antimony, called a donor impurity, has five valence electrons, only four of which can be shared in the covalent bonds (see Figure 1-1B). This extra electron is free to drift, ionizing the impurity atom. Materials with these excess electrons are called N-type materials. Phosphorus, also a pentavalent element, is generally used as the N-type impurity agent for silicon.

When a trivalent element such as indium is added to germanium (or boron to silicon), the three valence electrons are taken up in the covalent bonds leaving one of the electron bonds in the parent atom unsatisfied. In this manner, a positively charged hole exists which can capture electrons drifting by. This is known as P-type material Both N- and P-type materials are used in transistors and other semiconductor devices.

When P- and N-type materials are brought together, a PN junction is created. In actual practice, the PN junction is formed by growing a crystal of either P- or N-type material and in one area alloying or diffusing-in the type of impurity required to create the opposite type of material. When indium is alloyed into the N-type germanium, a small amount of the indium penetrates the germanium and overrides the effect of the antimony, causing areas of the semiconductor slab to become doped P-type. Although both P- and N-type materials are neutral in charge, the excess electrons in the N-type material are able to cross the interface and combine with the holes in the P-type material. When this occurs, the impurity atoms become ionized. The N-type, upon losing an electron, becomes positively charged and the P-type impurity atom, upon receiving an electron, becomes negatively charged. These ions then form a potential barrier which is negative on the P side and positive on the N side. This potential barrier inhibits further flow of charges across the interface and a state of equilibrium is reached.

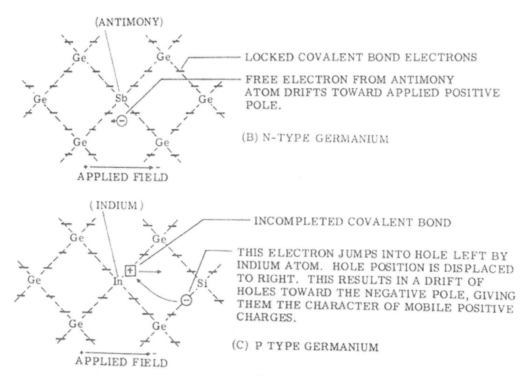

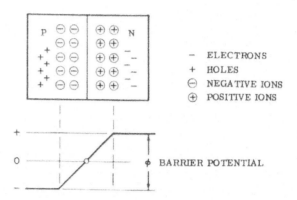

Figure 1-2 — Charge Distribution of PN Junction

It should be noted that the entire crystal is still electrically neutral but a sharp potential difference exists across the interface. At a given temperature only a certain number of electrons will have enough energy to diffuse across this barrier.

To increase the number of electrons that cross the interface, it is necessary to decrease this potential barrier. This can be done by applying a forward bias, using a battery with the positive terminal connected to the P side and the negative terminal connected to the N side. Then some of the ions on both sides lose their charge thereby lowering the barrier potential, as shown in Figure 1-3.

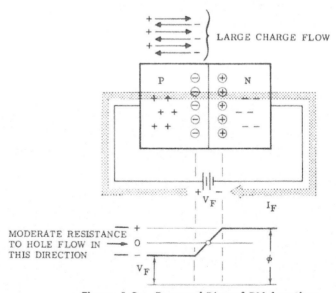

Figure 1-3 — Forward Bias of PN Junction

In Figure 1-4 we have an NP junction with a reverse bias applied: that is the negative terminal of the battery is connected to the P-type material and the positive terminal is connected to the N-type material. The result is an increase in the number of ionized atoms on each side of the interface. Consequently the barrier potential has been increased and the diffusion of charges across the interface is greatly reduced.

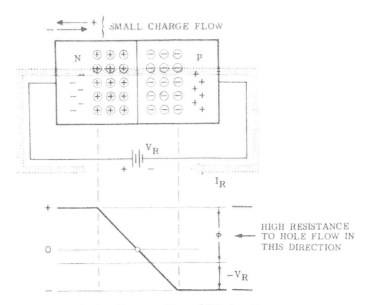

Figure 1-4 — Reverse Bias of NP Junction

When PN and NP junctions are combined, with the N-type region common to both as shown in Figure 1-5, a PNP transistor is created. With a forward bias applied to the PN junction, the number of carriers from the P region (or emitter) which diffuse into the N region (or base) can be modulated by varying the forward bias. If the thickness of the N region or base is small enough, the diffusion of positive carriers will continue through the NP interface. With a reverse bias applied across the NP interface, there is little resistance to the flow of positive carriers. Some of the positive carriers combine with electrons that have entered from the base lead, creating a slight base current flow, I_B. However,

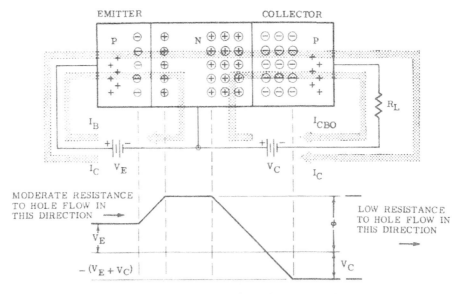

Figure 1-5 — Potential Profile of PNP Transistor

the great majority of positive carriers cross through the collector region into the external circuit. Note that the purpose of the collector bias voltage is not to create current flow but to allow usable power to be delivered to the load resistance. The transistor can be shown to have power gain since a small input power can control a large load power. Consider input power as $I_E^2 R_{in}$, where R_{in} is the input resistance of the emitter-base junction. Load power is $I_C^2 R_L$ and power gain is

$$G = \frac{P_o}{P_{in}} = \frac{I_C^2 R_L}{I_E^2 R_{in}}.$$

The emitter-base junction input resistance may be as low as a fraction of an ohm while the typical load resistance may be a thousand times as great. This explains why a transistor can provide a large power gain.

The ratio of I_C/I_E is called the common-base current gain, h_{fb}, which is normally 0.95 - 0.99. To attain higher power gains it is only necessary to increase R_L, as long as there is a specific minimum voltage maintained across the collector and base under D-C and A-C conditions. In the case of an A-C input, the collector voltage swings from a very low to a very high value, approaching the battery voltage. The gain is also a function of the emitter material, base width, and geometry of the device, especially the ratio of collector diameter to emitter diameter. There is a limit to the maximum voltage which can be placed across a junction; additional voltage will cause the charges to avalanche and become dependent upon voltage. At this point, which is known as the breakdown voltage, there is no longer any control of the transistor. This condition is not destructive, however, as long as the current is limited below the safe power point.

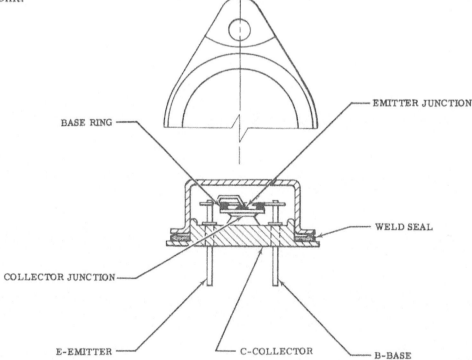

Figure 1-6 — Power Transistor Construction

Semiconductor Electronics

The P-type emitter is heavily doped and contains a large excess of holes or positive carriers. The N-type base contains a moderate excess of electrons and the collector a small excess of holes.

The interfaces between the regions of different types are considered to be very abrupt and thin, and base width, W, very small compared to the junction diameters.

Since there are many more holes at the interface of the P-type than there are electrons in the N-type, there is a high probability that many holes will penetrate the barrier and diffuse into the base. These will diffuse into the collector because of the very narrow base spacing.

The most common form of transistor is the PNP alloy-junction germanium type. These are fabricated by alloying a suitable impurity into both sides of the die. Other junction-forming techniques include barrier layer, diffused, grown junction, and mesa methods. These procedures are also used to produce NPN transistors.

In manufacturing the transistor, contacts to the die and junctions are made with wires or pins extending through a protective cover. The base contact is made to the N-type germanium die; the two junction contacts (called emitter and collector) are connected to the P-type alloyed regions.

The transistor shown in Figure 1-6 is a power transistor which will amplify, control, and dissipate relatively large amounts of power. These features are a result of the design geometry and the particularly efficient means provided to conduct heat away from the semiconductor junction.

The following chapter describes the physical and electrical characteristics of these versatile devices.

Chapter 2

*Transistor Characteristics . . . Mechanical . . . Electrical
Thermal . . . Characteristic Curves . . . Maximum Ratings*

To accomplish heat transfer, Motorola power transistors employ a copper mounting base to which the collector junction is soldered. (This feature will be discussed further under thermal resistance, Section 2-13). Because the collector of the transistor mechanically and electrically contacts the mounting base, the case serves as the collector terminal. The base and emitter pin terminals project through the mounting base and are insulated from it by glass "feed-throughs", which also provide a hermetic seal around the lead. The transistor assembly is completely sealed from external environment by a cap which is either hot or cold welded to the mounting base. While physical appearance may vary with the type of weld employed, the functioning of the seal is the same in either case.

2-2 — Electrical & Thermal Characteristics

To design a circuit, the engineer must take into account the various inherent electrical and thermal characteristics of transistors. A transistor consists of two PN junctions sharing a common, single-crystal base region. Figure 2-2 shows a typical PNP transistor, with the emitter PN junction forward-biased (positive on the emitter) and the collector PN junction reverse-biased (negative on the collector).

As the voltage V_{BE} across the emitter junction is varied, the number of "charge carriers" to the collector also varies. Thus by changing the input voltage, the output current is changed. There are certain basic electrical properties of transistor junctions which account for the relation between input voltage and current and output current and voltage. This relation can be shown by using the classical "black box" (Figure 2-3).

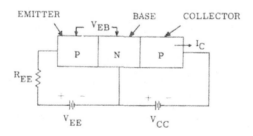

Figure 2-2 — Typical Biasing of PNP Transistor

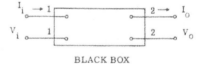

Figure 2-3 — Black Box
Equivalent of Transistor

If the transistor is represented as the "black box", then the relationships of the various voltages and currents may be represented by a number of circuit equations. When the output is short-circuited and the input open-circuited, the parameters which relate voltage to current are called "hybrid" or "h" parameters. The "h" parameter equations are:

$$v_1 = h_{11}i_1 + h_{12}v_2, \text{ and} \qquad (2\text{-}1)$$
$$i_2 = h_{21}i_1 + h_{22}v_2. \qquad (2\text{-}2)$$

When $v_2 = 0$ (Short Circuit output),

Then $\quad h_{11} = \dfrac{v_1}{i_1}$, and $\hfill (2\text{-}3)$

$$h_{21} = \dfrac{i_2}{i_1}. \qquad (2\text{-}4)$$

When $\quad i_1 = 0$ (Open Circuit input),

Then $\quad h_{12} = \dfrac{v_1}{v_2}$, and $\hfill (2\text{-}5)$

$$h_{22} = \dfrac{i_2}{v_2}. \qquad (2\text{-}6)$$

The subscript "11" represents the input (i), "21" a forward transfer (f), "12" a reverse transfer (r), and "22" the output (o). Conventional terminology of "h" parameters for small signal conditions is as follows:

Input impedance (ohms) $\qquad h_i = \dfrac{\partial v_1}{\partial i_1} \qquad (2\text{-}7)$

Forward current gain $\qquad h_f = \dfrac{\partial i_2}{\partial i_1} \qquad (2\text{-}8)$

Reverse voltage ratio $\qquad h_r = \dfrac{\partial v_1}{\partial v_2} \qquad (2\text{-}9)$

Output admittance (mhos) $\qquad h_o = \dfrac{\partial i_2}{\partial v_2} \qquad (2\text{-}10)$

The normal mode of operation is common emitter, signified by the addition of subscript "e"; for example, small-signal common-emitter current gain is h_{fe}. Similarly, common base is signified by a "b" subscript, and common collector by a "c". In addition to small-signal "h" parameters, large-signal and DC "h" parameters are commonly encountered. All of these are defined in Table 2-1

TABLE 2-1
("h" PARAMETERS FOR COMMON-EMITTER CIRCUIT)

Description	Small Signal	Large Signal	DC
Input Resistance	$h_{ie} = \dfrac{\partial V_{EB}}{\partial I_B}$	$H_{IE} = \dfrac{\Delta V_{EB}}{\Delta I_B}$	$h_{IE} = \dfrac{V_{EB}}{I_B}$
Current Gain	$h_{fe} = \dfrac{\partial I_C}{\partial I_B}$	$H_{FE} = \dfrac{\Delta I_C}{\Delta I_B}$	*$h_{FE} = \dfrac{I'_C - I_{CBO}}{I'_B + I_{CBO}}$

*Where I'_C and I'_B are the values read on a meter.

Since power transistors are usually operated at nearly short-circuit (AC) output, the h_{ie} and h_{fe} parameters are specified and may be used directly for circuit design. Because the input is rarely open-circuited, h_{re} and h_{oe} are seldom specified in data sheets on power transistors.

*Transistor Characteristics . . . Mechanical . . . Electrical
Thermal . . . Characteristic Curves . . . Maximum Ratings*

2-3 — Characteristic Curves

Static or DC curves relating input conditions, transfer functions, and output conditions show how the emitter and collector junctions control the output current. Some typical characteristic curves for Motorola power transistors appear later in this section. The "h" parameters can be obtained from the particular curve representing the same information because they are merely the slope at any point. For example, h_{fe} may be obtained from the I_C vs I_B curve as shown in Figure 2-6.

In addition to the "black box" information, other PN junction characteristics can be represented by a plot of variables. Such things as leakage current and breakdown voltage of the collector are best represented graphically. The effects of temperature on these curves are seen by plotting the curves at several different temperatures. Thus it is possible to completely characterize a transistor by "black box" theory, and voltage, current, and temperature plots. (It will be shown in Section 2-12 that curves also provide a visual description of the maximum ratings of the transistor.) Of course, static curves do not give any frequency information. The frequency cutoff point will be defined in Section 2-5.

2-4 — Special Specifications

End use determines the special Power Gain, Transconductance, and Distortion specifications associated with certain transistors. For example, the Motorola 2N176 Power Transistor was designed for use in the power output stage of automobile radios and hence requires a power gain specification in a specific circuit. Also distortion specification is required for this audio output stage. With switching transistors the important characteristics are DC or large-signal current gain and input resistance. In the latter case however, it is simpler to specify transconductance instead of input resistance. Transistor transconductance is defined as the ratio of collector current to base-emitter voltage, or:

$$g_{FE} = \frac{I_C}{V_{EB}} \quad (\text{note that } g_{FE} = \frac{h_{FE}}{h_{IE}}).$$

2-5 — Current Gain Frequency Cutoff

Current gain frequency cutoff (f_{ae}) for the common emitter configuration, (also called the beta cutoff frequency) is the frequency where the small-signal, forward-current gain is .707 of the current gain value to be found at a given reference frequency. The .707 point represents a 3 db reduction in current gain. The cutoff frequency is usually between 5kc and 10kc for power transistors. The common base frequency cutoff, f_{ab}, (generally not specified for power transistors) is approximately equal to h_{fe} times f_{ae}.

2-6 — Switching Characteristics

Switching characteristics involve delay time, rise time, storage time, and fall time. These time periods are derived from a display of the output pulse and a standard input pulse on an oscilloscope. Figure 2-4 is typical of such a display. In audio switching applications, nonsaturated rise and fall times t_r and t_f are related to f_{ae} according to the following empirical relations:

$$t_r \times f_{ae} = .3 \tag{2-11}$$

$$t_f \times f_{ae} = .6 \tag{2-12}$$

where t_r = nonsaturated rise time, the 10% to 90% points in microseconds,

t_f = nonsaturated fall time, the 10% to 90% points in microseconds, and

f_{ae} = common emitter cutoff frequency, cps.

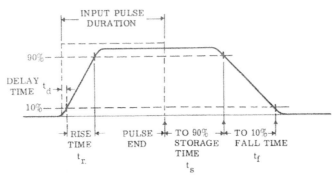

Figure 2-4 — Pulse Response Times

2-7 — Collector Cutoff Current

Collector cutoff current, I_{CBO}, (sometimes shortened to I_{CO}) is the small current that flows from the collector to the base because of the inverse collector potential, which exists when the transistor is cut off. This current is caused by random diffusion of charge carriers across the collector junction, plus leakage currents across the surface of the germanium die that composes the transistor assembly. Every transistor type has a maximum cutoff current value which helps define the range in which it can be used. Typical value of cutoff currents are much less than the maximum value given on data sheets.

I_{CBO} is one of the transistor parameters that is extremely temperature sensitive. Because power transistors generally operate at very high junction temperatures, changes in I_{CBO} at these temperatures can greatly affect stability. The leakage component of I_{CBO} is voltage dependent and therefore the total I_{CBO} is a function of voltage and temperature.

Variation of I_{CBO} with temperature and voltage, for a typical transistor is shown in Figure 2-5. At a given temperature and for a given collector junction area, diffusion (or saturation) component of I_{CBO} varies directly with base resistivity, the greater the resistivity, the greater the diffusion component. Thus this component is larger with higher voltage devices which have higher base resistivity.

2-8 — Emitter Cutoff Current

Emitter cutoff current (I_{EBO}) varies in the same manner as I_{CBO} and the curves are similar.

*Transistor Characteristics . . . Mechanical . . . Electrical
Thermal . . . Characteristic Curves . . . Maximum Ratings*

2-9 — Collector Saturation Voltage

Collector saturation voltage, $V_{CE\,sat}$, (Figure 2-9) is the minimum voltage necessary to sustain normal transistor action at a particular collector current. At this point the emitter-base voltage equals the collector-emitter voltage. At collector voltages lower than $V_{CE\,sat}$ the base-collector diode is forward-biased and the current-voltage relationship changes abruptly. Thus the saturation voltage is the minimum collector-emitter voltage required to maintain full conduction when enough base drive is supplied. Further application of base drive will reduce $V_{CE\,sat}$ with diminishing effect. Since the $V_{CE\,sat}$ vs I_C curve is almost a straight line, some transistor manufacturers list the characteristic as saturation resistance ($r_{CE\,sat}$). $V_{CE\,sat}$ is part of the output characteristic curve as shown in Figure 2-9.

2-10 — Collector Breakdown Voltage

Collector breakdown voltage is the inverse voltage at which the collector junction current begins to avalanche. Under some conditions of operation, especially with inductive loads, the actual voltage appearing at the collector may for a brief time greatly exceed the collector supply voltage, therefore the effects of inductive transients and surges must be taken into consideration. Different types of breakdown voltage characteristics are defined and discussed in Sections 2-16 - 2-19.

2-11 — Power Transistor Characteristic Curves

The important characteristic curves are as follows:

Temperature	Collector cutoff current vs temperature	(Figure 2-5)
Transfer	Collector current vs base current	(Figure 2-6)
Transfer	Collector current vs base-emitter voltage	(Figure 2-7)
Input	Base current vs base-emitter voltage	
Output	Collector current vs collector-to-emitter voltage with base current family	(Figure 2-8) (Figure 2-9)
Output	Collector current vs collector-to-emitter voltage with base-emitter voltage family	
Temperature	Current gain vs collector current and temperature	(Figure 2-10) (Figure 2-11)
Temperature	Transconductance vs collector current and temperature	

Some typical curves for Motorola devices, with an indication of their usefulness, are shown here. The composite curve of Figure 2-12 is an example of how transistor characteristic curves may be used to obtain input to output waveshape relations in a single-ended Class "A" audio amplifier.

Chapter Five -- Crystal Oscillators

A **crystal oscillator** is an electronic oscillator circuit that uses the mechanical resonance of a vibrating crystal of *piezoelectric* material to create an electrical signal with a precise frequency. This frequency is often used to keep track of time, as in quartz wristwatches, to provide a stable clock signal for digital integrated circuits, and to stabilize frequencies for radio transmitters and receivers. The most common type of piezoelectric resonator used is the quartz crystal; thus, oscillator circuits incorporating them became known as crystal oscillators, but other piezoelectric materials including polycrystalline ceramics are used in similar circuits.

Miniature 16MHz quartz crystal enclosed in a hermetically sealed HC-49/S, used as the resonator in a crystal oscillator

Electronic Symbol

An oscillating crystal is an electromechanical device operating on the piezoelectricity, resonance principle invented in 1918 by Alexander M. Nicholson and Walter Guyton Cady.

A crystal oscillator, particularly one made of quartz crystal, works by being distorted by an electric field when voltage is applied to an electrode near or on the crystal. This property is known as **electrostriction or inverse piezoelectricity**[20]. When the field is removed, the quartz - which oscillates at a precise frequency - generates an electric field as it returns to its previous shape, and this can generate a voltage. The result is that a quartz crystal behaves like an RLC circuit.

Quartz crystals are manufactured for frequencies from a few tens of kilohertz to hundreds of megahertz. Billions of crystals are manufactured annually. Most are used for consumer devices such as wrist watches, clocks, radios, computers,

100kHz crystal oscillators at the US National Bureau of Standards that served as the frequency standard for the United States in 1929

and cellphones. Quartz crystals are also found inside test and measurement equipment, such as counters, signal generators and oscilloscopes.

Piezoelectricity was discovered by Jacques and Pierre Curie in 1880. Paul Langevin first investigated quartz resonators for use in sonar during World War I. The first crystal-controlled oscillator, using a crystal of Rochelle salt,

was built in 1917 and patented in 1918 by Alexander M. Nicholson at Bell Telephone Laboratories, although his priority was disputed by Walter Guyton Cady. Cady built the first quartz crystal oscillator in 1921. Other early innovators in quartz crystal oscillators include G. W. Pierce and Louis Essen.

Quartz crystal oscillators were developed for high-stability frequency references during the 1920s and 1930s. Prior to crystals, radio stations controlled their frequency with tuned circuits, which could easily drift off frequency by 3–4kHz. Since broadcast stations were assigned frequencies only 10kHz apart, interference between adjacent stations due to frequency drift was a common problem. In 1925, Westinghouse installed a crystal oscillator in its flagship station KDKA, and by 1926, quartz crystals were used to control the frequency of many broadcasting stations and were popular with amateur radio operators. In 1928, Warren Marrison of Bell Telephone Laboratories developed the first quartz-crystal clock. With accuracies of up to 1 second in 30 years (30 ms/y, or 10^{-7}), quartz clocks replaced precision pendulum clocks as the world's most accurate

---

[20] https://www.hbm.com/en/3227/the-piezo-effect-and-its-applications/?gclid=CjwKCAjwiMj2BRBFEiwAYfTbCpJe4Ll0Vtebm-Nom34eHIrBb2PQ7LhdsiSPoNl-AnqZjMBYOForbKBoC3z8QAvD_BwE

timekeepers until atomic clocks were developed in the 1950s. Using the early work at Bell Labs, AT&T eventually established their Frequency Control Products division, later spun off and known today as Vectron International.

A number of firms started producing quartz crystals for electronic use during this time. Using what are now considered primitive methods, about 100,000 crystal units were produced in the United States during 1939. Through World War II, crystals were made from natural quartz crystal, virtually all from Brazil. Shortages of crystals during the war caused by the demand for accurate frequency control of military radios and radars spurred postwar research into culturing synthetic quartz, and, by 1950, a hydrothermal process for growing quartz crystals on a commercial scale was developed at Bell Laboratories. By the 1970s virtually all crystals used in electronics were synthetic.

In 1968, Juergen Staudte invented a photolithographic process for manufacturing quartz crystal oscillators while working at North American Aviation (now Rockwell) that allowed them to be made small enough for portable products like pagers and watches.

Although crystal oscillators still most commonly use quartz crystals, devices using other materials such as ceramic resonators are becoming more common.

Operation

A crystal is a solid in which the constituent atoms, molecules, or ions are packed in a regularly ordered, repeating pattern extending in all three spatial dimensions.

Almost any object made of an elastic material could be used like a crystal, with appropriate transducers, since all objects have natural resonant frequencies of vibration. For example, steel is very elastic and has a high speed of sound. It was often used in mechanical filters before quartz. The resonant frequency depends on size, shape, elasticity, and the speed of sound in the material. High-frequency crystals are typically cut in the shape of a simple rectangle or circular disk. Low-frequency crystals, such as those used in digital watches, are typically cut in the shape of a tuning fork. For applications not needing very precise timing, a low-cost ceramic resonator is often used in place of a quartz crystal.

Quartz has the further advantage that its elastic constants and its size change in such a way that the frequency dependence on temperature can be very low. The specific characteristics depend on the mode of vibration and the angle at which the quartz is cut (relative to its crystallographic axes). Therefore, the resonant frequency of the plate, which depends on its size, does not change much. This means that a quartz clock, filter or oscillator remains accurate. For critical applications the quartz oscillator is mounted in a temperature-controlled container, called a crystal oven, and can also be mounted on shock absorbers to prevent perturbation by external mechanical vibrations.[21]

Electromagnet

In 1825, British inventor William Sturgeon (1783-1850), introduced an invention that laid the foundation for a large scale revolution in electronic communications—the electromagnet. Sturgeon demonstrated the power of the electromagnet by lifting nine pounds with a seven ounce piece of iron wrapped with wires through which the current of a single cell battery was sent. However, the true power of the electromagnet comes from its role in the creation of countless inventions.

An electromagnet is a magnet that runs on electricity. Unlike a permanent magnet, the strength of an electromagnet can easily be changed by changing the amount of electric current that flows through it. The poles of an electromagnet can even be reversed by reversing the flow of electricity.

An electromagnet works because an electric current produces a magnetic field. The magnetic field produced by an electric current forms circles around the electric current.

If a wire carrying an electric current is formed into a series of loops, the magnetic field can be concentrated within the loops. The magnetic field can be strengthened even more by wrapping the wire around a core. The

---

[21] https://en.wikipedia.org/wiki/Crystal_oscillator

atoms of certain materials, such as iron, nickel and cobalt, each behave like tiny magnets. Normally, the atoms in something like a lump of iron point in random directions and the individual magnetic fields tend to cancel each other out. However, the magnetic field produced by the wire wrapped around the core can force some of the atoms within the core to point in one direction. All of their little magnetic fields add together, creating a stronger magnetic field.[22]

As the current flowing around the core increases, the number of aligned atoms increases and the stronger the magnetic field becomes --at least, up to a point. Sooner or later, all of the atoms that can be aligned will be aligned. At this point, the magnet is said to be saturated and increasing the electric current flowing around the core no longer affects the magnetization of the core itself.[23]

---

[22] https://education.jlab.org/qa/electromagnet
[23] Ibid

Chapter Six -- Telegraphy and Telephony

Emergence of Telegraph Systems

In 1830, an American named Joseph Henry (1797-1878), demonstrated the potential of William Sturgeon's electromagnet for long distance communication by sending an electronic current over one mile of wire to activate an electromagnet, causing a bell to strike.

Joseph Henry, (born December 17, 1797, Albany, New York, U.S.—died May 13, 1878, Washington, D.C.), one of the first great American scientists after Benjamin Franklin discovered several important principles of electricity, including self-induction, a phenomenon of primary importance in electronic circuitry.

While working with electromagnets at the Albany Academy (New York) in 1829, he made important design improvements. By insulating the wire instead of the iron core, he was able to wrap a large number of turns of wire around the core and thus greatly increase the power of the magnet. He made an electromagnet for Yale College that could support 2,063 pounds, a world record at the time.

Henry also searched for electromagnetic induction—the process of converting magnetism into electricity—and, in 1831, he started building a large electromagnet for that purpose. Because the room at the Albany Academy in which he wanted to build his experiment was not available, he had to postpone his work until June 1832, when he learned that British physicist Michael Faraday had already discovered induction the previous year. However, when he resumed his experiments, he was the first to notice the principle of self-induction.[24]

In 1837, British physicists, William Cooke and Charles Wheatstone, patented the telegraph using the same principle of electromagnetism.

However, it was Samuel Morse (1791-1872) who successfully exploited the electromagnet and improved Henry's invention. Morse started by making sketches of a "magnetized magnet" based on Henry's work. Eventually, he invented a telegraph system that was a practical and commercial success.

Samuel Morse

While teaching arts and design at New York University in 1835, Morse proved that signals could be trans-mitted by wire. He used pulses of current to deflect an electromagnet which moved a marker to produce written codes on a strip of paper. This led to the invention of Morse code.

The following year, the device was modified to emboss the paper with dots and dashes. He gave a public demonstration in 1838, but it wasn't until five years later that Congress, reflecting public apathy, awarded him $30,000 to construct an experimental telegraph line from Washington to Baltimore, a distance of 40 miles.

Six years later, members of Congress witnessed the transmission of messages over part of the telegraph line. Before the line had reached Baltimore, the Whig party held its national convention there and nominated Henry Clay on May 1, 1844. The news was hand-carried to Annapolis Junction, between Washington and Baltimore, where Morse's partner, Alfred Vail, wired it to the capitol. This was the first news dispatched by electric telegraph.

What Hath God Wrought?

The message, "What hath God wrought?," sent by Morse Code from the old Supreme Court chamber in the United States capitol to his partner in Baltimore, officially opened the completed line on May 24, 1844. Morse allowed Annie Ellsworth, the young daughter of a friend, to choose the words of the message and she selected a verse from Numbers XXIII, 23: "What hath God wrought?" to be recorded onto paper tape. Morse's early system produced a paper copy with raised dots and dashes, which were translated later by an operator.[25]

The Telegraph Spreads

---

[24] https://www.britannica.com/biography/Joseph-Henry
[25] https://www.thoughtco.com/the-history-of-the-electric-telegraph-and-telegraphy-1992542

Samuel Morse and his associates obtained private funds to extend their line to Philadelphia and New York. Small telegraph companies meanwhile began functioning in the East, South and Midwest. Dispatching trains by telegraph started in 1851, the same year Western Union began business. Western Union built its first transcontinental telegraph line in 1861, mainly along railroad rights-of-way. In 1881, the Postal Telegraph System entered the field for economic reasons and later merged with Western Union in 1943.[26]

Author's insertion: When the first transatlantic telegraph cable was laid in 1858 by businessman Cyrus Westfield, it operated for only three weeks; subsequent attempts in 1865 and 1866 were more successful. Although a telephone cable was discussed starting in 1920, to be practical it needed a number of technological advances which did not arrive until the 1940s. Starting in 1927, transatlantic telephone service was radio-based.

TAT-1 (Transatlantic No. 1) was the first transatlantic telephone cable system. It was laid between Gallanach Bay, near Oban, Scotland and Clarenville, Newfoundland between 1955 and 1956 by the cable ship Monarch. It was inaugurated on September 25, 1956, initially carrying 36 telephone channels. In the first 24 hours of public service there were 588 London–U.S. calls and 119 from London to Canada. The capacity of the cable was soon increased to 48 channels. Later, an additional three channels were added by use of C Carrier equipment. Time-assignment speech interpolation (TASI) was implemented on the TAT-1 cable in June 1960 and effectively increased the cable's capacity from 37 (out of 51 available channels) to 72 speech circuits. TAT-1 was finally retired in 1978. Later coaxial cables, installed through the 1970s, used transistors and had higher bandwidth. The Moscow–Washington hotline was initially connected through this system.

Current technology (21st Century)

All undersea cables presently in service use fiber optic technology. Many cables terminate in Newfoundland and Ireland, which lie on the great circle route (the shortest route) from London, UK, to New York City, USA.

There have been a succession of newer transatlantic cable systems. All recent systems have used fiber optic transmission, and a self-healing ring topology. Late in the 20th century, communications satellites lost most of their North Atlantic telephone traffic to these low cost, high capacity, low latency cables. This advantage only increases over time as tighter cables provide higher speed – the 2012 generation of cables drop the transatlantic latency to under 60 milliseconds, according to Hibernia Atlantic, deploying such a cable that year.

End insertion...[27]

The original Morse telegraph printed code on tape. However, in the United States, the operation developed into a process in which messages were sent by key and received by ear. A trained Morse operator could transmit 40 to 50 words per minute. Automatic transmission, introduced in 1914, handled more than twice that number. In 1900, Canadian Fredrick Creed invented the Creed Telegraph System, a way to convert Morse code to text.[28]

October 24, 1861

Western Union completes the first transcontinental telegraph line

On this day in 1861, workers of the Western Union Telegraph Company linked the eastern and western telegraph networks of the nation at Salt Lake City, Utah, completing a transcontinental line that, for the first time, allowed instantaneous communication between Washington, D.C., and San Francisco. Stephen J. Field, chief justice of California, sent the first transcontinental telegram to President Abraham Lincoln, predicting that the new communication link would help ensure the loyalty of the western states to the Union during the Civil War.

The push to create a transcontinental telegraph line had begun only a little more than a year before when Congress authorized a subsidy of $40,000 a year to any company building a telegraph line that would join the eastern and western networks. The Western Union Telegraph Company, as its name suggests, took up the challenge, and the company immediately began work on the critical link that would span the territory between the western edge of Missouri and Salt Lake City.

The obstacles to building the line over the sparsely populated and isolated western plains and mountains were huge. Wire and glass insulators had to be shipped by sea to San Francisco and carried eastward by horse-

---

[26] Ibid
[27] https://en.wikipedia.org/wiki/Transatlantic_communications_cable
[28] https://www.thoughtco.com/the-history-of-the-electric-telegraph-and-telegraphy-1992542

Invention of Photograph Transmission Equipment

Spurred by the prevailing emphasis on independent technological development, NEC began next the development of photograph transmission equipment, which is the basis of today's facsimile equipment.

In 1928 the coronation of the present emperor, Hirohito, was scheduled to take place in Kyoto. All newspaper companies planned to transmit the pictures taken at the ceremony from Kyoto to Tokyo by telephone wire. To accomplish this, most newspapers expected to import foreign equipment. NEC, however, attempted to develop its own system, under the direction of Yasujiro Niwa, chief engineer, and Masatsugu Kobayashi, engineer. It met the challenge splendidly, and a newspaper company quickly adopted NEC's telephotographic system. On coronation day only the NEC system was able to provide prompt photo coverage of the ceremony to readers in the Tokyo area.

Later, in 1936, experiments in transmitting wireless photographs between Tokyo and Berlin, Tokyo and London, and Tokyo and San Francisco were successful. At that time the Olympic Games were being held in Berlin, and pictures showing exploits of Japanese athletes were continuously transmitted to Japan to the great excitement of the public.

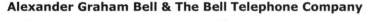
Photograph transmission equipment developed by NEC in 1928

drawn wagons over the Sierra Nevada. Supplying the thousands of telegraph poles needed was an equally daunting challenge in the largely treeless plains country, and these too had to be shipped from the western mountains.

Native American tribes also proved a problem. In the summer of 1861, a party of Sioux warriors cut part of the line that had been completed and took a long section of wire for making bracelets. Later, however, some of the Sioux wearing the telegraph-wire bracelets became sick, and a Sioux medicine man convinced them that the great spirit of the "talking wire" had avenged its desecration. Thereafter, the Sioux left the line alone, and the Western Union was able to connect the East and West Coasts of the nation much earlier than anyone had expected and a full eight years before the transcontinental railroad would be completed.[29]

**Note: Ten years prior to Western Union's introduction of the "fax" machine, in1928, in Japan, Nippon Electric Company introduced their "photograph transmission equipment."

Multiplex Telegraph, Teleprinters, & Other Advancements

In 1913, Western Union developed multiplexing, which made it possible to transmit eight messages simultaneously over a single wire (four in each direction). Teleprinter machines came into use around 1925 and, in 1936, Varioplex was introduced. This enabled a single wire to carry 72 transmissions at the same time (36 in each direction). Two years later, 1938, Western Union introduced the first of its automatic facsimile devices. In 1959, Western Union inaugurated TELEX, which enabled subscribers to the teleprinter service to dial each other directly.

Telephone Rivals the Telegraph

Until 1877, all rapid long-distance communication depended upon the telegraph. That year, a rival technology developed that would again change the face of communication—the telephone. By 1879, patent litigation between Western Union and the infant telephone system ended in an agreement that largely separated the two services.

While Samuel Morse is best known as the inventor of the telegraph, he is also esteemed for his contributions to American portraiture. His painting is characterized by delicate technique and vigorous honesty and insight into the character of his subjects.[30]

Alexander Graham Bell & The Bell Telephone Company

Predecessor to the Bell Company

The **Bell Patent Association** (February 27, 1875 – July 9, 1877, a name later assigned by historians), was not a corporate entity but a trusteeship and a partnership. It was established verbally in 1874 to be the holders of the patents produced by Alexander Graham Bell and his assistant Thomas Watson.

Approximate one-third interests were at first held by 1) Gardiner Greene Hubbard, a lawyer and Bell's future father-in-law; 2) Thomas Sanders, the well-to-do leather merchant father of one of Bell's deaf students (and who was the first to enter into an agreement with Bell); and finally by 3) Alexander Graham Bell. Hubbard

---

[29] https://www.history.com/this-day-in-history/western-union-completes-the-first-transcontinental-telegraph-line
[30] https://www.thoughtco.com/the-history-of-the-electric-telegraph-and-telegraphy-1992542

later registered some of his shares with two other family members. An approximate 10% interest of the patent association was later assigned by its principals to Bell's technical assistant, Thomas Watson, in lieu of salary and for his earlier financial support to Bell while they worked together creating their first functional telephones.[31]

Railroad Rights-of-Way and Easements

The Pacific Transcontinental Railroad Act, signed by President Abraham Lincoln, granting lands and powers to companies intending to construct and manage railroads is available on line if you are interested in some of the underlying issues upon which today's telecommunications networks have been funded and legislatively promoted.

Briefly summarizing what is an otherwise lengthy reading assignment, the congressional act cited in the above paragraph granted millions of free acres (from 1850 to 1871, the railroads received more than 175 million acres of public land – an area more than one tenth of the whole United States and larger in area than Texas) to private corporations whose founders and stockholders (as well as the politicians they supported) became some of the wealthiest men and families in America by "interpreting" the phraseology of the railroad specific acts.

While this entrepreneurial excess was no less devious nor onerous than today's political climate, it never-theless catapulted railroad real estate into an unpredicted star role in the telecommunications matinee.

Specifically addressed in the congressional acts referenced here is the requirement of those corporations constructing railroads to also reserve two hundred feet on each side of the rail beds for the specific purpose of providing telegraphy service. This, at the time seemingly obscure requirement, became the platform from which the Ma Bell/AT&T telephone system would deliver voice telephone service to America – particularly long distance and small town rural America. It is also one of the primary reasons why Ma Bell would lose her case when the Justice Department filed divestiture proceedings.

Breakup (divestiture) of the Bell System[32]

The **breakup of the Bell System** was mandated on January 8, 1982, by an agreed consent decree providing that AT&T Corporation would, as had been initially proposed by AT&T, relinquish control of the Bell Operating Companies that had provided local telephone service in the United States and Canada up until that point. This effectively took the monopoly that was the Bell System and split it into entirely separate companies that would continue to provide telephone service. AT&T would continue to be a provider of long distance service, while the now-independent Regional Bell Operating Companies (RBOCs) would provide local service, and would no longer be directly supplied with equipment from AT&T subsidiary Western Electric.

While divestiture was nothing new to AT&T, this divestiture was initiated by the filing in 1974 by the United States Department of Justice of an antitrust lawsuit against AT&T. AT&T was, at the time, the sole provider of telephone service throughout most of the United States. Furthermore, most telephonic equipment in the United States was produced by its subsidiary, Western Electric. This vertical integration led AT&T to have almost total control over communication technology in the country, which led to the antitrust case, *United States v. AT&T*. The plaintiff in the court complaint asked the court to order AT&T to divest ownership of Western Electric.

Feeling that it was about to lose the suit, AT&T proposed an alternative— the breakup of the biggest corporation in American history. It proposed that it retain control of Western Electric, Yellow Pages, the Bell trademark, Bell Labs, and AT&T Long Distance. It also proposed that it be freed from a 1956 antitrust consent decree, then administered by Judge Vincent Pasquale Biunno in the United States District Court for the District of New Jersey, that barred it from participating in the general sale of computers. In return, it proposed to give up ownership of the local operating companies. This last concession, it argued, would achieve the govern-

---

[31] https://en.wikipedia.org/wiki/Bell_Telephone_Company
[32] https://en.wikipedia.org/wiki/Breakup_of_the_Bell_System

ment's goal of creating competition in supplying telephone equipment and supplies to the operating companies. The settlement was finalized on January 8, 1982, with some changes ordered by the decree court: the regional holding companies got the Bell trademark, Yellow Pages, and about half of Bell Labs.

Effective January 1, 1984, the Bell System's many member companies were variously merged into seven independent "Regional Holding Companies," also known as Regional Bell Operating Companies (RBOCs), or "Baby Bells." This divestiture reduced the book value of AT&T by approximately 70%.

Post-breakup structure

The breakup of the Bell System resulted in creation of seven independent companies that were formed from the original twenty-two AT&T-controlled members.

At the time of the breakup, these companies were:

- NYNEX, acquired by Bell Atlantic in 1996, now part of Verizon Communications
- Pacific Telesis, acquired by SBC in 1997, now part of AT&T Inc.
- Ameritech, acquired by SBC in 1999, now part of AT&T Inc.
- Bell Atlantic, merged with GTE in 2000 to form Verizon Communications
- Southwestern Bell Corporation, rebranded as SBC Communications in 1995, acquired AT&T Corporation in 2005
- BellSouth, acquired by AT&T Inc. in 2006
- US West, acquired by Qwest in 2000, which in turn was acquired by CenturyLink in 2011

In addition, there were two members of the Bell System that were only partially owned by AT&T. Both of these companies, monopolies in their coverage areas, received Western Electric equipment and had agreements with AT&T whereby they were provided with long distance service. They continued to exist in their pre-breakup form after the antitrust case, but no longer directly received Western Electric equipment, and were no longer bound to use AT&T as their long distance provider. These companies were:

Cincinnati Bell, now the only Bell System member to remain independent, covering the Cincinnati metropolitan area

Southern New England Telephone (SNET), acquired by SBC in 1998, now part of Frontier Communications, covering Connecticut.

The breakup led to a surge of competition in the long distance telecommunications market by companies such as Sprint and MCI. AT&T's gambit in exchange for its divestiture, AT&T Computer Systems, failed, and after spinning off its manufacturing operations (most notably Western Electric, which became Lucent, then Alcatel-Lucent, now Nokia) and other misguided acquisitions such as NCR and AT&T Broadband, it was left with only its core business with roots as AT&T Long Lines and its successor AT&T Communications. It was at this point that AT&T was purchased by one of its own spin-offs, SBC Communications, the company that had also purchased two other RBOCs and a former AT&T associated operating company (Ameritech, Pacific Telesis, and SNET), and which later purchased another RBOC - BellSouth).

One consequence of the breakup was that local residential service rates, which were formerly subsidized by long distance revenues, began to rise faster than the rate of inflation. Long-distance rates, meanwhile, fell both due to the end of this subsidy and increased competition. The FCC established a system of access charges where long distance networks paid the more expensive local networks both to originate and terminate a call. In this way, the implicit subsidies of the Bell System became explicit post-divestiture. These access charges became a source of strong controversy as one company after another sought to arbitrage the network and avoid these fees. In 2002 the FCC declared that internet service providers would be treated as if they were local and would not have to pay these access charges. This led to VoIP service providers arguing that they did not have to pay access charges, resulting in significant savings for VoIP calls. The FCC was split on this issue for some time; VoIP services that utilized IP but in every other way looked like a normal phone call generally had to pay access charges, while VoIP services that looked more like applications on the internet and did not interconnect with the public telephone network did not have to pay access charges. However, an FCC order issued in December 2011 declared that all VoIP services would have to pay the charges for nine years, at which point all access charges would then be phased out.

Another consequence of the divestiture was in how national broadcast television (*i.e.*, ABC, NBC, CBS, PBS) and radio networks (NPR, Mutual, ABC Radio) distributed their programming to their local affiliated stations. Prior to the breakup, the broadcast networks relied on AT&T Long Lines' infrastructure of terrestrial microwave relay, coaxial cable, and, for radio, broadcast-quality leased line networks to deliver their programming to local stations. However, by the mid-1970s, the then-new technology of satellite distribution offered by other companies like RCA Astro Electronics and Western Union with their respective Satcom 1 and Westar 1 satellites started to give the Bell System competition in the broadcast distribution field, with the satellites providing higher video and audio quality, as well as much lower transmission costs.

However, the networks stayed with AT&T (along with simulcasting their feeds *via* satellite through the late 1970s to the early 1980s) due to some stations not being equipped yet with ground station receiving equipment to receive the networks' satellite feeds, and due to the broadcast networks' contractual obligations with AT&T up until the breakup in 1984, when the networks immediately switched to satellite exclusively. This was due to several reasons — the much cheaper rates for transmission offered by satellite operators that were not influenced by the high tariffs set by AT&T for broadcast customers, the split of the Bell System into separate RBOCs, and the end of contracts the broadcast companies had with AT&T.

AT&T's post-breakup strategy did not work out the way it had planned. Its attempt to enter the computer business failed, and it quickly realized that Western Electric was not profitable without the guaranteed customers the Bell System had provided. In 1995, AT&T spun off its computer division and Western Electric, exactly as the government had initially asked it to do. It then re-entered the local telephone business that it had exited after the breakup, which had become much more lucrative with the rise of dial-up internet access in the early 1990s. Even this, however, would not save AT&T Corporation. It would soon be absorbed by one of the Baby Bells, SBC Communications (formerly Southwestern Bell), which then co-opted the AT&T name to form the present-day AT&T Inc.[33]

Historical Perspective

A Bell System logo (called the Blue Bell), was used from 1889 to 1900. The Bell Telephone Company and its successors created the Bell System and drove its expansion.

The **Bell Telephone Company**, a common law joint stock company, was organized in Boston, Massachusetts on July 9, 1877, by Alexander Graham Bell's father-in-law, Gardiner Greene Hubbard, who also helped organize a sister company — the New England Telephone and Telegraph Company. The Bell Telephone Company was started on the basis of holding "potentially valuable patents," principally Bell's master telephone patent #174465.

The two companies merged on February 17, 1879, to form two new entities, the **National Bell Telephone Company** of Boston, and the International Bell Telephone Company, soon after established by Hubbard and

which became headquartered in Brussels, Belgium. Theodore Vail then took over its operations at that point, becoming a central figure in its rapid growth and commercial success.

The National Bell Telephone Company merged with American Speaking Telephone Company on March 20, 1880, to form the **American Bell Telephone Company**, also of Boston, Massachusetts.

Upon its inception, the Bell Telephone Company was organized with Hubbard as "trustee," although he was additionally its *de facto* president, since he also controlled his daughter's shares by power of attorney, and with Thomas Sanders, its principal financial backer, as treasurer. The American Bell Telephone Company evolved into the American Telephone & Telegraph Company (AT&T), at times the world's largest telephone company.[34]

---

[33] Ibid
[34] Ibid

Chapter Seven -- AT&T

AT&T Inc. is an American multinational conglomerate holding company headquartered at Whitacre Tower in Downtown Dallas, Texas. It is the world's largest telecommunications company, the second largest provider of mobile telephone services, and the largest provider of fixed telephone services in the United States through AT&T Communications. Since June 14, 2018, it is also the parent company of mass media conglomerate Warner-Media™, making it (at the time of this writing) the world's largest media and entertainment company in terms of revenue.

The Bell Telephone Company evolved into **American Telephone and Telegraph Company** in 1885, which later rebranded as AT&T Corporation. The 1982 *United States v. AT&T* antitrust lawsuit resulted in the divestiture of AT&T Corporation's ("Ma Bell") subsidiaries or Regional Bell Operating Companies (RBOCs, or "Baby Bells"), producing several independent companies including Southwestern Bell Corporation; the latter changed its name to SBC Communications Inc.™ in 1995. In 2005, SBC purchased its former parent, AT&T Corporation, and took on its branding with the merged entity naming itself AT&T Inc. and using its iconic logo and stock-trading symbol. In 2006, AT&T Inc. acquired BellSouth, the last independent Baby Bell company, making their former joint venture Cingular Wireless™ (which had acquired AT&T Wireless in 2004) wholly owned and rebranding it as AT&T Mobility™.

The current AT&T reconstitutes much of the former Bell System, and includes ten of the original 22 Bell Operating Companies along with the original long distance division.

Origin and growth (1882–1981)

AT&T can trace its origin back to the original Bell Telephone Company founded by Alexander Graham Bell after his patenting of the telephone. One of that company's subsidiaries was American Telephone and Telegraph Company (AT&T), established in 1885, which acquired the Bell Company on December 31, 1899, for legal reasons, leaving AT&T as the main company. AT&T established a network of subsidiaries in the United States and Canada that held a government-authorized phone service monopoly, formalized with the Kingsbury Commitment, throughout most of the twentieth century. This monopoly was known as the Bell System, and during this period, AT&T was also known by the nickname Ma Bell. For periods of time, the former AT&T was the world's largest phone company.

Breakup and reformation (1982–2004)

Southwestern Bell was one of the companies created by the breakup of AT&T Corp. The architect of divestiture for Southwestern Bell was Robert G. Pope. The company soon started a series of acquisitions. This includes the 1987 acquisition of Metromedia's™ mobile business and the acquisition of several cable companies in the early 1990s. In the latter half of the 1990s, the company acquired several other telecommunications companies, including some Baby Bells, while selling its cable business. During this time, the company changed its name to SBC Communications™. By 1998, the company was in the top 15 of the Fortune 500, and by 1999 the company was part of the Dow Jones Industrial Average (lasting through 2015).

Purchase of former parent and acquisitions (2005–2014)

In 2005, SBC purchased AT&T for $16 billion. After this purchase, SBC adopted the better-known AT&T name and brand, with the original AT&T Corp. still existing as the long-distance landline subsidiary of the merged company. The current AT&T claims the original AT&T Corp.'s history (dating to 1885) as its own, though its corporate structure only dates from 1983. It also retains SBC's pre-2005 stock price history, and all regulatory filings prior to 2005 are for Southwestern Bell/SBC, not AT&T Corp.

In September 2013, AT&T Inc. announced it would expand into Latin America through a collaboration with América Móvil. In December 2013, AT&T announced plans to sell its Connecticut wireline operations to Stamford-based Frontier Communications™.

Recent developments (2014–present)

AT&T purchased the Mexican carrier Iusacell in late 2014, and two months later purchased the Mexican wireless business of NII Holdings, merging the two companies to create AT&T Mexico.

In July 2015, AT&T purchased DirecTV™ for $48.5 billion, or $67.1 billion including assumed debt, subject to certain conditions. AT&T subsequently announced plans to converge its existing U-verse home internet and IPTV brands with DirecTV, to create AT&T Entertainment.

In an effort to increase its media holdings, on October 22, 2016, AT&T announced a deal to buy Time Warner for $108.7 billion.

AT&T also owns approximately a 2% stake in Canadian-domiciled entertainment company Lionsgate™.

On July 13, 2017, it was reported that AT&T would introduce a cloud-based DVR streaming service as part of its effort to create a unified platform across DirecTV and its DirecTV Now® streaming service, with U-verse® to be added soon. In October 2018, it was announced that the service is set to launch in 2019.

On September 12, 2017, it was reported that AT&T planned to launch a new cable TV-like service for delivery over its own or a competitor's broadband network sometime next year (2019).

On November 20, 2017, Assistant Attorney, General Makan Delrahim, filed a lawsuit for the United States Department of Justice Antitrust Division to block the merger with Time Warner, saying it "will harm competition, result in higher bills for consumers and less innovation." In order for AT&T to fully acquire Time Warner, the Department of Justice stated that the company must divest either DirecTV or Turner Broadcasting System.

As of 2017, AT&T is the world's largest telecommunications company. AT&T is also the second largest provider of mobile telephone services and the largest provider of fixed telephone services in the United States. On March 7, 2018, the company prepared to sell a minority stake of DirecTV Latin America through an IPO, creating a new holding company for those assets named Vrio Corp™. However, on April 18, 2018, just a day before the public debut of Vrio, AT&T canceled the IPO due to market conditions.

On June 12, 2018, AT&T was given permission by U.S. District Court Judge Richard J. Leon to go ahead with its $85 billion deal for Time Warner. The DOJ had attempted to stop the merger fearing it would harm competition. The merger closed two days after, becoming a wholly owned subsidiary and division of AT&T with a new name, WarnerMedia, announced the next day.

Three months after completing the acquisition and a year after reorganizing into four units, AT&T made its biggest move since 1984, reclassifying itself into a pure holding conglomerate and merging its RSNs, stakes in GSN, and Other, AT&T Audience into WarnerMedia's Turner, renaming DIRECTV Latin America to Vrio which is now part of the renamed AT&T Latin America (formerly AT&T International), moving wireline into Entertainment group, and renaming Consumer Mobility to simply Mobiliity.[35]

O.K., we know and probably admire those identified above for their genius, innovation, invention and contributions to our 21st Century lifestyle. So what? Why should we care?

"We stand on the shoulders of giants," declares Neil Degrasse Tyson. Understanding the platform on which our technologies stand, and who built them, is a minimum requirement if we are to prepare well for a successful career in telecommunications.

Historical Anecdote

Alexander Graham Bell

Alexander Graham Bell was born in Edinburgh, Scotland, on March 3, 1847. His course of study at the University of London was cut short when his parents, grieving the loss of Alexander's two siblings to tuberculosis, moved to Canada in 1870.

Bell died on August 2, 1922. On the day of his burial, all telephone service in the US was stopped for one minute in his honor.[36]

Serendipity Plays A Part

---

[35] https://en.wikipedia.org/wiki/AT%26T
[36] Copyright 1999, ScienCentral, Inc, and The American Institute of Physics.

Who really invented the telephone? Does it matter that Bell's patent was filed mere hours before a similar patent was filed by Elisha Gray? Does it matter that rumors of inappropriate coercion by Bell's attorney who was owed money by the patent officer who filed the patent circulate to this day; or, that there were men in Italy (Manzetti and Meucci), Germany (Reis) and France (Bourseul) whose work was preempted by Bell's patent?

Luck is defined as: "Preparation colliding with opportunity." But, what about unrelated coincidence and serendipitous (no observable or definable reason) influences without which events transpire differently than those recorded as genius, invention, commitment, dedication, etc.? It seems Mr. Bell had his share of these "circumstantial" influencers; but, who is to say that, without his preparation, these opportunities would have gone unheralded? Let's look at a few.

There is no disputing the historical indicators confirming work by those men mentioned above in pursuit of transmitting voice or audible sounds over wires or simply through the air. However, what is indisputable is the historical record verifying the first intelligible human vocal vibrations being sent over a wire between two separate rooms spoken by Alexander Bell: "Come here, Watson, I want to see you." And Watson hearing and responding to them.

With a surgeon's assistance, two years prior to filing his patent for the telephone, Bell, at the time a speech instructor in Canada, arranged a cadaver's eardrum to connect one side of it (the eardrum) to a straw and a shard of smoked glass attached to the other end of the straw. In this simple but ingenious experiment, Bell then yelled through a funnel directing his voice to the eardrum – voila! The straw vibrated scratching the smoke on the glass.

Bell reasoned, if a straw could work like this, why not an electric current? He further concluded the electric current would carry the sound vibrations as far as it went unimpeded down a wire and, with an eardrum attached to the current at the other end, the sound could be captured. This is not serendipity! This is genius in action.

However, is the fact that he conducted the experiment in his quest to assist the deaf because his wife, Mabel, was deaf, serendipitous?

Soon after making this discovery, Bell was visiting with his wife's father, Gardiner Hubbard, when he described his experiment and conclusions that voice could be carried long distances over a wire. To this outrageous declaration, his father-in-law and future investor responded: "Now you are talking nonsense! "

Serendipity? How about this?

The year was 1876.

The event was the Centennial celebration in Philadelphia of the founding of the United States.

Among inventions featured at the exhibition hall, Bell's device was granted a small table in a very obscure place overshadowed by, among others, a forty foot steam engine and a primitive typewriter.

Bell originally had no intention of attending the event. His fiancée at the time, however, had a train ticket to Philadelphia to visit her father and, on the platform prior to departure, convinced Bell to make the trip with her. Without a ticket, Bell jumped aboard.

Bell's invention had not garnered much attention during the two weeks it was on display. However, one of the exhibit judges, the emperor of Brazil, Dom Pedro Alcantra, whose interests in working with deaf people had introduced him to Bell's work in that field, recognized him and agreed to witness a demonstration of the device.

Upon hearing Bell's voice from across the room on his end of the device, he exclaimed: "My God, it talks!" This prompted the exhibit management to move the device into the spotlight where it became the highlighted invention of the convention. It was awarded a gold medal and thousands of admirers spread the news; thus, it was about as close to justifying the moniker "overnight success" as any invention ever.

Was it serendipity that Bell's sympathy for his deaf wife traveling alone made this opportunity available for his preparation? You be the judge.

Bell is recorded as having referred to his childhood for his original curiosity about sound vibrations. He described how his deaf mother preferred his method of pressing his lips against her forehead and speaking in low tones as a better way for her to "hear" than using the sound funnel popular at that time.

One Last Anecdote: The Queen's Speech

Not quite two years (1878) after the emperor of Brazil voiced his astonishment, Victoria, the queen of England sponsored a demonstration of Bell's device. Queen Victoria, always inquisitive and committed to maintaining contact with the scientific advances of the day, invited Bell to the Osborne House on the Isle of Wight for a demonstration.

The Demonstration

Monday, 14th January, 1878, a note in the queen's own hand: "After dinner we went to the Council Room and saw the Telephone. A Professor Bell explained the whole process, which is most extraordinary. It had been put in communication with Osborne Cottage, and we talked with Sir Thomas and Mary Biddulph, also heard some singing quite plainly. But it is rather faint, and one must hold the tube close to one's ear. The man, who was very pompous, kept calling Arthur 'Lord' Connaught! which amused us very much." (Arthur was **Duke** not 'Lord') of Connaught)."

From the Osborne House, where a second telephone was placed, to the Queen's residence was a fair distance; thus, a successful phone call was very impressive. The queen also heard a rendition of *Comin' Through The Rye* sung by Miss Kate Field from the Osborne House.

The Osborne Cottage terminal.

Other than the breach of royal etiquette, from all accounts, the Bell team performed admirably. However, taking full advantage of the opportunity, later that evening Bell connected the queen to Cowes for a selection of songs. Subsequently, calls went to Southampton for a bugle serenade then to London, a distance of seventy-four miles, to hear *God Save The Queen* accompanied by an organ.

You see here a copy of a letter to Bell from the Keeper of the Privy Purse, Major Biddulph. As you can read, he asked Bell if the queen could purchase the phones.

Bell replied:

"Dear Sir,

I feel highly honoured by the gratification expressed by Her Majesty, and by her desire to possess a set of Telephones. The instruments at present in Osborne are merely those supplied for ordinary commercial purposes, and it will give me much pleasure to be permitted to offer the Queen a set of Telephones to be made expressly for Her Majesty's use.

I am, dear Sir,
Yours very respectfully,

Alexander Graham Bell.

Chapter Eight -- Electromagnetism – Electromagnetic Spectrum

We have opened our study with the above glimpse into the history of some basic elements without which today's advanced networks, products and services could not exist hoping to whet your appetite for more and deeper information about the sciences, history and development of technologies and business interests that have delivered the advanced networks and devices we enjoy using in today's demanding environment. We will discover many more in our study; however, from this point, we will take a step back in time before telephony, to establish a firm foothold in the all-important physics of electromagnetics.

Electromagnetism

Lightning, thunder bolts of Zeus[37], – we know it as static electricity – is likely the first encounter man consciously had with the electromagnetic spectrum. All too often, Benjamin Franklin gets credit for identifying electricity; however, it behooves us to look a little deeper into this issue demanding total objectivity in our efforts.

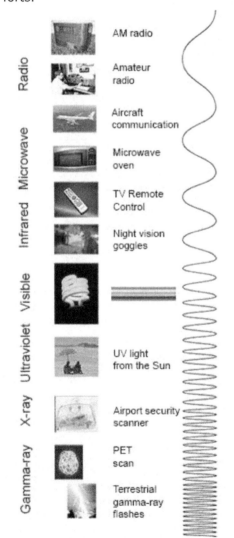

In the year 1600, English physician, William Gilbert, used the Latin word "electricus" to describe the force that certain substances exert when rubbed against each other. A few years later another English scientist, Thomas Browne, wrote several books and he used the word "electricity" to describe his investigations based on Gilbert's work.

In 1752, Ben Franklin conducted his experiment with a kite, a key, and a storm. This simply proved that lightning and tiny electric sparks were the same thing.

Italian physicist, Alessandro Volta, discovered that particular chemical reactions could produce electricity, and, in 1800, he constructed the *voltaic pile* (an early electric battery) that produced a steady electric current; thus, he was the first person to create a steady flow of electrical charge. Volta also created the first transmission of electricity by linking positively charged and negatively charged connectors and driving an electrical charge, or voltage, through them.[38]

The **history of electromagnetic theory** begins with ancient measures to understand atmospheric electricity, in particular lightning. People then had little understanding of electricity and were unable to explain the phenomena. Scientific understanding into the nature of electricity grew throughout the eighteenth and nineteenth centuries through the work of researchers such as Ampère, Coulomb, Faraday and Maxwell.

In the 19th century it had become clear that electricity and magnetism were related, and their theories were unified: wherever charges are in motion electric current results, and magnetism is due to electric current. The source for electric field is electric charge, whereas that for magnetic field is electric <u>current</u> (charges in motion).

The Electromagnetic Spectrum

The electromagnetic spectrum is the range of all types of electromagnetic radiation. Radiation is energy that travels and spreads out as it

---

[37] http://greekmythology.wikia.com/wiki/Lightning_Bolt; "The lightning bolts were the signature weapon and symbol of Zeus."
[38] https://www.universetoday.com/82402/who-discovered-electricity/

goes – the visible light that comes from a lamp in your house and the radio waves that come from a radio station are two types of electromagnetic radiation. The other types of electromagnetic radiation that make up the electromagnetic spectrum are microwaves, infrared, ultraviolet light, X-rays and gamma-rays.

You know more about the electromagnetic spectrum than you may think. This image shows where you might encounter each portion of the spectrum in your day-to-day life.

The electromagnetic spectrum is shown from lowest energy with the longest wavelength (at the top) to highest energy/shortest wavelength (at the bottom). (Credit: NASA's: *Imagine the Universe*)

Radio: Your radio captures radio waves broadcast by radio stations delivering your favorite tunes. Radio waves are also emitted by stars and gases in space. They also deliver the calls to your cellphone.

Microwave: Microwave radiation will cook your popcorn in just a few minutes, but is also used by astronomers to learn about the structure of galaxies.

Infrared: Night vision goggles pick up infrared light emitted by our skin and objects with heat. In space, infrared light helps us map the dust between stars.

Visible: Our eyes detect visible light. The sun, fireflies, light bulbs, and stars all emit visible light.

Ultraviolet: Ultraviolet radiation is emitted by the sun and is the reason skin tans and burns. "Hot" objects in space emit UV radiation as well.

X-ray: A dentist uses X-rays to image your teeth and airport security uses them to see through your bag. Hot gases in the universe also emit X-rays.

Gamma ray: Doctors use gamma-ray imaging to see inside your body. The biggest gamma-ray generator of all is the universe.

Is a radio wave the same as a gamma ray?

Radio waves, gamma-rays, visible light, and all the other parts of the electromagnetic spectrum are varying wave lengths of electro-magnetic radiation.

Electromagnetic radiation can be described in terms of streams of massless particles, called photons, each traveling in a wave-like pattern at the speed of light. Each photon contains a certain amount of energy. The different types of radiation are defined by the amount of energy found in the photons. Radio waves have photons with low energies, microwave photons have a little more energy than radio waves, infrared photons have still more, then visible, ultraviolet, X-rays, and, the most energetic of all, gamma-rays.

Measuring electromagnetic radiation

Electromagnetic radiation can be expressed in terms of energy, wavelength, or frequency. Frequency is measured in cycles per second, or Hertz. Wavelength is measured in meters. Energy is measured in electron volts. Each of these three quantities for describing electromagnetic radiation is related to each other in a precise mathematical way. But why have three ways of describing things, each with a different set of physical units?

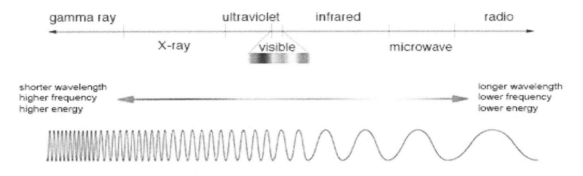

Comparison of wavelength, frequency and energy for the electromagnetic spectrum.

The short answer is that scientists don't like to use numbers any bigger or smaller than they have to. It is much easier to say or write "two kilometers" than "two thousand meters." Generally, scientists use whatever units are easiest for the type of electromagnetic radiation they work with.

Astronomers who study radio waves tend to use wavelengths or frequencies. Most of the radio part of the electromagnetic spectrum falls in the range from about 1 cm to 1 km, which is 30 gigahertz (GHz) to 300 kilohertz (kHz) in frequencies. Radio is a very broad part of the electromagnetic spectrum.

Infrared and optical astronomers generally use wavelength. Infrared astronomers use microns (millionths of a meter) for wavelengths, so their part of the spectrum falls in the range of 1 to 100 microns. Optical astronomers use both angstroms (0.00000001 cm, or 10^{-8} cm) and nanometers (0.0000001 cm, or 10^{-7} cm). Using nanometers, violet, blue, green, yellow, orange, and red light have wavelengths between 400 and 700 nanometers. (This range is just a tiny part of the entire spectrum, so the light our eyes can see is just a little fraction of all the electromagnetic radiation around us.)

The wavelengths of ultraviolet, X-ray, and gamma-ray regions of the spectrum are very small. Instead of using wavelengths, astronomers that study these portions of the spectrum usually refer to these photons by their energies, measured in electron volts (eV). Ultraviolet radiation falls in the range from a few electron volts to about 100 eV. X-ray photons have energies in the range 100 eV to 100,000 eV (or 100 keV). Gamma-rays are all the photons with energies greater than 100 keV.[39]

While all the information regarding the electromagnetic spectrum as defined above is important, our stated objective of studying who, what, when, where, why and how we achieved ubiquity for the advanced telecommunications products and services we enjoy in the 21st Century, is best served by focusing our attention on the radio frequency bands supporting what we will refer to as "commercial" two-way voice and data service with some consideration for the impact wireline telephony and the overwhelming dominance computers (dependent on semi-conductors and software) have had.

---

[39] https://imagine.gsfc.nasa.gov/science/toolbox/emspectrum1.html

Chapter Nine -- General Electric Research Lab & Charles Proteus Steinmetz

The General Electric Research Lab stands as a testament to the power of gathering engineers together with a common purpose. The lab was the first industrial research lab of its kind. Prior to the formation of the GE Research Lab, the only industrial research labs were German pharmaceutical labs. In the German labs like Bayer, scientists and researchers worked independently and competed with one another. At General Electric in Schenectady, New York, engineers and scientists were encouraged to share information and assist with problem solving. They were given great financial support to buy materials. The best machinists and craftsmen were employed to help build prototypes. From the tungsten light bulb to the computerized hybrid car it is no wonder that the Schenectady lab produced a great proportion of our world's technology.[40]

The idea for the laboratory was first promoted by Charles Proteus Steinmetz in the late 1890's. Steinmetz was GE's star engineer and kept in touch with associates back in Switzerland and Germany. Steinmetz was concerned that companies like Siemens, and independent researchers like Walther Nernst, were developing new forms of electric light that would damage GE's superiority in the market. Steinmetz and E.W. Rice explained to GE management that it was necessary to spend money on a lab and researchers who would work on the next big profitable item for the company. This investment would cost plenty, but would pay off in the longer term.

GE also had a measurements laboratory led by Lou Robinson. This lab maintained and created instrumentation to measure electricity. The new research lab would be far more than Robinson's lab in scale. E.W. Rice wanted Steinmetz to head the lab but Steinmetz refused. Rice then went to electrical pioneer Elihu Thomson in Lynn, MA. Thomson refused, he preferred to live close to the sea at the Lynn GE plant. Thomson suggested a young man named Willis Whitney at MIT.

With the help of President Coffin and Edwin Rice, the General Electric Research Lab was formed in 1900. The lab was temporarily located in Steinmetz's garage in his back yard.

It was clear that to make new inventions or innovations the company needed more scientifically trained engineers. Prior to this, inventions were simpler and could be discovered by trial and error methods of tinkerers. At that point in history the fields of physics, chemistry and mathematics progressed so rapidly that those who

graduated from universities in the early 1890's were far behind those who graduated just 5-10 years later; for this reason, management decided to hire young recruits.

Glass blowing apparatus for creation of experimental light bulbs was an early priority. Soon they hired William D. Coolidge and a handful of others to help improve the light bulb.

The early GE Research Lab team: Steinmetz on the left, the Hayden family, it might be Irving Langmuir with the bowtie in the center. This photo was taken in Steimetz's garage.[41]

As the lab expanded, it moved to the GE main plant west of downtown Schenectady. Researchers were given large rooms to work and a spirit of freedom developed. Researchers were loosely guided and could develop any idea they felt had potential. A brilliant young researcher from Brooklyn was hired. He, like many new recruits, was educated at the most advanced schools of science and engineering in Central Europe.

There was a large difference between Thomas Edison's Menlo Park, and the GE Research Lab.[42]

Historian George Wise stated that Edison's Menlo Park was more of an "invention factory." It was a place where inventors experimented to find marketable new products. Edison was a very strong personality and anyone he did not like did not last long. For example: C.S. Bradley, inventor of the first 3 phase AC generator, had worked for Edison for a short time. After some disagreements, he was let go and went on independently to change history. The GE Research Lab was managed by more balanced minds like Elihu Thomson, President

---

[40] https://edisontechcenter.org/GEresearchLab.html
[41] Ibid
[42] Ibid

Coffin, and E.W. Rice. They knew they had to create a warm atmosphere of collaboration to keep talent. In addition to this, the team had to be trained with the latest knowledge in physics, mechanics, and mathematics. Edison's team was not as well trained. It is no wonder that Edison's Menlo Park in Orange, New Jersey, failed to continue with the success achieved by the better managed and more adaptable GE Research Lab in Schenectady.

A sample of early successes

Ezekiel Weintraub and Hewitt discovered that mercury vapor causes the conversion of alternating current to direct current. The *Mercury Arc Rectifier* was used for many purposes including the powering of DC electric trains, battery chargers, and more.

Ernst F.W. Alexanderson worked on a single phase railway motor while Charles G. Curtis developed the most powerful and efficient steam turbine to date with the help of William LeRoy Emmet. The Curtis Turbine would revolutionize power generation worldwide. The first commercial sale of the turbine was to the Chicago Edison Company and it produced 5000 kilowatts of power in 1903. Later turbines would be able to produce increasing quantities of power with increasing efficiency.

Willis Whitney developed the GEM carbon filament lamp. This improved light output efficiency by 25%.

In 1908, William Coolidge discovered how to make ductile tungsten. Tungsten, the best material for an incandescent light bulb, was known; but, it was Coolidge's work that discovered how to make tungsten bendable and easily manufacturable. This significantly improved the life and durability of the light bulb and secured General Electric's position as the leader in incandescent light bulb manufacturing for the next 100 years. His tungsten was also used in the ignition of cars as a replacement for costly silver or platinum.

William Coolidge improved resolution of the X-ray by using his new tungsten targets in 1912.

Irving Langmuir developed early forms of the vacuum tube in the same year (1912).

Ernst Alexanderson's work on radio and television broadcast solidified him as the "Father of Radio and Television" and led to the formation of RCA and the big three networks. Alexanderson did not work directly in the lab; but, his labs were close to the others and all the engineers in radio/wireless worked together on problems.

Albert Hull's work created new vacuum tubes as well as the magnetron (microwave).

Legal Support

We could go on and on with the explosion in developments attained at the lab. The point is, for the first time, great minds were assembled and given the needed resources to do their work. The collaboration of minds and funding allowed the researchers to collaborate in the world of creativity.

It is no less important to acknowledge the contributions of the patent department. General Electric kept the best records of any other company at the time to record verifiable dates and times inventions were created. The large numbers of patent attorneys sorted out facts and proved/disproved claims.

Success of the Lab

The success of the lab can be attributed to the great collection of minds who were passionate about their work. In the environment of the early GE Research Lab, there was a great feeling of teamwork. Working for fortune or fame was not this lab's environment. While some engineers like Thomas Edison and Nikola Tesla endlessly craved credit and attention, the team in Schenectady worked quietly. Some, like Steinmetz, were even said to have created innovations on other team members' projects and refused to take credit.

C.W. Hewitt quietly helped C.W. Rice and Edward Kellogg develop the world's first powerful dynamic loudspeaker; yet, Hewitt wasn't credited until years later. The noncompetitive environment of the lab and undirected research continued until the 1950's when C. Guy Suits led a successful effort to change the structure of the lab.

Many pioneers worked at the lab. Some, like Ernst Alexanderson, had lifetime careers at the lab while others, like David Packard (of HP), participated in short term projects.

In 1955 the lab moved to Niskayuna, just a few miles north of Schenectady. Now high-paid researchers could live in the growing wealthy suburbs and commute easily to work, while the new property allowed for increased security and plenty of space for expansion. In the Cold War environment, it was important to restrict access to the lab by taking advantage of acres of natural fields with fences to separate the lab from nearby roads. Also, the new location gave direct access to the Mohawk River for increased water use and underwater experiments. During this time major advances took place including Bob Hall's semiconductor laser and a manmade diamond.

Director, Guy Suits, divided the lab into Metallurgy & Ceramics, Electron Physics, Chemistry, and General Physics. In this restructured environment, the lab continued to develop smaller vacuum tubes. So much was spent on miniaturizing the vacuum tube, the company opted out of the semiconductor research being done elsewhere.[43]

GE Lab Team led by Charles Proteus Steinmetz

A typical laboratory room at the downtown research lab. In this photo you see an experiment to create artificial lighting. The lighting was used to test the strength of insulators which would be subjected to real lightning strikes in the field.

---

[43] http://edisontechcenter.org/GEresearchLab.html

Chapter Ten -- Electromechanical Telephone-Switching[44]

This article was initially written as part of the IEEE STARS program.

Originally, all telephone calls required the participation of an operator. This began to change when a crude automatic switch, invented by Almon Strowger, was improved into the first practical automatic switch around 1900. The application of Strowger® switches, as well as panel, rotary, and crossbar switches, automated the telephone system. Automatic telephone switching was critical in making the telephone the influential mass market technology it became. It was also influential as an early and widespread example of automation of an electromechanical service.

In January 1878, less than two years after Alexander Graham Bell of Boston, Massachusetts received his first patent for the telephone, the world's first telephone exchange entered service in New Haven, Connecticut. Each of the twenty-one subscribers could call an operator at a central switchboard, who in turn could connect the calling subscriber to the desired targeted subscriber. Within a decade, such telephone exchanges, with many improvements along the way, were in operation in nearly every city in the United States. These were under license from American Bell Telephone, the holder of Bell's patents. There was similar, but somewhat later development, in most of the developed world. Every telephone call required the assistance of an operator or, as exchanges began to be connected to other exchanges, multiple operators. To a substantial extent, the story of innovations in telephony is an American story, in part because as late as the 1950s, the U.S. had more than half of the world's telephones.

The Strowger Switch

The photo is from Almon Strowger's original patent for an automatic telephone switch.

In 1889, Almon Strowger applied for a U.S. patent (which was issued in 1891) for what would be the basis for the first practical automatic telephone switch. (Fig. 1) In the Strowger switch, pulses generated at a subscriber's telephone directly moved electromagnetic contacts in a two-way motion in a stack of rotary contacts, thus selecting a telephone number, one digit at a time, without operator intervention. His original device was crude and impractical. Among other things, it had push buttons, and a subscriber had to, for example, push a button nine times to indicate a 9. A commonly told story explained that Strowger, an undertaker in Kansas City, was spurred to his invention by learning that the funeral of a friend was being handled by a competitor, whose family, Strowger was convinced, had been led to

---

[44] https://ethw.org/Electromechanical_Telephone-Switching

another undertaker by an unscrupulous telephone operator. Strowger and his backers formed a company, eventually known as the Automatic Electric Company, to develop the patent into a practical switch.

Fig. 2. Keith, Ericikson, and Erickson's patent for the telephone dial under the technical leadership of Alexander E. Keith, Automatic Electric produced a steady series of significant advances, which together yielded a commercially viable system. Perhaps the most notable of these advances was the invention of the dial phone in 1896. (Fig. 2) By 1900, these much improved Strowger switches had entered commercial use in a relatively small number of independent (that is, non-Bell) exchanges in the U.S., typically in small or medium sized cities. Advocates promoted the switch as private; detractors called it a lower grade of service. Their use spread. By 1904, some four percent of independent lines were on automatic exchange.

Fig. 3. shows a technician doing maintenance work on a Strowger switch bank, for the Dallas Telephone Co., Dallas, Texas,1919. In this photograph, twenty Strowger switches are visible. Each switch completes a circuit by selecting one of 100 switching contacts. These contacts are contained on 10 semicircular disks, and each disk has 10 contacts. The 10 disks are arranged vertically. The movable part of the switch is a rod bearing a metallic brush. The rod moves both vertically and rotationally, thus selecting the appropriate contact as directed by the customer's dialing. (Courtesy of AT&T Archives and History Center.)

In a Strowger switch, the subscriber's dial directly controlled the movement of the switch contacts that established the circuit, and this circuit was maintained for the duration of the call. As the switch had a 10 x 10 bank of contacts, the earliest switch could handle only 100 telephones. The development of multilevel switching at Automatic Electric greatly increased the switch capacity, initially to 6,000 and ultimately 10,000 telephones. (Fig. 3) But direct control of the switch by the subscriber remained an essential feature.

After 1910, Strowger switches began spreading to Europe. Additional improvements by Keith and others at Automatic Electric further improved the switch. By 1914, over 400,000 dial telephones were in use in the United States, 14 percent of the total phones in service. It was even adapted by Automatic Electric for the British Post Office to use in the largest British cities, beginning with London's Holborn exchange in 1927. The Strowger, or *step-by-step switch* as it also became known, remained the most widespread switch in use until the 1960s, and it was particularly common in non-urban exchanges.[45]

AT&T's Panel Switch

Although the large and well-established AT&T Bell System investigated automatic switching as early as 1903, it resisted adopting such switches for several reasons. Bell's strength was in the nation's large cities, with a large number of telephones and with a large percentage of calls requiring routing between exchanges within a city. Bell's studies showed that Strowger switches were slower than AT&T's improved manual switches in such applications. Also, Bell needed to make any switching innovations compatible with existing switches, as subscribers on any Bell automatic exchange would need to be able to efficiently contact subscribers still connected to manual exchanges.

---

[45] https://www.google.com/search?q=strowger+switch&oq=strowg&aqs=chrome.2.69i57j46j0l5.7678j1j8&sourceid=chrome&ie=UTF-8

AT&T and Western Electric, its equipment subsidiary, began research into alternative automatic switch designs better suited to urban needs. The first breakthrough was the invention of the translator by AT&T engineer Edward C. Molina in 1905. The translator, or the sender as an improved version would become known, introduced the concept of indirect control. That is, the pulses from the telephone dial would be translated into a different electromechanical code that could control a larger switching unit. This allowed for a subscriber's telephone to select from a larger number of possible circuits, and for the separation of the circuit used to set up the call from the circuit used for the call itself. This in turn led to the preliminary development of **two types of indirect control switches: the panel and the rotary**. Both of these featured continuously running motors and clutches that engaged to select electrical contacts.

Around 1910, Western Electric transferred further work on the rotary switch to its European division, after determining that there was more interest in it among European government-run telephone companies. In Europe, the urban exchanges tended to have fewer telephones and therefore lesser interoffice trunking requirements. Various versions of the rotary switch entered service in large cities in Europe, chiefly after World War I.

In the United States, Western Electric continued development of the panel switch, which was better suited for large cities with large volumes of interoffice calls. More than ninety percent of local calls in New York City involved phones connected to different local exchanges.

The panel switch was an extremely complex device, with tall panels covered with 500 rows of terminals. Each panel had an electric motor to drive its (usually sixty) selectors by electromagnetically controlled clutches. The selector moved continuously rather than in steps, and the selectors establishing contact points could move a considerable distance. Separate frames were used for the several parts of the telephone-calling process.

The Bell System's initial plan was for semiautomatic operation, where subscribers would still call operators, who in turn would enter the subscriber's desired number. Two such semiautomatic switches were installed in Newark, New Jersey in 1915. But the Bell System soon decided to move to fully automatic switching, partly because growth in the number of telephones was making manual interoffice trunking more difficult and partly because of changing labor conditions. With the growth of the telephone network, the recruitment and employment of a sufficient number of operators had become increasingly problematic.

The change to fully-automatic urban switching was made possible with a plan devised in 1916 by AT&T engineer W. G. Blauvelt. It allowed the transition to automatic dialing to take place without requiring every subscriber to get a new telephone number in addition to getting a new telephone with a dial. Blauvelt simply added letters to the numbers on the dial. Telephone numbers in large cities, such as New York, consisted of the exchange name and a 4-digit number. So instead of asking the operator for Pennsylvania 5000, the subscriber would dial PEN 5000. This also eased the connection between automatic and manual telephone exchanges, since the dialer could dial the entire number, and an operator could receive the number and know the manual exchange to which it should be forwarded.

Fig. 4. Part of a panel switch, Franklin Exchange, Chicago, Illinois, 1938.

Dozens of vertical rods are visible on the panel banks. These rods assume various positions and they move considerable distances to make the appropriate contacts for the call being connected. This is only one section of the complete switch, which, like all large electromechanical telephone switches, filled much of the telephone exchange building. (Courtesy of AT&T Archives and History Center.)

AT&T installed its first panel switch in Omaha, Nebraska, in December, 1921, and its second in the Pennsylvania exchange of New York City in October, 1922. By 1930 every telephone in Manhattan that connected to a central exchange was a dial telephone connected to a panel switch. (Fig. 4) Similar transitions occurred in major metropolitan areas throughout the country, but due to its cost, complexity, and high maintenance requirements, the panel switch was never adopted outside the United States.

For the operation of smaller, non-urban exchanges, AT&T in 1916 acquired a license from Automatic Electric to manufacture Strowger step-by-step switches, and also reached an agreement to purchase such switches. The first step-by-step switch in the Bell System entered service in Norfolk, Virginia in 1919.

AT&T's Crossbar Switch

AT&T began work on an alternative to the panel switch even before the first panel switch was installed. In 1913, J.N. Reynolds of Western Electric invented the crossbar selector in which a small number of magnets operated a large number of relay contacts in a coordinated array. This meant that there were only small mechanical motions and none of the large sliding movements required in the panel and Strowger switches. However, the crossbar selector proved too expensive at this time to be put into use.

About the same time, Gotthief A. Betulander of Televerket, the Swedish postal, telegraph, and telephone administration, began working on an all relay switch. It, like the panel switch, had separate circuits for selection and connection. In 1918, Betulander learned of Reynold's patent. Discovering that it required fewer relays, he combined it with the connection section of his design, thereby inventing the crossbar switch. He sold his invention to the Swedish company L. C. Ericsson, which had the resources to prepare it for manufacture. Ericsson was also developing its own variant of the rotary switch, the 500 switch and, in 1921, Televerket chose the latter for use in Swedish cities. However, Televerket did keep a version of the crossbar system alive, by using the crossbar selector in conjunction with Strowger switches in small rural exchanges, where they provided reliable service without on-site maintenance.

By the mid 1920s, the continued high costs of manufacturing, installing, and maintaining the panel switch had AT&T looking for an alternative design for large cities, but its researchers had not been able to produce a more cost-effective design. Then, in 1930, W. R. Mathies, of AT&T's research-and-development division, now known as Bell Telephone Laboratories, visited Sweden, and there he saw the crossbar selectors in use in rural exchanges. Convinced that such selectors could be adapted to large switches, Mathies had his group resume work. After they rejected the idea of simply replacing the selectors on the existing panel design they developed, beginning in 1934, an entirely new switch for urban use emerged. The new switch used the crossbar as well as some of their work from earlier in the decade.

Fig. 5. A technician doing maintenance work on a #1 crossbar switch, East 30th St., New York, New York, 1938. Each large link frame contains 20 crossbar switching units. These units contain electromechanical relays and involve no large mechanical movements, as in the panel switch. Indeed, the only mechanical movements are the opening and closing of the relays. (Courtesy of AT&T Archives and History Center.)

The first two crossbar switches went into service in 1938 in New York City. (Fig. 5) The crossbar switch achieved its goal of reducing costs for manufacturing and maintenance, and it had many innovative features that gave it a more flexible and adaptable design than panel or Strowger switches. An important feature was that the crossbar switch's basic building block, the link relay frame, required only small movements throughout. Because of its overall flexibility, the urban crossbar was named the #1 crossbar, in anticipation of the development of crossbar switches for other applications.

The units used to establish a call were not only separate from those used for the actual call path, as they had been in the panel, but were common control units. This meant that all selector frames were accessible to all of the phones, and after a call they were released for use on other calls. These "markers" as they became known, were fast, thus reducing connection time.

Also significant was that the crossbar was the first switch where both the originating and terminating traffic were combined on the same set of line switches. This made possible simpler connections from telephones to the switches, and also allowed the crossbar to be adapted, as it soon was, for use in **tandem switches**, that is, specialized switches used to route calls between multiple urban exchanges. **Crossbar tandems** for the first time allowed automatic alternative routing, when the direct route between exchanges was not available.

Crossbar switches were wired to allow for the separation of the two directions of transmission. These features combined to make the switch very adaptable, easy to modify for both new applications and the addition of peripherals for new features.

Thus, it proved easy for Bell Labs to adapt the crossbar switch for use as the first automatic switch in the long distance network. Previously, all long-distance calls required one or more operators at manual long distance switchboards; a subscriber dialed 211 to get a long distance operator. The first long distance crossbar switch, the #4 crossbar, was installed in Philadelphia, Pennsylvania, in 1943. Four additional #4 crossbars were installed in other metropolitan areas in the next five years. (The project to produce the #2 crossbar was cancelled, and the designation "#3 crossbar" was skipped for reasons that remain unclear.)

Customer-dialed Long Distance

Equipping the U.S. telephone system for customer-dialed long distance calls required several additional innovations. There needed to be a nationwide numbering plan; the now-familiar standard of 3-digit area code plus 7-digit local number was adopted. [emphasis author's] Also required was a device that would allow switches to recognize area codes and automatically determine whether a local or long distance call was being attempted. Finally, the #4 crossbar had to have a new device that would translate the area code and the exchange prefix into another code to designate the route the call needed to take.

Fig. 6. A toll crossbar switch, unknown location, 1955. This very large switch consists of many individual crossbar switching units and other components. (Courtesy of AT&T Archives and History Center.)

The numbering plan proved the easiest to design, but the more complex to administer, since it required for the first time that all telephone numbers, even in small towns, take seven pulls of the dial. The second was a new component for the crossbar switch, a so-called pre-translator, which acted after receiving the first three dialed digits. Since no local numbers had 0 or 1 for the second pull (since there were no letters above the 0 and 1 on the dial), all area codes had either 0 or 1 for the second digit. Thus, the pre-translator could react to the second digit. A new device for the #4 crossbar, known as the card translator, attached to the crossbar to perform the function. Western Electric named this modified design the #4A crossbar, and installed the first one in Albany, New York, in 1950. The #4A crossbars soon spread throughout the system. (Fig. 6) AT&T installed the 182nd and last #4A crossbar in Madison, Wisconsin, in 1976. Twenty additional #4A crossbars were installed by independent U.S. companies, and in Alaska and Canada.

New Versions of the Crossbar Switch

Bell Labs also redesigned the crossbar as a smaller switch for use in suburban and other non-urban exchanges where it replaced step-by-step switches. This new switch, the #5 crossbar, first went into service in Media, Pennsylvania, in 1948, and was the first to be designed and installed with an integral pre-translator for customer dialing of long distance calls. **The first customer-dialed long distance call in the United States was placed in 1951 between a telephone attached to a new #5 crossbar in Englewood, New Jersey, and one in Alameda, California. In the following years, the Bell System deployed #5 crossbars widely, and versions were produced by others for independent telephone companies. Pre-translators were also added to #1 crossbars.** [emphasis author's]

While use of the panel switch and #1 crossbar switch remained largely confined to the United States, the design of the #5 crossbar proved to have considerable interest globally, and, beginning in the mid-1950s, manufacturers throughout the world began producing their own crossbar switches adapted from the American designs. One version in particular, the Pentazona from ITT/France, introduced in 1964, was employed in more than 70 countries. By the early 1970s, crossbars were common everywhere, and together with hold-over older switches, chiefly Strowger switches, formed the backbone of the world's telephone exchanges.

The End of Electromechanical Switching

By the 1970s, it was clear that the days of the electromechanical switch were numbered; because, in 1965, AT&T had installed the first electronic switch, the #1 ESS (Electronic Switching System) in a local exchange in Succasunna, New Jersey. (The #1 ESS was an analog electronic switch; digital telephone switches came later.) Because its operations involved no

mechanical motions, electronic switches were faster and easier to maintain. And because electronic switches were essentially special purpose computers, they were more flexible and could allow for advanced features such as call waiting. But through its long history, automatic electromechanical switches, by reducing costs, decreasing labor requirements, and increasing efficiency played a major role in making the telephone a wide spread, almost ubiquitous technology. [emphasis author's]

Acknowledgments

The author thanks members of the STARS Editorial Board and others for review and constructive criticism of this article, with special thanks to Emerson Pugh, Ken Lipartito, and Rik Nebeker. The author also thanks Bill Caughlin of the AT&T Archives and History Center for the photographs used in this article.

Timeline

- 1878, The first manual telephone exchange opens in New Haven, Connecticut.
- 1889, Almon Strowger invents the first automatic telephone switch.
- 1891, Strowger receives US Patent 447918 for his invention.
- 1891, The Automatic Electric Co. is formed to develop a practical Strowger system.
- 1892, The first prototype of the Strowger system operates.
- 1896, Alexander Keith, John Erickson, and Charles Erickson invent the dial telephone.
- 1896, The first prototype of a dial telephone system operates.
- 1912, Gotthief A. Betulander invents the first all-relay telephone switch.
- 1913, John Reynolds invents the crossbar selector.
- 1916, William Blauvelt develops a telephone numbering plan for large cities.
- 1921, AT&T introduces the panel switch, designed for use in large cities.
- 1938, AT&T installs the first #1 crossbar switch in New York City.
- 1943, AT&T introduces the #4 crossbar switch, designed for long distance calls.
- 1948, AT&T introduces the #5 crossbar switch, designed for suburban exchanges.
- 1951, Customer dialing of long distance calls begins in the United States.
- 1965, AT&T installs the first all-electronic telephone switch.[46]

Telephone Companies' Central Office Switches

In telecommunications, an electronic switching system (ESS) is a telephone switch that uses solid-state electronics, (such as digital electronics) and computerized common control, to interconnect telephone circuits for the purpose of establishing telephone calls.

The generations of telephone switches before the advent of electronic switching in the 1950s used purely electro-mechanical relay systems and analog voice paths. These early machines typically utilized the step-by-step technique. The first generation of electronic switching systems in the 1960s were not entirely digital in nature, but used reed relay-operated metallic paths or crossbar switches operated by stored program control (SPC) systems. [emphasis author's]

First announced in 1955, the first customer trial installation of an all-electronic central office commenced in Morris, Illinois, in November, 1960, by Bell Laboratories. The first large-scale electronic switching system was the Number One Electronic Switching System (1ESS) of the Bell System, cut over in Succasunna, New Jersey, in May, 1965.

The adoption of metal–oxide–semiconductor (MOS) and pulse-code modulation (PCM) technologies in the 1970s led to the transition from analog to digital telephony. Later electronic switching systems implemented the digital representation of the electrical audio signals on subscriber loops by digitizing the analog signals and processing the resulting data for transmission between central offices. Time-division multiplexing (TDM) technology permitted the simultaneous transmission of

---

[46] Ibid

multiple telephone calls on a single wire connection between central offices or other electronic switches, resulting in dramatic capacity improvements of the telephone network. [emphasis author's]

With the advances of digital electronics starting in the 1960s telephone switches employed semiconductor device components in increasing measure.

In the late 20th century most telephone exchanges without TDM processing were eliminated and the term *electronic switching system* became largely a historical distinction for the older SPC systems.

The Number One Electronic Switching System (1ESS) was the first large-scale stored program control (SPC) telephone exchange or electronic switching system in the Bell System. It was manufactured by Western Electric and first placed into service in Succasunna, New Jersey, in May 1965. The switching fabric was composed of a reed relay matrix controlled by wire spring relays which in turn were controlled by a central processing unit (CPU).

The 1AESS central office switch was a plug compatible, higher capacity upgrade from 1ESS with a faster 1A processor that incorporated the existing instruction set for programming compatibility, and used smaller *remreed* (remnant reed) switches, fewer relays, and featured disk storage. It was in service from 1976 to 2017.

PBX – Private Branch Exchange

Definition: **PBX** stands for Private Branch Exchange, which is a private **telephone** network used within a company or organization. The users of the **PBX phone system** can communicate internally (within their company) and externally (with the outside world), using different communication channels like Voice over IP, ISDN or analog – within the parameters of this definition, cellular networks qualify as gigantic PBX networks (early [1983-85] local networks).

With a traditional PBX, you are typically constrained to a certain maximum number of outside telephone lines (trunks) and to a certain maximum number of internal telephone devices or extensions. Users of the PBX phone system (phones or extensions) share the outside lines for making external phone calls.

Switching to an IP PBX brings with it many benefits and opens up possibilities, allowing for almost unlimited growth in terms of extensions and trunks, and introducing more complex functions that are more costly and difficult to implement with a traditional PBX, such as:

- Ring Groups
- Queues
- Digital Receptionists
- Voicemail
- Reporting

Make no mistake about it, despite the growing desertion of local wireline telephone service by cell phone users, radio access to the PSTN using wireless devices depending on cellphone towers requires the PSTN (Public Switched Telephone Network) to make them viable communication devices. Like the indispensable electrical grid, the PSTN is the arterial component for cellphones to connect to landline phones.

Cellular MTSO (Mobile Telephone Switching Office): Connecting to the PSTN

The cellular "MTSO" – Mobile Telephone Switching Office – is the brain of cellular networks. Until an all electronic switch was readily available, one with massive computer power, cellular networks could not have delivered the minimum levels of service the public demanded. If the cell sites with their connections to the MTSO are the circulatory system, the MTSO is the brain of cellular networks – the body (network) and all its functions require both.

The advent of the internet/WWW has now rendered the term "PBX" associated with cellular networks obsolete requiring layer upon layer of qualifying statements to conclude that cellular networks today are no less PBX extensions to the PSTN than they were thirty years ago.

Interjecting here the encouragement to the reader to delve deeper into other similar issues impacting the interconnect issues that had to be resolved before today's wireless telecommunications could be as popular (indispensable) as they have become, we refer you to FCC, SEC, FTC, US Justice Dept. rulings and laws without which the wireless services we enjoy would likely be much different and more expensive.

In your research, study the history of Western Electric, AT&T Divestiture, the role of ITT before WWII and then after WWII, Hush-a-Phone, the Carterfone Decision of 1969, and the history of MCI.

Chapter Eleven -- Pre-cellular Mobile Telephones and Paging

Improved Mobile Telephone Service™ (IMTS™) was a pre-cellular VHF/UHF radio system wirelessly (RF) connecting mobile radio-telephones to the Public Switched Telephone Network (PSTN). IMTS™ was the radiotelephone equivalent of land dial phone service. It was introduced in 1964 as a replacement to Mobile Telephone Service® or MTS® and improved on most MTS systems by offering direct-dial rather than connections through a live operator.

The original Bell System US and Canadian mobile telephone system includes three frequency bands, VHF Low (35-44 MHz, 9 channels), VHF High (152-158 MHz, 11 channels in the U.S., 13 channels in Canada), and UHF (454-460 MHz, 12 channels). Alternative names were "Low Band", "High band" and "UHF." In addition to the Bell system (wireline incumbent) channels, another 7 channels at VHF, and 12 channels at UHF were granted to non-wireline companies designated as "RCCs" (Radio Common Carriers). These RCC channels were adjacent to the Bell System frequencies.

RCCs (including telcos) were also allowed to offer paging services to "beepers" or "pagers" on a secondary basis on the same channels; but soon, with the growth of paging, RCC mobile phone services were given lower priority. Some RCCs utilized IMTS technology; but, others adopted the "Secode-2805" signaling technology and a few obscure others.

A given provider might have offered service on one, two, or all three bands, although IMTS was never offered on low band (only MTS, but Whidbey Telephone in Washington State [and others] had a custom-designed direct dial system.) These were prone to network congestion and interference since the 'capture effect' allowed a radio closer to the terminal to capture the channel because of its stronger signal. Cellular networks remedied this problem by decreasing the area covered by one tower (a "cell") and increasing the number of cells. IMTS™ and MTS™ systems still exist in some remote areas, as it may be the only feasible way to cover a large sparsely populated area.

The basic operation of IMTS™ was advanced for its time, considering that integrated circuits were not commonly available. In a given city, one IMTS™ base station channel was "marked idle" by the transmission of a steady 2000Hz "idle" tone. Mobiles would scan the available frequencies and lock on to the channel transmitting the idle tone. When a call was placed to a mobile, the idle tone would change to 1800 Hz "channel seize" tone (the idle tone would appear on another frequency, if available), and the 7 digit mobile number (three digits of the NPA (Number Plan Area – Area Code) and the last four digits of subscriber number, the NXX was not sent) would be sent out as rotary dial pulses, switching between 2000 and 1800 Hz to represent digits. Any mobile recognizing the call was for someone else would resume scanning for mark idle tone, while the called mobile would then transmit 2150 Hz "guard" tone back to the base station. This would also initiate ringing at the mobile, and when the mobile subscriber picked up the phone, 1633 Hz "connect" tone would be sent back to the base station to indicate answer supervision and the voice path would be established. When the mobile disconnected, a burst of alternating 1336 "disconnect" and 1800Hz "seize" tones would be sent to allow the base station to service another call.

Mobiles originated calls by sending a burst of connect tone, to which the base station responded with a burst of seize tone. The mobile would then respond with its identification, consisting of its area code and last four digits of the phone number sent at 20 pulses per second, just as in inward dialing but with the addition of rudimentary parity checking.

Digits are formed with a pulse train of alternating tones, either connect and silence (for odd digits) or connect and guard (for even digits). When the base station received the calling party's identification, it would send dial tone to the mobile. The user would then use the rotary dial, which would send the dialed digits as an alternating 10 pulses per second pulse train (originally, directly formed by the rotary dial) of connect and guard tones.

Pre-cellular Mobile Telephony

IMTS™ systems typically had 25 watts of transmitter power at the mobile and 100-250 Watts at the terminal — unlike the first **cellular** car telephones that had maximum power output of 3 watts and modern cellular handsets with a maximum power output of 0.6 watts. Pre-cellular mobile installations normally consisted of a "head unit"—the telephone handset residing in a cradle with a direct dialing keyboard. These looked and functioned much like a landline, or hardwired, telephone. Unlike cellular handsets, these units passed through a dial tone when the receiver was lifted from the cradle and, in this way, seemed more like a landline telephone. There was a separate large radio transceiver chassis ("drawer unit"), typically measuring about 14"x20"x4", mounted either in the trunk, under the seats of an automobile or mounted behind the seats of pick-ups and trucks or busses. These transceivers were connected to the control head with a multi-conductor cable usually around .5" inch thick.

The mobile antennas almost always required a hole drilled in the body of the car to mount the antenna. Until the 1970s, there were no "on-glass" antennas - these were developed later for cellular car-mounted telephones. "Whip antennas," much like those used for CB radios, were about 19 in. long (1/4 wavelength at 155 MHz).

Pre-cellular radio/telephone mobiles required a large amount of power (10 to 15 amperes at 12 volts), supplied by thick power cabling connected directly to the automobile's battery. Therefore, it was quite possible, and not uncommon, for an IMTS™ telephone to drain an automobile's battery if used for moderate periods of time without the automobile engine running or if left on overnight. Optionally, these units were also connected to the car's horn and could honk the horn as a ringer to summon a user who was away from the car.

The IMTS™ units were *full duplex*, meaning that a user could both talk and hear the other party at the same time. This was an improvement over the earlier MTS™ systems, most of which were *half duplex*, allowing only one party to transmit at a time. The user had to "push to talk" to speak and then "unkey" the base station transmitter by releasing the PTT button to hear the other party on the line.

In 1960, General Electric introduced the "Progress Line" DTO- series MTS™ mobiles which were full duplex, although subscribers were still required to press the "push to talk" bar on the handset to speak.

There were also IMTS™ handheld transceivers (Yaesu's 1982 vintage Traveler™®) operating on 2-4 watts, and these were all half duplex. These were essentially modified "walkie-talkies" with a DTMF™ (dual tone multi-frequency) keypad attached on the front panel, which *fooled* the terminal into believing an IMTS™ mobile was using the system. These units were not very common or practical because they lacked the power to reliably connect to the base station over the distances common in the IMTS™ systems. A compromise existed with the briefcase phone which had nominally higher power in the range of 10 to 20 watts (depending on how much battery was in the briefcase), and which was full duplex. Typical IMTS™ briefcase phones were made by Canyon, GCS, SCM Melabs and Livermore Data Systems. While these manufacturers existed, the market was dominated by Motorola and GE. These two companies (and others) delivered fixed base station equipment as well as end-user mobile telephones and pagers to the phone companies and competing RCCs who leased the subscriber equipment to their customers.

Mobile Telephone System Base station

A single IMTS™ base station generally covered a licensed area within a 35-40 mile radius from its fixed antenna. This extended range was due to high transmitter power and, in many cases, high (100' to as much as 400-600') antenna placement. IMTS™ base stations in larger cities had as many as 7 or 8 channels while rural

stations had as few as one or two channels. Each telephone conversation (connection) required the exclusive use of a channel for the duration of each call. Because of this limitation, these systems had a much lower capacity than cellular systems and all channels busy conditions were common. In larger cities, this dictated a very limited number of simultaneous calls. Each subscriber was given a packet of dialing and use instructions. Roaming (receiving calls out of the "home area") was achieved by selecting the specific channels used by the network and service provider the user was traveling in and dialing a three-digit code, thereby logging the user's land number at that location. This process had to be repeated at each tower

which, as noted, usually had a range of 35-40 miles. Some areas only had half-duplex (one-way) communications and required the push-to-talk switch in the handset between the mouthpiece and the earpiece. Two lights on the "head" indicated busy (red) if no channels were idle and in-use (green) if connected to the tower, or depressing the push-to-talk switch. There was no encryption and all conversations were relatively easy to monitor.

Frequencies

The frequencies listed (in MHz in the chart below) are those formerly used (pre-cellular) in the US & Canadian Mobile Telephone Service and the Improved Mobile Telephone Service™. The low band "Z" prefixed channels were always operated in the MTS™, or manual mode. The "Z" channels were sold at auction by the FCC in approximately 2003 to other services and remain largely unused. The VHF and UHF frequencies have been opened to other services unrelated to mobile telephony and largely reassigned.

The two VHF high-band channels designated JJ and JW were used only in Canada, and were not available for use in the United States.

Limitations

IMTS™ technology severely limited the total number of subscribers. In the 1970s and the early 1980s, before the introduction of cellular phones, there were waiting lists of up to three years for those wishing to have mobile telephone service. These potential subscribers were waiting for other subscribers to disconnect their subscription in order to obtain a mobile telephone number and mobile phone service.

These limitations resulted in low quantity sales and production of IMTS™ phones and the mobile units were therefore very expensive ($2,000 to $4,000). Prior to the divestiture of AT&T in 1982, Bell System IMTS™ subscribers usually leased the equipment at a monthly rate of as much as $120. Availability of the channels was scarce; hence, airtime was also quite expensive at $0.70-1.20 per minute. Following the divestiture, customer-owned equipment was required by Bell companies and monthly rates then typically ran to $25 plus air time. Also, since there were so few channels, it was common for the phones to "queue up" to use a channel and IMTS™ manufacturers competed for the speed with which the units would seize an available channel.

The limit of customer numbers on MTS™ and IMTS™ was the driver for investment in cellular networks. In remote regions, this is not the case; in remote regions, obsolescence is the driver; but, the lack of a suitable and affordable alternative has resulted in regulatory obstacles. Customers did not want the MTS/IMTS™ service to be withdrawn. Increasing affordability of satellite service, and government investment in cellular expansion allowed MTS™ and IMTS™ to be removed.

FCC Spectrum Allocation

Channel	Base frequency	Mobile frequency
VHF Low Band		
ZO	35.26	43.26
ZF	35.30	43.30
ZM	35.38	43.38
ZH	35.34	43.34
ZA	35.42	43.32
ZY	35.46	43.46
ZR	35.50	43.50
ZB	35.54	43.54
ZW	35.62	43.62
ZL	35.66	43.66
VHF High Band		
JJ	152.48	157.74
JL	152.51	157.77
YL	152.54	157.80
JP	152.57	157.83
YP	152.60	157.86
YJ	152.63	157.89
YK	152.66	157.92
JS	152.69	157.95
YS	152.72	157.98
YR	152.75	158.01
JK	152.78	158.04
JR	152.81	158.07
JW	152.84	158.10
UHF Band		
QC	454.375	459.375

Paging Frequencies (Channels)

- 27.2550 Authorized in Part 95 of FCC rules. 25 watt power limit. Shared with Citizen's Band Radio service.
- 35.2200 to 35.6600 (40 kHz steps)
- 43.2200 to 43.6600 (40 kHz steps)
- 152.0075 Medical Paging
- 152.0300 to 152.8100 (30 kHz steps) - shared with land mobile in some cities
- **P5 – 152.240 – highest value channel**
- 157.4500 Medical Paging
- 157.7700 to 158.7000 (30 kHz steps) - shared with land mobile in some cities
- **P6 – 158.600 – 2nd highest value channel**
- 163.2500 Medical Paging
- 454.0125 to 454.5000 (12.5 kHz steps) - shared with land mobile in some cities
- 462.7500 to 462.9250 (25 kHz steps) - shared with low power land mobile services
- 465.0000
- 467.7500 to 467.9250 (25 kHz steps) - local paging - shared with low power land mobile services

QJ	454.40	459.40
QD	454.425	459.425
QA	454.45	459.45
QE	454.475	459.475
QP	454.50	459.50
QK	454.525	459.525
QB	454.55	459.55
QO	454.575	459.575
QR	454.60	459.60
QY	454.625	459.625
QF	454.65	459.65

The FCC's spectrum management dictated much of how today's wireless services have evolved. The frequencies in these two tables were set aside for the exclusive use of mobile telephone and paging services defined by Part 95 of the FCC Rules and Regulations. These specific channels were licensed as "Radio Common Carrier" frequencies.

Defined by the FCC, Radio Common Carriers were two competing entities: 1) legacy telephone companies (Ma Bell far and away the most dominant but there were many independent telcos who qualified for these RCC channels); 2) independent businesses whose FCC licenses authorized use of these channels as a means of delivering commercial paging and mobile radio services to the general public. In both instances, telcos and their competing RCCs, the legal right to charge the end user for using the "air time" on these allocated frequencies was extended by virtue of an FCC "Master Certificate." We will delve into more detail about RCCs and their role in advancing wireless telecom later in this work.

To understand how and why this distinction was necessary and became the basis upon which today's "common carriage," *i.e.*, cellular, PCS, 3G, 4G, & 5G are as prevalent, popular and economically lucrative as they are, we need to look back into some selective history of the FCC's role as well as the entrepreneurial activities we're referring to as "pre-cellular."

A glimpse into commercially viable radio services as they emerged from primitive broadcast systems (a single transmitter broadcasting news and entertainment to home radio receivers) will also aid in our deeper understanding of forces behind the cellular explosion as it was preceded by legacy mobile telephony.

It is impossible to overstate the impact and influence on modern day wireless telecommunications the GE Lab, led by Charles Proteus Steinmetz[47], and the later spin-off, Radio Corporation of America (RCA), have had in the application of physics and chemistry creating vacuum tubes, circuitry, transistors and other semiconductors (including Large Scale Integration [LSI] and Digital Signal Processing [DSP]), as well as microprocessors and microchips.

The GE Labs model Steinmetz championed, encouraging investment in research, subsequently copied by AT&T's creation of Bell Labs, is now taken for granted; however, looking back at the many corporations whose research labs, following Steinmetz' example, have delivered untold processes, products, services and economic contributions, we can appreciate the magnitude of the model. A few companies that come to mind include: IBM, Texas Instruments, Phillips, Ericsson, Motorola, Schlumberger, Fairchild, Siemens, Nippon Electric Co., Xerox Park, Intel, Hewlett-Packard, AMD, Texas Instruments and hundreds, if not thousands, more.

There are several discrete issues requiring multi-discipline combinations without which electronics and telecommunications as we know them today would not exist. A short list includes: 1) open, proprietary, *de facto* and *du jour* standards – what are they, why are they necessary, who governs them, and when did they arrive? 2) Numbering – when and why did numbering systems become an issue in telecommunications? 3) Modulation and signaling – what is it, how did it develop in wireless as a subset to telephony? 4) Circuit switching

---

[47] Author's note: Steinmetz, a graduate of the Sorbonne as a physicist, was a victim of spinal scoliosis. His deformity, coupled with an almost fatal flu infection, made him an "undesirable" immigrant. In the final stages of deportation at Ellis Island, he was rescued by a Catholic nurse who ushered him through the immigration process and nursed him to health after which he found refuge in western New York where his genius and ingenuity were recognized by Edison who put him in charge of the GE Lab.

vs packet switching – who cares? 5) Funding – demand and supply - the economic impact on research, development, manufacturing and distribution. In all cases, addressing these will be limited to their presence in telecommunications with only cursory mention of television and the greater computer universe. We will address them as factors a student of telecommunications basics needs to know and understand.

While all the early work we've seen by Hertz, Morse, Bell, Tesla, Edison, Marconi, Fessenden, Armstrong, and others in discovering, defining and articulating the physics of the electromagnetic spectrum is important, until we understand how their work resulted in various inventions spawning the radio industry, we won't understand today's telecommunications environment.

In many cases, despite wars, depressions and anti-technology social climates (Luddites), enough people found the money to fund early manufacturing of radios to ignite an industry. No small contributing factor was war and the taxes that purchased radios for military applications – particularly WWI and WWII.

Radio receivers were worthless to the general public without a transmitter broadcasting content the consumer was willing to pay to receive; thus, when the earliest radio stations began transmitting news and music, a boom in home radio 'sets' occurred.

There are many who claim "first" in broadcasting radio programming; however, large scale market acceptance began as an industry after WWI – effectively after 1920.

[48]After 1920: Large Corporations Began to Dominate the Industry

In 1919, Frank Conrad, a Westinghouse engineer, began broadcasting music in Pittsburgh. These broadcasts stimulated the sales of crystal sets. A crystal set, which could be made at home, was composed of a tuning coil, a crystal detector, and a pair of earphones. The popularity of Conrad's broadcasts led to Westinghouse establishing a radio station, KDKA, on November 2, 1920. In 1921, KDKA began broadcasting prizefights and major league baseball. While Conrad was creating KDKA, the *Detroit News* established a radio station. Other newspapers soon followed the Detroit newspaper's lead.

However, less well known were two stations in California who also lay claim to being first in the field. It is very likely many others, particularly in the mid-west were experimenting with home-based transmitters.

"Experimental radio broadcasting began in 1910 when Lee De Forest produced a program from the Metropolitan Opera House in New York City. Other experimental radio stations were started at the University of Wisconsin in Madison in 1915 and another in Wilkinsburg, Pennsylvania, a suburb of Pittsburgh, in 1916."[49]

RCA

The Radio Corporation of America (RCA), a spinoff of GE, was the government sanctioned radio monopoly formed to replace Marconi's American company. (Later, the government that had once considered making radio a government monopoly followed a policy of promoting competition in the radio industry). RCA was owned by a GE-dominated partnership that included Westinghouse, American Telegraph and Telephone Company (AT&T), Western Electric, United Fruit Company, and others. There were cross-licensing (patent pooling) agreements between GE, AT&T, Westinghouse, and RCA, which owned the assets of Marconi's company. Patent pooling was the solution to the problem of each company owning interdependent essential patents.[50]

For many years RCA and its head, David Sarnoff, were virtual synonyms. Sarnoff, who began his career in radio as a Marconi office boy, gained fame as a wireless operator and showed the great value of radio when he picked up distress messages from the sinking Titanic. Ultimately, RCA expanded into nearly every area of communications and electronics. Its extensive patent holdings gave it power over most of its competitors because they had to pay it royalties. While still working for Marconi, Sarnoff had the foresight to realize that the real money in radio lay in selling radio receivers. (Because the market was far smaller, radio transmitters generated smaller revenues.)[51]

---

[48] https://eh.net/encyclopedia/the-history-of-the-radio-industry-in-the-united-states-to-1940/
[49] https://law.jrank.org/pages/4873/Broadcasting-History-Radio.html#:~:text=Other%20experimental%20radio%20stations%20were,broadcasting%20on%20August%2020%2C%201920.
[50] Ibid
[51] Ibid

Financing Radio Broadcasts

Marconi was able to charge people for transmitting messages, but how was radio broadcasting to be financed? In Europe the government financed it. In the USA, it soon came to be largely financed by advertising. In 1922, few stations sold advertising time. Then the motive of many operating radio stations was to advertise other businesses they owned or to get publicity. About a quarter of the nation's 500 stations were owned by manufacturers, retailers, and other businesses, such as hotels and newspapers. Another quarter were owned by radio-related firms. Educational institutions, radio clubs, civic groups, churches, government, and the military owned 40 percent of the stations. Radio manufacturers viewed broadcasting simply as a way to sell radios. Over its first three years of selling radios, RCA's revenues amounted to $83,500,000. By 1930 nine out of ten broadcasting stations were selling advertising time. In 1939, more than a third of the stations lost money. However, by the end of World War II, only five percent were in the red. Stations' advertising revenues came both from local and national advertisers after networks were established. By 1938, 40 percent of the nation's 660 stations were affiliated with a network, and many were part of a chain (commonly-owned).[52]

Radio Networks

On September 25, 1926, RCA formed the National Broadcasting Company (NBC) to take over its network broadcasting business. In early 1927, only seven percent of the nation's 737 radio stations were affiliated with NBC. In that year a rival network whose name eventually became the Columbia Broadcasting System (CBS) was established. In 1928, CBS was purchased and reorganized by William S. Paley, a cigar company executive whose CBS career spanned more than a half-century. In 1934, the Mutual Broadcasting System was formed. Unlike NBC and CBS, it did not move into television. In 1943, the Federal Communications Commission forced NBC to sell a part of its system to Edward J. Noble, who formed the American Broadcasting Corporation (ABC). To avoid the high cost of producing radio shows, local radio stations purchased most of their shows, other than news, from the networks, which enjoyed economies of scale in producing radio programs because their costs were spread over the many stations using their programming.[53]

The Golden Age of Radio

Radio broadcasting was the cheapest form of entertainment, and it provided the public with far better entertainment than most people were accustomed to. As a result, its popularity grew rapidly in the late 1920s and early 1930s, and, by 1934, 60 percent of the nation's households had radios. One and a half million cars were also equipped with them. The 1930s were the Golden Age of radio. It was so popular that theaters dared not open until after the extremely popular *Amos 'n Andy* show was over. In the thirties, radio broadcasting was an entirely different genre from what it became after the introduction of television. Those who have only known the music, news, and talk radio of recent decades can have no conception of the big budget days of the thirties when radio was king of the electronic hill. Like reading, radio demanded the use of imagination. Through image-inspiring sound effects, which reached a high degree of sophistication in the thirties, radio replaced vision with visualization. Perfected during the thirties was the only new "art form" radio originated, the "soap opera," so called because the sponsors, usually soap companies, of these serialized morality plays targeted housewives, who were then very numerous.[54]

---

[52] Ibid
[53] Ibid
[54] ibid

The Growth of Radio

The growth of broadcast radio in the 1920s and 30s can be seen in Tables 1, 2, and 3 below, which give the number of stations, the amount of advertising revenue and sales of radio equipment.

> Author's Note: *Manufacturing and distributing broadcast receivers were dominated by Westinghouse, GE and RCA. However, what we call "boutique companies" today, were referred to as "loft" suppliers in the early days of broadcast receiver manufacturing and distribution. Among these, a fledgling company called Galvin Manufacturing, founded by Paul V. Galvin but operated by his brother, Joe, while Paul found outlets for sales, distribution, installation and repair, used these outlets to sell private labeled broadcast receivers before garnering a contract to supply battery powered two-way radios to the military for WWII.*
>
> *The Galvin Manufacturing Co., was renamed, Motorola, Inc., and became a world leader in two-way mobile communications as well as a major research and production facility for power transistors and microprocessors that are largely responsible for the leap in technology from vacuum tube dependent to transistorized high power mobile radios in the 450-512MHz and 800-970MHz commercial mobile radio bands.*
>
> *Steve Wozniak relied on Motorola's 6500 class microprocessors for his early Apple personal computers.*
>
> *A great deal of credit must also go to Motorola for their creation of a large block of Radio Common Carriers whose influence at the local level of major cities, as well as rural America, was a significant factor in the FCC decision to grant two competing cellular licenses per market and to assure competitive service to rural America by selecting the top 305 MSAs and then allocating spectrum for two RSA carriers per county outside the selected MSAs.*

Table 1
Number of Radio Stations in the US, 1921-1940

Year	Number
1921	5
1922	30
1923	556
1924	530
1925	571
1926	528
1927	681
1928	677
1929	606
1930	618
1931	612
1932	604
1933	599
1934	583
1935	585
1936	616
1937	646
1938	689
1939	722
1940	765

Table 3
Sales of Radio Equipment in Millions of Dollars

Year	Sales in Millions of $
1922	60
1923	136
1924	358
1925	430
1926	506
1927	426
1928	651
1929	843

Source: Douglas (1987), p. 75

Source: Sterling and Kittross (1978), p. 510.[55]

> Author's Note
> The Free-Speech Issue
> Was radio to be treated like news-papers and magazines, or were broadcasters to be denied free speech? Were radio stations to be treated, like telephone companies, as common carriers; that is, anyone desiring to make use of them would have to be allowed to use them, or would they be treated like newspapers, which are under no obligation to allow all comers access to their pages? It was also established that radio stations, like newspapers, would be protected by the First Amendment.
>
> Regulation and Legislation
> Government regulation of radio began in 1904 when President Theodore Roosevelt organized the Inter-departmental Board of Wireless Telegraphy. In 1910, the Wireless Ship Act was passed. That radio was to be a regulated industry was decided in 1912, when Congress passed a Radio Act that required people to obtain a license from the government in order to operate a radio transmitter. In 1924, Herbert Hoover, who was secretary of the Commerce Department, said that the radio industry was probably the only industry in the nation that was unanimously in favor of having itself regulated. Presumably, this was due both to the industry's desire to put a stop to stations interfering with each others' broadcasts and to limit the number of stations to a small enough number to lock in a profit. The Radio Act of 1927 solved the problem of broadcasting stations using the same frequency and the more powerful ones drowning out less powerful ones. This act also established that radio waves are public property; therefore, radio stations must be licensed by the government. It was decided, however, not to charge stations for the use of this property. This became a contentious and delaying factor when cellular and PCS licenses were being considered.   END

The practice of granting licenses with no charge eventually gave way to politicians' greed. Despite decades of demonstrated value and success with a policy of zero cost for the license, when the FCC allocated spectrum for the PCS band (1.9-2.2GHz), instead of granting the licenses at no cost, they auctioned them off generating $26B! It was a political coup for the politicians taking credit for extorting $26B from the treasuries of companies in the wireless telecommunications business; but, it was actually a tax. The costs of the licenses became the basis for cost-based subscriber rates resulting in monthly rates more than double what they would have been without the license cost. Further, this practice reduced cash resources otherwise available for research and development resulting in slower progress toward advanced network technologies.

Many years later, technologist, George Gilder, in his *Telecosm* article published in Forbes Magazine™ had a lot to say about the impact as well as motives of those who introduced and successfully promoted the abandonment of traditional spectrum licensing to auction spectrum for PCS (Personal Communications Service).

Article: *So, Stop The Auction*

The Steinbrecher radio can survey any existing swath of spectrum in real time and determine almost instantly which channels are in use and which are free. It is this capability that convinced McCaw to buy Steinbrecher data cells despite the commitment of McCaw's putative owner, AT&T, to deploy narrowband units made by Cirrus Logic's subsidiary, Pacific Communications Sciences Inc. (PCSI), which have to scan through channels one at a time. McCaw is using the Steinbrecher radios as sniffers that constantly survey the cellular band and direct data bursts to those channels that are not being used at a particular time.

Indeed, the immediate needs of the marketplace alone justify the adoption of Steinbrecher data cells. With modems and antennas increasingly available and even moving, sometime next year to PCMCIA slots the size of a credit card, demand for wireless data is likely to soar.

---

[55] Ibid

So, what does this have to do with the impending spectrum auction? Almost everything. Strictly speaking, the FCC is leasing 10-year exclusive rights to radiate electromagnetic waves at certain frequencies to deliver PCS. This entire auction concept is tied to thousands of exclusive frequencies alike and offer bandwidth on demand. It has no place for modulation schemes that do not need exclusive spectrum space. Continuing to use interference standards based on analog transmissions that are affected by every passing spray of radiation, FCC rules fail to grasp the far more robust nature of digital on-off codes with error correction. By the time the FCC gets around to selling its 2,500 shards of air, the air will have been radically changed by new technology.

The FCC is fostering a real estate paradigm for the spectrum. You buy or lease spectrum as you would a spread of land. Once you have your license, you can use it any way you want as long as you don't unduly disturb the neighbors. You rent a stretch of beach and build a wall.

PCSI is now shipping a quintuple-threat communicator that fits into the floppy bay of an advanced IBM ThinkPad® notebook or an Apple PowerBook®, enabling them to send and receive faxes, make wireless or wireline phone calls, dispatch data files across the existing cellular network or send CDPD® packets at 19.2 kilobits per second. Speech recognition capabilities from IBM and Dragon Systems will come next year to personal digital assistants, permitting them to read or receive E-mail by voice. Although the first Newtons® and Zoomers® have disappointed their sponsors, the market will ignite over the next two years as vendors adopt the essential form factor of a digital cellular phone with computer functions rather than providing a kluge computer with a vaporware phone.

Nonetheless, McCaw has more on its mind with Steinbrecher than merely gaining a second source for CDPD sniffers. By simultaneously purchasing some 10 percent of the company and putting chief technical officer Nicholas Kauser on the Steinbrecher board, McCaw is signaling not a tactical move but a major strategic thrust. The Steinbrecher rollout in fact represents McCaw's stealth deployment of broadband digital capability.

Today the rival CDPD equipment from PCSI, Hughes and AT&T all can be made to perform CDPD communications as an overlay to the existing cellular phone systems. However, only the Steinbrecher systems can be upgraded to perform all the functions of a base station and more, for voice, data and video. Only Steinbrecher allows the replacement of 416 radio transceivers, one for each channel, with one broadband radio and some digital signal processing chips. Only Steinbrecher can replace a $1.5 million, 1,000-square-foot cellular base station with a box the size of a briefcase costing some $100,000 but, thanks to Moore's Law, racing toward $10,000.

It remains to be seen only whether McCaw will have the guts to follow through on this initiative by completely rebuilding its network to accommodate the wideband radio being installed at its heart. Self-cannibalization is the rule of success in information technology. Intel and Microsoft, for example, lead the way in constantly attacking their own products. But this mode of life is deeply alien to the telephone business—even an entrepreneurial outfit like McCaw.

With new software and a simple upgrade to a MiniCell, the Steinbrecher DataCell® will allow the McCaw system to handle all modulation schemes simultaneously—AMPS, TDMA, CDMA and future methods such as Orthogonal Frequency Division Multiple Access—obviating the need for hybrid phones. The multiprotocol and aerobatic capabilities of broadband digital radios could enable McCaw to roll out a cornucopia of PCS services—for everything from monitoring vending machines or remote power stations to tracking trucks and packages, and linking laptops and PDAs—while the rest of the industry is still paralyzed by wrangles over incumbent users, regulatory procedures, frequency access and radio standards.

Making channel sizes a variable rather than a fixed function of radios, Steinbrecher systems offer the possibility of bandwidth on demand. They could open up the entire spectrum as one gigantic broadband pipe into which we would be able to insert packets in any empty space—dark fiber in the air.

The Steinbrecher system by contrast, suggests a model not of a beach but of an ocean. You can no more lease electromagnetic waves than you can lease ocean waves. Enabled by new technology, this new model is suitable for an information superhighway in the sky. You can use the spectrum as much as you want as long as you don't collide with anyone else or pollute it with high-powered noise or other nuisances.

In the Steinbrecher model, you employ the spectrum as you use any public right of way. You are responsible for keeping your eyes open and avoiding others. You cannot just buy a 10-year lease and then barge blindly all over the air in a high-powered vessel, depending on the government to keep everyone else off your territory and out of your way. The spectrum is no longer dark. The Steinbrecher broadband radio supplies you with lights as you travel the information superhighway. You can see other travelers and avoid them.

Even if Steinbrecher radios did not exist, however, the assumptions of the auction are collapsing in the face of innovations by Qualcomm and other spread-spectrum companies. Like Steinbrecher radios, CDMA modulation schemes allow you to use spectrum without interfering with others. To auditors without the code, calls seem indistinguishable from noise. But radios with the code can dig up signals from under the noise floor. Up to the point of traffic congestion where the quality of the signal begins to degrade gracefully, numerous users can employ the same frequencies at the same time. This property of CDMA has been tested in Qualcomm's CDMA Omnitracs® position locator and two-way communications system. Mainly used by trucking companies, it is now being extended to cars, boats, trains and other mobile equipment. Based on geosynchronous satellites, it operates all across the country, with some 60,000 units, under a "secondary license" that forbids Qualcomm to interfere with the primary license holders of the same frequencies. Qualcomm's transceivers on the tops of trucks use a small antenna that issues a beam six to 10 degrees in width. Because satellites are just two degrees apart, the Qualcomm beam can blanket several satellites. Other users, however, are entirely unconscious of the presence of the CDMA signal. Omnitracs has operated for some six years and has not interfered with anyone yet.

No More Blind Drivers on the Information Superhighway

With an increasing array of low-interference technologies available, the FCC should not give exclusive rights to anyone. Instead, it should impose a heavy burden of proof on any service providers with blind or high-powered systems that maintain they cannot operate without an exclusive license, that want to build on the beach and keep everyone else out of the surf. In particular, the FCC should make all the proponents of TDMA, whether in the American or European GSM systems, explain why the government should wall off spectrum. The wireless systems of the future will offer bandwidth on demand and send their packets wherever there is room.

At the same time that new technologies make hash of the need to auction off exclusive licenses, Qualcomm and Steinbrecher also radically attack the very notion of spectrum scarcity on which the auction is based. Steinbrecher's radio makes it possible to manufacture new spectrum nearly at will. By putting one of his MiniCells on every telephone pole and down every alley and in every elevator shaft, the cellular industry can exponentially multiply the total number of calls it can handle. At some $100,000 apiece and dropping in price, these MiniCells can operate at 900 megahertz or six gigahertz just as well as at the two-gigahertz range being auctioned by the government. It is as if Reed Hundt (FCC commissioner) is auctioning off beachfront property, with a long list of codicils and regulations and restrictive covenants, while the tide pours in around him and creates new surf everywhere.

Still more important in view of the coming auction, the wideband capability of the Steinbrecher radio joins CDMA in allowing the use of huge spans of spectrum that are ostensibly occupied by other users. The Steinbrecher radio can survey the gigahertz reserves of the military and intelligence services, UHF television and microwave, and direct usage to the many fallow regions. For example, the prime territory between 225 megahertz and 400 megahertz, consisting of some 3,000 25-kilohertz channels, is entirely occupied by government and air force communications. But most of the channels are largely unused. A Steinbrecher radio could sit on those frequencies and direct calls to empty slots.

An ideal system would combine Steinbrecher broadband machines with Qualcomm's modulation schemes. Steinbrecher supplies the lights and eyes to find space in already licensed spectrum bands. CDMA allows the noninvasive entry into spans of spectrum that are in active use.

Meanwhile, the Steinbrecher system changes the very nature of spectrum "ownership" or rental. Unrestricted to single band or range or frequencies, Steinbrecher radios can reach from the kilohertz to the high gigaherrz and go to any unoccupied territory. As Steinbrecher radios become the dominant technology, the notion of spectrum assignments allotted in 2,500 specific shards becomes a technological absurdity.

Wall Street is beginning to catch on. When Steinbrecher announced in January a private placement through Alex Brown, the company wanted to raise some $20 million. The response was overwhelming, and hundreds of frustrated investors were left wringing their hands as the new radio left the station. The sole proprietorship of the mid-1980s with revenues of $5 million or less was moving into sleek new headquarters off Route 128 in Burlington. Steinbrecher Corp. was becoming yet another of the Moore's Law monsters.

Meanwhile, the issue for Washington emerges starkly. Do we want a strategy for MiniCells or for Minitels?[56]

END Article

Mr. Gilder's assessment at the time Forbes published this article was spot on. However, despite Mr. Gilder's (and many others') attempts to prevent it, the auction he so eloquently dissected took place (see following reprint of Times article in 2000) and the politicians achieved their purpose at the expense of the wireless customers whose monthly costs for service doubled when it should have been significantly reduced by the introduction of Steinbrecher and Qualcomm broadband technologies as described by George Gilder in this article.

Regardless, the reason this article is presented here is to motivate the reader to think more like the teams representing Steinbrecher and Qualcomm and not like risk-averse telco engineers and executive management or politicians who use their influence to stifle innovation just to squeeze more money out of the general populace.

Clinton Orders A New Auction Of the Airwaves

By STEPHEN LABATON OCT. 14, 2000

With growing congestion of the airwaves threatening the development of a new generation of hand-held devices, President Clinton ordered the federal government today to review and then auction wide swaths of the spectrum now controlled by government agencies, as well as by private companies.

The extraordinary review is expected to lead to a fundamental reshuffling of how the spectrum is used and culminate in a huge auction in 2002 to award new licenses for companies to sell services like wireless telephones offering high-speed Internet connections.

The auction promises to raise tens of billions of dollars for the United States Treasury. It may also require the government to make huge payments to companies and to agencies including the Defense Department, law enforcement authorities and public safety organizations to shift their existing radio, phone and communications systems to new frequencies on the spectrum that are now underused but not considered useful for the newer hand-held devices.

Mr. Clinton's announcement follows months of dire predictions by communications experts that the United States might have already fallen behind Asian and European countries that had managed their airwaves more efficiently and had already conducted multibillion-dollar licensing auctions that would enable them to move ahead in the development of a wide array of innovative hand-held devices, from high-speed Internet telephones to wireless electronic credit cards.[57]

Author's Note: Editorial opinion: It is a classic case of political decisions by ignorant power mongers with little to no knowledge or understanding of the issues they're impacting. Unfortunately, this was not a new demonstration of politics interfering with the better interests of industry and consumers in the radio business. Similar cases occurred several times from 1920 to 2000 as politicians, who don't know an electron from a fig newton, lined their pockets and feathered their political nests by influencing vital FCC decisions.

Bottom line to the above action is: "This is a tax; plain and simple. If the costs of licenses passed through to end-users wasn't necessary, carriers would have had this cash to invest in infrastructure and subscriber equipment. To allow anyone to think the costs of licenses was not passed through to the customers is an exercise in contempt for the shrinking middle class whose better interests would have been served by continuing the legacy practice of no cost licenses. Better, more extensive networks sooner, advanced technologies and public service would have been accelerated rather than held back by the self-serving political interests."[58]

"An in-depth study of the origin and history of the Radio Manufacturing Association, led by Paul Galvin, Founder of Motorola, reveals astoundingly unselfish objective insistence by this early group for regulation of

---

[56] Forbes; ASAP, 1994: George Gilder's Telecosm: "Auctioning The Airwaves"
[57] https://www.nytimes.com/2000/10/14/business/clinton-orders-a-new-auction-of-the-airwaves.html
[58] Interview with Lee Horsman who argued this point at the FCC pre-licensing hearing in Palo Alto, CA - 1999

the radio spectrum by federal government intervention. However, despite their efforts, the FCC became a political grab bag as the value of spectrum grew exponentially following WWII and with the advent of ubiquitous cellular services."[59]

---

[59] Ibid

Chapter Twelve -- Radio Frequency (RF) Modulation

Modulation

RF is a naturally occurring resource – like the ocean or forests – in and of itself, it is unchanging, i.e,, it is what it is. Generating it (RF) with inventions doesn't change its properties; however, manipulating it bends it to the will of man. Manipulating it by imposing information on it alters its natural behavior. Imposing information on it is called "modulation." Technical information in the following paragraphs is intended to alert you, the student, to the many variations of modulating techniques. Advanced radio telecommunications technologies focus on these techniques as they represent the most effective ways to manipulate RF to serve its best purpose.

In electronics and telecommunications, **modulation** is the process of varying one or more properties of a periodic waveform, called the *carrier signal*, with a modulating signal that typically contains information to be transmitted. Most radio systems in the 20th century used frequency modulation (FM) or amplitude modulation (AM) to make the carrier frequency *carry* the radio broadcast.[60]

In general telecommunications, modulation is a process of conveying message signal; for example, a digital bit stream or an analog audio signal, inside another signal that can be physically transmitted. Modulation of a sine waveform transforms a narrow frequency range baseband message signal into a moderate to high frequency range passband signal, one that can pass through a filter.

A **modulator** is a device that performs modulation. A **demodulator** (sometimes *detector* or *demod*) is a device that performs demodulation, the inverse of modulation. A modem (from **mo**dulator–**dem**odulator) can perform both operations.[61]

The aim of **analog modulation** is to transfer an analog baseband (or low pass) signal, for example an audio signal or TV signal, over an analog bandpass channel at a different frequency, for example over a limited radio frequency band or a cable TV network channel.[62]

The aim of **digital modulation** is to transfer a digital bit stream over an analog communication channel, for example over the public switched telephone network (where a bandpass filter limits the frequency range to 300–3400Hz) or over a limited radio frequency band.[63]

Analog and digital modulation facilitate frequency division multiplexing (FDM), where several low pass information signals are transferred simultaneously over the same shared physical medium, using separate passband channels (several different carrier frequencies).[64]

The aim of **digital baseband modulation** methods, also known as line coding, is to transfer a digital bit stream over a baseband channel, typically a non-filtered copper wire such as a serial bus or a wired local area network.[65]

The aim of **pulse modulation** methods is to transfer a narrowband analog signal, for example, a phone call, over a wideband baseband channel or, in some of the schemes, as a bit stream over another digital transmission system.[66]

In music synthesizers, modulation may be used to synthesize waveforms with an extensive overtone spectrum using a small number of oscillators. In this case, the carrier frequency is typically in the same order or much lower than the modulating waveform (see frequency modulation synthesis or ring modulation synthesis).

---

[60] https://www.allaboutcircuits.com/textbook/radio-frequency-analysis-design/radio-frequency-modulation/the-many-types-of-rf-modulation-radio-frequency/
[61] Ibid
[62] Ibid
[63] Ibid
[64] Ibid
[65] Ibid
[66] Ibid

Analog Modulation Methods

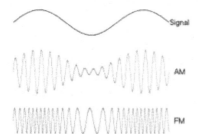

A low-frequency message signal (top) may be carried by an AM or FM radio wave.

This "waterfall plot" of a 146.52 MHz radio carrier, with amplitude modulation by a 1,000Hz sinusoid, shows two strong sidebands at + and − 1kHz from the carrier frequency.

FM, bottom, represents a carrier frequency modulated by a 1,000Hz sinusoid. The modulation index has been adjusted to around 2.4, so the carrier frequency has small amplitude. Several strong sidebands are apparent. In principle, an infinite number are produced in FM but the higher order sidebands are of negligible magnitude.

In analog modulation, the modulation is applied continuously in response to the analog information signal. Analog modulation techniques include:

- Amplitude modulation (AM) (here the amplitude of the carrier signal is varied in accordance with the instantaneous amplitude of the modulating signal)
- Double-sideband modulation (DSB)
- Double-sideband modulation with carrier (DSB-WC) (used on the AM radio broadcasting band)
- Double-sideband suppressed-carrier transmission (DSB-SC)
- Double-sideband reduced carrier transmission (DSB-RC)
- Single-sideband modulation (SSB, or SSB-AM)
- Single-sideband modulation with carrier (SSB-WC)
- Single-sideband modulation suppressed carrier modulation (SSB-SC)
- Vestigial sideband modulation (VSB, or VSB-AM)
- Quadrature amplitude modulation (QAM)
- Angle modulation, which is an approximately constant envelope
- Frequency modulation (FM) (here the frequency of the carrier signal is varied in accordance with the instantaneous amplitude of the modulating signal)
- Phase modulation (PM) (here the phase shift of the carrier signal is varied in accordance with the instantaneous amplitude of the modulating signal)
- Transpositional Modulation (TM), in which the waveform inflection is modified resulting in a signal where each quarter cycle is transposed in the modulation process. TM is a pseudo-analog modulation (AM) where an AM carrier also carries a phase variable phase f(ø). TM is f(AM,ø).[67]

Digital modulation methods

In digital modulation, an analog carrier signal is modulated by a discrete signal. Digital modulation methods can be considered as digital-to-analog conversion and the corresponding demodulation or detection as analog-to-digital conversion. The changes in the carrier signal are chosen from a finite number of M alternative symbols (the *modulation alphabet*).

A schematic representation of 4 baud (8 bit/s) data link containing arbitrarily chosen values is shown here.

A simple example: A telephone line is designed for transferring audible sounds; for example, tones, and not digital bits (zeros and ones). Computers may, however, communicate over a telephone line by means of modems, which are representing the digital bits by tones, called symbols. If there are four alternative symbols (corresponding to a musical instrument that can generate four different tones, one at a time), the first symbol

---

[67] Ibid

may represent the bit sequence 00, the second 01, the third 10 and the fourth 11. If the modem plays a melody consisting of 1000 tones per second, the symbol rate is 1000 symbols/second, or baud. Since each tone (*i.e.,* symbol) represents a message consisting of two digital bits in this example, the bit rate is twice the symbol rate, *i.e.,* 2000 bits per second. This is similar to the technique used by dial-up modems as opposed to DSL (more on this later) modems.

According to one definition of digital signal, the modulated signal is a digital signal. According to another definition, the modulation is a form of digital-to-analog conversion. Most textbooks would consider digital modulation schemes as a form of digital transmission, synonymous to data transmission. Very few would consider it as analog transmission.

Fundamental digital modulation methods

- The most fundamental digital modulation techniques are based on keying:
- PSK (phase-shift keying): a finite number of phases are used.
- FSK (frequency-shift keying): a finite number of frequencies are used.
- ASK (amplitude-shift keying): a finite number of amplitudes are used.
- QAM (quadrature amplitude modulation): a finite number of at least two phases and at least two amplitudes are used.

In QAM, an in-phase signal (or I, with one example being a cosine waveform) and a quadrature phase signal (or Q, with an example being a sine wave) are amplitude modulated with a finite number of amplitudes and then summed. It can be seen as a two-channel system, each channel using ASK. The resulting signal is equivalent to a combination of PSK and ASK.

In all of the above methods, each of these phases, frequencies or amplitudes are assigned a unique pattern of binary bits. Usually, each phase, frequency or amplitude, encodes an equal number of bits. This number of bits comprises the *symbol* that is represented by the particular phase, frequency or amplitude. If the alphabet consists of alternative symbols, each symbol represents a message consisting of *N* bits. If the symbol rate (also known as the baud rate) is symbols/second (or baud), the data rate is bit/second.[68]

For example, with an alphabet consisting of 16 alternative symbols, each symbol represents 4 bits. Thus, the data rate is four times the baud rate.

In the case of PSK, ASK or QAM, where the carrier frequency of the modulated signal is constant, the modulation alphabet is often conveniently represented on a constellation diagram, showing the amplitude of the I signal at the x-axis, and the amplitude of the Q signal as the y-axis, for each symbol.

Modulator and detector principles of operation

PSK and ASK, and sometimes also FSK, are often generated and detected using the principle of QAM. The I and Q signals can be combined into a complex-valued signal $I+jQ$ (where j is the imaginary unit). The resulting so called equivalent low pass signal or equivalent baseband signal is a complex-valued representation of the real-valued modulated physical signal (the so-called passband signal or RF signal).

These are the general steps used by the modulator to transmit data:

Group the incoming data bits into code words, one for each symbol that will be transmitted.

Map the code words to attributes, for example, amplitudes of the I and Q signals (the equivalent low pass signal), or frequency or phase values.

Adapt pulse shaping or some other filtering to limit the bandwidth and form the spectrum of the equivalent low pass signal, typically using digital signal processing (DSP).

Perform digital to analog conversion (DAC) of the I and Q signals (today all of the above are normally achieved using digital signal processing, DSP).

Generate a high-frequency sine carrier waveform, and perhaps also a cosine quadrature component. Carry out the modulation, for example by multiplying the sine and cosine waveform with the I and Q signals, resulting in

---

[68] Ibid

the equivalent low pass signal being frequency shifted to the modulated passband signal or RF signal. Sometimes this is achieved using DSP technology[69], for example direct digital synthesis using a waveform table, instead of analog signal processing. In that case, the above DAC step should be done after this step.

Amplification and analog bandpass filtering to avoid harmonic distortion and periodic spectrum.

At the receiver side, the demodulator typically performs:

Bandpass filtering.

Automatic gain control, AGC (to compensate for attenuation, for example fading).

Frequency shifting of the RF signal to the equivalent baseband I and Q signals, or to an intermediate frequency (IF) signal, by multiplying the RF signal with a local oscillator sine wave and cosine wave frequency (see the superheterodyne receiver principle).

Sampling and analog-to-digital conversion (ADC) (sometimes before or instead of the above point, for example by means of under-sampling).

Equalization filtering, for example, a matched filter, compensation for multipath propagation, time spreading, phase distortion and frequency selective fading, to avoid inter-symbol interference and symbol distortion.

Detection of the amplitudes of the I and Q signals, or the frequency or phase of the IF signal.

Quantization of the amplitudes, frequencies or phases to the nearest allowed symbol values.

Mapping of the quantized amplitudes, frequencies or phases to code words (bit groups).

Parallel-to-serial conversion of the code words into a bit stream.

Pass the resultant bit stream on for further processing such as removal of any error-correcting codes.[70]

As is common to all digital communication systems, the design of both the modulator and demodulator must be done simultaneously. Digital modulation schemes are possible because the transmitter-receiver pair has prior knowledge of how data is encoded and represented in the communications system. In all digital communication systems, both the modulator at the transmitter and the demodulator at the receiver are structured so they perform inverse operations.

Non-coherent modulation methods do not require a receiver reference clock signal that is phase synchronized with the sender carrier signal. In this case, modulation symbols (rather than bits, characters, or data packets) are asynchronously transferred. The opposite is coherent modulation.

List of digital modulation techniques

A list of digital modulation techniques would include the following:

- Phase-shift keying (PSK)
- Binary PSK (BPSK), using M=2 symbols
- Quadrature PSK (QPSK), using M=4 symbols
- 8PSK, using M=8 symbols
- 16PSK, using M=16 symbols
- Differential PSK (DPSK)
- Differential QPSK (DQPSK)

---

[69] A **digital signal processor** (**DSP**) is a specialized microprocessor chip, with its architecture optimized for the operational needs of digital signal processing.[1][2] DSPs are fabricated on MOS integrated circuit chips.[3][4] They are widely used in audio signal processing, telecommunications, digital image processing, radar, sonar and speech recognition systems, and in common consumer electronic devices such as mobile phones, disk drives and high-definition television (HDTV) products.[3]

The goal of a DSP is usually to measure, filter or compress continuous real-world analog signals. Most general-purpose microprocessors can also execute digital signal processing algorithms successfully, but may not be able to keep up with such processing continuously in real-time. Also, dedicated DSPs usually have better power efficiency, thus they are more suitable in portable devices such as mobile phones because of power consumption constraints.[5] DSPs often use special memory architectures that are able to fetch multiple data or instructions at the same time. DSPs often also implement data compression technology, with the discrete cosine transform (DCT) in particular being a widely used compression technology in DSPs.

[70] Ibid

- Offset QPSK (OQPSK)
- π/4–QPSK
- Frequency-shift keying (FSK)
- Audio frequency-shift keying (AFSK)
- Multi-frequency shift keying (MFSK)
- Dual-tone multi-frequency (DTMF)
- Amplitude-shift keying (ASK)
- On-off keying (OOK), the most common ASK form
- Vestigial, for example 8VSB
- Quadrature amplitude modulation (QAM), a combination of PSK and ASK
- Polar modulation like QAM a combination of PSK and ASK
- Continuous phase modulation (CPM) methods
- Minimum-shift keying (MSK)
- Gaussian minimum-shift keying (GMSK)
- Continuous-phase frequency-shift keying (CPFSK)
- Orthogonal frequency-division multiplexing (OFDM) modulation
- Discrete multi-tone (DMT), including adaptive modulation and bit-loading
- Wavelet modulation
- Trellis coded modulation (TCM), also known as Trellis modulation
- Spread-spectrum techniques
- Direct-sequence spread spectrum (DSSS)
- Chirp spread spectrum (CSS) according to IEEE 802.15.4a CSS uses pseudo-stochastic coding
- Frequency-hopping spread spectrum (FHSS) applies a special scheme for channel release

MSK and GMSK are particular cases of continuous phase modulation. Indeed, MSK is a particular case of the sub-family of CPM known as continuous-phase frequency shift keying (CPFSK) which is defined by a rectangular frequency pulse (*i.e.*, a linearly increasing phase pulse) of one-symbol-time duration (total response signaling).

OFDM is based on the idea of frequency-division multiplexing (FDM), but the multiplexed streams are all parts of a single original stream. The bit stream is split into several parallel data streams, each transferred over its own sub-carrier using some conventional digital modulation scheme. The modulated sub-carriers are summed to form an OFDM signal. This dividing and recombining help with handling channel impairments. OFDM is considered as a modulation technique rather than a multiplex technique since it transfers one bit stream over one communication channel using one sequence of so-called OFDM symbols. OFDM can be extended to multi-user channel access method in the orthogonal frequency-division multiple access (OFDMA) and multi-carrier code division multiple access (MC-CDMA) schemes, allowing several users to share the same physical medium by giving different sub-carriers or spreading codes to different users.

Of the two kinds of RF power amplifier, switching amplifiers (Class D amplifiers) cost less and use less battery power than linear amplifiers of the same output power. However, they only work with relatively constant-amplitude-modulation signals such as angle modulation (FSK or PSK) and CDMA, but not with QAM and OFDM. Nevertheless, even though switching amplifiers is completely unsuitable for normal QAM constellations, often the QAM modulation principle is used to drive switching amplifiers with these FM and other waveforms, and sometimes QAM demodulators are used to receive the signals put out by these switching amplifiers.

Automatic Digital Modulation Recognition (ADMR)

Automatic digital modulation recognition in intelligent communication systems is one of the most important issues in software defined radio (emphasis author's) and cognitive radio. According to incremental expanse of intelligent receivers, automatic modulation recognition becomes a challenging topic in telecommunication systems and computer engineering. Such systems have many civil and military applications. Moreover, blind recognition of modulation type is an important problem in commercial systems, especially in software defined radio. Usually in such systems, there are some extra information issues for system configuration, but considering blind approaches in intelligent receivers, we can reduce information overload and increase transmission performance. Obviously, with no knowledge of the transmitted data and many unknown parameters at the receiver, such as the signal power, carrier frequency and phase offsets, timing information, *etc.*, blind identification of the modulation is made fairly difficult. This becomes even more challenging in real-world scenarios with multipath fading, frequency-selective and time-varying channels.

There are two main approaches to automatic modulation recognition. The first approach uses likelihood-based methods to assign an input signal to a proper class. Another recent approach is based on feature extraction.

Digital Baseband Modulation or Line Coding

The term **digital baseband modulation** (or digital baseband transmission) is synonymous to line codes. These are methods to transfer a digital bit stream over an analog baseband channel (*aka* low pass channel) using a pulse train, *i.e.*, a discrete number of signal levels, by directly modulating the voltage or current on a cable or serial bus. Common examples are unipolar, non-return-to-zero (NRZ), Manchester and alternate mark inversion (AMI) coding.

Pulse Modulation Methods

Pulse modulation schemes aim at transferring a narrowband analog signal over an analog baseband channel as a two-level signal by modulating a pulse wave. Some pulse modulation schemes also allow the narrowband analog signal to be transferred as a digital signal (*i.e.*, as a quantized discrete-time signal) with a fixed bit rate, which can be transferred over an underlying digital transmission system, for example, some line code. These are not modulation schemes in the conventional sense because they are not channel coding schemes, but should be considered as source coding schemes, and, in some cases, analog-to-digital (A-to-D) conversion techniques.

- **Analog-over-analog methods**
- Pulse-amplitude modulation (PAM)
- Pulse-width modulation (PWM) and Pulse-depth modulation (PDM)

Analog-over-digital methods

- Pulse-code modulation (PCM)
- Differential PCM (DPCM)
- Adaptive DPCM (ADPCM)
- Delta modulation (DM or Δ-modulation)
- Delta-sigma modulation (ΣΔ)
- Continuously variable slope delta modulation (CVSDM), also called Adaptive-delta modulation (ADM)
- Pulse-density modulation (PDM) Miscellaneous modulation techniques – The use of on-off keying to transmit Morse code at radio frequencies is known as continuous wave (CW) operation.
- Adaptive modulation
- Space modulation is a method whereby signals are modulated within airspace such as that used in instrument landing systems.[71]

Author's Note: A central message I am attempting to convey to you, the student, is that bandwidth is a finite resource. Continuing to find new ways to cram more and more into less and less forces us to recognize the end game will absolutely end when modulation techniques alone can no longer fill a limited capacity pipe; thus, as we're seeing with q-bit computers, nano-technologies, super-conductors, quantum physics, fusion, *etc.*, telecommunications needs young men and women whose aptitudes and ambitions, fueled with early years of 'no boundaries fearlessness,' will think so far out of the box they will find new ways to wirelessly telecommunicate. If 20th Century think tank physicists whose interests included considering this approach have any merit (I can't list names here but they were/are geniuses at MIT, Stanford, Canadian labs funded by Research In Motion founders, and many others), there are possibilities other than traditional bandwidth expansion and modulation compression theories.

In this regard, the following article published in *Forbes ASAP* in 1994 presents a real world example of what you, the student contemplating a career in wireless telecommunications, may consider.

---

[71] https://en.wikipedia.org/wiki/Modulation

[72]Forbes, ASAP: 1994; George Gilder's Telecosm: "Auctioning the Airways"

Keep in mind, this was written in 1994.

Imagine it is 1971 and you are chair of the new [imaginary – author emphasis] Federal Computer Commission. This commission has been established to regulate the natural monopoly of computer technology as summed up in the famous Grosch's Law. In 1956, IBM engineer, Herbert Grosch, proved that computer power rises by the square of its cost and thus necessarily gravitates to the most costly machines.

According to a famous IBM projection, the entire world could use some 55 mainframes, time-sharing from dumb terminals and keypunch machines. The owners of these machines would rule the world of information in an ascendant information age. By the Orwellian dawn of 1984, Big Bre'r IBM would establish a new digital tyranny, with a new elite of the data-rich dominating the data-poor.

As head of the computer commission, you launch a bold program to forestall this grim outcome. Under a congressional mandate to promote competition for IBM and ensure the principle of universal computer service you ordain the creation of some 2,500 mainframe licenses to be auctioned to the highest bidders (with special licenses reserved for minorities, women and farmers).

To ensure widespread competition across all of America, you establish seven licenses in each metropolitan Major Trading Area and seven in every rural Basic Trading Area as defined by Rand McNally. To guarantee universal service, you mandate the free distribution of keypunch machines to all businesses and households so they can access the local computer centers

In establishing this auction in 1971, you had no reason at all to notice that a tiny company in Mountain View, CA, called Intel, was about to announce three new technologies together with some hype about "a new era of integrated electronics." After all, these technologies—the microprocessor, erasable, programmable read-only memory (EPROM); and a one-kilobit dynamic random access memory (DRAM)—were far too primitive to even compare with IBM's massive machines.

The likely results of such a Federal Computer Commission policy are not merely matters of conjecture. France pretty much did it when it distributed free Minitel terminals to its citizens to provide them access to government mainframes. While the United States made personal computers nearly ubiquitous—buying perhaps 100 million since the launch of the Minitel in the late 1970s—the French chatted through central databases and ended up with one-quarter as many computers per capita as this country, and one-tenth the number of computer networks. Today, PC networks are leading the U.S. economy to world dominance while Europe founders without a single major computer company, software firm or semiconductor manufacturer.

It is now 1994, and Reed Hundt, the new chairman of the Federal Communications Commission, is indeed about to hold an auction.

Rather than selling exclusive mainframe licenses, the current FCC is going to sell exclusive ten-year licenses to about 2,500 shards of the radio spectrum. Meanwhile, a tiny company called Steinbrecher Corp. of Burlington, Mass., is introducing the new microprocessor of the radio business.

In the world of radio waves ruled by the Federal Communications Commission, the Steinbrecher MiniCell is even more revolutionary than the microprocessor was in the world of computing. While Intel put an entire computer on a single chip, Steinbrecher has put an entire cellular base station—now requiring some 1,000 square feet and costing $1.5 million—in a box the size of a briefcase that costs $100,000 today. Based on a unique invention by Donald Steinbrecher and on the sweeping advance of computer technology, the MiniCell represents a far bigger leap forward beyond the current state of the art than the microprocessor did. What's more, this MiniCell is in fact much superior to existing cellular base stations. Unlike the 416 hard-wired radio transceivers (transmitter-receivers) in existing base stations, the MiniCell contains a single digital broadband radio and is fully programmable. It can accommodate scores of different kinds of cellular handsets.

Most important, the MiniCell benefits from the same technology as the microprocessor. Making possible the creation of this broadband digital radio is the tidal onrush of Moore's Law. In an antithesis of Grosch's Law, Gordon Moore of Intel showed that the cost-effectiveness of microchip technology doubles every 18 months.

---

[72] Forbes, ASAP; 1994; George Gilder's Telecosm: "Auctioning the Airways"; pp99-112

This insight suggested the Law of the Microcosm—that computing power gravitates not to the costliest but to the cheapest machines. Costing $100,000 today, the MiniCell will predictably cost some $10,000 before the turn of the century.

In time, these digital MiniCells will have an impact similar to that of the PC. They will drive the creation of a cornucopia of new mobile services—from plain old telephony to wireless video conferencing—based on ubiquitous client/server networks in the air. Endowing Americans with universal mobile access to information superhighways, these MiniCells can spearhead another generation of computer-led growth in the U.S. economy. Eventually, the implications of Steinbrecher's machines and other major innovation in wireless will crash in on the legalistic scene of the FCC.

And that's only the beginning of the story.

Going on the block in May will be 160 megaherts (millions of cycles per second) of the radio frequency spectrum, divided into seven sections of between 10 and 30 megahertz in each of 543 areas of the country, and devoted to enhanced Personal Communications Services (PCS).

Existing cellular systems operate in a total spectrum space of 50 megahertz in two frequency bands near the 800-megahertz level. By contrast, PCS will take four times that space in a frequency band near two gigahertz (billions of cycles per second). Because higher frequencies allow use of lower-power radios with smaller antennas and longer-lasting batteries, PCS offers the possibility of a drastically improved wireless system. Unfortunately, the major obstacle to the promise of PCS is the auction.

Amid the spectrum fever aroused by the bidding, however, new radio technologies are emerging that devastate its most basic assumptions. At a time when the world is about to take to information superhighways in the sky—plied by low-powered, pollution-free computer phones—the FCC is in danger of building a legal infrastructure and protectionist program for information smokestacks and gas guzzlers.

Even the language used to describe the auction betrays its fallacies. With the real estate imagery, analysts depict spectrum as "beachfront property" and the auction as a "land rush." They assume that radio frequencies are like analog telephone circuits: no two users can occupy the same spot of spectrum at the same time. Whether large 50-kilowatt broadcast stations booming Rush Limbaugh's voice across the nation or milliwatt cellular phones beaming love murmurs to a nearby base station, radio transmitters are assumed to be infectious, high-powered and blind. If one is on the highway, everyone else has to clear out. Both the prevailing wisdom and the entrenched technology dictate that every transmitter be quarantined in its own spectrum slot.

However, innovations from such companies as Steinbrecher and Qualcomm Inc. of San Diego overthrow this paradigm. Not only can numerous radios operate at noninterfering levels in the same frequency band, they can also see other users' signals and move to avoid them. In baseball jargon, the new radios can hit 'em where they ain't; in football idiom, they run for daylight. If appropriately handled, these technologies can render spectrum not scarce but abundant.

These developments make it retrograde to assign exclusive spectrum rights to anyone or to foster technologies that require exclusivity. Spectrum no longer shares any features of beachfront property. A wave would be a better analogy.

The New Rules of Waves

In the early decades of this century, radio was king. Electronics hackers played in the waves with a variety of ham, citizens band and shortwave machines. Experimenting with crystal sets, they innocently entered the domain of solid-state devices and acquired some of the skills that fueled the electronic revolution in the United States and the radar revolution that won World War II. The first point-contact transistor, created by John Bardeen and Walter Brattain at Bell Labs in 1948, functioned like a crystal radio. The first major solid-state product was a 1954 Texas Instruments pocket radio with six germanium transistors.

Over the following decades, the radio became a mass commodity. There are now some 230 million radios in the United States alone, not even including more than 16 million cellular phones (which are, in fact, portable two-way radios). Radios roll off Asian assembly lines at a rate that might be meaningfully measured in hertz (cycles per second), and they come in sizes fit for pockets, belts, watches and cars. But the romance of radio has died and given way to the romance of computers.

Today it is PC technology that engages the youthful energies previously invested in radio technology. The press trumpets a coming convergence between computers and TVs and games and films. But no one talks much about radios. For many years, we have been taking radios for granted.

As the foundation of wireless communications, however, radio—no less than TV or films—will burst into a new technoscape as a result of a convergence with computers. The hackers of the '50s and '60s are joining forces with the hackers of the '80s and '90s to create a new industry. Moore's Law is about to overrun the world of radio.

You double anything every 18 months and, pretty soon, you find yourself with a monster. During the 1970s and 1980s, Moore's Law overturned the established order in the computer industry and spawned some 100 million personal computers that are as powerful as million-dollar mainframes were when the revolution began. In the current decade, Moore's Law is upending the telephone and television industries with interactive *teleputers* that will be able to send, receive, shape and store interactive full-motion video. And, during the next five years, Moore's Law is going to transform exotic and costly radio equipment once consigned to the military and outer space into the basic communications access routes for the new world economy.

To understand this new world of radio, however, you must forget much of what you learned about the old world of radio. For example, these new radios differ radically from the radios of the past in the way they use spectrum, the way they interfere with one another and the way they are built.

For some 15 years, a hacker of the 1950s named Don Steinbrecher and a small group of students and associates have been making the world's most powerful and acrobatic radios. Steinbrecher radio gear can soar to spectrum altitudes as high as 94 gigahertz to provide radar "eyes" for smart bombs and planes, plunge down to the cellular band at 800 megahertz to listen in on phone calls or drop discretely to 30 megahertz—waves that bounce off the ionosphere—for remote over-the-horizon radar work identifying cocaine traffickers flying in low from Latin America. At the same time, some of these radios may soon command enough dynamic ranges of accurate broadband reception—rumored to be as high as 120 decibels (one trillion-to-one)—to detect a pin drop in a heavy-metal rock concert without missing a high-fidelity note or twang.

Like every radio transceiver, a Steinbrecher radio must have four key components: an antenna, a tuner, a modem and a mixer. The antenna part is easy; for many purposes, your metal shirt hanger will do the trick. But, without tuners, modems and mixers, nothing reaches its final destination—the human ear.

A tuner selects a desired carrier frequency, usually by exploiting the science of resonant circuits. A modem is a modulator-demodulator. In transmitting, it applies information to the carrier frequency by wiggling the waves in a pattern, called a modulation scheme, such as AM or FM. In receiving, the modem strips out (de-modulates) the information from the carrier wave.

The key to Steinbrecher radios is the broadband mixer. It surmounts what was long seen as an impossible challenge: moving a large array of the relatively high carrier frequencies on the antenna down to a so-called baseband level where they can be used without losing any of the information or adding spurious information in the process. Compared to FM carrier frequencies of 100 megahertz or even PCS frequencies of two gigahertz, baseband audio frequencies run between 20 hertz and 20 kilohertz.

Mixers were the basic Steinbrecher product, and, in 1978 and 1980, Steinbrecher acquired patents on a unique broadband mixer with high range and sensitivity called the Paramixer®. Even to its expected military customers, the Paramixer® was a hard sell because other radio components were unable to keep pace with its performance. Today, however, the Paramixer® is the foundation of the Steinbrecher radio in the MiniCell.

In the old world of radio, *transceiver* integrated all of these components—antenna, tuner, modem and mixer—into one analog hardware system. Because the radio is analog and hard-wired, its functions must be standardized. Each radio can receive or transmit only a very limited set of frequencies bearing information coded in a specific modulation scheme and exclusively occupying a specific spectrum space at a particular power range. If you are in the radio business—whether as an equipment manufacturer such as Motorola or Ericsson, a provider of services, such as McCaw or Comsat, or a broadcaster such as NBC or Turner—you care deeply about these hard-wired specifications, frequencies and modulation schemes.

How Digital Radios Can End The Spectrum Wars

To the people at Steinbrecher Corp., all these wrangles seem utterly unnecessary. With antennas, tuners, modems and mixers, wide-band digital radios perform all the same functions as ordinary radios. Only the antenna and mixer are in hardware, and these are generic; they don't care anymore about air standards than your shirt hanger does.

In Steinbrecher radios, all of the frequency tuning, all of the modulating and demodulating, all of the channelization, all of the coding and decoding that so embroil the politicians are performed by programmable digital signal processors and can be changed at a base station in real time. Strictly speaking, the tuner and modem are not part of the base station radio at all. The broadband radio in a Steinbrecher base station can send or receive signals to or from any handset or mobile unit operating within its bandwidth (in current cellular systems the full 12.5 megahertz of the band, in PCS, still larger bands of as much as 30 megahertz).

All the processing of codes, frequencies, channels and modulations, as well as all special mobile services, can move onto computers attached to the network. Steinbrecher technology thus can open up the spectrum for open and programmable client/server systems like those that now dominate the computer industry. Moore's Law, in fact, is changing radios into portable digital computers. The most pervasive personal computer of the next decade will be a digital cellular phone operating at least 40MIPS (million instructions per second).

Today the performance of analog-to-digital converters defines the limits of Steinbrecher radios. Even if the mixers are perfect, the system's performance can be no better than the accuracy of the A/D processors that transform the output of the mixers into a digital bit stream for the DSPs. Steinbrecher estimates that better broadband A/D converters—which can sample wave forms more accurately at high frequencies—could increase the performance of Steinbrecher systems by an amazing factor of 10. Pushed by demands and designs from Steinbrecher, Analog Devices and other suppliers are advancing converter technology nearly at a pace with Moore's Law, and Steinbrecher's broadband digital radios are rapidly approaching the ideal.

As Don Steinbrecher puts it, broadband A/D and DSP have changed wireless—"from a radio business to a computer business." At first, the computer portion of a broadband radio was very expensive. Until the early 1980s, military customers performed advanced broadband analog-to-digital conversion and digital signal processing on million-dollar custom supercomputers. In 1986, an advanced DSP system for graphics at Bell Labs entailed the use of 82 AT&T DSP32 chips and supporting devices in a custom computer that cost some $130,000. Today, these same functions are performed on an Apple Quadra 840AV using an AT&T 3210 running at 33 megaflops (million floating point operations per second) and 17 MIPS for under $20 in volume. This rising tide of advances in digital technology, propelled by Moore's Law, is about to sweep Steinbrecher's recondite radio company into the midst of a mass market in cellular telephony.

And the entire cellular and PCS industries will be beating a path to Steinbrecher's door. Just as millions of people today have learned the meaning of *MIPS* and *megabytes*, millions of people around the world, believe it or not, are going to come to understand the meaning of "*spurious-free dynamic range.*"

As a very rough analogy, imagine cranking the volume of your radio as high as possible without marring the desired signal with static and distortion. The spurious-free dynamic range of your radio would measure the distance between the lowest and the highest volumes with a clear signal. In more technical terms, spurious-free dynamic range is defined as the range of signal amplitudes that can simultaneously be processed without distortion or be resolved by a receiver without the emergence of spurious signals above the noise floor.

In building broadband radios with high dynamic range, however, Steinbrecher faced a fundamental technical problem. As a general rule, bandwidth is inversely proportional to dynamic range. You can have one or the other, but you can't have both. The broader the band, the more difficult it is to capture all of its contents with full accuracy and sensitivity or with full spurious-free dynamic range. An ordinary radio may command a high dynamic range of volumes because it is narrowband.

But Steinbrecher radio does not begin by tuning to one frequency alone; it grasps every frequency in a particular swath of spectrum. In some extreme Paramixer® applications (94-gigahertz radar, for example), the bandwidth could be 1- gigahertz—larger than the entire range of spectrum commonly used in the air, from submarine communications at 60 hertz to C band satellite at 6 gigahertz.

In most Steinbrecher applications that require high dynamic range, however, the bandwidth runs between a few megahertz and hundreds of megahertz (compared to 30 kilohertz in a cellular phone). Unless all of the frequencies captured by the broadband radio are really present in the band rather than as artifacts of the equipment—in technical jargon, unless the signals are spurious-free—the radio user cannot tell what is going on, cannot distinguish between spurs and signals.

Steinbrecher has devoted much of his career to the grail of spurious-free dynamic range. Soon after he arrived at Massachusetts Institute of Technology in September, 1961, to pursue work on device physics, he moved into the school's new Radio Astronomy Lab. The radio astronomers were using millimeter waves at 75 gigahertz to probe remote galaxies and pore through evidence of a big bang at the beginning of time. Because the return reflections from outer space were infinitesimal, the radio telescopes had to command a bandwidth of at least two gigahertz, a spurious-free dynamic range of more than 100 decibels (tens of billions – or even trillions-to-one) and noise levels of less than 10 decibels (millionths of a watt).

The telescope signals turned out not to be spurious-free. More than 90 percent of the receiver noise—the spurious signals—originated in the frequency converter or mixer, which translated the 75-gigahertz millimeter waves in cascading analog stages of diodes and transistors, fed by tunable local oscillators, down to baseband levels that could be usefully analyzed. This impelled Steinbrecher's obsession with spurious-free dynamic range in mixers.

To achieve high dynamic range in broadband mixers, Steinbrecher discovered, was chiefly a problem of the basic physics of diodes. At the University of Florida, at ECI Corp and at MIT, Steinbrecher had pursued studies in device physics focusing on the theory of P/N junctions—the positive-negative interfaces that create the active regions in diodes and transistors. How cleanly and abruptly they switch from on to off—how fully these switches avoid transitional effects—determines how well they can translate one frequency to another without spurs.

From this experience, Steinbrecher concluded, in 1968, that receivers could be built with at least a thousand times more dynamic range than was currently believed possible. He assigned his student, Robert Snyder, to investigate the issue mathematically, integrating the possible performance of each component into the performance of a mixer. Snyder's results stunningly confirmed Steinbrecher's hypothesis. They predicted that, in principle—with unlimited time and effort—the linearity and dynamic range of a radio could be improved to any arbitrary standard. In a key invention, Steinbrecher figured out how to create a diode circuit that could produce a perfect square wave, creating a diode with essentially zero switching time.

Steinbrecher then proceeded to put his theory into practice by developing the crucial diode and field-effect transistor arrays, mixers, amplifiers and other components necessary to build a working system of unparalleled dynamic range. Most of their advances required detailed knowledge of the behavior of P/N junctions To this day, the performance of Steinbrecher's equipment depends on adjustment to unexpected nonlinearities and noise sources that were discovered as part of Robert Snyder's work but are still not integrated into the prevailing models of diode behavior.

Beyond radio astronomy, the people who were interested in analyzing signals of unknown frequencies, rather than tuning into preset frequencies, were in the field of military intelligence. Enemies did not normally announce in advance the frequencies they planned to use or how they would modulate them. Steinbrecher Corp.'s first major contract came in the early 1980s for remote over-the-horizon radar (ROTHR) systems used to detect planes carrying drugs from Latin America. Steinbrecher also won contracts to supply MILSTAR satellite transceivers and 94-gigahertz "eyes" for smart munitions and jet aircraft.

In 1986, these large potential businesses began to attract venture capitalists, including EG&G Venture Partners, The Venture Capital Fund of New England and Raytheon. As often happens, the venture capitalists sought professional management. They pushed Steinbrecher upstairs to chairman and summoned a Stanford EE graduate named Douglas Shute to manage the company's move from a manufacturer of hard-sell mixers into a producer of revolutionary digital radios.

Still, Steinbrecher Corp. long remained a tiny firm occupying a dingy one-story building in a Woburn, Mass. industrial park, where it rarely pulled in more than $5 million in revenues. Not until the early 1990s, when its technology converged with Moore's Law, did the company begin to escape its niche.

Collision With Texas Instruments' DSP (Digital Signal Processing)

Indeed, strictly speaking, even Moore's Law was not enough to make this Pentagon turkey fly. Crucial was Texas Instrument's mid-1980s campaign to remake the digital signal processor into a commodity device comparable to Intel's microprocessor. Creating development systems and software tools, TI transformed the DSP from an exotic and expensive printed circuit board full of integrated circuits into a single programmable microchip manufactured in volume on the same factory floor the company used to produce hundreds of millions of dynamic random access memories. The results exceeded all expectations. Outpacing Moore's Law by a factor of nearly four for some eight years so far, DSP cost-effectiveness began soaring tenfold every two years. Pricing the devices for digital radios, Douglas Shute saw that the wideband digital radio had—"moved onto the map as a commercial product."

Also, in 1989, a secret contractor asked the company if its radios could snoop on calls in the cellular band. After gigahertz explorations in radio astronomy and military projects, the 12.5 megahertz of the cellular bandwidth seemed a piece of cake. Although this national security application never came through, the idea galvanized the company. If it should need a commercial market, cellular telephony was a good bet.

The pull of opportunity, however, is usually less potent than the push of catastrophe—which is the key reason for socialism's failure. Insulating the economy from failure, it also removes a key spur for success. For all the bureaucratic rigmarole of military procurement, producers for the Pentagon live in a relatively comfortable socialist world of cost plus contracts.

In 1989, however, just before the fall of the Soviet Union, Steinbrecher began to get clear signals from Washington that the market for his products was about to collapse. MILSTAR remained an experimental program, the ROTHR system was halted after the creation of just four stations with 1,600 mixers; and, suddenly, the cellular opportunity was not merely an attractive option—it was crucial for survival.

When Shute and Steinbrecher viewed the cellular scene in the United States, however, they became increasingly disdainful. These radio companies had no more idea of what was possible in radio technology than had the MIT engineering lab when he arrived in 1961. Indeed, Steinbrecher Corp.'s first potential customer—a wireless colossus—refused even to meet with Shute: The chief technologist said he had investigated digital radios several years before and determined they were unable to achieve the requisite dynamic range. Moreover, at scores of thousands of dollars apiece, digital signal processors were far too expensive. Most cellular executives, along with their Washington regulators, seemed stuck in a 1970s time warp when analog still ruled and DSP was a supercomputer.

Importing Obsolescence

As a result, the entire industry was convulsed by what Shute and Steinbrecher saw as a retrograde war over standards. Because Europe, in general, lagged far behind the United States in adopting analog cellular technology, the EEC had sponsored a multinational drive to leapfrog the United States by adopting a digital standard, which could then be exported to America. The standard they chose was called GSM (Global Services Mobile), a time-division multiple-access (TDMA) scheme that exceeded analog capacity by breaking each channel into three digital time slots. Racing to catch up, the American industry adopted a similar TDMA approach that also increased the current system's capacity by a factor of three. With McCaw Cellular in the lead, American firms quickly committed themselves to deploy TDMA as soon as possible.

Then, in 1991, Qualcomm unleashed a bombshell. Exploiting the increasing power of DSPs to process digital codes, the company demonstrated a spread spectrum, code division multiple access (CDMA) modulation scheme that not only increased capacity some twentyfold over analog, but also allowed use of the entire 12.5 megahertz of the cellular bandwidth in every cell. To prevent interference between adjoining cells, analog and TDMA systems could use a frequency in only one cell out of seven.

Much of the industry seemed paralyzed by fear of choosing the wrong system. To Shute and Steinbrecher, however, these fears seemed entirely feckless. Using wideband digital radios, companies could accommodate any array of frequencies and modulations schemes they desired—TDMA, CDMA, voice, data and, eventually, even video. Shute resolved to adapt Steinbrecher's advanced radio technology to these new markets. In mid-1992, Shute rushed ahead with a program to create a prototype cellular transceiver that could process all 12.5 megahertz of the cellular bandwidth and convert it to a digital bit stream.

The first major customer for the radios turned out to be ADC-Kentrox, a designer of analog cell extenders designed to overcome "dead zones" caused by large buildings in urban areas. This system was limited in reach to the few hundred meters the signals could be sent over analog wires without deterioration. By converting the signals to digital at the remote site, the Steinbrecher radio extended this distance from hundreds of meters to scores of kilometers and allowed the price of the product to remain at $100,000.

But these gains concealed the potential impact and meaning of the Steinbrecher technology. Once again, the Steinbrecher radios were being used to complement the existing system rather than overthrowing it. In a similar way, McCaw planned to buy some $30 million worth of Steinbrecher machines to carry through its cellular digital packet data (CDPD™) network. To be provided to 95 percent of McCaw's regions by the end of 1995, CDPD™ is a data overlay of the existing cellular system, which allows users of the current analog system to send digital data at a rate of 19.2 kilobits per second, compared to the 9.6-kilobit-per-second rate offered by most modems over twisted pair wires.[73]

FM Radio

One method of imposing speech and music on a continuous wave requires increasing or reducing the amplitude (modulating) the distance between radio waves' peaks and troughs. This type of transmission is called amplitude modulation (AM). FM (Frequency Modulation), in contrast to AM, appears to have first been thought of by John Stone Stone (this is not a typo) in 1892. Many years after Armstrong's invention of the super hetero-dyne, he solved radio's last major problem, static, by inventing frequency modulation (FM), which he successfully tested in 1933. A significant characteristic of FM as compared with AM is that FM stations using the same frequency do not interfere with each other. Radios simply pick up whichever FM station is the strongest. This means that low power FM stations can operate in close proximity.

Armstrong was hindered in his development of FM radio by a Federal Communications Commission (FCC) spectrum reallocation that he blamed on RCA.

Astute patent dealings were a must in the early radio industry. As was true of the rest of the electric industry, patent litigation was very common in the radio industry. One reason for the success of Marconi in America was his astute patent dealings. One of the most acrimonious radio patent suits was one between Armstrong and RCA. Armstrong expected to receive royalties on every FM radio set sold and, because FM was selected for the audio portion of TV broadcasting he also expected royalties on every TV set sold. Some television manufacturers paid Armstrong. RCA didn't. RCA also developed and patented an FM system different from Armstrong's that he claimed involved no new principle. So, in 1948, he instituted a suit against RCA and NBC charging them with willfully infringing and inducing others to infringe on his FM patents.

It was to RCA's advantage to drag the suit out. It had more money than Armstrong did and it could make more money until the case was settled by selling sets utilizing technology Armstrong said was his. It might be able to do this until his patents ran out. To finance the case and his research facility at Columbia, Armstrong had to sell many of his assets, including stock in Zenith, RCA and Standard Oil. By 1954, the financial burden imposed on him forced him to try to settle with RCA. RCA's offer did not even cover Armstrong's remaining legal fees. Not long after he received this offer, he committed suicide.[74]

In 1940, the Connecticut State Police adopted a VHF FM two way system in the 39 MHz band, manufactured by Fred M. Link's *Link Radio Corporation*. The Link contract was the first large scale two way FM VHF system in the country and was so successful that it was held out as a model for other departments to emulate. It should be noted that many articles, and Link's own advertising at the time, give the impression that Link was first with an FM VHF two way radio, but this is not actually the case. GE had purchased a license to pursue FM development from Major Armstrong, inventor of FM, and had produced working VHF FM equipment since approximately 1938, although it was essentially experimental without meaningful sales. This equipment had been examined by Professor Daniel Noble, consultant to the state police, who rented some of it (probably for "reverse engineering!") However, he found it "unsatisfactory" for reasons not fully disclosed. The Fred Link system was built to Noble's specifications, by modifying existing VHF AM equipment (the 8-UA receiver and 15-

---

[73] Forbes, ASAP; 1994: *George Gilder's: Telecosm: "Auctioning The Airwaves"*.
[74] Ibid

UBX transmitter). Noble would shortly thereafter join Galvin Corporation and supervise the production of Galvin's own line of two-way FM radios, which not coincidentally, looked very much like original Link equipment, and was in direct competition with it. This first line of Galvin FM equipment was dubbed the Motorola "Deluxe" line, and Galvin at that time ceased design of any new "Police Cruiser" receivers or T-69 series AM transmitting equipment (although production of both continued throughout the remainder of the 1940's.) Fred Link encountered financial difficulties and sold Link Radio in 1950, undoubtedly due to the competitive pressure from much better funded Motorola.

GE had already been building FM mobile equipment since 1938, well prior to Link and Noble's experiments, on a somewhat experimental basis, in coordination with Maj. Edwin Armstrong. Armstrong is usually referred to as the "inventor" of FM although at least one patent was taken out prior to 1910 describing FM transmission. Armstrong's patents, perhaps more correctly described, covered the first actual practical application of FM. GE had applied to the FCC for an experimental license for FM operation on 49 MHz which was granted on August 3, 1938.[75]

GE ran comparison tests of AM vs. FM (at 15 kHz +/- deviation) on September 28-29, 1939, with Maj. Edwin Armstrong in attendance, for the FCC Emergency Service administration. One of the persons in attendance was Professor Daniel E. Noble of Connecticut State College.[76]

A GE VHF FM two-way system was already in use by late spring, 1940, for the Douglas County, Nebraska Sheriff, consisting of a 250 Watt base station and a number of 25 Watt mobiles (see Radio-Craft, Sept. 1940 p. 137). Link's "first" FM system would have been being installed at relatively the same time, and despite attempts to whitewash it, was essentially a copy of the GE design. The Link Connecticut State Police system was the first large system to make use of FM, but the claim that it was the first VHF FM system is open to interpretation. Link's first FM equipment consisted of a modified 8UA VHF AM receiver and 15UBX AM transmitter from 1938.[77]

GE was one of the few manufacturers to respect Armstrong's patents on FM, and took out licenses to use that system, as did Link. Motorola did not, and was involved in litigation with Armstrong and Armstrong's widow (who eventually prevailed) well into the 1960's.[78]

Daniel Noble, an unsung genius of RF and semiconductor technologies

Daniel E. Noble (IRE Associate, 1925; Senior Member; and Fellow, 1947), born on 4 October 1901, in Naugatuck, Connecticut, received his B.S. degree in engineering from Connecticut State College (now University of Connecticut) in 1929. He studied at Harvard University summer school and attended Massachusetts Institute of Technology as a graduate student.

Afterward he taught at Connecticut State College, where he rose to the rank of Assistant Professor. During these years he was the designer, builder, operator and manager of the college broadcast station. The success of his effort at the college led Hartford stations WTIC and WDRC to ask him to build relay stations for them. With WDRC, Noble eventually built one of the early commercial FM broadcast stations.

On the heels of this success, the Connecticut State Police came to him for engineering assistance. Dr. Noble originated the systems planning for the State Police radio system and personally supervised every phase of site selection, testing and design detail. Completed in 1940, this was the first two-way state police system to be placed in operation and the first practical two-way FM radio telephone mobile system in the world.

Career with Motorola

When the success of the Connecticut system became widely known, Noble's work came to the attention of Paul V. Galvin, owner of the Galvin Manufacturing Corporation (later changed to Motorola, Inc.) in Chicago.

---

[75] http://www.wb6nvh.com/GE/GEhist1.htm
[76] Ibid
[77] Ibid
[78] Ibid

Although Noble was unsure of his permanent interest in industrial work, he joined Motorola as Director of Research in 1940.

His first work at Motorola included development of FM communications equipment for police and the U.S. Signal Corps. He was directly responsible for the systems concept and the direction of the development of the U.S. Army's SCR-300 FM Walkie-Talkie®.

After the war, Noble began work in solid state electronics. In 1949 he set up a solid state electronics research laboratory for Motorola in Phoenix. This was the start of Motorola's semiconductor work and would eventually lead to the establishment of the Semiconductor Products Division (now the Semiconductor Group) for the company.

Noble was deeply interested in the application of transistors for FM mobile systems and wished to develop power transistors and radio frequency transistors. At his request, Dr. Bill Taylor succeeded in developing the power transistor. Dr. Noble immediately set out to develop it further with the conviction that this was a possible method to design transistors for operation in UHF bands and beyond.

Noble deserved much of the credit for Motorola becoming a power in mobile communications. During his career at the company he held a variety of positions, including Director of Research; General Manager of the Communications Division; Vice President and Director of Motorola, Inc.; Vice President and Director in charge of the Communications Division; Group Executive Vice President and Vice Chairman of the Board and Chief Technical Officer of the Corporation. He went into semi-retirement in 1970.

Service and Personal Life

Dr. Noble authored many papers in his career and held nine patents on electronics. He was also a talented and thoughtful artist. As a painter his works were reproduced on book and magazine covers.

Noble served on many technical committees including the Chairmanship of Panel 13 (Mobile and Portable Radio Telephone Communications) of the Radio Technical Planning Board and as a member of the National Television Color Systems Committee, which established the transmission standards for color TV. He also served on the Boards of both IRE and IEEE. He was a member of the National Academy of Engineering and a Life Fellow of the IEEE and the Franklin Institute. He received the WEMA Medal of Achievement, the Franklin Institute's Stuart Ballantine Medal and the University of Connecticut Engineering Alumni Plaque. He was the 1978 IEEE Edison Medal Recipient "For leadership and innovation in meeting important public needs, especially in developing mobile communications and solid-state electronics."[79]

It is more than fair to credit Dr. Noble with advanced understanding of modulation techniques furthering the rise of mobile (wireless) communications.

Speaking of modulation

AM, FM, FSK, QPMSK – these four led the way. However, in the greater scheme of things, namely cellular and PCS, the two primary competitors are TDMA (Time Division Multiple Access [Global System for Mobile Communications]) and CDMA (Code Division Multiple Access). Let's look a little deeper; it's important if you are considering a career in telecommunications.

[80]Understanding Quadrature Phase Shift Keying (QPSK) Modulation

August 17, 2016 by Robert Keim

This technical brief covers the basic characteristics of a digital modulation scheme known as quadrature phase shift keying.

In the world of wired electronics, analog signals exhibit continuous variations whereas digital signals assume (ideally) one of two discrete states. This distinction can be extended to systems that transmit data *via* electromagnetic radiation instead of electric current traveling through wires.

---

[79] https://ethw.org/Daniel_Noble
[80] https://www.allaboutcircuits.com/technical-articles/quadrature-phase-shift-keying-qpsk-modulation/

When used for analog signals, frequency modulation and amplitude modulation lead to continuous variations in the frequency or amplitude of a carrier wave. When modulation techniques are used for digital communication, the variations applied to the carrier are restricted according to the discrete information being transmitted.

Examples of common digital modulation types are OOK (on/off keying), ASK (amplitude shift keying), and FSK (frequency shift keying). These schemes cause the carrier to assume one of two possible states depending on whether the system must transmit a binary 1 or a binary 0; each discrete carrier state is referred to as a symbol.

Quadrature phase shift keying (QPSK) is another modulation technique, and it's a particularly interesting one because it actually transmits two bits per symbol. In other words, a QPSK symbol doesn't represent 0 or 1—it represents 00, 01, 10, or 11.

This two-bits-per-symbol performance is possible because the carrier variations are not limited to two states. In ASK, for example, the carrier amplitude is either amplitude option A (representing a 1) or amplitude option B (representing a 0). In QPSK, the carrier varies in terms of phase, not frequency, and there are *four* possible phase shifts. We can intuitively determine what these four possible phase shifts should be: First we recall that modulation is only the beginning of the communication process; the receiver needs to be able to extract the original information from the modulated signal. Next, it makes sense to seek maximum separation between the four phase options, so that the receiver has less difficulty distinguishing one state from another. We have 360° of phase to work with and four phase states, and thus the separation should be 360°/4 = 90°. So our four QPSK phase shifts are 45°, 135°, 225°, and 315°.

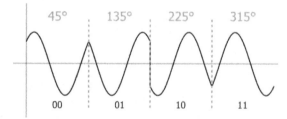

(Note: The phase-shift-to-digital-data correspondence shown is a logical though arbitrary choice; as long as the transmitter and receiver agree to interpret phase shifts in the same way, different correspondence schemes can be used.)

There's another reason why it makes sense to choose 45°, 135°, 225°, and 315°: they are easily generated using I/Q modulation techniques because summing I and Q signals that are either inverted or non-inverted results in these four phase shifts. The following table should clarify this:

Compared to modulation schemes that transmit one bit per symbol, QPSK is advantageous in terms of bandwidth efficiency. For example, imagine an analog baseband signal in a BPSK (binary phase shift keying) system. BPSK uses two possible phase shifts instead of four, and thus it can transmit only one bit per symbol. The baseband signal has a certain frequency, and during each symbol period, one bit can be transmitted. A QPSK system can use a baseband signal of the same frequency, yet it transmits *two* bits during each symbol period. Thus, its bandwidth efficiency is (ideally) higher by a factor of two.[81]

Traditionally, analog radio modulation methods such as AM and FM limited the amount of information conveyed within a given channel, and each channel could only host a single conversation at any one time—a pair of users, one transmitting and one receiving.

Analog modulation (AM) places a finite limit on the number of users that can occupy the radio spectrum, and does not cater well to today's expanding needs.

Digital radio, using various modulation schemes, is moving to alleviate this problem by increasing the amount of information that can be conveyed on a channel.

Digital radio has developed ways in which more than one conversation can be accommodated (multiplexed) inside the same physical RF channel. There are three common ways of achieving this:

---

[81] Ibid

1. Frequency Division Multiple Access (FDMA)
2. Time Division Multiple Access (TDMA)
3. Code Divisional Multiple Access (CDMA)

FREQUENCY DIVISION MULTIPLE ACCESS (FDMA)

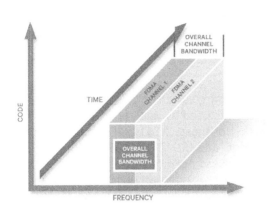

The RF (radio frequency) channel is split into several smaller sub-channels. For example, one 12.5kHz wide narrowband FM channel that previously carried only one conversation becomes two 6.25kHz sub-channels, each capable of carrying a separate conversation.

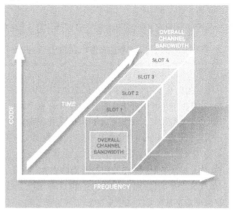

This technique has been around for decades and is used with either analog or digital radios. A 'telephone style conversation' can be set up if one sub-channel is used to transmit and one to receive.

The drawback of this is the more sub-channels you try to fit into the original channel, the more likely the users will suffer interference on the call. This is because the reduced channel spacing makes it harder to filter only the intended sub-channel and reject all the others at the receiver.

Consequently, dividing a single narrowband 12.5kHz channel frequency into more than two sub-channels becomes impractical.

2. TIME DIVISION MULTIPLE ACCESS (TDMA)

Instead of splitting the original RF channel into two RF sub-channels, it is instead split into timeslots. The transmitted RF frequency is identical in each slot, but each slot is still capable of carrying a separate conversation.

I	Q	phase shift of I+Q
noninverted	noninverted	45°
inverted	noninverted	135°
inverted	inverted	225°
noninverted	inverted	315°

In the diagram, the channel is split into four time slots, so in each slot, the speech is transmitted in a quarter of the time taken to say it.

This speech compression is possible using digital technology, but eventually practical near/far* (see below) limits are encountered that limits how many slots can be accommodated in a single RF channel before neighboring slots begin to overlap at the base station.

Again, a 'telephone-style conversation' can be set up, if certain slots are used for transmit and others for receive.[82]

3. CODE DIVISIONAL MULTIPLE ACCESS (CDMA)

Instead of splitting the RF channel into sub-channels or time slots, each slot has a unique code. Unlike FDMA, the transmitted RF frequency is the same in each slot, and unlike TDMA, the slots are transmitted simultaneously. In the diagram, the channel is split into four code slots.

---

[82] https://www.google.com/search?ei=Ft8mXMncHZajjwS27JP4Bg&q=gsm+vs+cdma+vs+lte&oq=GSM+vs+CDMA&gs_l=psy-ab.1.1.0l10.5373.9689..13683...1.0..0.73.757.12......0....1..gws-wiz.......0i71j0i67j0i131.gyQ1-DWci3Q

Each slot is still capable of carrying a separate conversation because the receiver only reconstructs information sent from a transmitter with the same code.[83]

However this does create a problem, as transmissions on the same frequency with different codes are still received and decoded but simply re-appear as noise. This means the greater the number of users, the higher the noise level on the system, which of course can affect coverage.

Near/far issues also require dynamic power control in CDMA systems to make sure all signals arrive at the base station at roughly the same level to ensure that signals from distant transmitters are not lost.

The near-far problem occurs when a transmitter sends a strong signal to a receiver which then makes it difficult for any weaker signals to be received.[84]

The top 4 wireless providers have all standardized on 4G LTE as their wireless communication standard, which has been deployed across the entire coverage; however, the LTE bands used by each provider remain largely incompatible. All 4 wireless providers also maintain legacy networks; of these, AT&T and T-Mobile use GSM and 3G UMTS (mostly converted to 4G HSPA+), while Verizon, Sprint, and U.S. Cellular use cdmaOne/EV-DO/1xRTT. While the top 4 wireless providers operate nationwide wireless networks which cover most of the population in the United States, U.S. Cellular and other smaller carriers provide native network coverage across selected regions of the United States while supplementing nationwide coverage through roaming agreements with other carriers.

As of 2016 all operators have adopted LTE, which includes provisioning of service through SIM cards. Verizon, AT&T, T-Mobile, and Sprint sell SIM cards through their retail channels in-store and online; however, the selection of devices compatible with Verizon and Sprint networks is limited. All carriers except Sprint have enabled VoLTE on their networks.

Each active SIM card is considered a subscriber. Wholesale customers include Machine to Machine and Mobile Virtual Network Operator customers that operate on the host network, but are managed by wholesale (Private Label partners, *e.g.*, Virgin Mobile, *etc.*). Verizon Wireless does not report wholesale subscriber count.

AT&T shut its GSM network down on December 31, 2016.

T-Mobile plans to reduce spectrum allocated for GSM and use the network mostly for nomadic and non-mobile GSM services through 2020. T-Mobile hopes to shut down its 3G network: "long before 2020." As of September 2016, 60% of calls were on VoLTE.

Verizon introduced the first LTE-only phone, LG Exalt LTE, in June 2017. Verizon plans to shut down CDMA 1xRTT network by the end of 2019. CDMA EV-DO was scheduled to operate until 2021 according to the plan announced in 2012. As of May 2017, half of voice traffic is on VoLTE.

The impact of CDMA introduced by Qualcomm has had on the cellular industry cannot be overstated.

The following is a detailed account describing the extraordinary contributions made by the Qualcomm brain trust.

The author, Daniel Nenni, has worked in Silicon Valley for the past 35 years with semiconductor manufacturers, electronic design automation software, and semiconductor intellectual property companies. He is the founder of SemiWiki.com™, the open forum for semiconductor professionals, a growing online community of people involved with the semiconductor design and manufacturing ecosystem. Since going online January 1st, 2011, more than 3,000,000 users have been recorded at www.SemiWiki.com. Daniel is an internationally recognized business development professional for companies involved with the fabless semiconductor ecosystem in regards to sales, marketing, funding, mergers, and acquisitions.

Mr. Nenni's research and extraordinary insight into the value of Qualcomm's contributions to the wireless telecommunications business will inform, enlighten and inspire you.

---

[83] Ibid
[84] https://blog.taitradio.com/2012/10/09/channel-sharing-explained-fdma-tdma-and-cdma/
To learn more about the basics of channel sharing, including channel spacing and a focus on FDMA vs TDMA, visit Tait Radio Academy for a series of short, free videos. Don't forget to register for the Academy to stay up-to-date on our latest videos and courses.

From the publication: **Mobile Unleashed: The Origin and Evolution of ARM Processors in our Devices**©
By Don Dingee and Daniel Nenni
<u>**Daniel Nenni**</u>
Published: 03-19-2018

On January 31, 1958, JPL's Project Deal – known to the outside world as Explorer I – achieved orbit. Life magazine featured a photo of Golomb and Viterbi in the JPL control room during the flight. On July 29, 1958, President Eisenhower signed the National Aeronautics and Space Act, creating NASA. JPL requested and received a move into the NASA organization in December, 1958.

Viterbi enrolled at the University Of Southern California (USC) to pursue his Ph. D., the only school that would allow him to continue working full time at JPL. He finished in 1962 and went to teach at the University of California, Los Angeles (UCLA). He recommended Golomb join the USC faculty in 1963. That started an influx of digital communications talent to USC that included Reed (who had moved to the Rand Corporation in Santa Monica in 1960), Lindsey (who joined JPL in 1962), Eberhardt Rechtin, Lloyd Welch, and others.

Lindsey would quip years later, "I think God made this group." Rechtin would say that together, this group achieved more in digital communications than any of them could have done alone. They influenced countless others.

Linked to San Diego

At the 1963 National Electronics Conference in Chicago, best paper awards went to Viterbi and Irwin Jacobs, a professor at MIT whose office was a few doors down from that of Claude Shannon. Jacobs and Viterbi had crossed paths briefly in 1959 while Jacobs visited JPL for an interview, and they knew of each other's work from ties between JPL and MIT.

Reacquainted at the 1963 conference, Jacobs suggested to Viterbi that he had a sabbatical coming up, and asked if JPL was a good place to work. Viterbi said that indeed it was. Jacobs' application was rejected, but Viterbi interceded with division chief Rechtin, and Jacobs was finally hired as a research fellow and headed for Pasadena. Viterbi was teaching at UCLA and consulting at JPL, and the two became friends in the 1964-65 academic year Jacobs spent working there.

After publishing the landmark text, "Principles of Communication Engineering," with John Wozencraft in 1965, Jacobs migrated to the West in 1966. He was lured by one of his professors at Cornell, Henry Booker, to join the faculty in a new engineering department at the University of California, San Diego (UCSD). Professors were valuable, and digital communication consultants were also in high demand. One day in early 1967, Jacobs took a trip to NASA's Ames Research Center for a conference. He found himself on a plane ride home with Viterbi and another MIT alumnus, Len Kleinrock, who had joined the UCLA faculty in 1963 and became friends with Viterbi. The three started chatting, with Jacobs casually mentioning he had more consulting work than he could handle himself.

Viterbi was finishing his masterpiece. He sought a simplification to the theory of decoding faint digital signals from strong noise, one that his UCLA students could grasp more easily than the complex curriculum in place. Arriving at a concept in March 1966, he refined the idea for a year before publication. In April 1967, Viterbi described his approach in an article in the IEEE Transactions on Information Theory under the title: "Error bounds for convolutional codes and an asymptotically optimum decoding algorithm."

The Viterbi Algorithm leverages "soft" decisions. A hard decision on a binary 0 or 1 can be made by observing each noisy received bit (or group of bits encoded into a symbol), with significant chance of error. Viterbi considered probabilistic information contained in possible state transitions known from how symbols are encoded at the transmitter. Analyzing a sequence of received symbols and state transitions with an add-compare-select (ACS) operation identifies a path of maximum likelihood, more accurately matching the transmitted sequence.

It was just theory, or so Viterbi thought at first. The algorithm reduced computations and error compared to alternatives, but was still intense to execute in real-time, and thought to require "several thousand registers" to produce low error rates. Several other researchers picked up the work, notably Jim Massey, David Forney, and Jim Omura. They were convinced it was optimum. Jerry Heller, one of Jacobs' doctoral students at MIT who had come with him to San Diego, was working at JPL. He decided to run some simulations during 1968 and 1969 and found Viterbi had been too pessimistic; 64 registers yielded a significant coding gain. That was still a rather large rack of computing equipment at the time.

The entrepreneurial thought Jacobs planted for a consulting firm had stuck. With an investment of $1500 (each man contributing $500) Linkabit was born in October, 1968, with an address of Kleinrock's home in Brentwood. Soon, offices moved to a building in Westwood near UCLA. At first, it was a day-a-week effort for Jacobs, Kleinrock, and Viterbi, who all kept their day jobs as professors.

There was even more business than anticipated. Linkabit's first new hire engineer in September, 1969, was Jerry Heller, soon followed by engineers Andrew Cohen, Klein Gilhousen, and Jim Dunn. Len Kleinrock stepped aside for a few months to pursue his dream project, installing the first endpoints of the ARPANET and sending its first message in October, 1969. According to him, when he tried returning to Linkabit, he was promptly dismissed, receiving a percentage of the firm as severance. With Kleinrock out and Viterbi not ready to relocate for several more years, Jacobs moved the Linkabit office to Sorrento Valley – the tip of San Diego's "Golden Triangle" – in 1970. His next hire was office manager, Dee Coffman (née Turpie), fresh out of high school.

Programming the Modem: "Coding is dead." That was the punchline for several speakers at the IEEE Communication Theory Workshop in 1970 in St. Petersburg, Florida. Irwin Jacobs stood up in the back of the room holding a 14-pin dual-in-line package – a simple 4-bit shift register, probably a 7495 in TTL families. "This is where it's at. This new digital technology out there is going to let us build all this stuff."

Early on, Linkabit was a research think tank, not a hardware company. Its first customers were NASA Ames Research Center and JPL, along with the Naval Electronics Laboratory in Point Loma, and DARPA. Linkabit studies around Viterbi decoding eventually formed the basis of deep space communications links used in JPL's Voyager and other programs. However, compact hardware implementations of Viterbi decoders and other signal processing would soon make Linkabit and its successor firm legendary.

Heller and Jacobs disclosed a 2 Mbps, 64 state, constraint length 7, rate ½ Viterbi decoder in October, 1971. It was based on a commercial unit built for the US Army Satellite Communications Agency. The Linkabit Model 7026, or LV7026, used about 360 TTL chips on 12 boards in a 19 inch rackmount, 4.5U (7.9") high, 22" deep enclosure. Compared to refrigerator-sized racks of equipment previously needed for the Viterbi Algorithm, it was a break-through.

Speed was also a concern. Viterbi tells of an early Linkabit attempt to integrate one ACS state of the decoder on a chip of only 100 gates – medium scale integration, or MSI. In his words, the effort: "almost bankrupted the company" through a string of several supplier failures. Almost bankrupt? It sounds like an exaggeration until considering the available alternatives to TTL. From hints in a 1971 Linkabit report and a 1974 Magnavox document, Linkabit was playing with fast but finicky emitter-coupled logic (ECL) in attempts to increase clock speeds in critical areas. Many companies failed trying things with ECL. Viterbi omitted names to protect the guilty, but the ECL fab suspects would be Fairchild, IBM, Motorola, and Signetics.

A different direction led to more success. Klein Gilhousen started tinkering with a concept for a Linkabit Microprocessor (LMP), a microcoded architecture for all the functions of a satellite modem. Gilhousen, Sheffie Worboys, and Franklin Antonio completed a breadboard of the LMP using mostly TTL chips with some higher performance MSI and LSI commercial parts in May, 1974. It ran at 3 MIPS. There were 32 instructions and four software stacks, three for processing and one for control. It was part RISC (before there was such a thing), part DSP.

Jacobs began writing code and socializing the LMP, giving lectures at MITLL and several other facilities about the ideas behind digital signal processing for a satellite modem. The US Air Force invited Linkabit to demonstrate their technology for the experimental LES-8/9 satellites. TRW had a multi-year head start on the spread spectrum modem within the AN/ASC-22 K-Band SATCOM system, but their solution was expensive and huge.

Linkabit stunned the MITLL team by setting up their relatively small system of several 19" rackmount boxes and acquiring full uplink in about an hour, a task the lab staff was sure would take several days just to get a basic mode running. In about three more hours, they found an error in the MITLL design specifications, fixed the error through reprogramming, and had the downlink working. Despite TRW's certification and production readiness, the USAF general in charge of the program funded Linkabit – a company that had never built production hardware in volumes for a defense program – to complete its modem development.

Besides the fact that the LMP worked so well, the reason for the intense USAF interest became clear in 1978. The real requirement was for a dual modem on airborne command platforms such as the Boeing EC- 135 and

Strategic Air Command aircraft including the Boeing B-52. The solution evolved into the Command Post Modem/Processor (CPM/P), using several LMPs to implement dual full-duplex modems and red/black messaging and control, ultimately reduced to three rugged ½ ATR boxes.

Linkabit was growing at 60% a year. Needing further capital to expand, they considered going public before being approached by another firm with expertise in RF technology, M/A-COM. In August 1980, the acquisition was completed. It radically altered the Linkabit culture from a freewheeling exchange of thoughts across the organization to a control-oriented, hierarchical structure. It didn't stop innovation. Several significant commercial products debuted. One was Very Small Aperture Terminal (VSAT), a small satellite communications system using a 4 to 8 foot dish for businesses. Its major adopters included 7-11, Holiday Inn, Schlumberger, and Wal-Mart. Another was VideoCipher, the satellite TV encryption system that went to work at HBO and other broadcasters. Jerry Heller oversaw VideoCipher through its life as the technology grew.

Jacobs and Viterbi had negotiated the acquisition with M/A-COM CEO, Larry Gould. As Jacobs put it, "We got along very well, but [Gould] went through a mid-life crisis." Gould wanted to make management changes, or merge with other firms – none of it making a lot of sense. The M/A-COM board of directors instead replaced Gould (officially, "retired") as CEO in 1982. Jacobs was an M/A-COM board member but was travelling in Europe and was unable to have the input he wanted in the decision or the new organizational structure. He subsequently tried to split the firm and take the Linkabit pieces back, going as far as vetting the deal with investment bankers. At the last moment, the M/A-COM board got cold feet and reneged on allowing Linkabit to separate. After finishing the three chips for the consumer version of the VideoCipher II descrambler, Jacobs abruptly "retired" on April 1, 1985. Within a week, Viterbi left M/A-COM as well and others quickly followed suit.

Let's Do It Again"

Retirement is far from all it's cracked up to be. For someone who hadn't wanted to run Linkabit day-to-day, Irwin Jacobs had done a solid job running it. Shortly after his M/A-COM departure, one of his associates asked, "Hey, why don't we try doing this again?" Jacobs took his family, who he had promised to spend more time with, on a car tour of Europe to think about it.

On July 1, 1985, six people reconvened in Jacobs' den – all freshly ex- Linkabit. Besides Jacobs, there was Franklin Antonio, Dee Coffman, Andrew Cohen, Klein Gilhousen, and Harvey White. Tribal legend says there were seven present; Andrew Viterbi was there in spirit, though actually on a cruise in Europe until mid-July, having agreed on a direction with Jacobs before departing. This core team picked the name Qualcomm, shorthand for quality communications, for a new company. They would combine elements of digital communications theory with practical design knowledge into refining code division multiple access, or CDMA.

In his channel capacity theorem, Shannon illustrated spread spectrum techniques could reliably transmit more digital data in a wider bandwidth with lower signal-to-noise ratios. CDMA uses a pseudorandom digital code to spread a given data transmission across the allocated bandwidth.

Different code assignments allow creation of multiple CDMA data channels sharing the same overall bandwidth. To any single channel, its neighbors operating on a different code look like they are speaking another language and do not interfere with the conversation. To outsiders without the codes, the whole thing is difficult to interpret and looks like background noise. This makes CDMA far more secure from eavesdropping or jamming compared to the primitive ideas of frequency hopping postulated by Nikola Tesla and later patented in 1942 by actress and inventor, Hedy Lamarr, and her composer friend George Antheil.

Unlike a TDMA system using fixed channels determining exactly how many simultaneous conversations a base station can carry in an allocated bandwidth, CDMA opens up capacity substantially. With sophisticated encoding and decoding techniques – enter Reed-Solomon codes and Viterbi decoding – a CDMA system can handle many more users up to an acceptable limit of bit error probability and cross-channel interference. In fact, CDMA reuses capacity during pauses in conversations, an ideal characteristic for mobile voice traffic.

Coding techniques also gave rise to a solution for multipath in spread spectrum applications. The RAKE receiver, developed by Bob Price and Paul Green of MITLL originally for radar applications,

used multiple correlators like fingers in a rake that could synchronize to different versions of a signal and statistically combine the results. RAKE receivers made CDMA practically impervious to noise between channels. [emphasis author's]

USAF SATCOM planners were the first to fall in love with CDMA for all its advantages, but it required intense digital computing resources to keep up with data in real-time. Jacobs and Viterbi realized they had some very valuable technology, proven with the digital signal processing capability of the LMP and the dual modem that had handled CDMA for satellite communications reliably. Could Qualcomm serve commercial needs?

Two things were obvious right from the beginning: cost becomes a much bigger issue in commercial products, and regulators like the FCC enter the picture for non-defense communication networks. So Qualcomm found itself picking up right where they left off at Linkabit – working government communication projects, trying to make solutions smaller and faster.

Those government projects spawned a single-chip Viterbi decoder. Finally, CMOS ASIC technology had caught up, ending the need for hundreds of TTL chips and exotic measures like ECL. Qualcomm had its first chip design ready in September, 1987: the Q1401, a 17 Mbps, 80 state, K=7, rate ½ decoder. It was fabbed by LSI Logic in 1.5 micron, estimated to be a 169mm 2 die in a 155 pin ceramic PGA. It was available in both commercial and military grades, slightly downgraded in speed at the wider military temperatures.

Space Truckin'

Just before Qualcomm opened for business, Viterbi received an interesting phone call. It was Allen Salmasi – who left JPL to start OmniNet™ in 1984 – asking if his firm could work with Qualcomm on a new location system for trucks.

The FCC allocated frequencies for RDSS (radio determination satellite service) in 1984. OmniNet held one RDSS license, competitor Geostar™ the other. Geostar's concept had position reporting and messaging from a truck to an L-band satellite, relayed to the trucking company. If OmniNet could deliver RDSS with a link from the trucking company back to the truck, it could be a huge opportunity.

Qualcomm wasn't too sure. Salmasi gave them $10,000 to study the situation – he had no customers, no venture capital (nobody believed it would work, not even Geostar who refused a partnership offer), and only "family and friends" money. OmniNet had to commercialize to survive, and Qualcomm was the best hope.

L-band satellites were scarce and expensive, partly because they used a processing payload that had to be mission customized. Ku-band satellites used for VSATs and other applications were ample, less expensive, allowed for ground signal processing, and could provide both uplink and downlink capability, but there was a catch. The FCC had licensed Ku-band for fixed terminals, with large ground parabolic dish antennae that had to be pointed within a degree or two. Secondary use permitted mobile if, and only if, it did not interfere with primary uses. A smaller ground dish antenna, especially one on a moving truck, would have both pointing and aperture issues almost certain to cause interference. Then Klein Gilhousen said, "We're using CDMA."

In theory CDMA and spread spectrum would solve any interference issues on the transmit side, and if antennae pointing were accurate enough, the receive side would work. Now the FCC were the ones not so sure. Qualcomm convinced the FCC to grant an experimental license, one that would cover 600 trucks. Jacobs and his teams created a unique directional antenna system that was compact at 10" in diameter and 6" tall, but highly accurate. A Communication Unit measuring 4"x8"x9" did the processing, and a Display Unit had a 40 character by four line read-out with a small keyboard and indicators for the driver. By January 1988, the system began limited operational testing on a cross-country drive.

Still without a customer, Salmasi was out of capital – so Qualcomm bought him, his company, and the entire system, launching it as OmniTRACS™ in August, 1988. With zero reports of interference, the FCC granted broader operating authority for the system. By October, Qualcomm had their first major customer in Schneider with about 10,000 trucks. OmniTRACS was on its way, with some 1.5 million trucks using the system today. This first important win provided income for Qualcomm to contemplate the next big market for CDMA.

Just Keep Talking

Gilhousen bent both Jacobs' and Viterbi's ears with the suggestion that Qualcomm go into cellular phones with CDMA. Viterbi found the idea familiar, having presented it in a 1982 paper on spread spectrum. Moving from defense satellite networks for several hundred B-52s and EC-135s to private satellite networks with 10,000 trucks and more had been straightforward, but a public cellular network presented a well-known problem.

While CDMA signals reduced interference between digital channels, there were still RF characteristics to consider with many transmitters talking to one terrestrial base station simultaneously. For satellite communication systems, every terminal on the earth is relatively far away and should have roughly the same signal strength under normal operating conditions.

In a cellular grid with low power handsets, distance matters and the near-far problem becomes significant. **Near-far relates to the dynamic range of a base station receiver. If all handsets transmit at the same power, the closest one captures the receiver and swamps handsets transmitting farther away from the cell tower making them inaudible in the noise.** [emphasis author's]

Viterbi, Jacobs, Gilhousen, and Butch Weaver set off to figure out the details. While they ran CDMA simulations, the Telecommunications Industry Association (TIA) met in January 1989 and chose TDMA in DAMPS as the 2G standard for the US. D-AMPS was evolutionary to AMPS, and some say there was a nationalistic agenda to adopt an alternative to the European-dominated GSM despite its head start. FDMA was seen as a lower-risk approach (favored by Motorola, AT&T, and others), but TDMA had already shown its technical superiority in GSM evaluations.

Few in the industry took CDMA seriously. The Cellular Telecommunication Industry Association (CTIA) pushed for user performance recommendations in a 2G standard with at least 10 times the capacity of AMPS, but also wanted a smooth transition path. DAMPS did not meet the UPR capacity goals, but was regarded as the fastest path to 2G.

Capacity concerns gave Qualcomm its opening. Jacobs reached out to the CTIA to present the CDMA findings and, after an initial rebuff, got an audience at a membership meeting in Chicago in June 1989. He waited for the assembled experts to shoot his presentation full of holes. It didn't happen.

One reason their presentation went so well was that they had been test driving it with PacTel Cellular since February 1989. After the TIA vote, Jacobs and Viterbi started asking for meetings with regional carriers. "All of a sudden, one day, Irwin Jacobs and Andy Viterbi showed up in my office. Honestly, I don't even know how they got there," said PacTel Cellular CEO Jeff Hultman.

However, William C. Y. Lee, PacTel Cellular chief scientist, knew why they had come. PacTel Cellular was experiencing rapid subscriber growth in its Los Angeles market, and was about to experience a capacity shortfall. Lee had been studying digital spread spectrum efficiency and capacity issues for years, comparing FDMA and TDMA.

What he saw with CDMA – with perhaps 20 times improvement over analog systems – and the risks in developing TDMA, were enough to justify a $1M bet on research funding for Qualcomm. Lee, like many others, needed to see a working solution for the near-far problem and other issues.

Just under six months later on November 7, 1989, Qualcomm had a prototype system. A CDMA "phone" – actually 30 pounds of equipment – was stuffed in the back of a van ready to drive around San Diego. There were two "base stations" set up so call handoff could be demonstrated.

Before a gathering of cellular industry executives, at least 150, and by some reports as many as 300, William C. Y. Lee made a presentation, Jacobs made his presentation, and Gilhousen described what visitors were about to see. Just before dismissing the group for the demonstration, Jacobs noticed Butch Weaver waving frantically. A GPS glitch took out base station synchronization. Jacobs improvised, and kept talking about CDMA for some 45 minutes until Weaver and the team got the system working.

Many attendees at the demonstration were thrilled at what they had seen. The critics said CDMA would never work, that the theory would not hold up under full-scale deployment and real-world conditions, and it "violated the laws of physics" according to one pundit. Additionally, there was the small problem of getting it to fit in a handset – a problem Qualcomm was prepared to deal with. Beyond a need for miniaturization and the basics of direct sequence spread spectrum and channelization, Qualcomm was developing solutions to three major CDMA issues.

First was the near-far problem. Dynamic power control changes power levels to maintain adequate signal-to-noise. CDMA handsets closer to base stations typically use less transmit power, and ones farther away use more. The result is all signals arrive at the base station at about the same signal-to-noise ratio. Lower transmit power also lowered interference and saved handset battery power. Qualcomm used aggressive open loop and closed loop power control making adjustments at 800 times per second (later increased to 1500), compared to just a handful of times per second in GSM.

Second was soft handoffs. In a TDMA system, dropped calls often happened when users transitioned from one base station to another due to a hard handoff. CDMA cells establish a connection at the next base station while still connected to the current one.

Third was a variable rate vocoder. Instead of on-off encoding used in GSM, a variable rate encoder adapts rapidly as speech naturally pauses and resumes, reducing the number of bits transmitted by handsets and effectively increasing overall capacity at the base station. This feature was not present in TDMA, since channels are fixed and un-sharable.

Get In and Hang On

If CDMA could be productized, Hultman had promised PacTel Cellular's support but other deals would be needed to reach critical mass. PacTel helped introduce Qualcomm to higher-level executives at the other Baby Bells and the major cellular infrastructure vendors, looking for markets where CDMA would be welcome. Qualcomm leadership also made a fateful decision on their business model: instead of building all the equipment themselves, they would license their CDMA intellectual property to manufacturers.

Another cellular market with looming capacity headaches was New York, home to NYNEX. Qualcomm carted its CDMA prototypes to Manhattan for field trials during February 1990. NYNEX already had AT&T looking at next-generation infrastructure specifics, and by early July, AT&T and Qualcomm had a license agreement for CDMA base station technology. On July 31, 1990, Qualcomm published the first version of the CDMA specifications for industry comments – the Common Air Interface. On August 2, NYNEX announced it would spend $100M to build "a second cellular telephone network" in Manhattan by the end of 1991, mostly to provide time for frequency allocation and base station construction. $3M would go to Qualcomm to produce CDMA phones.

Others held back. The two largest cellular infrastructure vendors, Ericsson and Motorola, had plans for TDMA networks. Motorola hedged its bet in a September, 1990, CDMA infrastructure cross licensing agreement with Qualcomm, but publicly expressed technical concerns. Carriers like McCaw Cellular (the forerunner of AT&T Wireless) and Ameritech were trying to postpone any major commitments to CDMA. Internationally, Europe was all in on GSM based on TDMA, and Japan was developing its own TDMA-based cellular network.

In the uncommitted column was Korea, without a digital solution. Salmasi leveraged introductions from PacTel's Lee in August, 1990, into rounds of discussion culminating in the May, 1991, ETRI CDMA joint development agreement. Although a major funding commitment with a lucrative future royalty stream, the program would take five years to unfold.

Even with these wins, Qualcomm was hanging on the financial edge. Every dollar of income was plowed back into more employees – numbering about 600 at the close of 1991 – and CDMA R&D.

PacTel continued with its CDMA plans, leading to the CAP I capacity trial in November 1991 – using commercial-ready Qualcomm CDMA chipsets. Five ASICs were designed in a two-year program. Three were for a CDMA phone: a modulator, a demodulator, and an enhanced Viterbi decoder. Two more were created for a base station, also used with the Viterbi decoder. These chipsets interfaced with an external microprocessor. The trials proved CDMA technology was viable on a larger scale, and could produce the capacity gains projected.

On the heels of disclosing the CAP I trial success and the ASICs at a CTIA technology forum, Qualcomm proceeded with its initial public offering of 4 million shares, raising $68M in December, 1991. PacTel bought a block of shares on the open market, and kicked in an additional $2.2M to buy warrants for 390,000 more shares, assuring CDMA R&D would continue uninterrupted.

Along with the Korean ETRI joint development deal, four manufacturers were onboard with Qualcomm and CDMA entering 1992: AT&T, Motorola, Oki, and Nortel Networks. Licensee number five in April, 1992, was none other than Nokia, the climax of a year and a half of negotiations directly between Jacobs and Jorma Ollila. Nokia had been observing the PacTel trials with keen interest, and had set up their own R&D center in San Diego to be close to the action with CDMA. One of the sticking points was the royalty: Nokia is thought to have paid around 3% of handset ASPs under its first 15-year agreement.

On March 2, 1993, Qualcomm introduced the CD-7000, a dual-mode CDMA/AMPS handheld phone powered by a single chip baseband: the Mobile Station Modem (MSM). The phone was a typical candy bar, 178x57x25mm weighing a bit over 340g (13 oz). The first customer was US West, with a commitment for at least 36,000 phones. Also, in March, 1993, plans for CDMA phones and infrastructure in Korea were announced with four manufacturers: Goldstar, Hyundai, Maxon and Samsung.

Qualcomm provided details of the new MSM baseband chip at Hot Chips in August 1993. The three basic CDMA functions of modulator, demodulator, and Viterbi decoder were on a single 0.8 micron, 114mm2 chip. It had 450,000 transistors and consumed 300mW, still requiring an external processor and RF circuitry to complete a handset. Qualcomm indicated a multi-foundry strategy, but didn't disclose suppliers – later reports named IBM as the source.

The TIA finally relented, endorsing CDMA with first publication of the IS-95 specification in July 1993, known commercially as cdmaOne. Cellular markets now had their choice of 2G digital standards in CDMA, and GSM.[85]

END

---

[85] https://www.semiwiki.com/forum/content/7353-detailed-history-qualcomm.html

Chapter Thirteen -- 2 Cellular Licenses per Market

Why did the FCC mandate two cellular carriers per MSA/RSA (Metropolitan Statistical Area/Rural Service Area)?

To answer this question, we must go back to a time when 2-way mobile communications systems were beginning to demand spectrum allocations exceeding the FCC's practical resources for managing the spectrum. Though the FCC's decision to grant licenses to specific entities without any fee contributed to accelerated growth of the radio industry, coordination of frequencies was an undeniable requirement if the spectrum was to be protected from congestion and confusion rendering it a useless natural resource.

Allocating specific spectrum bands to military (all branches), maritime (government and merchant marine), federal, state and local public safety and HAMs (amateur radio operators) created a knee jerk reaction by the powerful radio broadcast companies who saw government interference as a threat to their business and what they perceived as their divine right to all spectrum. Their self-serving reaction created a lobbying group devoted to protecting the broadcasters from encroachment into their spectrum by others whose business interests were considerably enhanced by utilizing wireless communications.

In response, early recognition by FCC engineers of limited commercially viable radio frequencies prompted what became the platform for allocating spectrum according to specific use profiles and establishing "coordinating agencies" whose task was to over-see allocated spectrum related to the very specific interests of those anticipating FCC licenses for commercial 2-way radio systems, mobile telephones and paging. Among the community of frequency coordinating agencies, 1) NABER (National Association of Business and Educational Radio) emerged as a significantly powerful lobbying force protecting the interests and rights of general businesses to their share of the useable radio spectrum. Additionally, other frequencies reserved for specific use included: 2) State & Local Public Safety represented by APCO, 3) Special Industrial Radio Services (SIRSA) became the lobbying power coordinating frequencies set aside for petroleum based business including asphalt/paving, oilfield exploration, drilling, production, well servicing, refining, distribution (think pipelines as well as over-the-road transport), ready-mix concrete companies and many others; 4) Industrial & Manufacturing; 5) Trucking; 6) Logging and Forestry; 7) Utilities; 8) Mining; 9) Public Conveyance and Livery; 10) Railroads; 11) public and private air traffic control and communications (see FAA); 12) television and others emerged.

However, for our purposes, the primary lobbying group to originally represent the Radio Common Carriers was called Telocator®. This organization became a powerful voice in Washington, D.C., and was a major force preventing Ma Bell from being a single source of telecommunications. Eventually, Telocator® joined CTIA® (Cellular Telecommunications Industry Association) and later, PCIA® (Personal Communications Industry Association).

Successfully lobbying congress, the FCC and the Justice Department, to reserve equal radio spectrum for Radio Common Carriers to compete with the telcos (not just Ma Bell but myriads of independent telcos, some of significant size (GTE, [Contel], Alltel, *etc.*), the competitive stage was set for companies like MCI (Jack Goeken), Metromedia (John Kluge), McCaw Cellular (Craig McCaw) and others to successfully challenge AT&T and Regional Bell Operating Companies (RBOCs) in the marketplace.

While FCC licenses were free, frequency coordination was not. Any entity applying for an FCC license was required to submit a certificate issued by the appropriate coordinating agency identifying the least congested frequency available in a specific geographic area recommended by that agency along with their license application before the FCC would grant a license. This coordination service required a "coordination fee" and a solicitation for membership. Assuming the licensee recognized the benefit of supporting this lobbying group's efforts on his behalf to protect his investment and be his representative for additional spectrum when it became available, the licensee could voluntarily join that lobbying organization. As a member, he would pay annual membership dues on a "per radio or pager" basis.

As it developed, the community of coordinating agencies responsible for mitigating congestion in specific blocks (bands) of radio spectrum became a major partner with the FCC in the development of wireless technology in an orderly and efficient use of radio spectrum. It is from this practice that the duopoly of cellular (it later became less of a duopoly as three to five additional carriers were granted licenses to compete in designated markets), was established.

We have introduced the term "Radio Common Carrier" in earlier discussions but it is important to understand the context and implications of this designation as it relates to all other FCC-licensed mobile systems.

"*The Rise Of The RCCs*," an article published in "*RCR Special Report: The First Decade of Cellular*,"[86] provides a glimpse into this issue:

"In 1949, the Justice Department filed an antitrust suit against AT&T™ and its Bell system. When the suit was finally settled in 1956, AT&T™ escaped with the Bell system intact, but was forced out of the mobile radio manufacturing business (Western Electric) because of a concession made in the Consent Decree. That particular concession [AT&T™ agreed to stop manufacturing mobile radio equipment] opened the door for Motorola, Inc. to become the dominant equipment supplier to the mobile radio industry. It also strengthened the position of a group of small independent operators called Radio Common Carriers."[87]

"The FCC ruled that independent operators should be allowed to offer mobile phone service."[88]

"The commission's decision was significant because, for the first time, it allowed competition into the telephone world and opened the door for an entirely new group of players."[89]

In this particular regard, a first-hand observer from that era delves into the issue a little deeper: "While animosity certainly developed between competing RCCs, they did, nonetheless, recognize they needed a single voice to represent them in their competitive struggle against the broadcast industry and the telephone companies; thus, Telocator®, a lobbying organization launched by the independent RCCs (we have to remember the telephone companies' mobile telephone spectrum was also considered radio common carriage), became the forum for annual conventions where issues common to all member companies could air their opinions, make suggestions for change and improvement and, above all, centralize a pool of cash and resources with which to combat the competition in the non-stop (often very distrustful) battles for spectrum and associated tariffing."[90]

By the time cellular arrived, the battle lines were clearly defined and the combatants were loathe to consider any kind of mutually beneficial compromise for cellular licensing. Here is another excerpt from the RCR Wireless Special report referenced earlier: "By the mid-1980s, wireline cellular companies found themselves unwelcome at Telocator® and joined to form what is now CTIA®. CTIA® would become the chief representative of the industry before the FCC, congress and the courts."[91]

"After several years of feuding with each other, CTIA® and Telocator® now [1993] peacefully co-exist and work together on some projects."[92]

"Robert Maher, President of CTIA from 1984-1991, played a major role in gaining federal interconnection and privacy rights for the cellular industry. Telocator®, too, was a driving force that helped carriers win big in the war to get fair and non-discriminatory interconnections with the landline telephone companies."[93]

"A master tactician, Maher also is credited with securing an additional 10 megahertz of 800MHz spectrum in 1986 for cellular carriers. That was a tremendous feat, according to Maher, considering that the industry was so young, competition for 800MHz frequencies was strong and regulators were toying with the idea of going with a non-specific flexible allocation around that time."[94]

---

[86] *The First Decade of Cellular*, 1983-1993, 05 April; An RCR Special Report; ppSR34-35; RCR Wireless; Arden Media Mailing Address: 3112 Windsor Drive A349, Austin, TX 78703
[87] Ibid
[88] Ibid
[89] Ibid; pSR35
[90] Interview: Lee Horsman; 37-year career in wireless telecom; Colorado Springs, 2018
[91] *The First Decade of Cellular*, 1983-1993, 05 April; An RCR Special Report; ppSR34-35; RCR Wireless; Arden Media Mailing Address: 3112 Windsor Drive A349, Austin, TX 78703
[92] Ibid
[93] Ibid
[94] Ibid

"But, being the caretaker, the new cellular organization had its challenges. 'There were no real experts,' Maher reflected. 'Everybody was learning.'"[95]

This off the cuff interview with Mr. Maher is an example of the ignorance telco industry mid-level managers, and those they hired, brought with them into the cellular arena. There were many very real experts in the non-wireline community but they were ignored by the risk averse wireline side as well as the media. Creativity and innovation in the early cellular business came from the non-wireline side. Had the telcos recognized the superior experience and management skills residing in the legacy RCC community, rather than maintaining their arrogance at the expense of the business, the industry could have advanced much more rapidly. The population of telco-oriented early cellular executive suite risk averse management was most obvious in their: "I can say 'no,' but I can't say, 'yes'", impotence. I am tempted to list them by name; however, in the interest of Christian charity and potential libel implications, I won't.

I am compelled to mention the names of genuine experts whose expertise, experience and management skills were ignored: 1) Jay Kitchen, NABER; 2) Van Carson, Motorola; 3) Ray Windle, NMI/NEC; 4) Bob Edwards, Radiophone; 5) Charlie Jackson, Gencom; 6) Tom Stanley, FCC; 7) Dr. Kobayashi, NEC.; 8) Wayne Schelle, ARTS/APC; 9) Jai Baghat, Skytel; 10) John Palmer, Skytel; 11) Bob White, Radiophone, of course Marty Cooper, Arlene Harris and others – Homer Harris, Carl Mathis, Stan Reubenstein, William Deford, Howard Hix, Lee Gopadze, Harry Brock, Bud Forrester, to name just a few. (This author apologizes to those who deserve to be on this list but he has failed to mention.)

"Unfortunately, high profile equated to assumed knowledge and, in the case of early cellular, this was a media-driven epidemic. From the time the FCC allocated spectrum for mobile telephones, and telcos were automatically assigned frequencies (channels); and, until equal spectrum was allocated for independent RCCs to compete with them establishing competitive mobile telephone service, telephone company executives pursued wireless as a necessary annoyance. By the time revenues from telco company mobile phone businesses were measureable, this sector of their enterprise was lost in the rounding of annual revenue reports. P&L from this business was so negligible it wasn't even included in the agendas for discussion at their quarterly and annual budget meetings. Thus, it was a great place to park managers whose skills had achieved the "Peter principle." These managers were good enough to keep but not good enough to be promoted; thus, they were assigned to the stepchild mobile business. It was a natural easy decision to populate their early executive cellular positions with these castoffs. Fortunately for those who enjoyed this promotion, unfortunately for the industry, they became the icons of genius and media darlings in an impossible to fail business."[96]

At the same time, visionaries like Marty Cooper, Craig McCaw, Wayne Schelle, Jay Kitchen and others provided leadership and fearless innovation while the risk averse telco executives watched and waited for results before jumping on board and subsequently taking credit for it (this is a particularly accurate reflection when the introduction of packet switched data was introduced – more on this later). It wasn't until McCaw's open commitment to pay any cellular licensee $80/pop, regardless of the market, that SBC (and it wasn't the cellular exec in office at the time but the President and Chairman of the board in St. Louis who made the decision) purchased non-wireline licenses in New York City, Philadelphia, Washington, DC, Boston, Houston, San Antonio and Chicago. They subsequently had to forfeit the NYC, Philadelphia and Boston licenses to be in compliance with FCC/Justice Dept. rules regarding majority ownership of more than one license by one entity per market."[97]

"The toughest issue we had to deal with [was] getting the A (non-wireline) and B (wireline) carriers to sit in the same room."[98] Robert Maher, Pres., CTIA

In large part because the vast majority of FCC licenses were granted for business use at no charge, the only licensees allowed to generate revenues from the air time for which they were licensed were the common carriers, *e.g.*, telcos and their competitors. The frequencies designated for Radio Common Carriers were the only FCC-licensed spectrum with which the licensee could legally charge his customer for "air time" – that amount

---

[95] Ibid
[96] Interview: Lee Horsman; 37-year career in wireless telecom; Colorado Springs, 2018
[97] Ibid
[98] *The First Decade of Cellular*, 1983-1993, 05 April; An RCR Special Report; ppSR34-35; RCR Wireless; Arden Media Mailing Address: 3112 Windsor Drive A349, Austin, TX 78703

of measureable time each individual customer was using the licensed frequency with a mobile telephone or pager. No other FCC-licensed entity could legally charge for air time on a frequency licensed to them for specific purposes. The operative word here is "legally." Far too many examples of violations were occurring utilizing systems at the time called "community repeaters," interconnected to the PSTN with a phone patch as well as private licensees who installed phone patches on their base stations and illegally allowed use of the systems for mobile radio PSTN interconnect. – *NOTE: We will address community repeaters and SMRs [Specialized Mobile Radio} frequencies (channels) [Nextel™] in detail later.*

Example: a taxi company, licensed to use a specific frequency for dispatch purposes, could not provide a radio to another entity like Uber™ and charge them for their use of that frequency. They could buy a radio, mark it up and sell or rent it but, if they charged for the use of the radio system, they were in violation of the FCC rules and regulations attendant to their license. Frequencies were monitored and some violators were prosecuted beyond simply forfeiting their FCC license.

However: "On October 22, 1986, the FCC released their long standing freeze on licensing for profit cooperatives on frequencies below 800MHz"[99].

"In simple terms, the ability to operate for profit cooperatives on frequencies below 800MHz opens new vistas of opportunity for the entrepreneurial dealer. A case in point involves the VHF Business Radio frequencies. In many areas, they are far less congested than their UHF counterparts. In fact, these frequencies are surprisingly clear in all but the very largest urban centers. The reason is obvious. As an industry, we have promoted an upward ascension of frequencies. First we moved the low band users to VHF, then the VHF users to UHF, then the UHF users to 800MHz. In our pell-mell exodus of the lower frequency bands, few gave any thought to what was being left behind. What was left behind was one of the most valuable resources in the radio spectrum. The problem is that we can't use the new high technology systems in VHF, or can we?"[100]

Reality check here: By 1986, the stampede to cellular was already in its third year. Abandoning private and semi-private two-way radio systems (including legacy RCC spectrum), even with phone patches and high capacity paging terminals, was in process and this FCC reaction was too little too late, and, for that matter, antithetical.

Trunked Specialized Mobile Radio (SMR/ESMR) frequencies were licensed as pseudo-common carriers to capitalize on perceived opportunities to compete with legacy RCCs. This spawned Nextel® and a few other hopefuls. Early success (and ultimate failure) of Nextel as a viable competitor to cellular depended on market acceptance of the "push-to-talk" instant connection feature in addition to automatic interconnect. Further consideration of Nextel and other businesses attempting to compete with cellular by building SMR/ESMR (and a few other) networks exceeds the scope of our objective; thus, deeper research is recommended if sufficient interest encourages it.

An RCC, on the other hand, was legally licensed to purchase equipment designed to produce revenues from the airtime a mobile telephone or pager used. These licenses became extremely valuable. While RCCs, including telcos, enjoyed lucrative revenue streams and their businesses created the platforms upon which today's ubiquitous wireless services stand, the FCC practice of licensing more than one RCC competitor in major markets backfired when cellular arrived. Companies who had fiercely competed with one another in lucrative markets were forced to join forces as the one "non-wireline" cellular licensee expected to compete with the telcos. It does not require great imagination to consider the implications as family owned businesses, some for two and three generations, competing with each other in lucrative markets, were forced to play nice in the cellular sandbox as the non-wireline cellular licensee. The lawyers had a heyday.

Attempting to mitigate the impact, the FCC declared a "head start" program. Because the telcos had excess cash and other resources in place, particularly single ownership of real estate, towers, strategically located large switches, sophisticated billing systems, decades of sales, marketing and customer service personnel, ar-

---

[99] A Primer on FCC Licensing; *Focus on Marketing: Networking In Ways You Never Thought Of*; 1987; Nu-Way Ltd., Birmingham, AL;
[100] Ibid – pp5-2

mies of field engineers and telephone-savvy technicians, the huge advantage they enjoyed over the non-wireline licensees had to be addressed. Thus, while the non-wireline licensees fought for their places, and the telcos built networks and launched service, the FCC concocted a half-baked "equalization" plan.

When the non-wireline companies launched a competitive network, the FCC mandated the telcos would voluntarily transfer half of their customers to the non-wireline switch data base! This was unprecedented and, as one would expect, failed to deliver the FCC's desired result. If you were mandated to voluntarily give your competitor half your subscribers, which half would you give them? Maybe the half that included all the deadbeats and slow pays? Regardless, it went into effect and, because the demand was so great, both licensees were successful beyond anything their business models projected.

The FCC decision to allocate spectrum reserved for common carriage is a major distinction that should be carefully studied. A great deal of detail not presented here should be thoroughly digested if understanding 21st century wireless telecommunications service is to be pursued. (See FCC-specific detail in later chapters.)

Commercial 2-Way Radio Service and Paging

Because we are attempting to address history, technologies, and distribution of telecommunications leading to 21st century ubiquitous wireless products and services, we will skirt other spectrum designees whose contributions to, and use of, RF deserves a text of their own. We refer to military, maritime, television, Amateur Radio, unlicensed citizens band, GPS, WiFi/WiMax, Bluetooth, satellite and others. In this regard, a study of RADAR, LIDAR (with all its subsets and advances in military as well as public safety applications) and narrowband satellite services (look for Equatorial) plus more popular satellite constellations for voice, data, and video applications is strongly recommended. As we approach the end of this work, we will address Iridium™, the cellular satellite constellation.

2-Way

Discussions with HAMs, military communications people and others will invariably include a lively discourse regarding how radio frequencies are defined in name and abbreviation, *e.g.,*ELF, LF, VHF, UHF, *etc.*

This table reflects the ITU Official designations:

Frequency range	Wavelength range	ITU designation		IEEE bands
		Full name	Abbreviation	
3–30 Hz	10^5–10^4 km	Extremely low frequency	ELF	N/A
30–300 Hz	10^4–10^3 km	Super low frequency	SLF	N/A
300–3000 Hz	10^3–100 km	Ultra low frequency	ULF	N/A
3–30 kHz	100–10 km	Very low frequency	VLF	N/A
30–300 kHz	10–1 km	Low frequency	LF	N/A
300 kHz – 3 MHz	1 km – 100 m	Medium frequency	MF	N/A
3–30 MHz	100–10 m	High frequency	HF	HF
30–300 MHz	10–1 m	Very high frequency	VHF	VHF
300 MHz – 3 GHz	1 m – 10 cm	Ultra high frequency	UHF	UHF, L, S
3–30 GHz	10–1 cm	Super high frequency	SHF	S, C, X, Ku, K, Ka
30–300 GHz	1 cm – 1 mm	Extremely high frequency	EHF	Ka, V, W, mm
300 GHz – 3 THz	1 mm – 0.1 mm	Tremendously high frequency	THF	N/A

In the interest of simplifying things, for our purposes, we will use the following designations:

Lo-band: 25-75MHz – a caveat here; any reference to Single Side Band will assume frequencies below 3MHz utilizing amplitude modulation. In the world of commercial radio service, SSB was/is generally used for extremely long transmissions as in from Dallas, Texas, to oil rigs in the Persian Gulf. Advanced understanding of solar activity and a technology called 'tropo-scatter' (RF waves angled at the troposphere are reflected at the same angles allowing a reasonably efficient level of control) have significantly improved charts for utilizing these frequencies during different seasons and times of day/night.

Hi-band (VHF): 150-175MHz –Rule of thumb here: dB-for-dB, foot-for-foot of antenna height, microvolt-for-microvolt of receiver sensitivity, and dollar-for-dollar of system equipment expense, this band is the most efficient for maximum coverage for most reasonable expense. As a matter of historical fact, the two most valuable paging frequencies during the pre-cellular hey-day of paging were P5 (152.240MHz) and P6 (156.800MHz).

UHF: 450-512MHz: Until semiconductors produced a high power transistor, mobile radios in this band required three power vacuum tubes in the final amplifier. In the early 1970s, a fully transistorized (solid state) 100W mobile radio designed for the UHF band demonstrated the efficacy of higher power for transmitting UHF and 800-900MHz. While this solid state breakthrough is impressive for all it meant to the two-way radio business, the implications for future miniaturization are incalculable. This is a historical mark you, the student, should lodge indelibly in your mind as one of the most critical breakthroughs leading to 21st Century ubiquitous telecommunications.

Cellular: 800-894MHz (50MHz within these bookends): While fixed cell site transmissions could legally pump out a maximum of 35W, ERP (Effective Radiated Power) was often as much as 250W. Subscriber equipment, however, was limited to 3W for mobiles and transportable "bag" phones. Hand-held phones that were held against the user's head/ear were limited to a maximum output power of .6W (600mW). This is necessary because, at these frequencies, the danger of human injury from 'near-microwave' (for all practical purposes simply microwave) energy was possible.

One of the most important engineering principles in commercial 2-way radio system design is that coverage must be calculated as a function of TALK BACK from the mobile to the base station. It does not matter if a mobile or portable radio can receive a strong signal from the base station if it is too far away to respond. Even high power (100-110W VHF) trunk mounted mobiles with high gain antennas mounted in the middle of an automobile's roof where maximum ground plane improves antenna gain, the mobile's ability to effectively reach the base station is considerably less than the base station's ability to reach the mobile.

This is no less true in cellular than it is in any other two-way radio system. However, at the microwave frequencies replacing and/or augmenting 800 & 900MHz in today's networks, there are far too many different power adjustments, physics and environment issues at play to attempt to address them in this context. Suffice it to say, the closer the subscriber's phone is to the cell site (or other fixed receiver) serving it at any given moment, the better the wireless experience will be. Signal strength bars on a phone are poor indicators of service quality.

FCC – Part 90 – Land Mobile

The Communications Act of 1934 created the FCC as we know it today. Earlier regulatory agencies were not adequately funded nor empowered to create and enforce rules and regulations necessary to protect, preserve, manage and promote efficient use of the electromagnetic spectrum.

Land mobile radio system (LMRS), also called public land mobile radio or private land mobile radio, is a wireless communications system intended for use by terrestrial users in vehicles (mobiles) or on foot (portables). Examples are two way radios in vehicles. Such systems are used by emergency first responder organizations such as police, fire, and ambulance services, public works organizations, dispatch services such as taxis, or companies with large vehicle fleets or numerous field staff and literally hundreds more such as railroads, forestry and too many more to list. Such a system can be independent, but often can be connected to other fixed systems such as the public switched telephone network (PSTN).

Wireless access to the World Wide Web as we enjoy it today is an extension of Land Mobile Radio as the technologies and regulatory management evolved. In this section, we will see who, where, when, why and how pre-cellular LMRS systems provided the platform for 21st Century telecommunications ubiquity.

Just as we have recognized giants of the past whose contributions in electricity, electromagnetism, telegraphy, telephony and, to some degree, radio frequency science and invention, have been critical to understanding, articulating and delivering fundamental theories as well as products, it is imperative that any discussion of the basis for advanced telecommunications as we enjoy them includes a fundamental recognition of two globally ubiquitous platforms: 1) the power grid; 2) PSTN (internationally interconnected Public Switched Telephone Network(s)) to which we will refer as the "fixed plant." Without these, ubiquitous telecommunications, including the internet, could not exist as it serves us today.

We will not delve into the electrical grid.

We will delve into the PSTN.

However, we will first dissect commercial 2-way radio systems in enough depth for you, the student, to understand its history, topology and much of its deliverables as a commercial enterprise constantly evolving until it delivered cellular and all that cellular has become as a ubiquitous interface to the Public Switched Telephone Network as well as public and private data networks allowing access to the internet.

Make no mistake, and don't allow anyone to convince you otherwise, MONEY, profit for corporations, was the reason for commercial 2-way radio systems to develop into ubiquitous wireless access to the PSTN. From early

AM dispatch systems designed and constructed for the Detroit Police Department's squad cars, followed by the first FM system installed for a Connecticut law enforcement application, two-way radio popularity resulted in demand that funded companies whose founders, shareholders, employees, suppliers and customers enjoyed great wealth, lifetime careers and productivity.

While there were others (Standard, Aertron, Kenwood, Maxon to name a few) in the US, the "Big Four" suppliers of pre-cellular commercial 2-way radios were: 1) Motorola; 2) GE; 3) RCA; 4) EF Johnson. For our purposes, we will settle on Motorola for simplifying the concepts. Do not confuse what we're referring to as "commercial 2-way radios" with Radio Common Carrier mobile telephones and paging. We will deal with this difference in greater detail later.

Before radio, police departments used telephone call boxes to contact headquarters. This delayed response, particularly critical emergency response. An early solution enjoined entertainment broadcast programming to interrupt whatever program was airing to send a message over their "airwaves." Of course this allowed anyone listening to involve themselves in the crime or emergency situation – not good; thus, it was quickly abandoned.

However, it demonstrated the need for two-way radio communications prompting Paul Galvin, founder of Motorola (and several others), to deliver a solution that became the platform on which he built a multi-billion dollar corporation and provided the model for utilizing radio to deliver the ubiquitous telecommunications service we enjoy in the 21st Century.

The impact of Mr. Galvin's leadership with the Radio Manufacturer's Association, insisting on federal regulation of radio spectrum, was an extraordinary demonstration of his vision for spectrum management without which it is unlikely wireless telecommunications as we enjoy them could have been developed.

The patent office's objective influence on the competitive environment, in concert with spectrum management promoting diversity, as well as delivering a firm foundation for effective application of a natural resource cannot be over-estimated.

In *The Founder's Touch – The Life of Paul Galvin of Motorola*[101], the early days of Motorola's leadership in commercializing radio is chronicled through the lens of author, Harry Petrakis. However, it is prudent to acknowledge investments by GE, RCA and peripheral industries (components, towers, antennas, coaxial cables & connectors, signaling devices, engineering services, test equipment, *etc.*) and to objectively credit a myriad of others, in many cases equal or superior to Motorola's contributions.

AM broadcast receivers were not invented by Mr. Galvin nor his company employees. Like others, he recognized the market opportunity and set about to capitalize on it. Like others of his time, ambition, coupled with extraordinary work ethic, fueled by survival instinct and capitalistic freedom, Mr. Galvin's force of will inspired those around him to deliver extraordinary results.

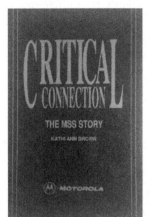

Quoting from the Galvin biography: "There is an art in business as there is in anything else, an art of anticipation and an acumen that comes out of experience plus a certain sensitivity. Galvin had this art. He knew that the eliminator [AC product eliminating a battery – author insert] was not going to provide them a market for very long. Even then AC radio was beginning to come into use with countless loft operators producing a variety of sets. Dominating the field was the competition of such strong producers as Atwater-Kent, Kennedy, Spartan, Majestic, Zenith, RCA and GE."[102]

"By 1929, radio was an 840 million dollar annual business, up 1400 *per cent* in just seven years. The screen grid tube had made it possible to give sets much greater sensitivity with fewer tubes. All new home radios were now AC operated.[103]

For a human interest look at what Mr. Galvin and his employees went through to deliver the first Motorola radio in a car, you are encouraged to read *The Founder's Touch*©. That first car radio required extraordinary imagination, creativity, experimentation, ingenuity and dedication that should impress you. Suffice it to say here, Mr. Galvin's demonstration of it at the Radio Manufacturer's Association Convention in Atlantic City in 1930, marks the beginning of an explosion in radio rivaled perhaps only by AC electricity, telephony the automobile and the PC/internet for its impact on life as we know it.

"The original model 5T71 auto radio that Galvin carried [installed and operating in his personal auto] to Atlantic City established the first of many "Motorola Firsts" in product designs that were to follow. This model sold for $110-130 with accessories including installation. It was designed to fit any of the popular cars of that period, and designed so it could be reproduced on a commercial basis. It has justifiably been called the "First Commercial Auto Radio."[104]

These next quotes from *The Founders Touch*© record what this author believes is possibly the single most impactful contribution Motorola made to the burgeoning wireless telecommunications juggernaut. It indelibly and irrefutably places into history the beginning of the MSS (Motorola Service Shop) organization which became a major factor in the heavyweight title fight between Ma Bell and independent RCCs without which 21st Century ubiquitous service would likely be very different. A book, *The Critical Connection*[105], has been written about it.

"During 1930, Galvin Manufacturing Corporation began selling the first models to be marketed under the Motorola label, a name that suggested both motion and radio, which seemed to Galvin striking and effective. The name Motorola had come to Galvin quite simply as an inspiration one morning while he was shaving."[106]

"But many of the shipments during this same period were unlabeled sets, sold as earlier home radios had been sold, with the dealer or distributor affixing his own label. While this distressed him, Galvin had neither the money nor the organization to demand recognition of his corporate or new trade name, "Motorola." But he

---

[101] Petrakis, Harry Mark; *The Founder's Touch – The Life of Paul Galvin of Motorola*; 1965©, McGraw-Hill, Inc.; Motorola University Press; JG Ferguson Publishing Co.; Chicago
[102] Ibid – pp64
[103] Ibid – pp74
[104] Ibid – pp92
[105] Kathi Ann Brown: *The Critical Connection-The MSS Story* (Motorola); 1992-Motorola University Press; 3701 E Algonquin Rd, Rolling Meadows, IL
[106] Ibid – pp93

also knew that the best kind of advertising was the radios themselves. Each set installed and operating became a "rolling demonstrator" that attracted many other potential customers within earshot along the street."[107]

"Yet, infuriated complaints about the difficulties of installing the radios continued to come in from the field."[108]

"Nobody around here knows how to put one of these sets into the car," a dealer calling Galvin from Texas said angrily. "How the hell can we sell them if nobody can install them?"[109]

"Galvin knew that their success in overcoming this technical problem might well determine whether the struggling company could survive. Without any sales or service organization to throw into the breach, he enlisted Elmer Wavering to join him as he traveled through the country selling car radios and holding sessions on their installation. They planned a campaign that would bring him into cities ahead of Wavering. Galvin would obtain an order for radios with a solemn promise that, "Our Mr. Wavering will follow up within a few days to provide your people a complete lesson in installation and maintenance." When Wavering arrived in town, groups were ready for his presentation. Later, in 1931, Galvin and Wavering would be joined by Bill Engle, Murray Yeomans, Dale Andrews and Johnny Rogers. This nucleus of an organization helped establish the first Authorized Motorola Installation Stations that would, within the space of just a few years, develop a countrywide army of men able to skillfully install car radios."[110]

It is prudent to emphasize here the car radios referenced above were broadcast receivers only; meaning they received radio programs from commercial radio stations broadcasting news, sports, music and the like. These car radios had no transmitters.

As the FCC's growing regulation of radio spectrum took on an enforceable role, the engineers there recognized the importance of specifying technical limiting factors on a per frequency basis. Identifying specific frequencies and allocating them with detailed lists of commercial services legally authorized to operate a transmitter on these specific frequencies also required technical specifications equipment manufacturers were expected to meet. Among these was to produce and sell only those radios featuring transmitters with frequency control devices that could, and would, maintain a "center carrier frequency" with a minimum amount of "drift" to prevent interference to adjacent frequencies. Because this was technically difficult, the FCC required that any radio sold and installed for use in a commercial application had to be inspected annually by a licensed technician and labeled with the date and technician's license ID certifying the transmitter was operating within the rigorous limits of its specified frequency – that its transmissions were not "drifting" outside the limits of the center frequency as specified by the FCC's rules and regulations.

Due to its early organizing for audio car radio installations, Motorola had a platform ready on which to build the service organization that dominated US Land Mobile Radio Service for many years. In addition to fielding teams of trainers to teach independent businessmen in rural areas, as well as the major population centers, these trainers became the largest group of FCC-approved licensing instructors ever assembled. As a result, every MSS had at least one technician with a "First Class FCC License" for certifying transmitter stability in every commercial Motorola two-way radio in the field. Try to imagine another way to get a full-fledged licensed technician in Podunk, Rural America, to ensure the local police department's communications systems would meet spec' and be reliable. There were many small towns with a radio shop (MSS and GE MRs + RCA & independent shops) that kept the utilities, police and fire departments' radio systems working.

When Motorola's commercial two-way business replaced broadcast receivers as their larger business product, the MSS organization was prepared to grow along with its supplier. Additionally, this same organization was also poised for expansion when the FCC allocated spectrum for paging and mobile telephone service to compete with the telephone companies. A captive community of technically astute businessmen, targeted by a special five-man team of experts fielded by Motorola to assist in applying for licenses as RCCs, accelerated what would otherwise have been a protracted process. This is not to say others, outside the MSS community, did not also participate in the early days of RCC paging and mobile telephone opportunities; but, the size and

---

[107] Ibid – pp93
[108] Ibid – pp93
[109] Ibid – pp93
[110] Ibid – pp94

experience represented by the MSS organization was without parallel. One does not need much imagination to recognize how and why Motorola dominated the state and local public safety markets as well as many commercial markets. The role this unsung activity played in the history and evolution of two-way radio into ubiquitous wireless services beginning with cellular and advancing to 21st Century networks, is another major factor in wireless telecommunications history.

Mobile two-way communications

Paul Galvin assigned his chief engineer, Don Mitchell, to develop a radio transmitter for cars. In August, 1939, Galvin Manufacturing introduced the Motorola model T6920 AM mobile transmitter, which broadcast in the 30-40MHz range. A model, P6912 VHF receiver and base station followed.

This Motorola two-way radio system was priced about one-fourth as much as the competition's, and the transmitters could be installed in cars that already had receivers in the same frequency band.

In 1940, the police department in Bowling Green, Kentucky, became the first customer for a complete Motorola AM two-way radio system. The radios were so well designed, Galvin Manufacturing produced the same models for several years – until FM technology replaced them in the 1940s.[111] For an in depth look at Motorola's early police mobile radios, go to the web at: *Directory of Motorola Police Radio 1942*.[112]

With this radio system, the transmitter and the receiver were two completely separate units connected by a very thick cable. This is also an early form of "duplex" service because, in order to prevent interference, transmit and receive frequencies were separated by a significant amount of bandwidth. This allowed the operator to hear incoming information through the speaker simultaneously with his talking on the microphone.

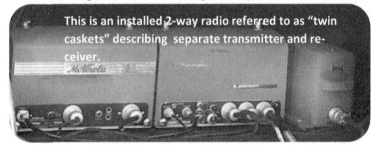
This is an installed 2-way radio referred to as "twin caskets" describing separate transmitter and receiver.

The transmitter, with its iron alloy heat sink, was so heavy the receiver had to be appointed with a lead weight to balance the weight for the squad car's suspension system. The most common installation had the two units, transmitter and receiver (called at the time, "twin caskets"), anchored in the trunk. A thick coaxial cable ran from the trunk to the dash where the microphone and speaker were fixed to the dash. When the microphone was keyed, the dynamotor revved up, the car's forward motion was almost like braking, and the headlights dimmed until the transmitter was up to power. It all must have been very exciting and perhaps even amusing. Fortunately, its life cycle was limited until new innovation replaced it and "transceivers," the combined transmitter and receiver in one case (a "drawer unit") replaced the twin caskets.

FM, frequency modulation, the dominant technology for commercial two-way radio systems, established itself as the most effective technology for cost-effective, reliable frequency-specific, non-interfering proliferation and market acceptance. Until digital technologies replaced it, FM was the standard for almost all commercial two-way radio systems.

Let's look at a few configurations of the most common two-way radio systems. For our purposes, we will ignore unlicensed CB (Citizens Band), WiFi, Bluetooth, and other limited application devices; nor will we delve into high power broadcasting radio and television station systems, military, aeronautics (air traffic control, Civil Air Patrol), marine and maritime systems, Global Positioning Satellite, weather, seismographic and other telemetry networks, HAM (Amateur Radio) systems, NOAA and other atmospheric and weather-related systems, and hosts of medical RF applications.

Base Station – Mobile Relay (Repeater – Community Repeater) – Control Station

Mobile Radio – Portable Radio – Pager

---

[111] Ibid
[112] https://www.wb6nvh.com/Moto42/Moto42.htm

What, exactly, is a base station?

Base station? Think "fixed;" no, not like fixed as in repaired; fixed as in a "fixed position," *i.e.*, "once in place, not intended to be moved." Part of the early FCC rules was the requirement of any licensed "fixed transmitter" to be identified with the latitude longitude coordinates of its residence. This was part of the licensing process resulting in the FCC granting a construction permit prior to issuing the license. All the information on the li-

cense application had to correspond exactly to the information on a frequency coordination filing form and this information included precise information relating to the physical location where any fixed base station or mobile relay (repeater) or control station would be located.

A base station, physically a cabinet containing a transmitter, receiver, power supply, tuning controls, a heat sink (radiator) and often other ancillaries, attached to a coaxial cable terminating on the opposite end with a "load" (antenna), powered by AC electricity from the grid with a converter to drive the electronics with DC, is the heart of any commercial two-way radio system.

A copy of the FCC license authorizing the installation and operation of a base station was required to be posted on or near the fixed radio.

The size and form of base stations vary considerably. From large cabinets (<>7'x40"x40") to smaller (<>30"x40"x24") and desk-top size, roughly, 14"x24"x24". These styles and types prevailed until rack mounting allowed greater flexibility and easier maintenance as decks with plug-in "cards" or "modules" were easier to replace than repairing electronics in the field.

In-door cabinets not requiring weatherproofing and racks for mounting decks were installed in shelters. Weatherproof outdoor cabinets could be installed directly on a tower in close proximity to the antenna system associated with it reducing signal loss due to excessively long cable runs; however, installing base stations at varying levels on a tower creates wind loading issues as well as inconvenient access for tech-

nicians maintaining the equipment. Most of the time, base stations were installed inside shelters (we will discuss shelters a little later) or as outdoor cabinets mounted on concrete slabs or galvanized steel frames in enclosed equipment compounds.

Prior to the introduction of manufactured shelters designed to prevent access to vandals and rodents, early "radio shacks" were primitive requiring any human visitor to approach and enter cautiously to avoid attack by wasps, snakes, spiders and rodents. To make this point, here is a photo of a mouse electrocuted while chewing on the grounding cable. As you can see, I found him with his teeth bonded to the copper conductor. These shacks were hot in the summer and cold in the winter. Dust, always a major factor in the deterioration of electronic circuits and devices, was problematic as was humidity and intense summer heat. Special care had to be taken to prevent rain, humidity condensation and snow melt from getting into the electrical circuits.

1970-1990 remote

When the radio system operator was close enough to the base station to have the microphone and speaker directly attached to the base station (usually a desk top transceiver), operation of the system was referred to as "local control." This was a fairly common configuration in rural areas; however, when the base station was located too far from the dispatcher (system operator) for local control, "remote control" devices were necessary. Do not confuse this with control stations we will discuss a little later.

1950-60 remote

"Remote control" often referred to a dispatcher's device located too far from the base station for local control. A "remote control" device had no radio components. It was a small device with a "push-to-talk – release to listen" button, volume control and other convenience features. It was most often connected to the base station *via* a leased telephone line. In the absence of a leased telephone line, it could be connected to the base station with a 960MHz microwave link referred to as "point-to-point." This was a relatively rare configuration for a simplex radio system.

Multi-frequency base stations required more complicated remote control systems. In-depth discussion of the complicated console systems common to 911, state and local police, fire, EMS and other large scale radio systems (think public transportation, ready-mix concrete fleets, garbage and waste disposal fleets, *etc.*) exceeds the scope of this discussion.

Mobile Relay – Repeater – Community Repeater[113]

Mobile Relay is the FCC identification for repeater. Essentially, repeaters are base stations designed to forward audio transmitted on one frequency by re-transmitting that same audio on a different frequency. This is usually done to increase the radio

---

[113] https://www.google.com/search?q=two+way+radio+repeater+systems&rlz=1C1CHZL_enUS725US725&sxsrf=ALeKk005jmb7a3li3srkTC12ZVd_fGkv0A:1591818542672&source=lnms&tbm=isch&sa=X&ved=2ahUKEwjFjKGWgvjpAhXTHM0KHdMDDegQ_AUoAnoECA4QBA&biw=1920&bih=937#imgrc=6RJ-EVAALg7oDM

range of mobile-to-mobile, portable-to-portable or portable to mobile communications.

If the repeater and the mobiles/portables/control station(s) are equipped with two sets of frequencies, the user enjoys the full radius of coverage provided by the base station, (*i.e.*, repeater) because contact with the repeater from the mobiles and portables is repeated at the height of the base station/repeater antenna. If Mobile #1 transmits on frequency 454.375MHz, the repeater receives on 454.375MHz. By virtue of being directly wired to a transmitter on frequency 459.375MHz, Mobile #1 talks to Mobile #2 when the repeater re-transmits the audio transmitted by Mobile #1 459.375 which is one of two receive frequencies residing in all mobiles/portables. When Mobile #2 responds, it transmits on a different frequency, 460.182MHz, the repeater receives on 460.182MHz and re-transmits the audio on frequency 454.375MHz which is received by Mobile #1 on receive frequency 454.375MHz. See diagrams and more detailed description in following pages.

Community repeaters are mobile relay base stations with squelch decks allowing users to avoid listening to traffic on channels licensed to shared users. This technology is referred to as CTCSS, Private Line™, Digital Private Line™, Channel Guard™ and a few others (see more detail below). These base stations (CRs – community repeaters) were an early answer to the problem of small companies or private individuals whose business and professional needs for communications could not justify the expense of ownership associated with the radio systems necessary to provide the wide area coverage required. A CR (Community Repeater) was commonly owned by a radio manufacturing company or radio shop whose interest in selling and maintaining radio systems were enhanced by a tower delivering the antenna height from which wide area coverage could be achieved. These companies could legally sell equipment (mobiles, portables, control stations, telemetry devices, paging, mobile telephone service equipment) to small companies and professionals who could afford to rent space on the repeater.

If you were a realtor in Podunk, USA, and you specialized in farm property, your area of interest could conceivably cover thousands of square miles. Your safety could be a major concern and communicating with your office as well as customers was likely worth a monthly rental for time on a CR plus the cost of a mobile radio or pager. You would also be willing to share the channel with your neighbors.

The squelch decks on CRs are designed to allow channel monitoring; thus, those who share a community repeater, usually no more than six mobiles per deck with a maximum of six decks, agree to press the monitor switch on the microphone before activating the PTT (push-to-talk) switch avoiding "walking" on someone currently transmitting. You see, the frequencies (channels) are shared. To keep all the users from annoying noise unrelated to their interests, the squelch tones/digits assigned to each user allow only audio from the mobiles/portables/ control station from that user to be heard by that user until the monitor switch is activated opening the receivers.

It is not difficult to imagine the costs associated with towers exceeding the budgets of professionals and small businesses. Large metropolitan areas also enjoyed the benefits of CRs. Tall buildings centrally located in major cities were prime sites for CRs. When these weren't available, towers were erected. These sites delivered communications service to many professionals and small businesses when early mobile telephone systems could not.

In the early days of cellular, small businesses reluctantly began replacing their legacy two-way systems with more expensive cellular phone service. In many cases, their remorse was palpable since the cellular technologies were less reliable than their licensed radio service from a community repeater. As cellular service improved, remorse has become euphoria and associated expenses are acceptable.

In some cases, large companies purchased their own repeaters, licensed them and either erected their own towers bearing all the expenses or rented space on someone else's tower, skyscraper, water tower or other high structure for their repeater. These privately owned and licensed repeaters served dozens of mobiles (utility providers, ready-mix, garbage collection, *etc.*). They too were equipped with squelch suppression features to eliminate co-channel chatter. In some rare cases, they legally installed phone patches on these repeaters allowing mobile interconnect with the PSTN (Public Switched Telephone Network). The problem this created was channel use. Generally speaking, two-way conversations such as dispatch information and mobile/portable location reporting were very brief allowing any given mobile almost instant access to the channel; however, if a company executive had access to the PSTN *via* a phone patch on the repeater, his conversations tied

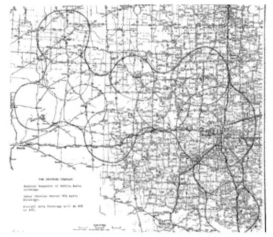

Western Co Oklahoma Micor Repeater System Coverage Map

up the channel until he ended his call. You don't have to be a genius to imagine the internal strife this created; thus, phone patches on privately owned repeaters, while legal, were relatively rare.

Pursuing this a little more, there were many unscrupulous sales people who promoted phone patches on CRs! Not only was this illegal, it was self-defeating unless that CR was dominated by a single company – like a real estate agency. The frequencies assigned to business CRs were explicitly exempt from delivering "air-time for sale." It was illegal for any entity to install a repeater licensed for specific use or general business use with a phone patch and charge for the time that phone patch was connected to the PSTN for phone calls from associated mobile or portable radios. Many were shut down by the FCC but many also escaped and were handsomely rewarded for their nefarious activity. Privately owned and licensed systems provided a level of communications unavailable from rented time on a CR. As an example, let's imagine an oil well servicing company (think Halliburton™, Schlumberger™, Dowell™ The Western Co.™) whose business justified an investment in a wide area wireless two-way communication system.

Your engineers, in concert with a supplier's engineering resources, design a system similar to the one shown here utilizing the **450MHz** band. Each circle represents coverage delivered by a repeater. Anywhere in this coverage area, mobiles may connect with other mobiles for voice communications. However, let's say an oil field worker with a **VHF** (150.000-175.000MHz) hand-held portable radio working away from his vehicle needs to talk to a dispatcher, another portable or mobile somewhere in this coverage area but they are out of range of his portable. If we have installed a VHF mobile in his service vehicle that is also equipped with a 450MHz radio, we can hard wire the two radios to create an "in-band repeater." The portable, operating on 153.155MHz transmits to the VHF (153.155MHz) mobile in the vehicle that the low power portable can reach. By virtue of special wiring, the audio from the portable is fed through the 450MHz mobile which transmits to the repeater and allows the portable to communicate with any mobile or dispatcher in the system. Actual use of this configuration is a little more complicated than this but you get the idea.

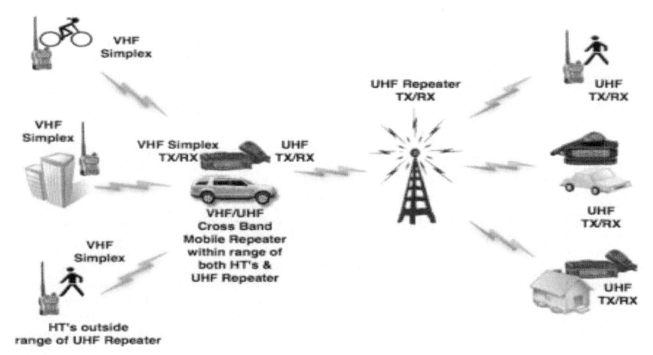

Towers

Let's talk radio towers, *e.g.*, towers designed to facilitate mounting antennas and the cables and ancillary equipment required to produce wireless telecommunications deliverables—human voice communications, data (internet access, text, e-mail, voice mail, *etc.*), video, photos, credit card processing, and a wide variety of telemetry applications (smart home remote monitoring and controls, GPS, personal fitness monitoring & reporting and many others.)

Fundamentally, there are two kinds of radio towers: 1) self-supporting; 2) guyed (stabilized and secured in place with guy wires).

There are sub-sets to these two categories:

In the self-supporting category:

Free standing lattice – three legs (triangle) or four legs

Free standing monopoles – two kinds:

Tapered slip-joint monopoles

Step-tapered monopoles

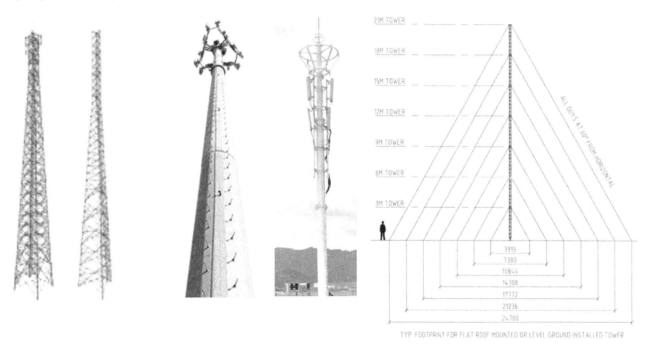

In guyed towers, the styles, varieties and options exceed the scope of this effort. You need to know there are many tower manufacturers and distributors of tower accessories for erecting, supporting, appointing with mounts and cable ladders to accommodate antennas and coaxial cables, facilitate technicians who need to climb them, elevators, lighting (any tower higher than ninety-nine feet requires a top beacon), antenna mounts of many descriptions, clamps, guy wires, foundation materials, large industrial turnbuckles, anchors, ice bridges (protective covers to prevent falling ice from damaging equipment and cable), platforms, gin poles, and far too many more miscellaneous pieces to attempt listing them.

The wireless industry enjoys a universe of contractors staffed with experts for foundation construction, tower erection and installation of antennas for all types of radio systems including advanced cellular/PCS, WiMAX, as well as 3G, 4G, & 5G networks. These contractors are often large companies with lucrative careers available for mechanical and civil engineers as well as climbers and technicians with technical skills and trade school education.

In addition to towers, antennas are mounted on water towers, power grid utility towers, roof tops, spires, chimneys, smokestacks, barns, windmills, church steeples, bell carillon towers, silos, granaries, light standards, and myriad more.

Stealth towers are structures camouflaged to blend into the surrounding environment (trees, cacti, *etc.*) or to be concealed within familiar structures like crosses, church steeples, *etc*.

See below some guyed towers.

Specially designed towers

Sutro Tower in San Francisco

designed to withstand earthquakes

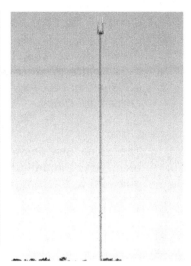

2000' tower in downtown Kansas City

Chapter Fourteen -- Antennas (not *antennae*)

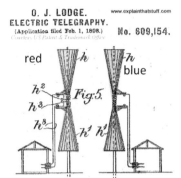

Artwork: Oliver Lodge's illustration of sending radio waves through space from a transmitter (red) to a receiver (blue) some distance away, taken from his 1898 patent US 609,154: Electric Telegraphy. Courtesy of US Patent and Trademark Office.

Who invented the radio antenna?

There's no easy answer to that question because radio evolved into a useful technology through the second half of the 19th century thanks to the work of quite a few different people—both theoretical scientists and practical experimenters.[114]

Who were these pioneers? Scottish physicist **James Clerk Maxwell** figured out a theory of radio around 1864, and **Heinrich Hertz** proved that radio waves really did exist about 20 years later (they were called Hertzian waves in his honor for some time afterward). Several years later, at a meeting in Oxford, England on August 14, 1894, English physicist, **Oliver Lodge**, demonstrated how radio waves could be used for signaling from one room to another in what he later described (in his 1932 autobiography) as "a very infantile kind of radio-telegraphy." Lodge filed a US patent for "electric telegraphy" on February 1, 1898, describing apparatus for "an operator, by means of what is now known as 'Hertzian-wave telegraphy' to transmit messages across space to any one or more of a number of different individuals in various localities..." Unknown to Lodge at that stage, **Guglielmo Marconi** was carrying out his own experiments in Italy around the same time—and ultimately proved the better showman: many people think of him as the "inventor of radio" to this day whereas, in truth, he was only one of a group of forward-thinking people who helped turn the science of electromagnetic waves into a practical, world-changing technology.[115]

None of the original radio experiments used transmitters or receivers that we would instantly recognize today. Hertz and Lodge, for example, used a piece of equipment called a spark-gap oscillator: a couple of zinc balls attached to short lengths of copper wire with an air gap in between them. Lodge and Marconi both used Branly coherers (glass tubes packed with metal filings) for detecting the waves they'd transmitted and received, though Marconi found them "too erratic and unreliable" and eventually designed his own detector. Armed with this new equipment, he carried out systematic experiments into how the height of an antenna affected the distance over which he could transmit a signal[116]

From these inauspicious beginnings, the science of antennas has delivered a wide range of sizes, shapes, electrical designs, radiating patterns and amazing miniature, as well as large scale array, antenna systems. For you, the student, you would be well advised to consider focusing your engineering interests, talents and study to antenna design and applications. The future will require antennas to challenge conventional thinking at the same levels the miniaturization of cellphones, as well as large scale array systems and the incredibly difficult Iridium™ antennas, presented in past challenges.

From simple half or quarter wave dipoles and omni-pattern antennas (fig 1 below), to enormous collectors like the SETI (Search for Extraterrestrial Intelligence) dish at Stanford University (fig 2 below) to the Very Large Array System in New Mexico (fig 3 below) – a group of rail-mounted large collecting dishes focused on deep space designed to work together to deliver images to the central computer that stitches together all the data files collected into one coherent image, to extremely low frequency (ELF) "long wire" troposcatter and moon reflector antenna systems (fig 4 below), to multiple designs (one of many) for GPS receivers (fig 5 below), to the panel antennas we see on cellular towers and smaller PCS antennas (fig 6 below) as well as antennas mounted on light standards facilitating (fig 7 below) 5G networks – the possibilities for a satisfying career in antenna engineering are exciting. The following images are included to motivate you to consider this field of engineering as a career opportunity.

---

[114] https://www.explainthatstuff.com/antennas.html
[115] Ibid
[116] https://www.explainthatstuff.com/antennas.html

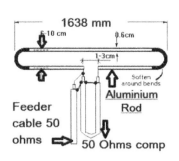  

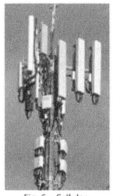  

Fig: 6 – Cellular Panel Antennas Fig: 7 – 5G Light Standard SETI antenna Microwave Antenna Fig: 3 – Very Large Array

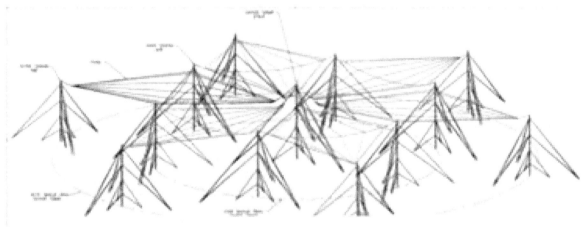

Fig: 4 – ELF Long Wire Antenna

Fig: 5 - GPS

Gallium Arsenide (GaAs) for Antennas

As an aspiring engineering student likely hoping to participate in an exciting new frontier, the following information is intended to provide insight into a fun-filled future of technical challenges. Opportunities in space requiring new discoveries to maintain and control spacecraft, robot rovers, and eventually continual contact with space travelers will require new discoveries in antenna design, materials, installation, *etc*.

While the layman may not be familiar with GaAs (Gallium Arsenide), it has been used to build solar cells for over four decades. That is because the chemical and physical properties of GaAs make it the undisputed choice for high-efficiency solar cells. For this reason, the space program has used GaAs solar cells for over 25 years, starting with the Mir space station and continuing to this day, with virtually every space bound vehicle incorporating GaAs solar cells. These types of cells are also used in terrestrial solar concentrating systems because of their ability to efficiently convert the sun's energy into electricity.

GaAs has the ability to deliver the highest energy conversion efficiencies, which is a measure of how much of the sun's energy is converted to electricity. In fact, all of the world records for high-efficiency solar cells are held by some form of a GaAs solar cell. The unique properties of GaAs that lead to high efficiency include a direct band gap for efficient conversion of photons to electron–hole pairs. It turns out that the best GaAs solar cells operate very much like an LED, being almost equally capable of converting electricity to light as they are of converting light to electricity.

Under real-world conditions, where changing levels of illumination and temperature are common, GaAs is a true standout compared to other materials. GaAs operates near its full efficiency at levels of illumination that are only one tenth of a sun, a level where most semiconductor materials have long since stopped operating as efficient solar cells. GaAs also has a temperature coefficient that is a mere one fifth of silicon and only one third of CIGS (Copper Indium Gallium Selenide) or CdTe (Cadmium Teluride). That means that at high temperature, GaAs continues to deliver energy at near its rated output, while the energy output of a silicon cell declines by 30% or more. The advantages of GaAs as a material for solar cell applications as discussed thus far can be summarized in the following manner.

1. *Low temperature coefficient*: the temperature coefficient is a measure of performance (efficiency) loss versus temperature relative to 25°C. Most widely used solar materials, such as Si, lose a lot of efficiency when the temperature rises. GaAs, however, has a low temperature coefficient and thus experiences very little efficiency loss at higher temperatures.

2. *Good low-light performance*: In most solar cells, the energy available in weak illumination (low light) leaks away, but this does not happen in the case of high quality GaAs. The wide bandgap and low-defect crystal structure of GaAs solar cells also results in a lower leakage current and more rapid voltage buildup with illumination. Additionally, the wider bandgap of GaAs also means it is much better tuned to the wavelengths of LED and fluorescent light, relative to silicon. This is important because GaAs solar cells can therefore be used in an office or warehouse environment to generate power.

3. *High efficiency*: GaAs is the highest efficiency solar material currently available. This means it produces more power for a given surface area than any other solar technology. This is very important when surface area is limited, such as on an aircraft, cars, or on small satellites. For example, triple junction GaAs solar is 37%+ efficient while silicon solar is around 21% efficient at best.

4. *Excellent UV radiation and moisture resistance*: GaAs is inherently resistant to damage from moisture, radiation, and ultraviolet light. These properties make GaAs an excellent choice for aerospace applications where there is increased UV and other forms of potentially harmful and detrimental radiation.

5. *Flexible and lightweight*: GaAs solar is highly efficient even when very thin layers are used, which keeps overall solar material weight low. Alta Devices™ uses a thin GaAs layer placed on a thin flexible substrate to maintain its light weight and flexible properties. Si is not as good an absorber of sunlight, so a relatively thick layer is required, making it very brittle and heavier. Rigid brittle glass is usually placed on top of the silicon, which further increases weight.

One of the major problems with GaAs is that the material itself is expensive. However, it is possible to grow extremely thin layers of GaAs that use just miniscule amounts of material, keeping the cost down. At the same time, these thin layers of semiconductor material actually get more efficient as they become thinner.

The opposite is true for most other solar cell technologies. And a side benefit of these thin cells is that they are completely flexible and can be incorporated into any of today's commercially available encapsulating materials. Even better, the flexible nature of these cells opens up the potential for a whole new generation of innovation in solar cells from factors that can dramatically reduce the cost of solar electricity.[117]

We will delve deeper into the Iridium cellular satellite system later; however, the GaAs-based antennas delivering wireless telephone (voice and data) coverage to every square mile of surface space on earth are operating beyond all performance and life expectancy specifications predicted. The following is an excerpt from *Creating Iridium*[118] by Durrell Hillis, Team Leader of Iridium. [Presented here with permission by the publisher, Vesuvius Publishing, Phoenix, AZ]

"One of the biggest challenges on the program was the development and production of the Main Mission Antenna for the Iridium satellite to provide the communications link with Iridium handsets on the surface of the earth."[119]

"It required state-of-the-art small modules that both transmit and receive signals from an Iridium handset by projecting 'beams' onto the earth. The technical challenge was to shape the beams so there would be complete coverage of the earth from the 66 satellites. The power efficiency of the modules was also critical due to the power limitations on the satellite. Use of a special semiconductor material, (gallium arsenide) was needed to meet those difficult requirements and Raytheon™ happened to be one of the few antenna suppliers in the country that had its own gallium arsenide factory."[120]

"With its extensive experience developing sophisticated antenna systems for DOD, (for the Patriot missile for example), Raytheon was the clear choice to join the Iridium team, but even they had never built an antenna that was this difficult."[121]

"There is nothing even now that does what Iridium does. There is still nothing that switches like this thing. That's pretty impressive, especially for something that was designed more than two decades ago—amazing."[122]

Assuming today's anticipated Mars missions are successful, where will we go from there? It's a sure bet that, regardless of beyond Mars missions, communications will be critical and engineers who understand GaAs technologies will likely be in high demand.

Does this interest you?

Nuts & Bolts

Radio Communications Equipment Shelters

In the early days of commercial two-way radio systems deployment, the most common practice for installing fixed (base station) equipment required a building to protect the radio equipment from the elements and vandalism. Eventually, the base station equipment manufacturers, as well as ancillary industry companies, produced weatherproof "outdoor" cabinets; however, regardless of technological progress, indeed because of technological progress, equipment shelters became a central issue for radio system (cellular/PCS) network operators to consider in their deployment budgets.

Radio equipment shelters in rural areas were often ramshackle affairs, poorly constructed and often less effective than they needed to be; thus, the term "radio shack" became popular jargon. While this term reflected the condition of many single purpose shelters providing electricity from the grid, access to telephone lines, a stable platform, usually space for more than one (often many) base stations and their ancillary companions (battery banks with uninterruptible power supply equipment, filters, duplexers, diplexers, *etc.*), some degree of lightning protection (very ineffective in the early years) and access to coaxial cable connecting antennas

---

[117] https://www.sciencedirect.com/topics/materials-science/gallium-arsenide
[118] *Creating Iridium – How a Remarkable Team Made Space History*; Durrell Hillis; Copyright © March 10, 2016; Vesuvius Press, 4806 S 40th St., Phoenix, AZ 85040.
[119] Ibid
[120] Ibid
[121] Ibid; pp109
[122] Ibid; pp111

mounted on accompanying towers to the fixed RF equipment, the term "radio shack" often also referred to the technicians' shops where they kept tools, test equipment and supplies and a bench for repairing and maintaining customer equipment. Additionally, the term was picked up by Tandy Corp™, and the retail chain of Radio Shack™ stores became a household term.

As common carrier networks began to replace privately owned and licensed two-way systems, protecting the equipment became a significant opportunity for manufacturers of ready-made fixed equipment buildings with advanced lightning protection "halo" systems with heavy duty grounding pre-installed as well as more reliable weather protection, back-up power generators, climate control to maintain constant temperature and humidity, microwave cable driers, ample room for ancillary equipment, access controls requiring pre-authorized access only, cable (ladder) racks to facilitate accurate and effective wiring maintenance and/or repair and aesthetically pleasing exterior treatment also serving as advanced protection of the interior from vandals with rifles as well as other means of damaging or destroying valuable electronic equipment.

The shelter manufacturing industry became a significant factor in advanced network deployment. While the compounds you see constructed to facilitate access security of cell sites generally featuring one or more towers are rapidly replacing shelters because radio equipment down-sizing and miniaturizing encourage less expensive mounting frames accommodating weather-proof cabinets, "pre-fab" buildings continue to be in demand.

The most common pre-manufactured shelters feature exterior concrete walls with a variety of finishes.

As you can easily imagine, shelters constructed in place, rather than pre-manufactured, represent a wide variety of sizes, shapes, materials, appearances and supporting facilities. Just take a minute to imagine effective protection on very high mountain sites, extremely cold or hot conditions like Alaska or the rain forests, deserts with high winds and blowing sand, swamps, salt saturated humidity of coastal areas, *etc*.

Rule: **All legally installed operating commercial 2-way radio systems require a "CP," (Construction Permit) requiring an FCC license which requires frequency coordination by a "Frequency Coordinator" before the license is granted.**

Shelter manufacturers require engineers.

Chapter Fifteen -- Let's Talk Radio

Simplex – Push To Talk, Release To Listen

T1R1 = Transmit frequency – Receive the same frequency

Example: Transmit: 43.08MHz – Receive: 43.08MHz – Co-ordinated by SIRSA

Inside the house in Diagram A is a base station with a transmitter, receiver, speaker and microphone. A coaxial cable is connected to the base station on one end and to the antenna mounted on the tower at the other end.

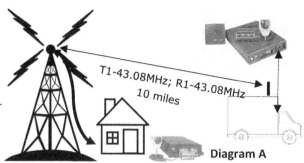
Diagram A

The truck has a radio mounted behind the driver's seat. This radio (transceiver) is connected to the truck's electrical system and an antenna mounted on the top of the truck.

When the dispatcher presses the PTT (push-to-talk) button on the microphone and speaks into it, the radio transmits the speech. The modulated signal travels up the cable to the antenna which radiates frequency 43.08MHz. The receiver in the truck recognizes the incoming RF signal and the speaker in the truck delivers the dispatcher's voice message.

Inside the truck, to respond to the dispatcher's message, a person takes the microphone 'off hook,' pushes the PTT button "keying" the mobile radio's transmitter which generates the same frequency it received on the incoming signal. The operator of the mobile speaks into the microphone and the mobile radio, which is physically connected *via* coaxial cable to the antenna mounted on the top of the truck, transmits the modulated signal to the antenna which radiates at the same frequency, 43.08MHz, sending the message from the truck back to the antenna on the tower. The message is carried down the cable from the antenna to the receiver in the fixed *base station* in the dispatcher's office. Inside the radio, the information carried by the RF is stripped from the carrier, sent to the speaker where it vibrates a cone resonating at human hearing frequencies and the dispatcher hears the truck operator's response to the original message.

Diagram B

Diagram B, portable-to-portable, presents a simpler "simplex" application than the above base to mobile requiring a high antenna to achieve greater coverage; however, portable to portable in this graphic is the same simplex principle – both radios transmit and receive the same frequency and require push to talk, release to listen.

In the mobile system above, two (or more) vehicles appointed with radios featuring the same transmit and receive frequencies are equipped to communicate directly as long as they are within radio range of each other. However, in the case of multiple portables or mobiles, only one may transmit at a time. Two or more radios transmitting simultaneously will create interference preventing successful reception by any other radio(s) within range operating on that same frequency.

Keep in mind, "simplex," identifies only the process when a single frequency is in effect. Frequencies in all three bands, HF, VHF and UHF, are available for employment in simplex systems. It is the simplest two-way "E&M" example we will address – believe it or not, "E&M" is as officially recognized in wireless telecom jargon as "POTS" is in telephony. "E&M" simply means, "ear-and-mouth." "POTS" is the abbreviation for "plain old telephone service."

In addition to the simplex system above described, there are many different configurations of land mobile radio systems. We will limit our study of legacy two-way systems to simplex and to the privately licensed system design allowing the most users to use a set of frequencies to enjoy the greatest base-to-mobile – mobile-to-mobile system at the least expense, *i.e.*, a community repeater with associated mobiles/portables.

It does not require a technical degree to understand the economics driving this design. Imagine the investment required to own or lease a parcel of land large enough to accommodate a tower tall enough to justify its investment by providing radio coverage to a wide enough area to be of value. For example, in any large city where businesses were managed more efficiently by the use of radio communications, a limited number of tall buildings ideally located in the center of the city allowed building managers to charge fees for the use of their building's roof as an antenna site. A common alternative was adopted by radio communications companies, particularly those whose business involved the sale of radio products, to solve this problem by erecting towers in strategic areas. For the customers of these radio sales organizations large enough to purchase and maintain their own fixed base station equipment, space on the towers high enough to deliver radio coverage required by the installation of base stations and their related ancillary equipment. These "shelters" or "radio shacks" were specially designed for this purpose with weather proof protected ports through which coaxial cable attached to the radio equipment (base stations) to be attached to tower legs or cable ladders on the tower facilitating attachment to the antenna(s) at the top (or elsewhere on the tower) were installed. Additionally, lightning suppression was often provided as well as security.

Community Repeater (LMRS) Land Mobile Radio System

A community repeater relieves the licensee of expenses associated with the land, tower, base station equipment and ancillaries while allowing him to enjoy the benefits of wide area coverage for a two-way radio communications system. In lieu of purchasing the base station and leasing space on a building or tower, he takes advantage of base station (community repeater) equipment the company from whom he is purchasing his mobile radios and fixed dispatch equipment provides under a leasing contract – usually a monthly charge assessed on a per mobile basis.

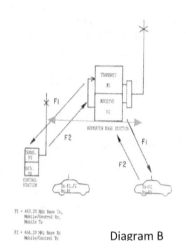
Diagram B

While there are several technical issues we could address here, understanding the basics of a single mobile or hand-held portable utilizing two frequencies is all we need to consider for understanding how today's radio technologies, commonly referred to in a universally vague context of "cellular," are fundamentally an extension of legacy two-way radio frequency theory and application.

Study Diagram B. Note the transmitter and receiver in the "repeater" are hard-wired together. Also, note in Diagram B, the remote control station, often referred to as a 'dispatcher,' is connected to the base station with either a leased phone line or an RF link and that, if it is by RF, the remote control station is configured with the same set of transmit and receive frequencies as the mobiles.

It is easy to confuse the difference between the dispatcher's communications with the mobiles using the leased line or RF to access the repeater with 'mobile-to-mobile' direct communications. We refer to the 'mobile-to-mobile' in a repeater system like the one presented in Diagram C as 'talk-around' because, if communications is direct car-to-car, the mobiles are not dependent on the repeater.

Utilizing the community repeater, the dispatcher and mobiles of different companies enjoy wide area coverage by sharing frequency pairs requiring FCC licenses for each

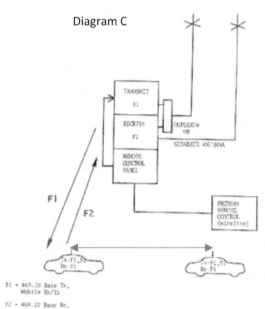
Diagram C

company's control stations and mobiles as well as being licensed to use the community repeater. However, squelch "decks" assigned to each different company prevent voice traffic from annoying their RF neighbors sharing the repeater. This translates to requiring each company's mobile operators, as well as dispatchers, to monitor the channel before keying their transmitters. These "decks" are a function of "squelch" (see below) utilizing unique analog tones or digital codes that allow designated radios to unmute for passing audio to the speaker. In this way, each customer's radio with its unique squelch tone/code reduces annoying audio meant only for one customer to be heard by others on the same frequencies until they manually monitor the channel by taking the microphone "off hook" or pressing the monitor feature on the microphone.

Community repeaters are equipped with one set of two frequencies separated by enough bandwidth (in diagram B it is 5MHz) to prevent one frequency from interfering with the other. Ex: Downlink transmit: 463.20; Uplink: 468.20

Keeping in mind the repeater's two channels are hard-wired avoiding any opportunity for either frequency to interfere with the other while receiving a signal from the remote control (dispatch) radio or from a mobile. The received signal is sent *via* the wired connection to the transmitter for simultaneously re-transmitting; thus, 468.20 and simultaneously transmitting that received signal on frequency 463.20 delivering the message from the sending radio to the receiving radios.

Why is it important to understand this concept if we are pursuing the whys and hows of advanced "cellular" phone network technologies?

Answer: The issue is *space diversity* to prevent interference by the same frequencies operating in the same network. Pre-cellular, as in these examples, required significant bandwidth to provide buffer zones – a waste of spectrum - as well as radio equipment with the sole purpose of dealing with the physics problem. Solving this problem with a cellular concept was not easy nor was it inexpensive. Understanding the issue as 1) a legacy technological issue, 2) FCC regulatory challenge and 3) business problem enhances the student's ability to contemplate advanced methods for resolving these issues.

Bandwidth and Squelch

From what we've studied about radio thus far, by now you, the student, should be having some of your own thoughts and questions about a few things we have not yet touched upon. For instance, in our presentation of the simplex system operating on frequency 43.08MHz, do we assume this is the only two-way radio system licensed to operate on that frequency in the area surrounding it?

Are we caught in a limited world of one circuit-one call on a telephone line or a single frequency with two (or more) radios capturing it exclusively until they somehow abandon it making it available for another user?

If a conversation is occurring on the simplex channel, 43.08MHz, can anyone with radios on that same frequency eavesdrop? Does every radio receiver tuned to 43.08MHz in the surrounding area respond to the same transmissions on that frequency forcing everybody to listen? Ponder these questions and draw your own conclusions.

Squelch

In telecommunications, *Continuous Tone-Coded Squelch System or CTCSS,* is a circuit that is used to reduce the annoyance of listening to other users on a shared two-way radio communications channel. It is sometimes referred to as tone squelch. It does this by adding a low frequency audio tone to the voice. Where more than one group of users is on the same radio frequency (called *co-channel users*), CTCSS circuitry mutes those users who are using a different CTCSS tone or no CTCSS. It is sometimes incorrectly referred to as a sub-channel because no additional channels are created. All users with different CTCSS tones on the same channel are still transmitting on the identical radio frequency, and, if transmitted simultaneously, their transmissions interfere with each other; however, the interference is masked under most (but not all) conditions. The CTCSS feature also does not offer any security.

A receiver with just a carrier or noise squelch unmutes for any sufficiently strong signal; in CTCSS mode, it unmutes only when the signal also carries the correct sub-audible audio tone. The tones are not actually below the range of human hearing, but are poorly reproduced by most communications-grade speakers and, in any event, are usually filtered out before being sent to the speaker or headphone. CTCSS can be regarded as a form of in-band signaling.[123]

Digital-Coded Squelch

CTCSS is an analog system. A later Digital-Coded Squelch (DCS) system was developed by Motorola under the trademarked name Digital Private Line (DPL)™. General Electric responded with the same system under the name of Digital Channel Guard (DCG)™. The generic name is CDCSS (Continuous Digital-Coded Squelch System).

The use of digital squelch on a channel that has existing tone squelch users precludes the use of the 131.8 and 136.5Hz tones as the digital bit rate is 134.4 bits per second and the decoders set to those two tones will sense an intermittent signal (referred to in the two-way radio field as "falsing" the decoder).[124]

Harnessing the electromagnetic spectrum represents one of the greatest technological leaps in human history. So many luxuries and necessities, products, services, and systems we take for granted are all, in some way, linked to electromagnetic technologies – more specifically, to those which make use of the RF spectrum. But, as anyone who works in the industry knows, the first order of business when designing a new product or system is to determine what part of RF spectrum will be the best fit for the application.

Radio Coverage or "Range"

How far can two radios be from each other before they can no longer communicate? It's all about ERP (Effective Radiated Power). To make this topic a little easier to study, allow me to relate an event that actually happened during the time this author was a two-way radio salesman.

The year was 1973. I was in an auditorium with about 800 other sales people listening to several speakers introduce the latest in two-way radio equipment they insisted was so much better than any our competitors had in their catalogs and we were all drinking their Kool-Aid™.

The year before this conference, the manufacturer I represented had constructed a 1,000' radio tower south of Dallas to support a large number of base station and community repeater antenna systems. At three different levels of the tower, platforms were constructed allowing fixed equipment to reside closer to the antennas than they could be if they were installed in a radio shack on the ground. This is an effective way of reducing signal loss otherwise created by excessively long cable and associated connectors.

At the conference, we heard the following announcement: "Our next speaker will introduce you to a technology promising to deliver greater coverage and greater capacity by using lower power and lower towers. It will be called cellular and it is the radio communications of the future."

What?! We had been loading a 1000' tower at a furious pace and this guy says it will be replaced with a technology that uses lower power and lower antennas? NO WAY! IMPOSSIBLE! It was all we could do to stay seated and listen to such nonsense!

The speaker came on and immediately projected a strange looking honeycomb design onto the big screen: "This is a cellular radio network concept," he proclaimed. "Designed by Bell Labs, they have called it AMPS – Advanced Mobile Phone Service – and, by re-using the same frequency several times in the same geographic coverage area and, by handing off the mobile as it moves across the area from one cell to another, it promises to handle more traffic from more customers than current mobile telephone systems will ever provide."

We were all stunned.

Now, almost fifty years later, we take it for granted; of course, a cellular frequency re-use network with a computer managing the traffic, what's the big deal?

Well, for one thing, coverage is a big deal. Because we now take it for granted that our phones enjoy coverage anywhere and everywhere, it may be difficult to understand why coverage in legacy two-way was such a barrier for customers to overcome.

---

[123] https://en.wikipedia.org/wiki/Continuous_Tone-Coded_Squelch_System
[124] Ibid

Even with a 1000' tower and 100W mobiles, reliable radio communications were limited to a radius from the tower of less than fifty miles. Someone may say something akin to: "Hey, with special high gain antennas that deliver coverage by varying radiation patterns, this fifty-mile radius could extend another 25 miles."

OK, under certain circumstances, different antenna patterns do increase coverage but nothing close to cellular networks no matter how high the antenna may be mounted on a terrestrially fixed tower.

Let's look at the way legacy two-way systems were designed for maximum coverage.

Effective Radiated Power

ERP, the amount of power actually radiated from the antenna is rarely the same power generated by the transmitter; so, what is it?

Legacy two-way radio guys refer to the "link budget" when discussing the gain (or more often loss) in determining ERP or anticipated range of operation for two-way radio communications. In our anecdote above, we recognized platforms on the 1000' tower and noted this was an effective way for the base station to be in closer proximity to the antenna than it would be if was installed at ground level requiring coaxial cable to connect the fixed equipment on the ground to the antenna on the tower. Fundamentally, closer proximity equals less loss created by cable length (also size, *i.e.*, 7/8' diameter, 1.5/8" diameter, *etc.*) as well as less cable to pay for. Additionally, the link budget had to consider loss from ancillary equipment such as diplexers, duplexers, cavity filters, *etc.*, connectors, jumper cables (usually .5" connecting the larger coax to the antenna) and the antenna's designed gain.

The most common error made by the unschooled is this unchanged fact: Coverage is a function of the mobile or portable radio's ability to talk BACK to its associated fixed station. This is no less true in cellular than it is with legacy commercial two-way radio, military, and any other two-way radio system. Thus, higher power mobiles or portables with gain antennas were as critical to achieving maximum reliable and clear communications as the base station. It is also imperative to keep in mind that free space loss and interference are the greatest factors in two-way radio system coverage.

Without delving too deeply into the technicalities of ERP and associated antenna patterns, suffice it to say the ERP issue in cellular networks, while fundamentally as critical as it ever was in legacy two-way, has been addressed very differently and the link budgets are calculated differently in advanced digital technologies. System or network balance is a much greater issue now and attempting to address it here exceeds the scope of this text.

It is enough for you to know that ERP is measured in decibels. It is affected by as many interruptions in a continuous train of waveguide required to deliver maximum signal strength from the transmitter and to the receiver as there are disparate elements affecting its delivery, *e.g.*, ancillary base station equipment, connectors, coaxial cable, more connectors, jumpers, more connectors and finally the antenna or antennas.

Just FYI, while most coaxial cable is manufactured with a center "conductor," this is technically a misnomer. RF is not conducted within a conductive medium like electricity. In the truest sense of the word, RF is "guided" along the surface of the conductor usually sandwiched between insulation and the center conductor. Yes, it's a trivial point but you need to know there is a difference between "conduction" and "wave guiding."

Bandwidth

The electromagnetic spectrum is classified into different segments based on the frequency of signals in those ranges. Signals with a frequency between 3 kHz and 300 GHz are considered to be within the RF spectrum.

The RF spectrum is utilized by governments, military forces, broadcasting companies, and private individuals alike. But, when too many people are all using the same frequency ranges for different things, it creates interference and poor performance.

To deal with these problems, regulatory bodies like the Federal Communications Commission (FCC) began partitioning the RF spectrum, designating certain frequency ranges for specific uses by the public and private sectors. The most widely used frequencies are those that fall somewhere between 25MHz and 6GHz because they offer a well-rounded series of advantages in terms of transmission range, ability to support high rates of data, antenna size and associated costs.

Bandwidth allocation has simplified the matter of determining which part of the spectrum is ideal for a given application because it's not just a matter of engineering, it is also about complying with the law. Countries which are members of the International Telecommunications Union (ITU) have their own regulatory bodies which allocate spectrum bandwidth for different applications. In the United States, the FCC oversees private sector use of the RF spectrum, while a lesser-known body called the National Telecommunications and Information Administration (NTIA) handles frequencies reserved for military and government use.

Of course, even with all these agencies, interference can still happen, and so, every three years, different nations send representatives to the World Radio Communications Conference (WARC) to resolve disputes over bandwidth allocation and other issues pertaining to the use of the RF spectrum.

Let's say you are an RF engineer working in the United States looking at a radio spectrum chart. It may first seem like it's simply a matter of following the chart to determine which frequency range your design should be operating in. Well, for a long time, it *was* pretty simple. Today? Not so much...

The Challenges of Interference in a Crowded RF Spectrum

With the rapid growth of new technologies and industries, especially mobile phones, the RF spectrum has become increasingly crowded. The challenge currently facing RF engineers is that we're simply running out of available bandwidth. New technologies like 5G and the *Internet of Things* (IoT) will require even more bandwidth.

One solution to this has been to expand the use of higher frequencies in the RF spectrum.

New developments have allowed companies and governments to make much greater use of the millimeter wave (3-30 GHz) and the Extremely High Frequency (EHF) ranges (30-300 GHz). In addition to new consumer goods, these advances are also enabling the next generation Electronic Warfare (EW) systems, space-based Wi-Fi and other SATCOM applications, and much more.[125]

Baseband bandwidth.

In this diagram, the bandwidth equals the upper frequency.

Bandwidth is the difference between the upper and lower frequencies in a continuous band of frequencies. It is typically measured in hertz, and depending on context, may specifically refer to *passband bandwidth* or *baseband bandwidth*.

Passband bandwidth is the difference between the upper and lower cutoff frequencies of, for example, a bandpass filter, a communication channel, or signal spectrum.

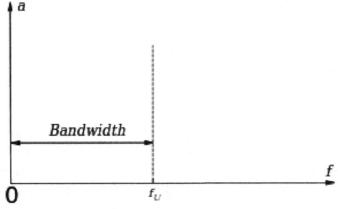

---

[125] Ibid

Bandwidth in hertz is a central concept in many fields, including electronics, information theory digital communications, radio communications, signal processing, and spectroscopy. It is one of the determinants of the capacity of a given communication channel.

A key characteristic of bandwidth is that any band of a given width can carry the same amount of information, regardless of where that band is located in the frequency spectrum. For example, a 3kHz band can carry a telephone conversation whether that band is at baseband (as in a POTS telephone line) or modulated to some higher frequency.[126]

RF Bandwidth *vs* Data Rate as a Function of Modulation

RF bandwidth and data rate are related by the modulation format. Different modulation formats will require different bandwidths for the same data rate. For FM modulation, the bandwidth is approximately 2*(df + fm) where df is the maximum frequency deviation and fm is the frequency of the message. FSK is basically FM where the message signal is a square wave. The highest frequency component of a binary bit sequence transmitted serially occurs when the sequence is 01010101. This component is one half of the bit rate. So for FSK, the bandwidth is approximately Δf + r where Δf is the separation

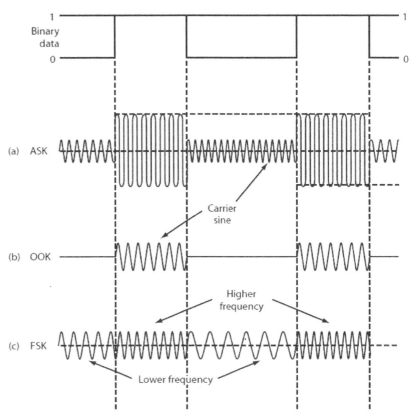

1. Three basic digital modulation formats are still very popular with low-data-rate short-range wireless applications: amplitude shift keying (a), on-off keying (b), and frequency shift keying (c). These waveforms are coherent as the binary state change occurs at carrier zero crossing points.

between the two frequencies and r is the bit rate. The reason this is bigger than Δf is because, whenever the frequency is changed, extra frequency components are generated. Switching between frequencies more often (higher data rate) results in more power in these extra frequency components. Now, these can be filtered out to some extent, but if you filter more of them than Δf + r, the result will be too distorted to reliably extract the original bit stream.[127]

Think about it this way: a pure sinewave consumes zero bandwidth, but it also contains zero information. As soon as you start changing a characteristic of a pure sinewave (frequency, phase, amplitude, *etc*.) its bandwidth must increase accordingly. In the case of amplitude modulation, modulating the amplitude of a sinewave of frequency *fc* at frequency *fm* will result in a signal with components at *fc*, *fc+fm*, and *fc-fm*. If the message contains components all the way down to DC, then the resulting modulated signal will have twice the bandwidth of the message signal. FSK is basically transmitting two AM signals at the same time on different frequencies, so the bandwidth will naturally be increased by the separation of these two carrier frequencies.[128]

For FSK, the bit rate and the symbol rate are the same. But for higher order modulations like QPSK and QAM, each transmitted symbol can code for more than one bit so the bit rate can be significantly higher than the symbol rate. This means that the required transmit bandwidth is less than what would be required for AM or

---

[126] https://en.wikipedia.org/wiki/Bandwidth_(signal_processing)
[127] https://electronics.stackexchange.com/questions/92237/rf-bandwidth-vs-data-rate-modulation
[128] Ibid

FSK. QPSK and QAM have higher spectral efficiency. However, QPSK and QAM are more susceptible to noise and distortion and therefore require a relatively higher SNR (signal-to-noise ratio).[129]

Also, for FSK, you want the two frequencies to be integer multiples of the data rate. This will result in an integer number of cycles in each bit period so that the carrier always ends up at the same level on data bit transitions. This probably won't be done at RF, though. Generally the FSK signal would be generated at an intermediate frequency which would then be mixed up to the actual RF carrier frequency.[130]

System/network capacity drives telecom engineers to utilize or otherwise invent technologies to maximize available bandwidth. Predicting traffic demand by measuring it in *erlangs*, is a fundamental tool in maximizing spectrum efficiencies.

An erlang is the unit of measure for traffic density in a telecommunications system or network and it is widely used for measuring load and efficiency.[131]

For our purposes, the following information regarding digital modulation standards and the implications of bandwidth will suffice until we address cellular system topologies in subsequent chapters.

Rule of thumb regarding channel bandwidth:

- Land Mobile Radio Service = 25kHz
- Narrow band LMRS = 12.5kHz
- AMPS (analog cellular) = 30kHz
- TDMA/GSM = 200kHz÷8=25kHz
- GSM-850 uses 824 - 849 MHz to send information from the Mobile Station to the Base Transceiver Station (uplink) and 869 - 894 MHz for the other direction (downlink). Channel numbers 128 to 251.
- CDMA = 1.25MHz

Here's an axiom that will serve you well: advanced communications are the result of modulation and signaling technologies applied to radio frequencies selectively carved from the radio spectrum. While electro-mechanically generating a specific frequency the FCC has licensed for commercial use is no small modern techno-logical miracle, the RF itself, a naturally occurring element of the electromagnetic spectrum, is not the discipline from which advanced wireless telecommunications have evolved. Imposing information on specific frequencies or bands by modulation technologies allowing radio to deliver information wirelessly is the greater achievement.

There is a great deal more to understand about how today's advanced telecommunications has employed TDMA/GSM, CDMA, HSPA and others to cost-effectively and bandwidth efficiently deliver the capacities required by 21st Century wireless services market demand. We will not pursue it further at this time but we will delve into it in greater depth a little later. Until then, understanding the difference between circuit switching and packet switching will be our immediate focus.

Standards – Open, Proprietary, *De Facto, Du Jour*

NOVEMBER 18, 2014|Carl Henning[132]

I'm a fan of open standards like PROFINET and PROFIBUS. But there are other kinds of standards out there. Here's a continuum of standards from proprietary to open to too open… and in between.

Open Standards

Wikipedia definition: "An open standard is a standard that is publicly available and has various rights to use associated with it, and may also have various properties of how it was designed (*e.g.* open process). There is

---

[129] Ibid
[130] Ibid
[131] https://www.electronics-notes.com/articles/connectivity/erlang/what-is-an-erlang-formula.php
[132] https://us.profinet.com/open-standards-proprietary-standards/

no single definition and interpretations vary with usage." They also provide 20 additional definitions! That proves their "no single definition" point.

PROFINET fits this definition. The specification is available to everyone for purchase from IEC (International Electro-technical Commission). There are no further barriers to anyone developing a product just from the spec. The specification was created, and has evolved, in PI Working Groups. Many PI members participated in that work. PI membership is not required to develop a PROFINET product, although I certainly encourage it! PI members who have their product certified are entitled to use the PROFINET logo.[133]

Perhaps a better example of the difference between an 'open' standard and a 'proprietary' standard is to consider Apple and Microsoft. Apple's proprietary operating system requires any application developer whose interests require an Apple device to pay a license fee.

Windows™, Microsoft's 'open' standard, is shared with any application developer at no charge. Thus, we see many different manufacturers of computer devices utilizing the Windows 'open' standard but Apple, and only Apple, producing and distributing Apple Computers.

Proprietary (Closed) Standards

Proprietary standards have been around a long time – DH+ for example. A proprietary standard is owned by one company and they exercise sole discretion as to who may use it and under what terms (and at what cost). There are probably many current examples. What about Emerson's Charms? Is that a proprietary fieldbus? EtherCAT™ is a definite example of a proprietary fieldbus. It is owned by one company – Beckhoff. They retain ownership and have opted to make it available to everyone with only a small royalty to Beckhoff for every node.[134]

Too Open Standards

How can a standard be "too open"? It can be so open that there is no assurance that devices will interoperate. Modbus™ is a good example here. It just moves bits and bytes that can represent anything you want them to. Many companies adopted their own rules for how the data should be arranged. Remember Enron Modbus™? Special IO Servers had to be created to allow the user to modify packets, swap bytes, and other gyrations when unique data arrangements were encountered.[135]

In Between Standards

What do you call a standard that you can buy from IEC, but you have to sign a contract to develop a product? I've called it an "in between" standard – kind of open, kind of closed. EtherNet/IP™ falls into this category.[136]

In its infancy, cellular networks worked well because AT&T & Bell Labs made AMPS an "open source" for design, operation and for the manufacturing of compatible mobile telephones.[137]

The analog platform of original AMPS utilized 40MHz of spectrum divided equally between two carriers per market (we will address this in depth a little later). Three years following its introduction, demand prompted the FCC to open an additional 10MHz in the same band it had held in reserve. This resulted in enough spectrum to equally divide 50MHz between two carriers per market.

As it compared to legacy pre-cellular mobile telephone networks, there were three primary issues cellular AMPS employed earlier systems could not deliver: 1) frequency re-use within the same geographic area; 2) individual call hand-off when the moving mobile created inadequate signal strength requiring hand-off to another channel in an adjacent "cell," 3) universal roaming.

Despite the competition between two licensed carriers per market, the phones were compatible with either network. While this created political and business problems, it did, nevertheless, promote sharing and "net

---

[133] Ibid
[134] https://us.profinet.com/open-standards-proprietary-standards/d
[135] Ibid
[136] Ibid
[137] Ibid

revenue" settlement as competitive networks provided service for any 'roaming' customer; this process became known as "in collect," and "out collect." As rural cellular networks came on line, this practice accelerated the popularity of wireless communication more than any other single issue.[138]

Advanced Mobile Phone Service (AMPS™) Standard

Advanced Mobile Phone Service (AMPS) is [was] a standard system for analog signal cellular telephone service in the United States and is also used in other countries. It is based on the initial radio spectrum allocated for cellular service by the Federal Communications Commission (FCC) in 1970.[139]

Commercially introduced by AT&T in 1983, AMPS became the most widely deployed cellular system in the United States.

AMPS is designed for frequency ranges within the 800 and 900 Megahertz (MHz) spectrum. Each service provider can use half of the 824-849 MHz range for **receiving** signals from cellular phones and half the 869-894 MHz range for **transmitting** to cellular phones. The bands are divided into 30kHz sub-bands, called *channels*. The receiving channels are called *reverse channels* and the sending channels are called *forward channels*. The division of the spectrum into sub-band channels is achieved by using frequency division multiple access (FDMA).

The signals received from a transmitter cover an area called a cell. As a user moves out of the cell's area into an adjacent cell, he is switched to a new cell's channel. The signals in the adjacent cell are sent and received on different channels than the previous cell's signals so the signals don't interfere with each other.[140]

The introduction of digital to cellular, coupled with voice demand never anticipated by early AMPS designers, followed by data applications, made AMPS obsolete. Thus, TDMA (GSM), CDMA, 3G, 4G, 4GLTE and 5G prevail.

From its earliest recorded reference in 1946 to 1985, only the most forward thinking insiders thought mobile telephone service would ever facilitate anything but voice communications. As a matter of historical fact, as late as 1994, many carrier executives facing market demands for "data over cellular" were still insisting: "voice will always be king."

However, in 1984, an audaciously presumptuous start-up modem company in Dallas, Texas, Spectrum Cellular™, introduced a cellular modem with three patented features: 1) the ability to fool the switch into thinking a hand-off had not occurred until the connection was re-secured solidly enough to maintain a data connection; 2) forward error correction for packets delivered on AMPS cellular networks; 3) dynamic packet sizing on circuit switched cellular channels.

The difference between data packets carried over "circuits" and packets delivered on a "packet switched" network is like automobiles carried piggyback on railroad flat cars [circuit switched] and automobiles carrying passengers being delivered to their final destination by cars on highways [packet switched].

From the late 1980's through the mid-nineties, competition for wireless delivery of non-verbal (data) raged. Of the many proposed solutions, only cellular represented the ubiquitous coverage demanded by the market.

---

[138] Ibid
[139] https://searchmobilecomputing.techtarget.com/definition/Advanced-Mobile-Phone-Service
[140] Ibid

Radio-based Packet Data Service/Platform Providers

	Cellular Data, Inc.	ARDIS	RAM Mobile Data	SMRs EX.: Cvrg. Plus
Major Sponsor	Venture Capital	IBM/Motorola	RAM/Ericsson/BellSouth	Motorola
Stage of Development	Field Test Completed by GTEMC in Houston Published Acceptance	Mature--15 years	Licensed in 1989, Systems Under Construction in Major Cities	1 Year of Commercial Applications On Line
Svc. Areas & Coverage	4 cities by EOY '92 300 cities by EOY '95	400 systems in 50 states	<>10 cities in various stages of construction; Los Angeles announced as completed	<>400 systems (SMRs)
Potential Coverage	Same as Cellular Voice Coverage	Top 500 cities in U.S. Limited Rural & Highway Coverage	60 Major Cities Announced as Goal	U.S. & Canada
Current Subscribers	None	20,000	<>1000	Unknown
Channels Available	Up to 4,800 per CGSA (Cellular Geographic Service Area)	1-3	10-30	20
Subscriber Capacity	30 Million +	130-260 Million	250-500 Million	500,000-1,000,000
Services Limitations	Fixed & Mobile Urban & Rural	Fixed & Mobile Urban	Mobile Urban & Rural	Mobile Urban & Rural
Data Speed: Reference: Actual:	2400 bps 1200-1700 bps	(19.2 announced) 4800 bps 2400 bps	8000 bps 4,640 bps	4800 bps 2400 bps
Service Costs	Variable per Application; Examples: POS = $.035/xctn. Alarm = $15/mo. Field Sales = $.50/xctn	$.08/packet + $.04/100 character + $32/mo. minimum access	$15-30/mo. + $.03-.0125/packet	$35/vehicle/mo. + $.07/packet
CPE Costs	$125-500--varies as stand-alone or imbedded into application-specific platforms	$3300	Varies per platform with different vendors producing a wide variety of devices: estimated range: $1500-5000.	Varies per application-specific platform/system integrator: estimated range: $1500-5000.
Average Monthly Service Charges per Device	$46.00	$125.60	$102.50	$85.00
Current Applications	Point-of-Sale Alarm/Security Vending Machines Notebook Computers	Dispatch Field Sales & Svc. Public Safety Notebook Computers	Dispatch Public Safety Point-of-Sale	Dispatch Public Safety
Future Applications	Telemetry ATMs Auto. Vehicle Location Personal Services Consumer Services E-Mail Route Services Demand-side Load Mgmt. Public Safety	Dispatch Field Sales & Svc. Public Safety Notebook Computers	Dispatch Public Safety Point-of-Sale	Dispatch Public Safety

Sources: Datacomm Research Co., LaPose Associates, Dataquest, Mobile Data Report, Company Files

This chart contains descriptions of wireless companies competing for the wireless packet data market before the cellular companies' *"voice will always be king"* myopia recognized the magnitude of the opportunity.

Notably absent from this chart are: 1) Research In Motion's® Blackberry™ operating in the SMR bands with Mobitex™ architecture and 2) Metrocast™, a San Diego based company created to receive and forward alpha numeric paging. Both of these companies limited their offerings to message services and neither of them had a fraction of the ubiquity cellular networks represented. However, other than CDPD™ and CDI™, none of those listed in the chart had a fraction of the ubiquity of cellular.

Because in 21st Century wireless telecommunications we take for granted e-mail, texting, video, graphics, streaming, voice mail, social media and myriad apps PLUS voice communications – all delivered by cellular technologies – it is difficult for anyone who did not experience the early years of cellular to understand and appreciate the value and impact efforts by companies like those mentioned and listed in the chart had on the cellular network owner/operators. However, for those of us who spent entire careers in the wireless industry, both in pre-cellular legacy two-way businesses then abandoning that segment to participate in the advent and growth of cellular/PCS, we feel it is imperative that the real story be told accurately and objectively.

For instance, few people in today's wireless industry know that Quintron™, a small company founded in Quincy, Illinois, later purchased by Glenayre™, produced the first commercially viable VHF/UHF digital transmitters with the minimum stability required for transmitting digital codes (POCSAG) to digital receivers (pagers). Motorola's PURC transmitters appeared a full year after Quintron's equipment led the United States into the digital paging industry.

Optional PM-250C Power Monitor/Alarm Panel provides continuous measurement of forward or reflected power. Includes low power & high SWR alarm relays & front panel LED indicators.

Single tube, conduction cooled, conservatively designed power amplifier, continuous duty rated up to 300 Watts without fans or blowers.

Filter on output port insures low harmonic output.

Oversize power amplifier heatsink for cool reliable operation.

All solid state exciter is designed for easy access to all components. Convenient multiple test points and LED indicators simplify trouble-shooting and maintenance.

Rugged solid state driver for long trouble-free life.

Regulated filaments on final amplifier tube insures longest possible tube life.

All solid state power supply with large voltage and current safety factors. Built-in single function DC remote control with automatic high voltage reset.

performance specifications

Frequency Range: 148 to 174 MHz, Export. 150 to 160 MHz, U.S.
Channels: 1 Crystal controlled. For multiple channel, see bulletin on PMX-16 Programmable Master Oscillator
Output Impedance: 50 ohms, 1.5 SWR Max
Emission: 16F3, 15F2
Deviation: ±5kHz w/built-in limiter. (Also incorporates defeatable ALC amplifier on QT-7500)
Audio Input: 600 ohms, balanced, -25 to +15 dBm, adjustable. QT-7500 tone input 4.7 Kohms, unbalanced, 1.7V rms for 1kHz deviation. QT-7501 tone input, 5 Kohms, 0.5V to 5.8V rms for ±4.5 KHz deviation. Digital pulse width 0.33ms to 4.0ms max. Both have std. subtone inputs.
Audio Response: ±1dB of a 6dB/octave pre-emphasis curve, 300-3000Hz, or strappable to flat, ±1 dB.
Audio Distortion: 3% on QT-7500, 2% on QT-7501. At ⅔ deviation and 1000 Hz.
Spurious & Harmonics: -85dB
Sideband Noise: QT-7500 adjacent channel: -85dB, -105dB optional. At ±90kHz or more: -95dB, -109dB optional. Measured in a 15kHz band width. (See Note 1.) QT-7501 adjacent channel: -80dB.
Turn-on Time: 10 milliseconds, max.
Duty Cycle: continuous at full power.
Power Requirements: 107-128 Volts, 60Hz, single phase. 220 Volts and 50Hz optional.

Model Number	Power Out (Watts)	Frequency Stability	Line Current @120V		F.C.C. Type Designation	D.O.C. Type Approval No.
			Standby	Full Power		
QT-7500	50-300	±0.0002% or ±0.000005%	1.0A	6.0A	QT-7500	237 192 063C
QT-7501			1.2A	6.6A	BFL907QT-7501	237 192 085C

* Also available with multiple channel using PMX 16, add suffix -PMX to model and FCC type designation.
* For simulcasting, specify QT-7501 in systems where mixed with QT-6501, use QT-7500 where mixed with QT-6500.

mechanical specifications

Size: Less Cabinet: Overall, 19" rack width × 29¾" H, 17 Rack Units. Sub-units - RF Unit: 19" W × 6" D × 19¼" H; Spacer: 19" W × 1¾" H, Power Supply: 19" W × 15¼" D × 8⅝" H. QT-7501 exciter is 19" W × 8" D × 7"H.
Shipping Weight: Less Cabinet - 97 lbs. for QT-7500, 115 lbs. for QT-7501
All transmitters are complete with operating tube, technical manual, crystal oscillator and are tuned and tested to your operating power level and frequency. See cabinet bulletins for details on cabinet dimensions.
Notes: 1. -109dB is limit of measurement capability. Actual value should be considerably lower.

Specifications subject to change without notice.

NEC's line of digital pagers, marketed exclusively by National Marketing, Inc., seeded the market a year ahead of Motorola.

As we have reviewed the early history of radio-based (wireless) telecommunications and acknowledged that the first use of radio spectrum to carry information was, in its purest form, digital – or as many would argue, data – *i.e.*, dots and dashes representing intelligible information, a student beginning his or her career in telecommunications engineering or related physical science could be excused for wondering why the evolution of ubiquitous service did not always recognize and include "data" as a fundamentally sound commercially desirable element of early cellular networks and deliverables.

It is no less confounding to consider the lagging interest by cellular (particularly wireline "B" side) network operators in delivering data services as a natural deliverable equal to – or as is now recognized in the 21st Century superior to – voice as a source of revenues to be hotly pursued when the HAMS (amateur radio operators) had been demonstrating the utility and efficacy of wireless data communications and telemetry for decades.

We will review the cellular wireless packet data issue in greater detail later; however, reflecting on the risk aversion of B-Side wireless network management's acknowledging the market potential, unnecessarily delaying deployment almost ten years, prompts me to recognize those on the non-wireline A-Side whose wisdom and appreciation for innovative ideas produced early packet data delivery platforms. Beginning with the IBM team in Boca Raton led by Jim Robinson and Rob Wolf, invited by forward thinking Dane Ershin, MTSO switch manager at Cell One in Chicago, early experiments in imposing data packets on a channel where idle time is available (*channel sniffing*), produced the first cellular network packet-switched data deliverables. These experiments were successful enough to convince Nick Kauser, CTO of McCaw Cellular, to deploy it on a commercial basis. McCaw Cellular (Cellular One) announced wide area deployment and CDPD™ (Cellular Digital Packet Data) became the first large-scale packet switched commercial service delivered on cellular networks. Other key technologists associated with development and deployment of CDPD™ deserving mention include: Muhammad Ali, Advanced Technology engineer at Southwestern Bell, Bill Frezza, MIT engineer and RAM Mobile Data expert, Rob McHaley, McCaw, and Gary Brunt, Cell One – Washington, DC.

Chapter Sixteen -- Paging

Let's look at paging.

Why?

Well, if there was a pre-cellular ubiquitous communication technology in the United States, it was paging. However, while pagers (commonly referred to as "beepers") are still in use, in the pre-cellular world, they were indispensable to many different professionals and businesses as well as public safety (law enforcement, fire and EMS officers) medical professionals and realtors. Furthermore, digital RF was given a great boost by ubiquitous paging networks.

From earliest "single tone" systems, paging signaling evolved through several stages trying to squeeze more pagers into fixed channels with limited bandwidth. To pursue this line without boring you to death, we will review it through the anecdotal reflections of someone whose career included several years in the paging industry including the critical intersection where analog signal schemes were replaced by digital formats – primarily Golay® (Motorola's proprietary standard) and POCSAG® (a universal open standard – Post Office Code Standardization Advisory Group as a European standard) featured by NEC pagers distributed by National Marketing, Inc. For all practical purposes, these two companies, Motorola and NEC – Motorola about 80%, NEC <> 20% -- dominated the paging industry in its heyday prior to its demise resulting from cellular's debut.

Interview with Lee Horsman[141]

Paging, by definition, is the one-way transmission of signaling and message (numeric and/or alpha) information to pagers (beepers). The term, "two-way paging," is a misnomer. If the receiving device is equipped with a transmitter allowing it to respond to a paging signal, it is no longer a pager ... it is a two-way radio. Yes, two-way radios were capable of receiving paging alerts; however, a two-way radio is a two-way radio and a pager is a pager – they are two different devices – a one-way receiver is a pager. A two-way radio equipped to receive a paging signal is still a two-way radio.

Frequencies assigned by the FCC intended to be used as one-way RF transmission carriers are considered paging frequencies. With a few insignificant exceptions, these frequencies were transmitted by sophisticated paging systems with no facility (base station transmitters with receivers) for any response from a pager. The systems deployed to facilitate paging over extended coverage areas were the domain of the telephone companies and their competitors, the Radio Common Carriers. Private carrier paging systems, EMS and a few others enjoyed limited success but, for all practical purposes, the overwhelming dominance of paging service was delivered by the telcos and their competitors, the RCCs.

While the RF technologies for these wide area systems made ubiquitous service common and affordable, the signaling techniques were subject to more advanced technologies and were a harbinger of what would facilitate future cellular technologies. From extremely limited single tone encoders to advanced digital signaling, digital paging and associated simulcast technologies conclusively demonstrated the efficacy of digitized RF for large scale deployment of wireless networks preceding cellular to fully exploit available bandwidth.

Paging and pre-cellular mobile radiotelephone spectrum assigned by the FCC and identified as "common carrier" channels, was licensed to the telephone companies and their competitors, local companies whose businesses relied on selling, leasing or renting mobile telephones and pagers to their customers. The mobile devices (pagers and mobile phones) were supported by fixed network equipment requiring significant capital as well as technical management and maintenance.

The RCCs often also provided answering services creating an ideal combination of services to compete with the large telcos. This, of course, was prior to the advent of answering machines that evolved into "voice-store-and-forward" systems that ultimately became the ubiquitous voice messaging technologies we enjoy in this, the 21st Century.

---

[141] Interview with Lee Horsman, 37-year career in wireless telecommunications

A major factor in the evolution of paging from its analog legacy systems to the digital systems that increased the number of users per channel from a maximum of 1250 numeric pagers to a theoretical maximum of three million, was the advent of simulcast broadcasting coupled with rapidly developing computer technologies allowing paging terminals to manage the traffic as well as automatic customer billing and accounting records.

Simulcasting required digital RF transmitters with oscillating tolerances no less than five parts per million. This level of precision, achieved by a "simulcast controller," prevented corruption that would otherwise render useless the ability of pagers to respond to the POCSAG or Golay formatting. Fundamentally, what I'm describing is the ability of multiple transmitters to broadcast a paging code sequence simultaneously within five parts per million tolerances. Considering delays varying with distance as leased phone lines and microwave systems connected the transmitters to the terminal and simulcast controller, you (the student) should be able to imagine the difficulty in synchronizing as many as fifteen or twenty transmitters located in a large metropolitan area (Los Angeles, NYC, *etc.*) to reliably signal a single pager that would display a calling number on its LCD screen – one pager out of as many as several thousand.

I will digress here to emphasize a salient point I am convinced will be lost in the history of wireless telecommunications if I fail to address it.

In the 1940's, 50's, 60's and 70's, licensed mobile telephone service and paging services providers enjoyed lucrative businesses because there was a greater demand for personal communications by individuals whose needs could not be satisfied by purchasing, installing and maintaining their own privately owned and licensed two-way radio system just to have access to the PSTN (Public Switched Telephone Network) than existing licensed systems could support. Doctors, lawyers, real estate sales people, architects, and executives who needed wireless communications could not justify a privately licensed 2-way system; thus, the FCC set aside groups of frequencies in different spectrum for delivering wireless communications to this class of potential users they referred to as "common carriage" channels.

Yes, we've introduced this earlier; however, it is a significant issue if you, the student, are to understand why and how cellular evolved as it did. As much as RF technologies, the political and practical issues are no less critical to your appreciation for and understanding of the historical backdrop from which advanced cellular/PCS networks and their accompanying end-user devices have emerged.

In the 70's, we attempted to conduct sales training classes intended to produce knowledgeable sales people; thus, we simplified the technicalities as much as possible. For instance, one of our more common ways of explaining the need for "common carriage" was to ask: "How do the butcher, the baker and the candlestick maker use FCC licensed spectrum if all they need is one device that is accessed by a landline phone?" Of course this was a way to make the point that the benefits of wireless communications should be enjoyed by all; therefore, the FCC carved out spectrum to serve those who could not take advantage of privately licensed systems.

Demand exceeded bandwidth availability – particularly in early analog mobile telephone and paging networks.

Digital was an answer but, for mobile phones, digital alone was inadequate and the cellular concept, coupled with innovative genius applied to digital modulation, provided the solution.

However, had it not been for the radio shops in small town America who had the entrepreneurial motivation to build, service and market wireless mobile telephony and paging, even the cellular concept would have been dramatically slower in its advance across America.

The FCC was able to take advantage of this presence when it announced its "duopoly" strategy for each market then divided the fifty states into two categories: 1) MSA = 300-305 Metropolitan Statistical Areas; 2) RSA

= Rural Service Areas. The designated MSAs and RSAs would each be granted an equal amount of spectrum, at first 40MHz followed three years later with an additional 10MHz to be divided equally between two licensed operators, both of whom who were to deploy Bell Lab's Advanced Mobile Phone (AMPS) standards for the fixed plant – no exceptions!

Existing antenna support structures all across America, built and maintained by local companies as well as the mammoth telcos were in place. Engineers and FCC-licensed certified technicians were ready to install and maintain the cellular networks.

For all its foresight and success, this FCC strategy introduced many extremely thorny business issues as well as political and legal briar patches introducing a whole new level of opportunities for attorneys to complicate the process resulting in huge unnecessary expenses and construction delays.

You may have heard the phrase: "not in my back yard" or simply, "NIMBY?" Until the attorneys pointed out this *unfair invasion*, most cities, municipalities and small towns were eager to have a cell tower as close as possible for the obvious call quality it would deliver. Unfortunately, NIMBY became a small town moniker for extorting cash from cellular operators who passed on these expenses in their rate plans and the townspeople watched as towers were built farther away, costs escalated and attorneys prospered.

Back to paging,

The term "critical communication" has become the identifier for paging systems serving emergency service providers, particularly medical doctors, EMS personnel and other "critical" service providers whose need for absolute reliability in being wirelessly contacted can't rely on cellular. Paging continues to be the preferred technology for these specialized services. This is especially true in Small Town, USA where cellular coverage continues to suffer from inadequate fixed plant and volunteer fire fighters and EMS personnel require reliable communication alerts.

The following is an excerpt of an article published in *The Wireless Messaging News*™, a trade publication covering a variety of wireless services including current paging activity. The author of the article, Jim Nelson, CEO of Prism-IPX, LLC, is, in this author's opinion, the most experienced and knowledgeable expert on the history, technical engineering, equipment evolution, application and business impact of paging in the world today. A pioneer in paging, but, more specifically, digital and simulcast technologies, his opinions and expertise are rarely equaled. It is presented here with permission by the publisher of *The Wireless Messaging News*, Brad Dye, who co-authored the article.

The Wireless Messaging News©

Is Paging Going Away? By Jim Nelson, CEO, Prism-IPX, LLC

September 23, 2016; Issue 725 -- Reprint[142]

In the spirit of the 2016 Presidential campaign it is time for someone to speak up about the status of paging use without regard for being politically correct. As a veteran of the paging industry for nearly 50 years I feel qualified to present the facts.

For many years I have heard people say that Paging is going away and being replaced by smartphones but that simply is not true. Paging systems continue to be sold and new pagers put into service every month. Paging is still being used along with cellphones for many reasons. It is true many people try using cellphones for messaging and for non-crucial messaging and it might satisfy them — until they miss an important message. Many that have experienced a serious cellphone service outage due to terrorist acts, natural disasters or other emergencies are using paging again as it has been proven over and over again that Paging works.

---

[142] https://www.google.com/search?rlz=1C1CHZL_enUS725US725&sxsrf=ALeKk038V64wnOEtvjJ3_O4dupINZtt-nag%3A1585271747828&ei=w1N9XumBMsSO9PwP6OuZ4AY&q=Wireless+Messaging+News+Is+Paging+Going+Away&oq=Wireless+Messaging+News+Is+Paging+Going+Away&gs_lcp=CgZwc3ktYWIQAzIFCCEQqwIyBQghEKsCMgUIIRCrAjoECCMQJzoICCEQFhAdEB46BQghEKA-BUL_5AljqmQNgiKcDaABwAHgAgAGAAYgB_Q-SAQQxNi42mAEAoAEBqgEHZ3dzLXdpcGeg&sclient=psy-ab&ved=0ahUKEwip75q7vbnoAh-VEB50JHeh1BmwQ4dUDCAs&uact=5

For professionals, especially those involved in providing critical services, a missed message can mean life or death. The very reasons why paging was created still exist today, *i.e.,* fast, dependable notification with short messages on a device that is not cluttered with games and has an unmistakable sound that signifies importance.

In a recent study sponsored by (read PAID FOR) TigerText and utilizing research conducted by HIMSS Analytics and other industry research, an attempt was made to discredit paging use by claiming it is too expensive. The study surveyed 200 hospitals and discovered that 90% of these organizations still use pagers. Now considering there are 5,627 registered hospitals in the US, if this percentage holds true then 5064.3 of them use paging. Does that sound like paging is going away?

The article states their research surveyed 200 users with results clearly intended to minimize the value of paging and makes me wonder why HIMSS chose to support one vendor (TigerText) over the entire paging community which ALSO attends, markets and exhibits at HIMSS conferences! Doesn't it make you wonder if favorable research results are for sale?

There is no argument that smartphones are very useful and convenient for general messaging and searching for information. That use is far different from the role pagers play in critical messaging. And if you are going to use a mobile app on your smartphone wouldn't it make sense to use one that the professional messaging (Paging) companies designed? Several paging service providers offer mobile phone apps for text messaging. Many of their apps have all the considerations for what makes messaging reliable and worthy of consideration.

Many people today, including those in the medical community, have never used a pager and have no incentive to do so until they have an unfortunate experience caused by service outages or system failures which is almost inevitable during severe weather or cell-site outages.

In spite of the evidence, the debates will continue so here are some points that must be considered.

Who uses pagers? Doctors, nurses, E911 first responders, firefighters, police, energy producer's emergency response teams, energy distribution systems, industrial alarm monitoring systems, to name a few.

Many critical communications systems for Public Safety, Fire Brigades and First Responders around the world use pagers because they know they work and can be depended on.

Recent articles claim that about 85 percent of hospitals still rely on pagers. (Doesn't that make a statement about how valuable they are?)

In a recent article a doctor stated he has used a pager for urgent messages every day for nearly 20 years and it is still the most dependable messaging device today.

In spite of their claims, reporters and mobile app vendors have no idea of how many pagers are used today. The limited surveys that are cited in published articles are anti-Paging and almost always written as advertisement for a mobile app vendor. (That is not professional journalism.)

Some articles claim pager users receive so many pages they cannot do their work effectively. That is not the fault of the pager. If you used a phone you still could not answer all the calls.

Many mobile text messaging application vendors are self-promoting their products with no concern for immediate patient care.

Many mobile text messaging application vendors try to convince hospital administrators and CIOs[1] to replace pagers by citing cost and efficiency of phones over pagers. This is very debatable but even if that were true is "user convenience" more important than fast, dependable patient care? (If your answer is yes I'm not coming to your hospital!)

Pagers still fill a need that cellphone and smartphone technologies fail to address adequately.

Transmission of critical or emergency messages must be reliable, yet cellular and Wi-Fi networks are often disabled due to catastrophes, natural disasters or even technical problems.

Data breaches put patient information at risk. For example, over 90% of US hospitals experienced a data breach in 2012 and 75% of hospitals are not sufficiently securing devices with patient data. Dealing with these

HIPAA violations is very expensive. Paging systems can provide complete security for message data transport and encryption on the pagers."[143] End Article

Here is a golden opportunity to alert you, the student, to a basic technical issue related to coverage or range of RF service. From its earliest days, the radio manufacturers emphasized the importance of managing coverage expectations of their two-way radio service customers by calculating range as a function of "talk back," the ability of a mobile radio to "talk back" to its companion fixed (base) station. It is no secret that a high gain antenna mounted on a high fixed structure with a high power transmitter (25-110W), high gain antenna, enjoying AC power from the grid (as opposed to a battery) can deliver an RF-carried signal great distances. Of course these coverage parameters are impacted by the specific radio frequencies with lower bands reaching farther than higher bands but modulation is also a variable affecting range. Regardless, for a fixed station to transmit high power from an antenna mounted on a high structure to a mobile many miles away is relatively easy; however, for a low power (.8-110W) mobile or hand-held radio with a limited antenna moving across a coverage area to reliably "talk back" to the base station is a miraculous achievement and it is this aspect of paging that is most responsible for the reliability difference between paging networks and all other RF networks – but especially cellular and PCS. It is also why signal strength indicators ("bars") on cellphones rarely deliver reliable indications of service quality. Receiving "five bars" of signal strength has very little influence on the ability of the cellphone to make equally strong contact with the cell site delivering the indicated signal strength on the phone.

This is also a good time to repeat our earlier reference to *link budget*, a legacy technical term referring to calculations for determining how much signal loss is introduced into a system by various components – antennas, connectors, cable, and ancillary equipment like duplexers, diplexers, filters, *etc*.

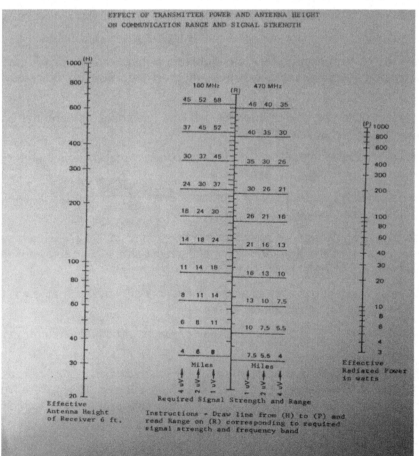

There is no enemy equal to energy dissipation (*free space loss*) for its deleterious impact on the quality of a radio signal as it is transmitted and received. *Free space loss* is the chief component in the link budget determining the distance a mobile may be from the base station receiver to enjoy reliable communication. Following free space loss, RF delivered to an antenna requires cables, connectors and ancillary equipment all contributing to the reduction of reliable communication between the base station (cell site) and the mobiles/portables it is serving. Thus, the science for coverage calculations is a critical discipline in all commercial and military RF communications networks designs.

A basic term associated with coverage potential is "ERP" (Effective Ra-

---

[143] http://www.braddye.com/paging_english.html; Brad Dye Publisher: *The Wireless Messaging News*; *Wireless News Aggregation*; Friday, Sept. 23, 2016; Issue #725 – Reprint; Nelson, Jim: *Is Paging Going Away?*

diated Power). This term refers to the amount of power radiated from the antenna. As a rule of thumb, in legacy two-way radio, mobile telephony and paging systems, the higher the antenna with respect to the surrounding terrain, the greater the coverage. ERP of the base station and, reciprocally, the base station's ability to receive weaker signals from its mobiles, is proportional to the square of antenna height. If antenna height is doubled, the ERP is quadrupled. If antenna height is tripled, ERP is multiplied nine times. This accounts for the familiar sight of antennas mounted on the tallest buildings and mountains for VHF and UHF mobile radio and paging systems.

The graphic image above is a *nomograph.* Using it, we may understand the respective range differences between mobile units and base stations of varying power ratings and associated tower heights.

The scale on the left side of the nomograph represents the effective antenna height above average terrain. It may generally be assumed that a one hundred foot tower located on average terrain will have an effective antenna height of one hundred feet above average terrain. If this same one hundred foot tower was installed on the top of a three hundred foot hill or building, the effective antenna height would be four hundred feet.

On the nomograph, the center scale is used to denote varying degrees of received signal strength. The fact that a receiver is capable of ¼-microvolt sensitivity, affected by RF noise, interference, attenuation, *etc.*, impacts the otherwise assumed ¼-microvolt sensitivity feature. In general practice, a 1-microvolt signal is considered to be the lowest useable signal in high band (150-175MHz) and UHF (450-512MHz). Under normal (this is a difficult measurement definition to rationalize) conditions, a 2-microvolt signal would be about what you could expect for a good voice quality signal acceptable to the average user of communications equipment. In areas of severe intermodulation interference, random RF noise, *etc.*, a signal of 4-microvolts would be required.

The scale on the right side is the ERP in watts. This could be used on the mobiles or base station. Let's assume we wish to make a system calculation utilizing a 30-foot tower and 45-watt VHF mobiles and a 45-watt base station transmitter. If this design included a 5.8db omnidirectional antenna and low loss transmission line, it could be assumed the ERP would be about 180 watts. Conversely, the mobile would be heard at the station just as if it were a 180-watt mobile simply because of the base station antenna gain.

To determine the predicted range, you would draw a line from the 30 mark on Scale H (left side of nomograph) to the 180 mark on Scale P on the right side. You would then refer to the center scale at the point where the line crosses. In this example, a predicted range of approximately 13.5 miles is indicated for VHF assuming a 2-microvolt received signal.

If we replace the 5.8db gain antenna with a unity gain, the station power is not multiplied which produces an ERP of only 45 watts. To calculate the range, we draw a straight line between the 30 mark on Scale H to 45 on Scale P. By referring to the center scale, we note the range is reduced to about eleven miles.

Now let's suppose the 45 watt mobiles are replaced with 5 watt portables. The reception range will remain at eleven miles because we haven't changed anything at the receiver. However, the ERP drops to 5 watts. Talk back range is now reduced to less than seven miles.

The nomograph graphically shows the benefits of high power, tower height and antenna gain.

Important "take-away!" The variable with the greatest impact on coverage (range) is tower height! An additional one hundred feet of base station antenna height added to the original system increases range to over twenty-one miles. More expensive, one hundred watt mobiles increases range to a mere sixteen miles.

Another important fact: Coverage calculated as a function of ERP with the above described techniques does not equate to coverage engineering techniques for cellular networks. While ERP is an important factor in cellular network quality of service (QOS) design, it is only one of many included in very sophisticated "system balance" metrics.

As noted earlier, paging systems were not impacted by the limited ability of mobiles to talk back to the fixed station antenna; thus, ERP from the transmitter(s) is singularly primary in range calculations. Paging systems in hospitals, large hotels, office buildings, warehouses, manufacturing plants and rural areas were more reliable for critical communications because portable receivers inside buildings, and far from the fixed station, did not rely on a transmitter to talk back to the base station. It does not require a great deal of imagination to understand why a limited power transmitter in a portable radio has more difficulty talking out of a building or complex than a high power base station equipped with a high gain antenna has talking into the same building or complex.

In legacy 2-way radio systems, and to a slightly lesser degree since the introduction of fiber optic cable, radio systems typically required coaxial cable to connect the radios to their companion antennas/antenna systems. Inherent in this design, was the "impedance" properties of the cable affecting the amount of RF generated by the transmitter compared to the strength of the original transmission compared to the strength of that same signal received by the antenna after traveling the length of the cable and negotiating the resistance properties of various elements introduced along the way – connectors, jumpers, splitters, amplifiers, duplexers, diplexers, cavity filters, *etc.* The science involved in engineering systems to take maximum advantage of the various elements to produce the best results was primarily the responsibility of those companies who manufactured and distributed coaxial cable, connectors, antennas and the various components listed above.

Studying and understanding the terms listed below will be of great value to you.

Attenuation

In a general sense, the word, attenuation, simply means weakening or diminution; however, in its application to radio engineering, it means the loss of signal measured against its original transmission usually resulting from free space, transmission line properties affected by interrupting factors along the length of the cable from the radio transmitter to the RF energy radiated from the associated antenna(s).

In physics, **attenuation** or, in some contexts, **extinction,** is the gradual loss of flux intensity through a medium. For instance, dark glasses attenuate sunlight, lead attenuates X-rays, and water and air attenuate both light and sound at variable attenuation rates.

Hearing protectors help reduce acoustic flux from flowing into the ears. This phenomenon is called acoustic attenuation and is measured in decibels (dBs).

In electrical engineering and telecommunications, attenuation affects the propagation of waves and signals in electrical circuits, in optical fibers, and in air. Electrical attenuators and optical attenuators are commonly manufactured components in this field.[144]

Coaxial and general RF cables

Attenuation in a coaxial cable is a function of the materials and the construction. The most common coaxial cable is manufactured to a precise 50 ohm impedance specification. Some are 75 ohm.

Andrew Corporation (now Commscope™) designed, manufactured and delivered innovative and essential equipment and solutions for the global communications infrastructure market.[145]

In the early days of commercial two-way radio, "Doc" Andrew founded Andrew Corporation, a coaxial cable company dedicated to manufacturing and marketing high quality transmission cable and associated hardware.

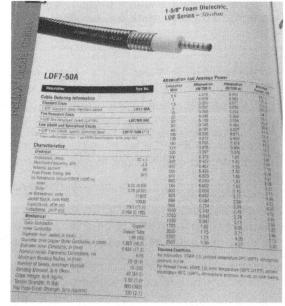

---

[144] https://en.wikipedia.org/wiki/Attenuation
[145] https://www.commscope.com/NewsCenter/PressReleases/CommScope-to-Acquire-Andrew-for-$2-6-Billion/

For many years, (1947-2007) Andrew Corp. set the standard for coaxial cable and pioneered many advanced products to serve the radio industry – broadcast, land mobile, TV, microwave and others. The following information as well as the photo and specification page shown here are lifted from **Catalog 38**©, Andrew Corp's. catalog published before they were acquired by Commscope™. There is no other source for this information more precisely articulated and reliable than this. In its day, it was considered the sacred book of errorless instruction for engineers and field technicians designing, installing and maintaining radio systems of all types. No published document was more treasured or carefully protected by those whose careers depended on the best information for designing and maintaining antenna transmission systems than this catalog. The internet has not replaced this catalog for its instantly available, comprehensive, succinct, reliable information regarding antenna transmission design. The following excerpts from the catalog published in 2000 are presented here to help you, a budding engineer, understand the issues to be addressed when selecting transmission system components is the task. We will address antennas in more detail later in this text.

Andrew Corporation; Orland Park, Il; Catalog 38

"HELIAX™ is the Andrew brand name that stands for the most complete, cost effective, high performance coaxial cable systems in the world."

"For more than forty years, Andrew Corporation has led the industry in meeting the need for semi-flexible RF transmission line. In land mobile, broadcast, cellular, military, terrestrial microwave, HF, earth station, personal communication, and many other applications, HELIAX™ coaxial cable products, including **air and foam dielectric** cable, are the industry standard of excellence. The unique feature that makes HELIAX™ coaxial cable the best in the world is a solid copper, corrugated outer conductor which gives it strength, durability, flexibility and complete shielding. These outstanding coaxial cables are complemented by our compatible connectors, hangers, grounding systems and other installation accessories to form a complete RF transmission line system. This broad range of coaxial cable and cable products means that Andrew can provide the right fit for any application you may have from a single component to a complete integrated cable system. It also means that all of your transmission line needs can be met by just one vendor—Andrew."

"When you purchase HELIAX™ coaxial cable from Andrew, you're buying more than just cable. You're buying quality and performance that will save you money over the life of your system investment. You receive:

- Outstanding Electrical Performance
- Long Service Life
- Simplified System Planning
- Lower Installation Costs
- ISO 9001 Certified"

"Here's a closer look at the benefits:

"Outstanding Electrical Performance"

"HELIAX™ coaxial cable, connectors and accessories are designed to provide optimum electrical performance for a wide range of RF applications. You can be certain that HELIAX™ coaxial cable systems will perform as you expect—no surprises."

"HELIAX™ connectors are designed exclusively for use with HELIAX™ coaxial cables to provide excellent electrical performance for the complete transmission line system."

Low Attenuation

"The low attenuation of HELIAX™ coaxial cable results in highly efficient signal transfer which maximizes overall system performance."

"Complete Shielding"

"Because HELIAX™ cable has a solid copper outer conductor, you get continuous RFI/EMI shielding to minimize interference and maximize system security."

"Low VSWR"

"HELIAX™ feeder cables. LDF4-LDF7 and VXL series cables now feature a maximum VSWR of 1.13:1 in the cellular and PCS bands. This specification applies to bulk length cable and includes straight DIN or N-Type connectors."

"Also available are lower VSWR options, or low VSWR in other frequency bands. Refer to the low VSWR specifications tables for each cable type."

"Excellent Intermodulation Performance"

"The solid inner and outer conductors of HELIAX™ cable virtually eliminate intermodulation generation. Connectors minimize intermodulation by ensuring high contact pressure at the connector to cable interface."

"High Power Rating"

"The low attenuation and excellent heat transfer properties of HELIAX™ cables combined with temperature stabilized dielectric materials result in safe long term operation at the high average power levels often required for broadcast, military and other applications."

"Long Service Life"

"When it comes to reliability, HELIAX™ coaxial cables have built-in quality features to protect your investment and provide long term cost effective performance. Service and maintenance costs are avoided because HELIAX™ cable systems are designed to last."

"All HELIAX™ coaxial cables are jacketed for direct burial or for corrosive environmental conditions. Standard jacketing material is weather-resistant polyethylene suitable for use in extreme climates. Operational fire retardant CATVX , CATVR, and CATVP rated jacketed cables are available to meet safety regulations for indoor installations. The fire retardant cables are UV stabilized and do not require additional UV protection during outdoor storage. [See Page 631 for information on cable and connector temperature ratings.]"

"Strong and Flexible"

"HELIAX™ cable's solid copper, corrugated outer conductor gives it great strength, durability and flexibility. This assures long life as well as ease of installation."

"Weatherproof and Durable"

"HELIAX™ cable's standard black polyethylene jacketing is weatherproof and ultraviolet stabilized making it suitable for outdoor applications. HELIAX™ cable is directly buriable and highly resistant to crushing. It is exceptionally corrosion resistant helping to provide a long term, trouble-free, cable system. Many users have been in operation for more than twenty years with the same HELIAX™ cable."

"Reliable"

"The availability of HELIAX™ cable in long continuous lengths eliminates the need for joints which can affect reliability."

"Simplified System Planning"

"Selecting a HELIAX™ cable system will make system planning easy and cost-effective. With Andrew, you have the advantage of our outstanding engineering resources and comprehensive product line. Look at the system planning benefits you receive when you purchase HELIAX™ coaxial cable:

One-stop shopping – with Andrew one-stop shopping, all of your transmission line needs-- quality cable, connectors, accessories and service – are available from one vendor. You avoid the problems of delivery delays, out of sequence deliveries, and non-compliant materials which are frequently the result of dealing with multiple vendors. At Andrew, all of our cable components are engineered to work together as a HELIAX™ cable system."

"Fast Delivery"

"Product delivery is critical when you have a weather emergency or last minute design change that could result in down time and lost revenue. In such situations, we respond quickly to get you on the air. Rapid product availability allows Andrew to be a real problem solver for you at installation time. With schedules to meet, you need to avoid delivery delays, contain costs, and get your system operating on time. With HELIAX™ coaxial cable, from Andrew, you can do it."

"Large Variety Of Sizes And Types"

"The wide variety of HELIAX™ cable sizes and types lets you select the best cable for your application allowing more cost effective planning. Optional fire-retardant non-halogenated jacketing is available to meet safety regulations for indoor installations."

"Factory Connector Attachment"

"For your convenience, HELIAX™ cables can be ordered cut to length and factory fitted with connectors per your specifications. This service helps you avoid field assembly and testing."

"Free Software and Product Information"

"To help plan your system, Andrew provides a number of software packages. In addition, you can obtain 'Installation Instruction Bulletins,' 'Special Publications,' and 'Product Specifications,' *via* Fax-On-Demand and the Andrew web site."

"Snap-Clean™ Foam Dielectric"

"Snap-Clean Foam Dielectric™ sets a new standard for quick, easy connector installation. With a simple twist, the foam dielectric snaps free of the inner conductor, leaving the solid inner conductor ready for connector attachment with no foam or adhesive residue. Additional cleaning and scraping of the cable are not required. This saves time, money and results in superior electrical performance of the cable and connector. 'Snap-Clean™' is featured on HELIAX™ foam cables with a solid inner conductor."

"Lower Installation Costs"

"The HELIAX™ cable product line helps lower your field installation costs."

"Long Continuous Lengths"

"This simplifies installation and eliminates the costs of splicing. Cable lengths can be conveniently stocked on site and cut to required lengths."

"Flexibility"

"HELIAX™ cable's corrugated copper outer conductor gives it flexibility which makes shipping, handling and installation easier and more cost-effective than rigid line."

"Ease Of Connector Attachment"

"Connectors for HELIAX™ coaxial cable can be easily attached in the field with standard hand tools. HELIAX™ connectors provide high resistance to connector 'pull-off' and 'twist off' as well as excellent electrical contact."

"Whatever your transmission line needs may be, HELIAX™ coaxial cables, connectors and accessories made exclusively by Andrew consistently provide you with outstanding electrical performance, long service life, simplified system planning, and lower installation costs."

"ISO 9001 Certified"

"ISO 9001 is the internationally recognized standard for quality systems. It was designed to provide a thorough yet flexible model for quality system design and implementation. Andrew facilities have successfully completed the requirements of ISO 9001, the most stringent portion of the standard. This certification resulted from a consistent quality system that involves everyone in the organization in improving both internal and external quality."

CommScope™, Inc. (NYSE: CTV –www.commscope.com) is a world leader in infrastructure solutions for communication networks. Through its SYSTIMAX® Solutions™ and Uniprise® Solutions brands, CommScope is the global leader in structured cabling systems for business enterprise applications. It is also the world's largest manufacturer of coaxial cable for Hybrid Fiber Coaxial applications and one of the leading North American providers of environmentally secure cabinets for DSL and FTTN applications. Backed by strong research and development, CommScope™ combines technical expertise and proprietary technology with global manufacturing capability to provide customers with high-performance wired or wireless cabling solutions.[146]

Standing Wave Ratio (SWR) – Voltage Standing Wave Ratio (VSWR often referred to as [viz-war]

In telecommunications, standing wave ratio (SWR) is a measure of impedance matching of loads to the characteristic impedance of a transmission line or waveguide. Impedance mismatches result in standing waves along the transmission line, and SWR is defined as the ratio of the partial standing wave's amplitude at an *antinode* (maximum) to the amplitude at a node (minimum) along the line.

The SWR is usually thought of in terms of the maximum and minimum AC voltages along the transmission line, thus called the voltage standing wave ratio or VSWR (sometimes pronounced "vizwar"). For example, the VSWR value 1.2:1 denotes an AC voltage due to standing waves along the transmission line reaching a peak value 1.2 times that of the minimum AC voltage along that line. The SWR can as well be defined as the ratio of the maximum amplitude to minimum amplitude of the transmission line's currents, electric field strength, or the magnetic field strength. Neglecting transmission line loss, these ratios are identical.

The power standing wave ratio (PSWR) is defined as the square of the VSWR, however, this deprecated terminology has no physical relation to actual powers involved in transmission.

SWR is usually measured using a dedicated instrument called an SWR meter. Since SWR is a measure of the load impedance relative to the characteristic impedance of the transmission line in use (which together determine the reflection coefficient), a given SWR meter can only interpret the impedance it sees in terms of SWR if it has been designed for that particular characteristic impedance. In practice most transmission lines used in these applications are coaxial cables with an impedance of either 50 or 75 ohms, so most SWR meters correspond to one of these.

Checking the SWR is a standard procedure in a radio station. Although the same information could be obtained by measuring the load's impedance with an impedance analyzer (or "impedance bridge"), the SWR meter is simpler and more robust for this purpose. By measuring the magnitude of the impedance mismatch at the transmitter output it reveals problems due to either the antenna or the transmission line.[147]

Ohm (Ω) – electrical resistance measurement

In 1861, Latimer Clark (1822–1898) and Sir Charles Bright (1832–1888) presented a paper at the British Association for the Advancement of Science meeting suggesting that standards for electrical units be established and suggesting names for these units derived from eminent philosophers, 'Ohma', 'Farad' and 'Volt'. The BAAS in 1861 appointed a committee including Maxwell and Thomson to report on standards of electrical resistance. Their objectives were to devise a unit that was of convenient size, part of a complete system for electrical measurements, coherent with the units for energy, stable, reproducible and based on the French metrical system. In the third report of the committee, 1864, the resistance unit is referred to as "B.A. unit, or Ohmad". By 1867 the unit is referred to as simply *ohm*.[148]

The standard unit of electrical resistance in the International System of Units (SI), formally defined to be the electrical resistance between two points of a conductor when a constant potential difference applied between these points produces in this conductor a current of one ampere. The resistance in ohms is numerically equal to the magnitude of the potential difference. *Symbol*: Ω[149]

Transmission Line – in radio systems, most commonly coaxial cable

Coaxial cable (see photos above)

Coaxial cable, or coax is a type of electrical cable that has an inner conductor surrounded by a tubular insulating layer, surrounded by a tubular conducting shield. Many coaxial cables also have an insulating outer sheath

---

[146] https://en.wikipedia.org/wiki/Standing.wave_ratio
[147] Ibid
[148] https://en.wikipedia.org/wiki/Ohm
[149] dictionary.com/browse/ohm

or jacket. The term coaxial comes from the inner conductor and the outer shield sharing a geometric axis. Coaxial cable was used in the first (1858) and following transatlantic cable installations, but its theory wasn't described until 1880 by English physicist, engineer, and mathematician Oliver Heaviside, who patented the design in that year (British patent No. 1,407).

Coaxial cable is a type of transmission line, used to carry high frequency electrical signals with low losses. It is used in such applications as telephone trunk lines, broadband internet networking cables, high speed computer data busses, carrying cable television signals, and connecting radio transmitters and receivers to their antennas. It differs from other shielded cables because the dimensions of the cable and connectors are controlled to give a precise, constant conductor spacing, which is needed for it to function efficiently as a transmission line.

Paging Encoders and Terminals

Single tone, two-tone sequential and 5-6 tone signaling schemes dominated paging technology prior to the advent of digital (POCSAG and Golay™). These analog modulation techniques limited the number of pagers per channel. Introducing voice on a paging channel further reduced the number of users any single channel could accommodate. Roughly, in the heyday of analog paging, a "tone only" paging channel could support about 1200 pagers. If a channel was dedicated to tone and voice paging, the 1200 was reduced to about 750. These limitations affected very few hospitals, clinics, hotels, airport terminals, high rise office buildings, manufacturing complexes, and others whose paging systems were privately licensed. However, to the telcos and RCCs whose businesses relied on paying customers, these limitations had a severe impact on the profitability of their businesses. Competition for channels was fierce and, until digital debuted, spectrum for paging was the highest priority of the business.

Early paging systems required manual encoding. Encoding equipment was primitive but effective. Following the first single tone encoders, second generation encoders featured two rows of buttons an operator had to depress to send two distinct tones carefully timed over the radio channel to activate reeds in a pager which would trigger a "beep" audible tone (or vibration) prompting the user to find a telephone from which to call a pre-determined home, office, client, *etc*. Automating this process became a high priority for paging service providers – particularly common carriers.

A machine to generate paging codes associated with an incoming call identified as a viable paying customer with a pager to be alerted was an imperative in the pre-cellular days when paging was the only reliable ubiquitous wireless service available.

The first integrated terminal, AMCOR's™ product, dominated the RCC/telco paging services market by coupling customer records to individual subscriber pagers. This allowed the RCC/telco operator to bill his customers for the time each subscriber unit utilized the RF channel assigned to his device. The following reference to the AMCOR™ terminal was lifted from the website noted below.

THE **PORTLAND RADIO GUIDE** HOME PAGE
©1995-2014 /FREQUENTLY ASKED QUESTIONS/ARCHIVE/CONTACT
http://archive.pdxradio.com/2009-14/topic/450-453-mhz/page/5;
archive2009-14.pdxradio.com; *Portland radio, the world & beyond*
ARCHIVE2009-14.PDXRADIO.COM»PORTLAND RADIO

"The original paging terminal (I guess we'd call it a server these days!) arrived in 1974. It was all TTL logic with no microprocessor and required a huge 20 amp linear power supply."

"Probably an AMCOR terminal. (Big brown and tan cabinet)"

"They had a core memory board in the back that had to be 18" x 18" that had a bazillion little ferrite beads "cores" on them. They had the schematics on blueprint size paper and Glen Day had put funny things into them that always made looking at them enjoyable. One that comes to mind was a side view of one of the cards and where the little lever at the top of the card was for removing it there were moose antlers instead of the lever!"

"That device was replaced in the early 80's with something that had SEVERAL microprocessors -- one on each board." Probably a BBL terminal. (big blue cabinet with a smoked plastic front door)"

"They were top of the line in their day. Ours had the paging terminal module, the voice storage module and the mobile telephone module. The voice storage module had four 14", 66 Mb Winchester hard drives that cost $33,000 each!"

"They were great terminals!"

"BBL stood for Bill, Bob and Lloyd. Those were the first names of the 3 guys that started the company!"

PSTN trunks were selectively distributed by the terminal to serve specific numbers assigned to the subscribers; thus, the terminal, equipped with banks of two-tone sequential and 5-6 tone generators could connect an account number with any number of pagers assigned to a customer and keep track of which pagers were signaled how many times during a billing cycle. This was a major breakthrough for high volume paging businesses. It also ushered in an era of competitive equipment companies vying for leadership in the arena. But, until digital RF and digital modulation standards were adopted, limited channel capacity and limited number of FCC-licensed channels did not justify the investment in computerized terminals.

With the advent of digital paging, Amcor, as well as Motorola's terminal products and Secode's paging signaling equipment were woefully inadequate. Single channels could now facilitate as many as three million pagers and the digital signaling codes, POCSAG and Golay™, required terminals capable of generating these (and a few minor others) on this scale. Additionally, the need for managing this number of incoming calls from the PSTN as well as customer records became the basis for large scale computerized terminals. New companies emerged to fill this need. Among them, Day, Glenayre, BBL (later purchased by Glenayre), Unipage (purchased by Motorola), Commterm (Canadian), Zetron, and a few others.

Voice messaging we take for granted today has a unique history with the paging industry playing a significant role. Paging terminals featured "store and forward" service allowing paging subscribers to respond to pages by retrieving stored voice messages. This was a major feature responsible for much of the demise of the answering service businesses. However, the overwhelming weight of the telcos once again produced the scale necessary to deliver voice mail to the masses when they integrated Octel's technology and products into the PSTN. See the history of voice mail and Octel™ below.

Also, recognizing the impact answering services had on the development of message delivery, storage and retrieval can't be over-emphasized. PSTN trunking theory and management by businesses other than the phone companies were early test beds for telephone services being extended by entrepreneurial interests.

Very large businesses were built to accommodate the demand for professional services' needs for remote messaging. Early punch board systems gave way to automation igniting invention of automatic recording machines. Early recorders featured reel-type tapes that quickly moved to smaller tape cassettes sparking residential voice recording encouraging the phone companies to invest in large banks of recorders allowing them to add voice messaging to their service offerings. Telco-based message services, with the investment resources of Ma Bell, resulted in digital switch-based messaging service on the scale we enjoy today.

Chapter Seventeen – The Invention of Voice Mail

http://www.everyvoicemail.com/vm-history.htm[150]

THE INVENTION OF VOICE MAIL

Voice mail was the brainchild of Gordon Mathews, a successful entrepreneur who held 35 US and foreign patents at the time of his death on February 23, 2002.

In the late seventies, Matthews began working on the technology that would eventually be called "voicemail." In 1979, Matthews took his technology and formed a company called VMX™, which stands for Voice Message Express™. He applied for a patent in 1979 to cover his voicemail invention and sold the first system to 3M. A few years later, in 1982, the patent for his invention was awarded. His "Voice Message Exchange" managed electronic messages in a digital format. (As a side note: Mathews' wife, Monika, recorded the first greeting on this first commercial voicemail.)

Matthews eventually left VMX in 1989. The company had hit rough financial waters and VMX was later sold to Octel Communications™, which in turn was purchased by Lucent Technologies™ and spun off into a new company called Avaya™. To this day [2020], there are companies that still use VMX systems to meet their voice mail needs.

Voice Mail for the Masses

For the first few years after voice mail had been introduced to the world, not many companies could take advantage of it. The proprietary VMX systems were very expensive and consequently voice mail was only available to the largest corporations. The playing field was leveled with the introduction of PC-based voice processing boards manufactured by companies like Dialogic Corporation™.

Dialogic Communications Corporation™ was founded in 1982 and quickly became an industry leading manufacturer of voice processing equipment. Their products allowed software developers to create voice mail software that would work on industry standard personal computers. This development significantly lowered the cost to manufacture a voice mail system and led to an explosive growth of voicemail.

Today, voice mail has become an integral part of operating a successful business. Companies large and small rely on voicemail to efficiently and effectively communicate with their customers.[151]

http://www.fundinguniverse.com/company-histories/octel-communications-corp-history/

Octel Communications Corp.™ was the leading manufacturer and provider of voice-mail products and services. The firm has grown enormously during its brief history as the voice-mail market has expanded dramatically.

Octel was founded by Robert Cohen, a product manager for a computerized instrumentation equipment company, and Peter Olson, an engineer. They met in 1981 when Cohen called Olson to fix a problem with a piece of electronic equipment that worked in the lab but not in the field. Cohen was so impressed with Olson's abilities that he suggested they start a company together.

The duo drew up a list of possible areas of specialization in the technology field and settled on voice mail because they thought it a good market niche. At the time, most voice-mail systems were made by giants like International Business Machines, whose products were large, expensive, and unpopular. Some smaller companies existed, but Olson and Cohen felt they were not geared toward dealing with businesses in a professional manner. Olson and Cohen designed a product to fit this niche. Their business plan called for a voice-mail machine that would cost $10,000 to make and $50,000 to sell. They wanted it to take up no more space than a closet and to be compatible with the top ten telephone systems then being used. Competing voice-mail systems generally worked only with the manufacturer's telephone system, and none worked with all 80 PBX systems on the market. So whereas AT&T could sell its voice-mail system only to businesses owning an AT&T phone system, the Octel system could be sold to anybody.

---

[150] http://www.everyvoicemail.com/vm-history.htm
[151] Ibid

With this business plan, Octel raised about $2 million in venture capital, effectively selling half of the company to various investors in the process. When finished, the firm's system took up as much room as a large suitcase and sold for $55,000. A competing system from IBM™ was the size of a small room and cost $250,000. Despite its small size, the Octel system was powerful; Olson had used advanced microprocessors made by Intel™ and Zilog™ and wired them to run in parallel.

After spending another $4 million, Octel had the system ready in early 1984. However, corporate purchasing departments usually took about a year to order new systems, a fact that was overlooked in Octel's business plan. By fall of that year, the company had sold only about 10 systems. The firm had to cut costs and raise another $7 million in venture capital. By 1985, however, orders for Octel's system began arriving. Voice mail was becoming more popular in corporate America and, thanks to its universal compatibility, the Octel system sold very well for a first product by a new company.

Voice-mail machines essentially are computers dedicated to the purpose of answering telephones and recording the human voice. Voice-mail systems translate voices into digital information and store it. To keep file sizes small, much of the information is stripped out, which can lead to a tinny quality that some users find objectionable. Also, telephone answering machines were relatively new, and many people were reluctant to leave messages with machines. However, voice mail offered many advantages. Because information is digital, messages can be copied or manipulated like other computer data. Thus an executive can send ten messages simultaneously or forward a message to someone else. Using touch-tone telephones, callers can select from menu options and route their calls without using a human operator.

Octel's system also offered options such as slowing down or speeding up a message during playback and automatic call-forwarding. Corporations were first beginning to evaluate the benefits of such systems when Octel's system came to market, and its low price tag generated interest and orders.

The firm became profitable in 1986, considered a fast takeoff for a start-up technology firm. A 1987 court ruling changed telecommunications regulations to allow the regional Bell telephone companies to begin offering telecommunications services like voice mail. They were, however, not allowed to manufacture their own equipment, and several decided to use Octel's equipment in their systems.

Propelled by its sales to the Bells, Octel became the largest manufacturer of voice-mail systems in 1988, just four years after offering its first product. Its sales grew from $19 million in 1986 to $48 million in 1987. The voice-mail market was booming, growing 50 percent a year by some estimates, to reach $270 million in 1987. In February, 1988, Octel went public, raising $7 million by selling 15 percent of the company. The firm was looked over carefully by the financial community because it was one of the first high-technology companies to go public after the stock market crash of October 1987. Later that year, in a sign of the growing importance of both Octel and the voice-processing industry, electronics giant, Hewlett-Packard™, bought 10 percent of Octel. Its new link with HP gave the young company a marketing boost and a quick presence in Europe, where its products were to be sold under the Hewlett-Packard name. It also led to increased integration of Octel's products with Hewlett-Packard's electronic-mail and computer systems.

At the time, Octel was offering two voice-mail systems: 1) Aspen Systems™ were designed for large businesses and could contain up to 7,500 mailboxes; 2) the VPC 100®, for smaller customers, contained up to 100 mailboxes.

In 1990, Cohen resigned as chief executive officer, citing the need to spend more time with his family; he remained on Octel's board. Douglas Chance, a 24-year veteran of Hewlett-Packard who had served on Octel's board, became CEO. Octel earned $18 million on sales of $160 million for 1990; voice-mail sales for its nearest competitor, AT&T, were $140 million.

With computer technology constantly improving, Octel's systems were rapidly becoming more sophisticated, providing the link between employees (who could be at a touch-tone telephone anywhere in the world) and their employer's computer systems. Universities were using the firm's PowerCall™ system for student registration. With it, the schools recorded course descriptions for students, who could then check whether a particular class was available and register for it over the phone.

In 1991, Octel introduced a device that attached to voice-processing systems and turned telephones into terminals, allowing users to interact with computers through the number pads on their telephones. The system, called the Voice Information Processing Server®, let callers access databases, voice messages, and electronic mail and carried caller data throughout the call so that information—an identification number, for instance--did not have to be reentered.

By 1992, Octel not only held 20 percent of the voice-mail market but had 36 percent of the market for voice-information services (in which telephone service providers buy voice-mail systems, then rent voice-mail services to customers). In fact, Octel was the first company to enter this business, which had exacting standards because of the high volume of calls that were processed and because the systems themselves were attached to equipment located in the central office of a telephone company. The quickly growing cellular telephone market accounted for many of the firm's voice information services sales. The firm had installed 6,500 voice-mail machines, many at Fortune 500 companies.

The firm announced plans to introduce a universal mail box, a system that would collect messages from many sources: voice mail from a subscriber's business, home, and cellular telephones, as well as paper mail. It would also receive data, like faxes, to be printed out or viewed later.

In late 1992, Octel bought Tigon™, Ameritech Corp.'s Dallas-based voice messaging subsidiary. Ameritech agreed to buy voice-processing services from Tigon. Octel made Tigon a wholly owned subsidiary and renamed it Octel Network Services™. Ameritech had bought Tigon in 1988 but could not operate it at enough of a profit. At the time of Octel's purchase, Tigon had large corporate customers in most major U.S. cities, as well as some in Japan, Taiwan, Britain, Australia, and Canada. Because of the purchase, Octel quickly became the world's largest voice mail outsourcing company. Octel Network Services managed clients' voice-mail networks and engaged in disaster recovery, operations management, systems administration, and project management. These operations brought Octel a large source of recurring revenue to help balance the one-time profit of selling a voice-mail system.

Ameritech became one of the most important clients for Octel Network Services, which operated the voice-mail services Ameritech offered to residential and small-business customers. By 1994, 400,000 Ameritech residential customers were using the system, with thousands joining up every month.

In 1993, with the use of faxes proliferating in corporate America, Octel released three products for its Voice Information Processor: Faxagent®, Faxbroadcast®, and Faxstation®. Each consisted of a card and software. The same year, the firm began a joint venture in Israel, hoping to gain access to some of that country's technical specialists. Also in 1993, Robert Cohen rejoined the firm as president and CEO. Total revenue for the year came to $338.5 million.

Octel saw an opportunity for operating voice-mail systems in developing countries, and by the mid-1990s, it had major installations operating in Brazil and China. In these countries millions of customers wanted their own telephones but could not get them; thus, many simply bought their own mailbox and checked messages from pay phones. The firm hoped this system would catch on in developing countries and become a major source of revenue.

In early 1994, Octel took over the industry's first voice-mail company when it merged with VMX Inc. in a stock swap valued at about $150 million. Octel's first move was to write software allowing the two systems to network and to port VMXworks®, a software application, to Octel's systems. Several VMX vice-presidents took similar titles in related areas at Octel.

Octel now had the two most popular user interfaces for voice mail. Analysts expected the acquisition to help Octel as voice processing became based less on the telephone and more on the personal computer. The purchase also brought on VMX's Rhetorex™ subsidiary, which designed and manufactured voice-processing components.

Octel had an installed base of 37,000 systems including those that came with the VMX deal. With new applications like fax products the firm hoped to capitalize on this market to make secondary sales. Meanwhile, Octel continued to win customers. In 1994, data-processing giant, Electronic Data Systems™ (EDS – Ross Perot), which had purchased voice-mail systems from Octel in the past, chose to use Octel's voice-processing services. The seven-year contract called for Octel to provide facilities management and services for over 100 Octel systems at Electronic Data Systems locations. Octel also signed long-term contracts with Kodak™, Blockbuster Entertainment™, and Texas Instruments™.

In 1994 Octel finished its new corporate headquarters, a five-building complex in Milpitas, California, with 368,000 square feet of space. VMX employees also moved into the space.

With the increasing prevalence of electronic mail and the increasing power of personal computers, the creation of voice-mail products for the personal computer became more important. In 1994, Octel released Visual Mailbox®, a software program that allowed users on local area networks to use personal computers to access voice mail and faxes. The computers did not need built-in multimedia support, although the software required users to be on a system using Octel's VMX 200/300 voice-mail system.

Octel believed that voice mail would likely be provided on local area networks as they became more powerful and considered the moves an important way to prepare for future market changes. In 1995, Octel demonstrated add-ons for Microsoft's Exchange® messaging server that enabled users to integrate voice, fax, and e-mail. Also in 1995, Bell Atlantic signed a three-year agreement to use Octel's OptiMail®, which permitted the outsourcing of voice and fax messaging services.

In the mid-1990s, Octel was the leading company in its field and many industry analysts believed it was well positioned for future growth. In 1990, Lucent Technologies™ (originally AT&T's manufacturing corporation, Western Electric), purchased Octel-VMX. In 1997, Alcatel purchased Lucent Technologies. In 2015, Nokia purchased Alcatel.[152]

https://en.wikipedia.org/wiki/Avaya[153]

Avaya (/əˈvaɪ.ə/) is an American multinational technology company headquartered in Santa Clara, California, that specializes in business communications, specifically unified communications (UC), contact center (CC), and services. Serving organizations at 220,000 customer locations worldwide, Avaya is the largest pure-play UC and CC company, ranking No. 1 in CC and No. 2 in UC and collaboration. The company had FY17 revenues of $3.3 billion, 78% of which was attributed to software and services.

In 1995, Lucent Technologies was spun off from AT&T, and Lucent spun off units of its own in an attempt to restructure its struggling operations.

Avaya was then spun off as its own company in 2000. It remained a public company from 2000 to 2007, when it was purchased by private equity firms.

In 2001, the Mark Avaya Interaction Center for customer relationship management began, enabling businesses to draw multi-platform call centers to multimedia, multi-site contact centers. A proposed "converged communications" road map focused on the role that applications would play in making communications improve business performance.

On December 15, 2017, it again became a public company, trading under the stock ticker AVYA.

Acquisition and return to private corporation

In October 2007, Avaya was acquired by two private-equity firms, TPG Capital and Silver Lake Partners, for $8.2 billion and the company was delisted on the New York Stock Exchange. The following year, Avaya Speech to Text (enabling voicemail messages to be read on mobile devices or computers) and Avaya Unified Communications (focusing on role-based communications for teleworkers, home agents, small-business mobile workers, branch-office integration, retail stores and branch banking) were introduced, and Kevin Kennedy became the company's CEO and president.

In 2009, the Avaya Aura® for integrated communications was introduced, and in December, the company acquired Nortel Enterprise's assets for $900 million. The following year, Avaya was the converged-network equipment supplier for the 2010 Winter Olympics and Paralympics, and Avaya Aura Contact Center was introduced. In June 2011, Avaya filed an application with the U.S. Securities and Exchange Commission to raise up to $1 billion in an initial public offering. On October 4, 2011, the company reported that it was acquiring Sipera Systems™ for its session border controller (SBC) and unified communications security applications. On

---

[152] http://www.fundinguniverse.com/company-histories/octel-communications-corp-history/
[153] https://en.wikipedia.org/wiki/Avaya

October 19, 2011, it was reported that Avaya would buy Aurix™. Shareholders approved the acquisition of Radvision™ for about $230 million on April 30, 2012, and the deal closed in June.

Bankruptcy (2016–2017).

According to May 2016 news articles citing "internal sources," Avaya's private-equity owners (Silver Lake Partners and TPG Capital) considered a sale of the company valued at $6 to $10 billion including debt. During the company's earnings call that month, CEO Kevin Kennedy had confirmed that Goldman Sachs was helping Avaya evaluate expressions of interest received relative to specific assets and explore other potential opportunities. In November, Avaya considered Chapter 11 bankruptcy while trying to sell its call-center business. On January 19, 2017, Avaya filed for bankruptcy protection under Chapter 11, saying that its foreign operations would be unaffected. In its petition, the company listed $5.5 billion in assets and $6.3 billion in debts.

In an effort to monetize its assets during the bankruptcy period, Avaya announced, in March 2017, it would sell its networking business and associated products to Extreme Networks™ for US$100 million. The sale was finalized in July 2017.

Acquisitions

Since 2001, Avaya has sold and acquired several companies, including VPNet Technologies™, VISTA Information Technologies™, Quintus™, Route Science™, Tenovis™, Spectel™, NimCat Networks™, Traverse Networks™, Ubiquity Software Corporation™, Agile Software NZ Limited™, Konftel™, Sipera™, Aurix™, Radvision™ and Esnatech™.

Through Nortel's bankruptcy proceedings, assets related to their Enterprise Voice and Data business units were auctioned. Avaya placed a $900 million bid, and was announced as the winner of the assets on September 14, 2009.

Chapter Eighteen -- Big RF (cellular/PCS) Systems Manufacturers

Nortel

A Brief History of Nortel Networks[154]

Nov. 27, 2008

Nortel Networks was created in 1895 when Montreal-based Bell Canada divested its manufacturing division under the name Northern Electric and Manufacturing Co. The purpose of the reorganization was to circumvent government restrictions prohibiting diversification of its manufacturing operations.

For the first 60 years of its existence, controlling equity stakes were owned by Bell Canada and Western Electric, the manufacturing arm of AT&T Corp. As a preferred supplier to Bell Canada, Nortel's core business was manufacturing telephone equipment according to designs licensed from Western Electric – which, in turn, received a royalty on Nortel's sales.

Nortel took full advantage of the freedom to diversify its production. By 1900, it was the largest manufacturer in the world of sleigh bells. It also became the dominant supplier of electrical appliances in Canada (a business it left in the 1950s).

The boom in the 1920s caused employment at Nortel to soar from 2,500 to 7,000 persons. But the depression of the 1930s hit hard and employment was cut back drastically to 2,500. Nortel was saved from bankruptcy thanks to a loan from Western Electric.

In 1956, AT&T signed an antitrust agreement with the U.S. Justice Department that loosened Western Electric's monopolistic influence in the manufacture of telephone equipment. This led to Western Union withdrawing from the Canadian market and the sale of its Nortel stake to Bell Canada in 1962.

Over the 1970s, Bell Canada funded research at Nortel in the development of digital switches. By the early 1980s, it was first to market with this new technology for switching calls on the telephone network. [emphasis author's]

The timing was perfect: the recent breakup of AT&T's monopoly allowed the regional Bells to buy equipment from suppliers other than Western Electric. During the severe recession of the early 1980s, Nortel's stock was one of the few to rise appreciably, as purchase orders flooded in from the regional Bell companies.

In the late 1980s, Nortel's fiber-optics product line emerged from "skunk work" projects initiated by Rudolph Kriegler (who was awarded the Order of Canada in 2008). In the early 1990s, John Roth led Nortel's foray into wireless communications.

The Internet emerged as a force in the 1990s and to adapt, Nortel took a "right-angle turn" – a centerpiece of which was an aggressive acquisition program carried out under John Roth. At the peak of Nortel's fortunes in 1999, Mr. Kriegler told a journalist: "I never thought Nortel would do so well." Bell Canada sold off most of its Nortel stake in 2000.

Shortly after, the tech bubble burst and Nortel's shares collapsed with it. An accounting scandal dispelled early signs of recovery. A financial crisis in 2008 dimmed hopes for a turnaround under CEO Mike Zafirovski.

As referenced above, in the subsequent bankruptcy proceedings, Nortel became part of Avaya.

---

[154] https://seekingalpha.com/article/108227-a-brief-history-of-nortel-networks

Ericsson[155]

Ericsson introduced the world's first fully automatic mobile telephone system, MTA, in 1956. It released one of the world's first hands-free speaker telephones in the 1960s. In 1954, it released the *Ericofon*. Ericsson crossbar switching equipment was used in telephone administrations in many countries. In 1983, the company introduced the ERIPAX® suite of network products and services.

1995–2003: emergence of the Internet

In the 1990s, during the emergence of the Internet, Ericsson was regarded as slow to realize its potential and falling behind in the area of IP technology. But the company had established an Internet project in 1995 called Infocom Systems® to exploit opportunities leading from fixed-line telecom and IT. CEO, Lars Ramqvist, wrote in the 1996 annual report that in all three of its business areas – Mobile Telephones and Terminals, Mobile Systems, and Infocom Systems – "we will expand our operations as they relate to customer service and Internet Protocol (IP) access (Internet and intranet access)."[156]

Ericsson GH337 (1995) and Ericsson T28 1999) mobile phones

The growth of GSM, which became a *de facto* world standard, combined with Ericsson's other mobile standards, such as D-AMPS and PDC, meant that, by the start of 1997, Ericsson had an estimated 40% share of the world's mobile market, with around 54 million subscribers. There were also around 188 million AXE lines in place or on order in 117 countries. Telecom and chip companies worked in the 1990s to provide Internet access over mobile telephones. Early versions such as Wireless Application Protocol (WAP) used packet data over the existing GSM network, in a form known as GPRS (General Packet Radio Service), but these services, known as 2.5G, were fairly rudimentary and did not achieve much mass-market success.

The International Telecommunication Union (ITU) had prepared the specifications for a 3G mobile service that included several technologies. Ericsson pushed hard for the WCDMA (wideband CDMA) form based on the GSM standard, and began testing it in 1996.

Japanese operator, NTT DoCoMo, signed deals to partner with Ericsson and Nokia, who came together in 1997 to support WCDMA over rival standards. **DoCoMo was the first operator with a live 3G network, using its own version of WCDMA called FOMA.** Ericsson was a significant developer of the WCDMA version of GSM, while US-based chip developer, Qualcomm, promoted the alternative system CDMA2000, building on the popularity of CDMA in the US market. This resulted in a patent infringement lawsuit that was resolved in March 1999 when the two companies agreed to pay each other royalties for the use of their respective technologies and Ericsson purchased Qualcomm's wireless infrastructure business and some R&D resources.

Once the Qualcomm conflict was settled, Ericsson continued to be involved in mobile Internet. It announced a partnership with Microsoft to combine its web browser and server software with Ericsson's mobile Internet technologies. The subsequent joint venture was dissolved in 2001 in the aftermath of the Internet and telecom crashes.

Ericsson got caught up in the dot-com bubble of the late 1990s. The company's market value increased; its share price peaked at SEK 825 in March 2000, from a low of SEK 20 at the start of the 1990s. Lars Ramqvist resigned as CEO in January 1998, and later became chairperson of the board. Sven-Christer Nilsson took over as CEO in early 1998, and led the company in a clearer IP direction. Under his leadership, the company's acquisitions included a share in US router company, Juniper™.

Ericsson had become a leading player in networks and the production of mobile telephones, sharing top place with Nokia and Motorola during 1997. Services were becoming increasingly important; Ericsson had offered network rollout services for many years, and had operated networks but, at the end of the 1990s, the service operations were amalgamated into a services unit.

---

[155] https://en.wikipedia.org/wiki/Ericsson

[156] Ibid

In June 1999, Kurt Hellström, the head of Ericsson's mobile division, replaced Nilsson as CEO. Worldwide hype around the potential of the internet – and for Ericsson, in particular, the mobile internet – had inflated industry expectations. Operators in many westernized countries used much of their capital bidding for 3G licenses, and could not afford the new networks required to use the spectrum they had acquired. The order intake that Ericsson and other telecom vendors had expected, and invested in preparing for, was disappointing, causing job losses and consolidations across the industry.

Ericsson issued a profit warning in March 2001. Over the coming year, sales to operators halved. Mobile telephones became a burden; the company's telephones unit made a loss of SEK 24 million in 2000. A fire in a Philips chip factory in New Mexico in March 2000 caused severe disruption to Ericsson's phone production, dealing a *coup de grâce* to Ericsson's mobile phone hopes. Mobile phones would be spun off into a joint venture with Sony, Sony Ericsson Mobile Communications, in October 2001. Ericsson launched several rounds of restructuring, refinancing and job-cutting; during 2001, staff numbers fell from 107,000 to 85,000. A further 20,000 went the next year, and 11,000 more in 2003. A new rights issue raised SEK 30 billion to keep the company afloat. The company had survived as mobile Internet started growing. With record profits, it was in better shape than many of its competitors.

2003–2018: rebuilding and growing

The emergence of full mobile Internet began a period of growth for the global telecom industry, including Ericsson. After the launch of 3G services during 2003, people started to access the Internet using their telephones.

Ericsson's position as a supplier of GSM equipment to many major operators, and its pioneering role in the emerging 3G standards and associated technology, placed it at the forefront of many of the changes to come. The cutbacks that followed 10 consecutive quarters of losses meant the company could return to profit in Q3 2003, and begin to grow again. After announcing in 2003 that it had returned to growth, new CEO Carl-Henric Svanberg said the company was to concentrate on operational excellence, a wide-ranging push for efficiency and better return on investment that dominated Ericsson's corporate culture for several years.

During the cutbacks, Ericsson had reduced its CDMA organization. This standard, used largely in North America, Japan and mainland Asia, was a rival to GSM, and Ericsson had a global market share of 25%, but the overall volumes were too low so Ericsson wound down its CDMA commitment, ending it completely by 2006. Ericsson started a series of acquisitions to strengthen its position in key technologies and market segments. The first of these was Marconi™, a company dating back to the dawn of radio whose assets included a strong portfolio in transmission, fiber optic and fixed network services.

Further acquisitions included Redback Networks™ (carrier edge-routers), Entrisphere™ (fiber) and LHS Telekommunikation™ (customer care services) in 2007, and Tandberg Television™ in 2008. Ericsson sold its enterprise PBX division to Aastra Technologies™ the same year. Ericsson re-entered the CDMA market after acquiring North American vendor Nortel's CDMA operations and assets in 2009. The acquisitions followed Ericsson's general strategy of expanding into next-generation network technologies and multimedia, a combined offering that became more important as video became the dominant form of data traffic on mobile broadband networks. 40% of the world's mobile traffic is carried over Ericsson networks. Ericsson created a division to develop its multimedia business in early 2007.

Ericsson was working on ways to improve WCDMA as operators were buying and rolling it out; it was the first generation of 3G access. New advances included IMS (IP Multimedia Subsystem) and the next evolution of WCDMA, called High-Speed Packet Access (HSPA). It was initially deployed in the download version called HSDPA; the technology spread from the first test calls in the US in late 2005 to 59 commercial networks in September 2006. **HSPA would provide the world's first mobile broadband**.

In July 2016, Hans Vestberg stepped down as Ericsson's CEO after heading the company for six years. Jan Frykhammar, who had been working for the company since 1991, stepped in as interim CEO while Ericsson searched for a full-time replacement.

On 16 January 2017, following Ericsson's announcement on 26 October 2016, new CEO Börje Ekholm started and interim CEO Jan Frykhammar stepped down the following day.

In June 2018, Ericsson, Inc. and Ericsson AB agreed to pay $145,893 to settle potential civil liability for an apparent violation of the International Emergency Economic Powers Act (IEEPA) and the Sudanese Sanctions Regulations, 31 C.F.R. part 538 (SSR).

Nokia

1865–1967[157]

Nokia's history dates to 1865, when Finnish-Swede mining engineer Fredrik Idestam established a pulp mill near the town of Tampere, Finland (then in the Russian Empire). A second pulp mill was opened in 1868 near the neighboring town of Nokia, offering better hydropower resources. In 1871, Idestam, together with friend Leo Mechelin, formed a shared company from it and called it *Nokia Ab* (in Swedish, *Nokia Company* being the English equivalent), after the site of the second pulp mill.

Idestam retired in 1896, making Mechelin the company's chairman. Mechelin expanded into electricity generation by 1902 which Idestam had opposed. In 1904 Suomen Gummitehdas (*Finnish Rubber Works*), a rubber business founded by Eduard Polón, established a factory near the town of Nokia and used its name.

In 1922, Nokia Ab entered into a partnership with Finnish Rubber Works and Kaapelitehdas (*the Cable Factory*), all now jointly under the leadership of Polón. Finnish Rubber Works Company grew rapidly when it moved to the Nokia region in the 1930s to take advantage of the electrical power supply, and the cable company soon did too.

Nokia at the time also made respirators for both civilian and military use, from the 1930s well into the early 1990s.[23]

1967–1990

In 1967, the three companies – Nokia, Kaapelitehdas and Finnish Rubber Works – merged and created a new Nokia Corporation, restructured into four major businesses: forestry, cable, rubber and electronics. In the early 1970s, it entered the networking and radio industry. Nokia also started making military equipment for Finland's defense forces (*Puolustusvoimat*), such as the Sanomalaite M/90 communicator in 1983, and the M61 gas mask first developed in the 1960s. Nokia was now also making professional mobile radios, telephone switches, capacitors and chemicals.

After Finland's trade agreement with the Soviet Union in the 1960s, Nokia expanded into the Soviet market. It soon widened trade, wranging from automatic telephone exchanges to robotics among others; by the late 1970s the Soviet Union became a major market for Nokia, helping to yield high profits. Nokia also co-operated on scientific technology with the Soviet Union. The U.S. government became increasingly suspicious of that cooperation after the end of the Cold War détente in the early 1980s. Nokia imported many US-made components and used them for the Soviets, and according to U.S. Deputy Minister of Defense, Richard Perle, Nokia had a secret co-operation with the Pentagon that allowed the U.S. to keep track of technology developments in the Soviet Union through trading with Nokia. This was a demonstration of Finland trading with both sides, as it was neutral during the Cold War.

In 1977, Kari Kairamo became CEO and he transformed the company's businesses. By this time, Finland was becoming what has been called "Nordic Japan." Under his leadership Nokia acquired many companies including television maker Salora™ in 1984, followed by Swedish electronics and computer maker Luxor AB™ in 1985, and French television maker Oceanic™ in 1987. This made Nokia the third-largest television manufacturer in Europe (behind Philips™ and Thomson™). The existing brands continued to be used until the end of the television business in 1996.

Mobira Cityman 450, 1985

---

[157] https://en.wikipedia.org/wiki/Nokia

In 1987, Nokia acquired Schaub-Lorenz™, the consumer operations of Germany's Standard Elektrik Lorenz™ (SEL), which included its "Schaub-Lorenz®" and "Graetz®" brands. It was originally part of American conglomerate, International Telephone & Telegraph™, (ITT), and after the acquisition products were sold under the "ITT Nokia" brand, despite SEL's sale to Compagnie Générale d'Electricité™ (CGE), the predecessor of Alcatel, in 1986.

On 1 April 1988, Nokia bought the computer division of Ericsson's Information Systems, which originated as a computer division of Swedish aircraft and car manufacturer Saab called Datasaab™. Ericsson Information Systems made Alfaskop terminals, typewriters, minicomputers and Ericsson-branded IBM compatible PCs. The merger with Nokia's Information Systems division—which, since 1981, had a line of personal computers called MikroMikko®—resulted in the name Nokia Data™.

Nokia also acquired Mobira™, a mobile telephony company, which was the foundation of its future mobile phones business. In 1981, Mobira launched the Nordic Mobile Telephone™ (NMT) service, the world's first international cellular network and the first to allow international roaming. In 1982, Mobira launched the Mobira Senator® car phone, Nokia's first mobile phone. At that time, the company had no interest in producing mobile phones, which the executive board regarded as akin to James Bond's gadgets: improbably futuristic and niche devices. After all these acquisitions, Nokia's revenue base became US $2.7 billion. CEO Kairamo committed suicide on 11 December, 1988.

In 1987, Kaapelitehdas discontinued production of cables at its Helsinki factory after 44 years, effectively shutting down the sub-company.

Nokia Bell Labs

Bell Labs, a division of Alcatel-Lucent, brought to Nokia an unparalleled history of technological innovation including: lasers, transistors, and UNIX. Bell labs researchers led analog, digital and mobile shifts in communication technology; the development of the Internet; and the innovation of wavelength division multiplexing (DWDM*) enabling huge increases in network capacity.

In fiber-optic communications, **wavelength-division multiplexing** (**WDM**) is a technology which multiplexes a number of optical carrier signals onto a single optical fiber by using different wavelengths (*i.e.*, colors) of laser light. This technique enables bi-directional communications over one strand of fiber, as well as multiplication of capacity.

The term WDM is commonly applied to an optical carrier, which is typically described by its wavelength, whereas frequency-division multiplexing typically applies to a radio carrier which is more often described by frequency. This is purely conventional because wavelength and frequency communicate the same information. Specifically, frequency (in Hertz, which is cycles per second) multiplied by wavelength (the physical length of one cycle) equals the velocity of the carrier wave. In a vacuum, this is the velocity of light, usually denoted by the lower case letter, c. In glass fiber, it is substantially slower, usually about 0.7 times c. The data rate, which ideally might be at **the carrier frequency, in practical systems, is always a fraction of the carrier frequency** (emphasis author's)

Nokia Networks™ (formerly **Nokia Solutions and Networks** (**NSN**) and **Nokia Siemens Networks** (**NSN**)) is a multinational data networking and telecommunications equipment company headquartered in Espoo, Finland, and wholly owned subsidiary of Nokia Corporation. It started as a joint venture between Nokia of Finland and Siemens of Germany known as Nokia Siemens Networks. Nokia Networks has operations in around 120 countries. In 2013, Nokia acquired 100% of Nokia Networks, buying all of Siemens shares. In April 2014, the NSN name was phased out as part of a rebranding process.

2006

The company was created as the result of a joint venture between Siemens Communications (minus its Enterprise business unit) and Nokia's Network Business. The formation of the company was publicly announced on 19 June 2006. Nokia Siemens Networks™ was officially launched at the 3GSM World Congress in Barcelona in February 2007. Nokia Siemens Networks then began full operations on 1 April 2007 and has its headquarters in Espoo, Greater Helsinki, Finland.

2008

In January, 2008, Nokia Siemens Networks acquired Israeli company *Atrica™*, a company that builds carrier-class Ethernet transport systems for metro networks. The official release did not disclose terms; however, they are thought to be in the region of $100 million. In February, 2008, Nokia Siemens Networks acquired *Apertio™*, a Bristol, UK-based mobile network customer management tools provider, for €140 million. With this acquisition Nokia Siemens Networks gained customers in the subscriber management area including Orange, T-Mobile, O_2, Vodafone, and Hutchison 3G.

2009

In 2009, according to Siemens, Siemens only retained a non-controlling financial interest in NSN, with the day-to-day operations residing with Nokia.

2010

On 19 July 2010, Nokia Siemens Networks announced it would acquire the wireless-network equipment of Motorola. The acquisition was completed on 29 April, 2011, for $975 million in cash. As of the transaction, approximately 6,900 employees transferred to Nokia Siemens Networks.

2011

On 23 November, 2011, Nokia Siemens Networks announced it would refocus its business on mobile broadband equipment, the fastest-growing segment of the market. This refocus resulted in the restructuring of the company and the planned layoffs of 17,000 employees. The plan reduced the company's work force by 23% from its 2011 level of 74,000, and helped the company trim annual operating expenses by $1.35 billion by the end of 2013.

On 12 December, 2011, ADTRAN, Inc.™ announced it would acquire Nokia Siemens Networks' fixed line Broadband Access business. This caused around 400 jobs to move to ADTRAN as part of the deal.

After the restructuring process, Nokia Siemens Networks brought in a positive turn around to its businesses. The bottom line and operating margins rose to approximately 10%, which was a significant shift from the previous sub-zero margins, with positive cash flows for six continuous quarters.

2013

On 7 August, 2013, Nokia completed the acquisition of Siemens' stake in the company and rebranded as *Nokia Solutions and Networks™*. After this acquisition, NSN became a fully owned subsidiary of Nokia.

2014

On 29 April, 2014, Nokia announced that NSN would henceforth be known as *Nokia Networks™*. It was also announced that Rajeev Suri, the CEO of NSN would be appointed as President and CEO of Nokia Corporation, effective May 1, 2014.

2015

On April 15, 2015, Nokia announced its intent to purchase Alcatel-Lucent for €15.6 billion in an all-stock deal. The acquisition aimed to create a stronger competitor to the rival firms Ericsson and Huawei, whom Nokia and Alcatel-Lucent had surpassed in terms of total combined revenue in 2014. The acquisition was expected to be completed in early 2016, and was subject to regulatory and shareholder approval. Regulatory approval was obtained in October 2015 and shareholder approval was announced on January 4, 2016.

2016

On 3 November, 2016, Nokia completed the acquisition of Alcatel-Lucent and it was merged into their Nokia Networks division.

The company owns licenses to operate a cellular communications network in the 1900MHz (PCS) and 1700MHz (AWS) bands with coverage in many parts of the continental U.S., Alaska, Hawaii, Puerto Rico and the U.S. Virgin Islands, as well as licenses in the 700MHz band (block A mostly) available in certain parts of the country.

Lucent

Alcatel-Lucent was formed when Alcatel (originally short for the Société **Al**sacienne de **C**onstructions **A**tomiques, de **T**élécommunications et d'**É**lectronique, a small company in Mulhouse absorbed by CGE in 1966) merged with Lucent Technologies on December 1, 2006. However, the predecessors of the company have been a part of telecommunications industry since the late 19th century. The company has roots in two early tele-communications companies: La Compagnie Générale d'Electricité (CGE) and the Western Electric Manufacturing Company.

Western Electric began in 1869 when Elisha Gray and Enos N. Barton started a manufacturing firm based in Cleveland, Ohio, US. By 1880, the company had relocated to Chicago, Illinois, and become the largest electrical manufacturing company in the United States. In 1881, the American Bell Telephone Company, founded by Alexander Graham Bell and forerunner of American Telephone & Telegraph (AT&T), purchased a controlling interest in Western Electric and made it the exclusive developer and manufacturer of equipment for the Bell telephone companies.

Bell Telephone Laboratories was created in 1925 from the consolidation of the R&D organizations of Western Electric and AT&T. Bell Labs would make significant scientific advances including: the transistor, the laser, the solar cell, the digital signal processor chip, the Unix operating system and the cellular concept of mobile telephone service. Bell Labs researchers have won 7 Nobel Prizes.

Also in 1925, Western Electric sold its International Western Electric Company subsidiary to ITT Corporation. CGE purchased the telecommunications part of ITT in the mid-1980s.

AT&T re-entered the European telecommunications market in 1984 following the Bell System divestiture. Philips promoted the venture in part because its PRX public switching technology was aging and it sought a partner to help fund the development costs of digital switching. The joint company used the existing manufacturing and development facilities in The Hague, Hilversum, Brussels and Malmesbury as well as its U.S. resources to adapt the 5ESS system to the European market. The joint venture company, AT&T & Philips Telecommunications BV™, doubled annual turnover between 1984 and 1987, winning major switching and transmission contracts, mainly in the effectively captive Netherlands market. In 1987, AT&T increased its holding to 60% and, in 1990, it purchased the remainder of the Philips' holding.

In 1998, Alcatel Alsthom™ shifted its focus to the telecommunications industry, spinning off its Alsthom™ activities and changing the company's name to Alcatel. AT&T spun off Lucent Technologies in April 1996 with an initial public offering (IPO).

In April 2004, TCL Corporation™ and Alcatel announced the creation of a mobile phone manufacturing joint venture: Alcatel Mobile Phones™. A year later, Alcatel sold its share in the joint venture but licensed the Alcatel brand name to TCL, which continues to this day under Nokia.

Facing intense competition in the telecommunications industry, Alcatel and Lucent Technologies merged on November 30, 2006.

On 5 April 2006, Alcatel announced that it would swap its shares of Alcatel Alenia Space™ and Telespazio™ for €673 million and a 12.1% stake in Thales™, a key player in the French defense industry. This increased Alcatel's stake in Thales to 20.8%.

Alcatel-Lucent acquired Nortel's UMTS radio access business at the end of 2006. During 2007, the company acquired Canadian metro WDM networking supplier Tropic Networks, Inc.™; enterprise services gateway products developer NetDevices™; IPTV software company Tamblin™; and the telecommunications consulting practice, Thompson Advisory Group, Inc.™ Alcatel-Lucent acquired Motive, Inc.™, a provider of service management software for broadband and mobile data services in 2008. They formerly had a joint venture with Dutch company Draka Holding N.V.™ for manufacturing optical fibre, but Draka bought out Alcatel-Lucent's 49.9% stake for €209 million in December, 2007.

Ben Verwaayen was appointed as chief executive officer in September 2008 after Alcatel-Lucent's first CEO, Patricia Russo, and first chairman, Serge Tchuruk, resigned. In May 2009, Alcatel-Lucent's stake in Thales was acquired by Dassault Aviation™. Alcatel-Lucent announced the acquisition of OpenPlug™ on September 1, 2010.

For 2010, the company had revenues of €16 billion and a reported net loss of €334 million.

In October 2011, Alcatel-Lucent sold its call-centre services business Genesys™ unit to Permira™, a private equity group, for $1.5 billion—the same amount the company bought the business for in 2000. Alcatel-Lucent needed funding for the Franco-American business, which made annual losses from 2007 to 2011.

For 2011, revenues were €15 billion, net loss of €1.1 billion. For 2012, revenues were €14.4 billion and net loss of €1.4 billion. After seven consecutive years of negative cash flows, in October 2013, the company announced plans to slash 10,000 employees, or 14% of the total current 72,000 workforce, as a part of a €1 billion cost reduction effort.

In April 2013, Michel Combes succeeded Verwaayen as CEO. On 19 June, 2013, Combes announced "The Shift Plan," a three-year plan including portfolio refocusing on IP networking, ultra-broadband access and cloud; 1 billion Euro in cost savings; selective asset sales intended to generate at least 1 billion Euro over the period of the plan; and the restructuring of the group's debt.

On 1 October, 2014, it announced it had closed the sale of its subsidiary Alcatel-Lucent Enterprise (ALE) to China Huaxin Post & Telecommunication Economy Development Center.

In 2014, the Italian labs for the management system for terrestrial networks (1350 OMS) and two families of equipment for fiber optic telecommunications—OMSN (Optical Multi-Service Node) and TSS (Transport Service Switch)—were transferred to a new dedicated company, SM Optics, a subsidiary of the Siae Microelettronica group.

On 15 April, 2015, Finnish telecommunications firm Nokia announced its intent to purchase Alcatel-Lucent for €15.6 billion in an all-stock deal. The acquisition aimed to create a stronger competitor to the rival firms Ericsson and Huawei, whom Nokia and Alcatel-Lucent had surpassed in terms of total combined revenue in 2014. The acquisition was expected to be completed in early 2016, and was subject to regulatory and shareholder approval. Combes left in September and was replaced by Philippe Camus as interim CEO. Regulatory approval was obtained in October 2015 and shareholder approval was announced on 4 January 2016. The Bell Labs division would be maintained but the Alcatel-Lucent brand would be replaced by Nokia.

On 14 January, 2016, Alcatel-Lucent started operating as part of the Nokia Group. The sale to Nokia was finalized in November and the company was merged into Nokia Networks.

Motorola

Motorola, Inc., American manufacturer of wireless communications and electronic systems. In 2011 it split into two companies: Motorola Mobility and Motorola Solutions. Its headquarters are located in Schaumburg, Illinois.

The company was founded in 1928 in Chicago by brothers Paul and Joseph Galvin as the Galvin Manufacturing Corporation. Its first product was the "battery eliminator," a device that connected direct-current, battery-powered radios to the alternating current then found in almost two-thirds of U.S. households. In 1930 the company began selling a low-cost automobile radio, called the Motorola, that became the most popular new-car option, as well as a successful aftermarket kit. In 1937 the company diversified into home tabletop radios and introduced the first car radio to offer push-button dialing.

During the Great Depression, Galvin Manufacturing cut its workforce by two-thirds and saw its revenues drop by more than one-third. To sustain the company during the later years of the Depression, the Galvin brothers, who opposed unions, took on work from other companies, such as the Philco Corporation in 1938, whose workers were on strike. In defense of these actions, the Galvins claimed that their starting wage of 40 to 60 cents per hour surpassed the industry average of 25 to 35 cents per hour.

In 1940 the company introduced a pair of two-way radio communications products for the police and military. The first was an AM-band police radio system adopted later that year in Bowling Green, Kentucky; the second was the Handie-Talkie®, an AM-band, handheld device with a long antenna that ultimately was used by soldiers during World War II. Both AM-based systems were quickly superseded by FM technologies. The most notable replacement occurred in 1943, when Galvin Manufacturing invented the FM Walkie-Talkie. This device was carried by battlefield soldiers in special backpacks and could communicate over longer distances and with far less static interference than its AM-based predecessor. The two-way radio saw action on all fronts during the war and is credited as being a decisive factor in many Allied victories in the field.

In 1943, the company sold stock to the public for the first time, and, in 1947, it changed its name to Motorola, Inc., which was by then a well-known brand name. The next year, Motorola extended its role in the U.S. consumer market by introducing the first television set for under $200, the Golden View®. Its seven-inch round picture tube helped Motorola secure 10 percent of the U.S. television market by 1954. In 1953, the company, like other television makers, created its own program, the *Motorola TV Hour*® (see Youtube videos)[158], to boost interest in the new medium. Robert Galvin, Paul Galvin's son and a vice president of the company, hosted the weekly drama series. Motorola's consumer product line branched into high-fidelity phonographs in the mid-1950s.

After licensing the design for transistors from Bell Laboratories in 1952, Motorola began experimenting with them to replace its large, heavy, and expensive radio power supplies. By 1956, the company began to sell hybrid radios with both vacuum tubes and transistors—its first successful foray into electronic products. That same year the company began to sell its transistors to other manufacturers and established its Semiconductor Products Division in Phoenix, Arizona. By 1962, the company had more than 4,000 different electronic components on the market. One of the largest early markets was for automobiles, whose manufacturers used electronic components to build alternators, which replaced generators in most cars sold in the 1960s. Together with the Ford Motor Company and the Radio Corporation of America (RCA), Motorola developed the eight-track tape player for cars in 1965.

Robert Galvin became president of the company in 1956. Despite Motorola's ongoing success and strong brand recognition in consumer products, he shifted the company's strategy toward selling directly to business and government. In 1962, Motorola began supplying radio communications gear to the unmanned Mariner and later to the manned Gemini space programs. Apollo astronaut Neil Armstrong's 1969 message from the moon was carried over a Motorola-designed transponder.

In 1974, the company sold its Quasar® television line to Matsushita Electrical Industrial Co., Ltd.™, of Japan, ending most of its historic consumer business. That same year, Motorola released its first microprocessor for sale to computer makers. Its most popular computer chips, the MC680x0 series, were used in all of the early Apple Macintosh computers and in workstation computers built by Sun Microsystems, Inc., and Silicon Graphics, Inc., throughout the 1980s and early '90s. In 1993, the company developed the first consumer RISC (**R**educed-**I**nstruction-**S**et **C**omputing) chip, the PowerPC, with IBM Corporation and Apple Computer, Inc. (now Apple Inc.), in an unsuccessful attempt to unseat Intel Corporation as the leading seller of microprocessors.

Motorola was more successful in the market for embedded microprocessors, which became ubiquitous in automotive control units, industrial control systems, and such common items as kitchen appliances, pagers, electronic game systems, routers, laser printers, and handheld personal digital assistants (PDAs). In this market Motorola became the leading manufacturer.

In 1977, Motorola developed a handheld wireless telephone* that was able to communicate with the public telephone network through a system of short-range "cells." By 1985, most major cities in the world were installing cellular systems and, in 1989, the company introduced the MicroTAC™**flip cellular phone, which quickly became an international status symbol as well as a useful personal communications device. The overwhelming success of cellular telephony inspired the development of Iridium, a system of 66 (became 77) small satellites deployed in low Earth orbit that enabled communications over virtually the entire surface of Earth.

---

[158] https://www.facebook.com/watch/?v=365586653981831

Operational in 1998, Iridium linked existing terrestrial communications systems, including faxes, pagers, computers, and telephones. **(Author's Note: Iridium will be discussed later in this work.)**

*The Motorola DynaTAC 8000X®, introduced in 1983, was the world's first portable commercial handheld cellular phone.© *Motorola, Inc., Heritage Services & Archives*

**Motorola's MicroTAC® flip cellular phone, introduced in 1989.©*1999 Motorola Museum*

Although sales of its semiconductor-based businesses and the introduction of the well-received RAZR V3® cellular telephone in 2004 improved the company's bottom line, Motorola continued to lose money and market share to rival cellular telephone manufacturers. However, the declining sales began to turn around when, in 2009, Motorola introduced smartphones running Android®, an operating system released by the search engine company Google, Inc. In 2011, Motorola split into two independent companies. Motorola Mobility™, the cellular telephone and home networking components, made smartphones, tablet computers, digital cable television boxes, and modems. Motorola Solutions™, the business and government components, made two-way radios and bar code scanners and assembled computer networks. In 2012, Google bought Motorola Mobility for $12.5 billion. Google then sold Motorola Mobility in 2014 to the Chinese computer company Lenovo™ for $2.91 billion but retained many of the company's patents.

Huawei

Huawei Technologies Co. Ltd. is the world's largest telecom equipment maker and China's largest telephone network equipment maker. With 3,442 patents, Huawei became the world's No. 1 applicant for international patents in 2014.

According to the company founder Ren Zhengfei, the name *Huawei* comes from a slogan he saw on a wall, *Zhonghua youwei* meaning: "China has promise" (中华有为, *Zhōnghuá yǒuwéi*), when he was starting the company and needed a name. *Zhonghua* or *Hua* means China, while *youwei* means "promising to show promise". *Huawei* has also been translated as "splendid achievement" or "China is able" which are possible readings to the name. In Chinese pinyin, the name is *Huáwéi*, and pronounced [xwaˇwéi] in Mandarin Chinese; in Cantonese, the name is transliterated with Jyutping as *Waa-wai* and pronounced [waːˋwěi]. However, pronunciation of *Huawei* by non-Chinese varies in other countries, for example "Hoe-ah-wei" in the Netherlands. The company had considered changing the name in English as it was concerned that non-Chinese may find the name hard to pronounce, but decided to keep the name, and launched a name recognition campaign instead to encourage a pronunciation closer to "Wah-Way" using the words "Wow Way."

During the 1980s, the Chinese government tried to modernize the country's underdeveloped telecommunications infrastructure. A core component of the telecommunications network was telephone exchange switches, and in the late 1980s, several Chinese research groups endeavored to acquire and develop the technology, usually through joint ventures with foreign companies.

Ren Zhengfei, a former deputy director of the People's Liberation Army engineering corps, founded Huawei in 1987 in Shenzhen. The company reports that it had RMB 21,000 in registered capital at the time of its founding.

Ren sought to reverse engineer foreign technologies with local researchers. At a time when all of China's telecommunications technology was imported from abroad, Ren hoped to build a domestic Chinese telecommunication company that could compete with, and ultimately replace, foreign competitors.

During its first several years, the company's business model consisted mainly of reselling private branch exchange (PBX) switches imported from Hong Kong. Meanwhile, it was reverse-engineering imported switches and investing heavily in research and development to manufacture its own technologies. By 1990, the company had approximately 600 R&D staff and began its own independent commercialization of PBX switches targeting hotels and small enterprises.

The company's first major breakthrough came in 1993 when it launched its C&C08 program controlled telephone switch. It was by far the most powerful switch available in China at the time. By initially deploying in small cities and rural areas and placing emphasis on service and customizability, the company gained market share and made its way into the mainstream market.

Huawei also won a key contract to build the first national telecommunications network for the People's Liberation Army, a deal one employee described as "small in terms of our overall business, but large in terms of our relationships." In 1994, founder Ren Zhengfei had a meeting with party general secretary Jiang Zemin, telling him that "switching equipment technology was related to national security, and that a nation that did not have its own switching equipment was like one that lacked its own military." Jiang reportedly agreed with this assessment.

In the 1990s, Canadian telecom giant, Nortel, outsourced production of their entire product line to Huawei. They subsequently outsourced much of their product engineering to Huawei as well.

Another major turning point for the company came in 1996 when the government in Beijing adopted an explicit policy of supporting domestic telecommunications manufacturers and restricting access to foreign competitors. Huawei was promoted by both the government and the military as a national champion, and established new research and development offices.

Foreign expansion

Huawei Offices

In 1997, Huawei won a contract to provide fixed-line network products to Hong Kong company, Hutchison Whampoa. Later that year, Huawei launched its wireless GSM-based products and eventually expanded to offer CDMA and UMTS. In 1999, the company opened a research and development (R&D) center in Bangalore, India to develop a wide range of telecom software.

In May 2003, Huawei partnered with 3Com on a joint venture known as H3C, which was focused on enterprise networking equipment. It marked 3Com's re-entrance into the high-end core routers and switch market, after having abandoned it in 2000 to focus on other businesses. 3Com bought out Huawei's share of the venture in 2006 for US$882 million.

In 2005, Huawei's foreign contract orders exceeded its domestic sales for the first time. Huawei signed a Global Framework Agreement with Vodafone. This agreement marked the first time a telecommunications equipment supplier from China had received Approved Supplier status from Vodafone Global Supply Chain. Huawei also signed a contract with British Telecom (BT) for the deployment of its multi-service access network (MSAN) and transmission equipment for BT's 21st Century Network (21CN).

In 2007, Huawei began a joint venture with U.S. security software vendor Symantec Corporation™, known as Huawei Symantec™, which aimed to provide end-to-end solutions for network data storage and security. Huawei bought out Symantec's share of the venture in 2012, with *The New York Times* noting that Symantec had fears that the partnership: "--would prevent it from obtaining United States government classified information about cyberthreats."

In May 2008, Australian carrier, Optus™, announced it would establish a technology research facility with Huawei in Sydney. In October 2008, Huawei reached an agreement to contribute to a new GSM-based HSPA+ network being deployed jointly by Canadian carriers, Bell Mobility™ and Telus Mobility™. Joined by Nokia Siemens Networks, Huawei delivered one of the world's first LTE/EPC commercial networks for TeliaSonera™ in Oslo, Norway, in 2009.

In July 2010, Huawei was included in the Global Fortune 500 2010 list published by the U.S. magazine *Fortune* for the first time, on the strength of annual sales of US$21.8 billion and net profit of US$2.67 billion.

In October 2012, it was announced that Huawei would move its UK headquarters to Green Park, Reading, Berkshire.

In September 2017, Huawei created a NarrowBand IOT city-aware network using a "one network, one platform, N applications" construction model utilizing IoT, cloud computing, big data, and other next-generation information and communications technology. It also aims to be one of the world's five largest cloud players in the near future.

In April 2019, Huawei established Huawei Malaysia Global Training Centre (MGTC)™ at Cyberjaya, Malaysia, which is Huawei's first training center outside of China.

In September, 2019, Huawei filed a defamation lawsuit against a French researcher and a television show which had hosted her. The researcher, with the Foundation for Strategic Research, had noted that Ren Zhengfei was a former PLA member and that Huawei functions as an arm of the Chinese government. This was the first time Huawei had sued a researcher for defamation for stating common opinions and recognized facts.

Recent performance

As of the end of 2018, Huawei sold 200 million smartphones. They reported that strong consumer demand for premium range smart phones helped the company reach consumer sales in excess of $52 billion in 2018.

Huawei announced worldwide revenues of $105.1 billion for 2018, with a net profit of $8.7 billion. Huawei's Q1 2019 revenues were up 39% year-over-year, at US$26.76 billion.

In 2019, Huawei reported revenue of US$122 billion.

Political Controversies

Further information: Criticism of Huawei

Huawei has been at the center of espionage allegations over Chinese 5G network equipment.

In 2018, the United States passed a defense funding bill that contained a passage barring the federal government from doing business with Huawei, ZTE, and several Chinese vendors of surveillance products, due to security concerns.

On 1 December, 2018, Huawei vice-chairwoman and CFO Meng Wanzhou, daughter of company founder Ren Zhengfei, was arrested in Canada at the request of U.S. authorities. She faced extradition to the United States on charges of violating sanctions against Iran. On 22 August, 2018, an arrest warrant was issued by the U.S. District Court for the Eastern District of New York. Meng was charged with: "conspiracy to defraud multiple international institutions," according to the prosecutor. The warrant was based on allegations of a conspiracy to defraud banks which were clearing money that was claimed to be for Huawei, but was actually for Skycom™, an entity claimed to be entirely controlled by Huawei, which was said to be dealing in Iran, contrary to sanctions. None of the allegations have been proven in court. On 11 December, 2018, Meng was released on bail.

On 28 January, 2019, U.S. federal prosecutors formally indicted Meng and Huawei with 13 counts of bank and wire fraud (in order to mask sale of U.S. technology in Iran that is illegal under sanctions), obstruction of justice, and misappropriating trade secrets. The Department also filed a formal extradition request for Meng with Canadian authorities that same day. Huawei responded to the charges and said that it: "denies that it or its subsidiary or affiliate have committed any of the asserted violations," as well as asserted Meng was similarly innocent. The China Ministry of Industry and Information Technology believed the charges brought on by the United States were "unfair."

In November 2019, Huawei announced it will pay RMB2 billion (US$286 million) in bonuses to its staff, and double their October salaries as a reward for their efforts to counter the effect of recent U.S. trade sanctions on their supply chain.

Shortly after Meng's detention, Chinese authorities arrested Canadian former diplomat, Michael Kovrig, and consultant, Michael Spavor, on charges of espionage. This was widely seen as a retaliatory move, and other subsequent arrests were also questioned. These arrests have been viewed as hostage diplomacy, as has the subsequent arrest of Australian, Yang Hengjun.

"Canada is not the only one grappling with the Gordian knot of national security, global alliance and competitive market issues that Huawei represents," wrote the Financial Post, noting that Australia and New Zealand have banned Huawei equipment, Britain is weighing its options, and the situation in the United States is "complicated."

In September 2019, Microsoft's top lawyer and President, Brad Smith, expressed concern about the continued US ban of Huawei products and services. In an interview with Bloomberg Businessweek®, he remarked that the ban shouldn't be imposed without a, "sound basis in fact, logic, and the rule of law." Microsoft Corporation, which supplies Windows 10 for Huawei PCs, says the allegations by the Trump administration that Huawei is a genuine national security threat to the US are not supported by any evidence.

In February 2020, US government officials claimed that Huawei has had the ability to covertly exploit backdoors intended for law enforcement officials in carrier equipment like antennas and routers since 2009. The US Department of Justice (DoJ) and the Federal Bureau of Investigation (FBI) charged Huawei with racketeering and conspiring to steal trade secrets from six US firms.

By now, you should have recognized how many of today's technologies we take for granted, *e.g.*, voice mail, e:mail, text, voice-to-text, text-to-voice, language translation –as well as basic voice and text—and so many more can be traced backward in time to the early pioneers listed above as well as multitudes not listed.

The companies presented above represent only the largest and most influential in the evolution of wireless from its earliest days to about the turn of the century. In addition to these, there were other smaller but significantly influential companies founded and staffed by experts in wireless technology, deliverables and marketing. Among these, NEC™, Sinclair™, Freeman™ and Plexsys™ played significant roles, particularly in international arenas where special circumstances dictated unique network and system designs as well as fully portable deployment for military as well as other special applications.

Chapter Nineteen -- Major Carriers

T-Mobile

Cellular network

The company's predecessor, VoiceStream Wireless™, began building a regional 2G, 1900MHz GSM, circuit switched, digital cellular network in 1994 and first offered service in 1996 in Honolulu and Salt Lake City. From that starting point, the network has expanded in size through acquisitions of other cellular-network operators and additional spectrum purchases. The network has also expanded in capabilities through the introduction of new technologies. VoiceStream upgraded the 1900MHz network to include packet switching *via* General Packet Radio Service (GPRS), then increased packet switched data transmission speeds *via* Enhanced Data Rates for GSM Evolution. In 2006, the company spent $4.2 billion to purchase 120 D, E or F block 1700MHz AWS licenses and began rolling out 3G UMTS services in those frequency bands. The company upgraded network equipment and back-haul capabilities to enable HSPA (High Speed Packet Access), and later HSPA+ and LTE services.

Packet-switched data upgrade

Packet-switched data service first became available to users in the form of General Packet Radio Service (GPRS) (Author note: This reference requires qualification—see CDPD™ and CDI™.). Packet-switched data speeds increased when Enhanced Data Rates for GSM Evolution (EDGE) was incorporated into the network. EDGE coverage was available within at least forty percent of the GSM footprint.

Both voice capacity and packet-switched data speeds improved when 3G Universal Mobile Telecommunications System (UMTS) equipment was installed in the network. On January 5, 2010, the company announced it had upgraded its entire 3G network to HSPA 7.2 Mbit/s, an improvement from its previous peak of 3.6 Mbit/s. It also said that it planned to be the first U.S. carrier to deploy HSPA+ across its network by mid-2010. The company had finished HSPA+ trials in Philadelphia, Pennsylvania, and had begun deploying HSPA+ across its network.

3G upgrade / discontinuation

In September 2006, the Federal Communications Commission (FCC) auctioned licenses in the first Advanced Wireless Services band. This band was an area of wireless spectrum, half in the 1700MHz (1.7GHz) and half in the 2100MHz (2.1GHz) frequencies, that was already in use by government services. The spectrum was planned to become available after the government users migrated to different frequencies.

The auction made numerous licenses available in overlapping market-areas, economic-areas, and regional levels. Each license was individually bid upon, and T-Mobile USA was the winner in 120 license auctions, at an aggregate price of $4.18 billion. As part of its winnings, T-Mobile USA gained nationwide coverage of 1.7GHz and 2.1GHz, with numerous areas being supplemented with additional licenses. Examples include New York City, Chicago, and Boston where T-Mobile USA acquired one-third (33 percent) of the available spectrum, or San Francisco, Houston, and Miami where they acquired 45 percent of the available spectrum.

October 6, 2006, two weeks after confirming its winning bids, the company announced its intentions to create a UMTS third-generation, or 3G, cellular network with the spectrum it had won. It said it would utilize and build on the experience of T-Mobile International's European subsidiaries, which already implemented 3G networks. At the time of initial roll-out, the company intended to offer 7.2 Mbit/s service, making the company's 3G network the fastest in the U.S. The upgrade was forecast to cost $2.6 billion, in addition to the $4.12 billion spent to acquire the spectrum licenses.

In the same announcement, the company indicated it had already begun to deploy about half of the upgraded equipment, beginning in major markets such as New York City. With the equipment in place, it would be able to activate its network as soon as the government agencies vacated the spectrum. The company had hoped to have its network activated by mid-2007, but as of September 2007, the government users had not vacated the AWS band.

The company began selling its first 3G-capable phone, the Nokia 6263, in November 2007, and announced in February 2008, that its 3G network would finally be activated "within the next few months" and released in the New York City market on May 1, 2008.

By 2009, the company had launched its 3G network in more than 200 markets, covering some 208 million points of presence (POPS). Throughout 2015, T-Mobile began re-farming UMTS/HSPA services from the original AWS band to their PCS band to expand bandwidth available for LTE. This rendered a select number of T-Mobile 3G devices inoperable on the 3G network.

HSPA/HSPA+ upgrade

On June 28, 2010, the company announced it would begin to upgrade its network from HSPA+ 21 to HSPA+ 42 beginning sometime in 2011. T-Mobile marketed HSPA+ services as 4G.

4G LTE upgrade

On February 23, 2012, during the Q4 Earnings Call, T-Mobile laid out the future of their 4G upgrade path. They would roll out the LTE network on the AWS spectrum, and transition their HSPA+ network to the PCS band. To achieve compatibility with other networks and phones in the US, T-Mobile began this transition in March 2013, and the rollout of LTE is currently underway as T-Mobile expands to more markets. Due to the failed acquisition of T-Mobile USA by AT&T, T-Mobile USA received additional UMTS frequency band IV (AWS) spectrum. On March 26, 2013, T-Mobile began rolling out LTE in 7 markets: Baltimore, San Jose, Washington, D.C., Phoenix, Las Vegas, Kansas City, and Houston.

On August 21, 2012, the FCC approved a deal between T-Mobile and Verizon in which T-Mobile gained additional AWS spectrum licenses in 125 Cellular Market Areas.

On February 25, 2014, T-Mobile announced in their Q4 2013 earnings call that their 4G LTE network covered 209 million people in 273 metro areas. They also planned to start rolling out their 700MHz A-Block spectrum by the end of 2014, which, by the end of the rollout, would cover 158 million people. This spectrum led to improved LTE coverage overall in these areas, particularly indoors.

On March 13, 2014, T-Mobile announced a new plan to upgrade its entire 2G/EDGE network to 4G LTE. They expected 50% to be done by the end of 2014, and it to be "substantially complete" by the middle of 2015.

On December 16, 2014, T-Mobile announced during CEO John Legere's *Un-carrier 8.0 interview* that their 4G LTE network covered 260 million people and their 700 MHz Band 12 LTE had been rolled out in Cleveland, Colorado Springs, Minneapolis, and Washington, D.C. They expected to cover 280 million with LTE by mid-2015 and 300 million by the end of 2015. They also stated that they covered 121 metro areas with their Wideband LTE.

On October 27, 2015, T-Mobile announced in its Q3 2015 earnings call that they covered over 300 million people with LTE, reaching their 2015 end of year goal months ahead of schedule. They had 245 markets with Wideband (at least 15+15MHz) LTE. They also had 204 markets with Extended Range 700MHz Band 12 LTE covering around 175 million people. Their coverage map revealed that they now had new native LTE coverage in Montana, the Dakotas, Eastern West Virginia, and Northern Michigan.

On May 25, 2016, T-Mobile announced it will be purchasing the 700MHz A-block license (LTE band 12) for the Chicago metro area. When this transaction closes, together with several other pending 700MHz license acquisitions, T-Mobile expects to possess 700MHz licenses covering a total of 272 million people, or 84% of the US population – including 10 of the top 10 largest US metro areas. T-Mobile refers to its 700MHz low-band network as 'Extended-range LTE' and claims it penetrates buildings and reaches out farther than its PCS and AWS only network. In September 2016, T-Mobile launched 4x4 MIMO and 3 channel carrier aggregation allowing theoretical speeds of 400 Mbit/s, and also announced the company's LTE network reaches over 312 million potential subscribers.

In early 2017, T-Mobile purchased 45% of available 600MHz spectrum in the US, covering 100% geographically of the US. They started rollout of LTE on this band on August 15, 2017.

In 2018, T-Mobile has stated they will not discontinue rollout and upgrades of LTE in favor of 5G. Instead, they will continue to grow and support their LTE network to work simultaneously with 5G.

As of January 22, 2019, the LTE-Advanced upgrade has been deployed in 6,000 cities and towns.

As of October 28, 2019, LTE now covers 326 million people.

As of February 6, 2020, the 600MHz network reaches 8,900 cities and towns, covering 248 million people.

5G NR upgrade

On February 26, 2018, T-Mobile announced it would roll out 5G to 30 cities by the end of 2018, with compatible handsets delivering early 2019. They also stated their 5G network will be able to work simultaneously with their 4G LTE network, delivering faster speeds and broader range.

On June 25, 2018, T-Mobile and Nokia completed their first bi-directional 5G NR transmission in the 28GHz frequency compliant with 3GPP 5G New Radio (NR) standards, showing a big step forward to building a nationwide 5G Network.

On July 30, 2018, T-Mobile and Nokia announced a $3.5 billion contract for equipment and software to build out a nationwide 5G network that will be compliant with 3GPP 5G New Radio (NR) standards. The network will use the 600MHz and 28GHz frequency bands.

On September 11, 2018, T-Mobile and Ericsson announced a $3.5 Billion contract for equipment to build out a nationwide 5G network that will be compliant with 3GPP 5G New Radio (NR) standards. The network will use the 600MHz and 28GHz frequency bands. This marks $7 Billion already invested in T-Mobile's 5G network, which will use both companies' equipment.

On November 20, 2018, T-Mobile and Nokia completed their first downlink 5G NR transmission in the 600MHz frequency compliant with 3GPP 5G New Radio (NR) standards in Spokane, Washington. 28GHz only reaches roughly 1 square mile (2.6 km^2), whereas 600MHz can reach hundreds of square miles. This marks one step closer to a rural 5G network, one highly sought improvement with 5G technology (high-speed data in rural areas).

On January 7, 2019, T-Mobile and Ericsson completed the first audio and video call using a live NR network using 3 separate frequency bands; 600MHz, 28GHz, and 39GHz. This was also the first live network test with successful uplink and downlink.

On June 28, 2019, T-Mobile officially launched their 5G mmWave network with the launch of their first commercially available 5G NR device, the Galaxy S10 5G. The network has launched in 6 cities; Los Angeles, NYC, Atlanta, Dallas, Las Vegas, and Cleveland.

On July 11, 2019, T-Mobile and Ericsson completed their first n71 (600MHz) data session in their lab in Bellevue, Washington, on a commercial 5G modem, the Snapdragon X55™, which is the first commercial 5G modem to feature the n71 band. However, the modem was pre-market and not in any commercially available device.

On November 7, 2019, T-Mobile announced that it's 600MHz 5G network will launch on December 6, 2019. The network will launch alongside the first 2 600MHz 5G devices, the Samsung Galaxy Note 10+ 5G and the OnePlus 7T Pro 5G McLaren Edition.

On December 2, 2019, T-Mobile officially launched its 600MHz 5G network. It launched with an initial coverage of 200 million people and over 5,000 cities or towns.

Roaming

T-Mobile has roaming arrangements with a number of national and regional mobile network operators, including AT&T Mobility.

As of 2008, prepaid customers have almost all of the postpaid domestic roaming privileges and restricted international roaming to Canada and Mexico.

In 2009, T-Mobile USA began removing AT&T Mobility roaming coverage in many locations across the country, and updated its on-line coverage maps to reflect the smaller coverage area. AT&T Mobility roaming remains available in select locations, primarily on smaller carriers that were acquired by AT&T Mobility after long-term roaming contracts were in place between T-Mobile and the smaller carriers, including Centennial Wireless and Edge Wireless.

On June 29, 2010, the company launched voice service in the Gulf of Mexico on GSM *via* roaming agreement through Broadpoint™. T-Mobile USA™ was scheduled to launch data service in Fall 2010. Also in 2010, T-Mobile US became a member of the FreeMove alliance.

On October 9, 2013, T-Mobile announced Simple Global®, a service included with eligible Simple Choice plans. This service allows the subscriber to roam in over 100 countries with unlimited text and speed-limited data, and make calls at $0.20/minute. High-speed data passes will be available for purchase. On March 7, 2014, T-Mobile announced this number will be increasing to 122 countries. If one is connected to WiFi in one of these countries, and their phone supports WiFi calling, all calls and texts to and from the USA are free, and work the same as if they were on the cellular network.

On July 15, 2015, T-Mobile launched *Mobile Without Borders*®, a service included with all new T-Mobile plans and available as an add-on to grandfathered or promotional plans for $10. This service allows the user to use his normal voice, text message, and data allotments while roaming in Mexico and Canada. Most T-Mobile services are available while roaming, with the notable exception of using the data in one's Data Stash®.

In August 2015, T-Mobile joined the Competitive Carriers Association's Data Services Hub, enabling the company to expand roaming partnerships with over a dozen rural and regional carriers. Smaller carriers will now be able to access T-Mobile's LTE network for roaming and T-Mobile will be able to expand roaming partnerships and extend its footprint with members whose network technologies had previously been incompatible.

In October 2017, T-Mobile announced that, starting November 12, 2017, LTE-speeds will be limited at 5 GB (with speeds at 128 kbit/s or 256 kbit/s on some plans) while data roaming in Canada and Mexico still remains unlimited. However, calling and texting in these countries still remain free from roaming charges. T-Mobile also announced a partnership with US Cellular in California, Iowa, Washington, and Wisconsin to expand 4G LTE coverage – compatible device required.

AirTouch[159]

AirTouch Communications was formed when Pacific Telesis spun off PacTel Cellular in 1994.

In July 1994, AirTouch Communications and US West formed a joint venture to eventually merge their cellular operations.

In May 1996, US West New Vector Group rebranded US West Cellular as AirTouch Cellular.

In April 1997, AirTouch tried to buy US West New Vector but missed the Morris Trust filing deadline by one day.

In February 1998, AirTouch Communications bought US West New Vector from US West Media for $5.7 billion. This made AirTouch the second largest wireless company in the US.

In January 1999, Vodafone bid $62 billion for AirTouch.

In June 1999, Vodafone Group Plc merged with AirTouch Communications, creating **Vodafone Airtouch Plc**.

In September 1999, Bell Atlantic and Vodafone Airtouch agreed to merge their U.S. wireless operations (Bell Atlantic Mobile, AirTouch Cellular) to form Verizon Wireless.

In April 2000, Verizon Wireless began operations—the creation of the Verizon Wireless brand marked the end of the AirTouch brand.

In June, 2006, Verizon Wireless sold its paging division to American Messaging Services.

---

[159] https://en.wikipedia.org/wiki/AirTouch

GTE[160]

In 1918, Wisconsin public utility accountants John F. O'Connell, Sigurd L. Odegard, and John A. Pratt pooled $33,500 to purchase the Richland Center Telephone Company, serving 1,466 telephones in Wisconsin's dairy belt. In 1920, the three accountants formed Commonwealth Telephone Company as the parent of Richland Center Telephone, with Odegard as president, Pratt as vice-president, and O'Connell as secretary. In 1922, Pratt resigned as vice-president and was replaced by Clarence R. Brown, a former Bell System employee.

Commonwealth Telephone expanded across southern Wisconsin and made its first purchase outside the state later in the decade when it bought Belvedere Telephone Company in Illinois. It also diversified by acquiring two electric utilities in Wisconsin. Expansion was stepped up in 1926, when Odegard secured an option to purchase Associated Telephone Company of Long Beach, California. Later that year, Commonwealth Telephone and Associated Telephone merged as Associated Telephone Utilities.

During its first six years, Associated Telephone Utilities acquired 340 telephone companies in the West, Midwest and East, which were consolidated into 45 companies operating more than 437,000 telephones in 25 states. By the time the stock market bottomed out in October 1929, Associated Telephone Utilities was operating about 500,000 telephones with revenues approaching $17 million.

In January 1930, a new subsidiary, Associated Telephone Investment Company, was established. Designed to support its parent's acquisition program, the new company's primary business was buying company stock in order to bolster its market value. Within two years, the investment company had incurred major losses, and a $1 million loan had to be negotiated. Associated Telephone Investment dissolved, but not soon enough to keep Associated Telephone from lapsing into receivership in 1933.

General Telephone

The company was reorganized that same year, and two years later was reorganized as General Telephone Corporation, operating 12 newly consolidated companies. John Winn, a 26-year veteran of the Bell System, was named president. In 1936, General Telephone created a new subsidiary, General Telephone Directory Company, to publish directories for the parent's entire service area.

Like other businesses, the telephone industry was under government restrictions during World War II, and General Telephone was called upon to increase services at military bases and war production factories. Following the war, General Telephone reactivated an acquisitions program that had been dormant for more than a decade and purchased 118,000 telephone lines between 1946 and 1950. In 1950, General Telephone purchased its first telephone equipment manufacturing subsidiary, Leich Electric Company, along with the related Leich Sales Corporation.

General Telephone's holdings included 15 telephone companies across 20 states by 1951, when Donald C. Power (attorney, utilities commissioner and former executive secretary for Ohio Governor, John Bricker) was named president of the company under chairman and long-time GT executive Morris F. LaCroix, replacing the retiring Harold Bozell (president 1940 - 1951). Power proceeded to expand the company through the 1950s principally through two acquisitions.

In 1955, Theodore Gary & Company, the second-largest independent telephone company, which had 600,000 telephone lines, was merged into General Telephone, which had grown into the largest independent outside the Bell System. The merger gave the company 2.5 million lines. Theodore Gary's assets included telephone operations in the Dominican Republic, British Columbia, and the Philippines, as well as Automatic Electric, the second-largest telephone equipment manufacturer in the U.S. It also had a subsidiary, named the General Telephone and Electric Corporation, formed in 1930 with the Transamerica Corporation and British investors to compete against ITT.

In 1959, General Telephone and Sylvania Electric Products merged, and the parent's name was changed to General Telephone & Electronics Corporation (GT&E). The merger gave Sylvania - a leader in such industries

---

[160] https://en.wikipedia.org/wiki/GTE

as lighting, television and radio, and chemistry and metallurgy- the needed capital to expand. For General Telephone, the merger meant the added benefit of Sylvania's extensive research and development capabilities in the field of electronics. Power also orchestrated other acquisitions in the late 1950s, including Peninsular Telephone Company in Florida, with 300,000 lines, and Lenkurt Electric Company, Inc., a leading producer of microwave and data transmissions systems.

In 1960, the subsidiary GT&E International Incorporated™ was formed to consolidate manufacturing and marketing activities of Sylvania™, Automatic Electric™, and Lenkurt™, outside the United States. Power was named CEO. and chairman in 1961, making way for Leslie H. Warner, formerly of Theodore Gary[161], to become president. During the next several years, the scope of GT&E's research, development, and marketing activities was broadened. In 1963, Sylvania began full-scale production of color television picture tubes, and within two years, it was supplying color tubes for 18 of the 23 domestic U.S. television manufacturers. About the same time, Automatic Electric began supplying electronic switching equipment for the U.S. defense department's global communications systems, and GT&E International began producing earth-based stations for both foreign and domestic markets. GT&E's telephone subsidiaries, meanwhile began acquiring community-antenna television systems (CATV) franchises in their operating areas.

In 1964, Warner orchestrated a deal that merged Western Utilities Corporation™, the nation's second-largest independent telephone company, with 635,000 telephones, into GT&E. The following year Sylvania introduced the revolutionary four-sided flashcube, enhancing its position as the world's largest flashbulb producer. Acquisitions in telephone service continued under Warner during the mid-1960s. Purchases included Quebec Telephone in Canada, Hawaiian Telephone Company, and Northern Ohio Telephone Company and added a total of 622,000 telephone lines to GT&E operations. By 1969, GT&E was serving ten million telephones.

In the late 1960s, GT&E joined in the search for a railroad car Automatic Car Identification system. It designed the KarTrak® optical system, which won over other manufacturer's systems in field trials, but ultimately proved to need too much maintenance. In the late 1970s, the system was abandoned.

In March 1970, GT&E's New York City headquarters was bombed by a radical antiwar group in protest of the company's participation in defense work. In December of that year, the GT&E board agreed to move the company's headquarters to Stamford, Connecticut. **In 1971, GT&E undertook an identity change and became simply GTE**, while Sylvania Electric Products became GTE Sylvania™. The same year, Donald C. Power retired and Leslie H. Warner became chairman of the Board. Theodore F. Brophy was brought in as president.

After first proposing to build separate satellite systems, GTE and its telecommunications rival, American Telephone & Telegraph, announced in 1974 joint venture plans for the construction and operation of seven earth-based stations interconnected by two satellites. Also in 1974, Sylvania acquired name and distribution rights for Philco television and stereo products. GTE International expanded its activities during the same period, acquiring television manufacturers in Canada and Israel and a telephone manufacturer in Germany.

In 1976, newly elected chairman, Theodore F. Brophy, reorganized the company along five global product lines: communications, lighting, consumer electronics, precision materials, and electrical equipment. GTE International was phased out during the reorganization, and GTE Products Corporation™ was formed to encompass both domestic and foreign manufacturing and marketing operations. At the same time, GTE Communications Products was formed to oversee operations of Automatic Electric, Lenkurt, Sylvania, and GTE Information Systems. In 1979, another reorganization soon followed under new president, Thomas A. Vanderslice. GTE Products Group was eliminated as an organizational unit and GTE Electrical Products, consisting of light-

---

[161]https://en.wikipedia.org/wiki/Theodore_Gary_%26_Company **Theodore Gary & Company** was a 20th-century independent telephone firm in the United States. Among its subsidiaries was the Associated Telephone and Telegraph Company, which controlled telephone companies in Latin America and telephone manufacturing interests in Europe in the 1920s and 1930s. In that capacity, Associated, formed in 1925, was the only other serious U.S. rival of International Telephone and Telegraph in Europe before World War II. Associated also exercised influence over the telephone networks in the Dominican Republic and Columbia. In 1930 it formed a new subsidiary, the General Telephone and Electric Corporation, with Transamerica Corporation and British investors, to strengthen overseas manufacturing and operations in competition with ITT. This was headed by Theodore Gary's son, Hunter Larrabee Gary. It would ultimately merge into the General Telephone Corp. (later known as GTE) in 1955.

ing, precision materials, and electrical equipment, was formed. Vanderslice also revitalized the GT&E Telephone Operating Group in order to develop competitive strategies for anticipated regulatory changes in the telecommunications industry.

In 1979, GTE purchased Telenet™ to establish a presence in the growing packet switching data communications business. GTE Telenet™ was later included in the US Telecom™ joint venture.

1980s

GT&E sold its consumer electronics businesses, including the accompanying brand names of Philco and Sylvania to Philips in 1981, after watching revenues from television and radio operations decrease precipitously with the success of foreign manufacturers. Following AT&T's 1982 announcement that it would divest 22 telephone operating companies, GT&E made a number of reorganization moves.

In 1982, the company adopted the name GTE Corporation and formed GTE Mobilnet Incorporated™ to handle the company's entrance into the new cellular telephone business. In 1983, GTE sold its electrical equipment, brokerage information services, and cable television equipment businesses. That same year, Automatic Electric and Lenkurt were combined as GTE Network Systems™.

GTE became the third-largest long-distance telephone company in 1983 through the acquisition of Southern Pacific Communications Company. At the same time, Southern Pacific Satellite Company was acquired, and the two firms were renamed GTE Sprint Communications Corporation™ and GTE Spacenet Corporation™, respectively. **Through an agreement with the Department of Justice, GTE conceded to keep Sprint Communications**™ **separate from its other telephone companies and limit other GTE telephone subsidiaries in certain markets**. In December, 1983, Vanderslice resigned as president and chief operating officer.

In 1984, GTE formalized its decision to concentrate on three core businesses: telecommunications, lighting, and precision metals. That same year, the company's first satellite was launched, and GTE's cellular telephone service went into operation; GTE's earnings exceeded $1 billion for the first time. In 1986, GTE acquired Airfone Inc.™, a telephone service provider for commercial aircraft and railroads, and Rotaflex plc™, a United Kingdom-based manufacturer of lighting fixtures.

Beginning in 1986, GTE spun off several operations to form joint ventures. That same year, GTE Sprint™ and United Telecommunication's long-distance subsidiary, US Telecom™, agreed to merge and form US Sprint Communications Company™, with each parent retaining a 50 percent interest in the new firm. That same year, GTE transferred its international transmission, overseas central office switching, and business systems operations to a joint venture with Siemens AG of Germany, which took 80 percent ownership of the new firm. The following year, GTE transferred its business systems operations in the United States to a new joint venture, Fujitsu GTE Business Systems, Inc.™, formed with Fujitsu Limited, which retained 80 percent ownership.

In April 1988, after the retirement of Theodore F. Brophy, James L. "Rocky" Johnson was promoted from his position as president and chief operating officer to CEO of GTE, he was appointed chairman in 1991. Under his leadership, GTE divested its consumer communications products unit as part of a telecommunications strategy to place increasing emphasis on the services sector. The following year (1989) GTE sold the majority of its interest in US Sprint to United Telecommunications and its interest in Fujitsu GTE Business Systems to Fujitsu.

In 1989, GTE and AT&T formed the joint venture company, AG Communication Systems Corporation, designed to bring advanced digital technology to GTE's switching systems. GTE retained 51 percent control over the joint venture, with AT&T pledging to take complete control of the new firm in 15 years.

With an increasing emphasis on telecommunications, in 1989 GTE launched a program to become the first cellular provider offering nationwide service and introduced the nation's first rural service area, providing cellular service on the Hawaiian island of Kauai. **The following year (1990), GTE acquired the Providence Journal Company's cellular properties in five southern states for $710 million and became the second largest cellular-service provider in the United States.**

1990s

In 1990, GTE reorganized its activities around three business groups: telecommunications products and services, telephone operations, and electrical products. That same year, GTE and Contel Corporation announced merger plans that would strengthen GTE's telecommunications and telephone sectors.

Following action or review by more than 20 governmental bodies, in March 1991, the merger of GTE and Contel was approved. Over half of Contel's $6.6 billion purchase price, $3.9 billion, was assumed debt. In April 1992, James L. "Rocky" Johnson retired after 43 years at GTE, remaining on the GTE board of directors as Chairman Emeritus. Charles "Chuck" Lee was named to succeed Johnson. Lee's first order of business was reduction of that obligation. He sold GTE's North American Lighting business to a Siemens affiliate for over $1 billion, shaved off local exchange properties in Idaho, Tennessee, Utah, and West Virginia to generate another $1 billion, and divested its interest in Sprint in 1992. In 1994, he sold its GTE Spacenet satellite operations to General Electric and sold Contel of Maine to Oxford Networks, which placed the company into a newly created subsidiary, Oxford West Telephone.

The Telecommunications Act of 1996 promised to encourage competition among local phone providers, long distance services, and cable television companies. Many leading telecoms prepared for the new competitive realities by aligning themselves with entertainment and information providers. GTE, on the other hand, continued to focus on its core operations, seeking to make them as efficient as possible.

Among other goals, GTE's plan sought to double revenues and slash costs by $1 billion per year by focusing on five key areas of operation: technological enhancement of wireline and wireless systems, expansion of data services, global expansion, and diversification into video services. GTE hoped to cross-sell its large base of wireline customers on wireless, data and video services, launching Tele-Go®, a user-friendly service that combined cordless and cellular phone features. The company bought broadband spectrum cellular licenses in Atlanta, Seattle, Cincinnati and Denver, and formed a joint venture with SBC Communications™ to enhance its cellular capabilities in Texas. In 1995, the company undertook a 15-state test of video conferencing services, as well as a video dial tone (VDT) experiment that proposed to offer cable television programming to 900,000 homes by 1997. GTE also formed a video programming and inter-services joint venture with Ameritech Corporation, BellSouth Corporation, SBC, and The Walt Disney Company in the fall of 1995.

Foreign efforts included affiliations with phone companies in Argentina, Mexico, Germany, Japan, Canada, the Dominican Republic, Venezuela and China. The early 1990s reorganization included a 37.5 percent workforce reduction, from 177,500 in 1991 to 111,000 by 1994. Lee's fivefold strategy had begun to bear fruit by the mid-1990s. While the communication conglomerate's sales remained rather flat, at about $19.8 billion, from 1992 through 1994, its net income increased by 43.7 percent, from $1.74 billion to a record $2.5 billion, during the same period.

Acquisition by Bell Atlantic

Bell Atlantic acquired GTE on June 30, 2000, and named the new entity Verizon Communications™. The GTE operating companies retained by Verizon are now collectively known as **Verizon West** division of Verizon (including east coast service territories). The remaining smaller operating companies were sold off or transferred into the remaining ones. Additional properties were sold off within a few years after the merger to CenturyTel™, Alltel™, and Hawaiian Telcom™. On July 1, 2010, Verizon sold many former GTE properties to Frontier Communications™. Other GTE territories in California, Florida, and Texas were sold to Frontier in 2015 and transferred in 2016, thus ending Verizon's landline operations outside of the historic Bell Atlantic footprint. Verizon still operates phone service in non-Bell System areas in Pennsylvania under Verizon North, and in non-Bell System areas in Virginia and Knotts Island, North Carolina under Verizon South.

Verizon[162]

---

[162] google.com/search?rlz=1C1CHZL_enUS725US725&sxsrf=ALeKk02leFkUne4VLs7uo_YrCEi8YmSnWg%3A1585520958155&ei=PiGBXuuL-CZa5tQbX6IDYBQ&q=verizon+history&oq=Verizon+history&gs_lcp=CgZwc3ktYWIQARgFMgYIABAHEB4yBggAEAcQHjIGCAAQBxAeMgYIABAHEB4yBggAEAcQHjICCAAyBggAEAcQHjIGCAAQBxAeMgYIABAHEB4yBggAEAcQHjoECAAQR1CIJVjNL2CpX2gAcAF4AIABXYgBmASSAQE3mAEAoAEBqgEHZ3dzLXdpepeg&sclient=psy-ab

Verizon Communications Inc. is an American multinational telecommunications conglomerate and a corporate component of the Dow Jones Industrial Average. The company is based at 1095 Avenue of the Americas in Midtown Manhattan, New York City, but is incorporated in Delaware.

In 1984, the United States Department of Justice mandated AT&T Corporation to break up the Bell System into seven companies, each a Regional Bell Operating Company (RBOC), commonly referred to as "Baby Bells." One of the Baby Bells, Bell Atlantic, came into existence in 1984, consisting of the separate operating companies New Jersey Bell, Bell of Pennsylvania, Diamond State Telephone, and C&P Telephone, with a trading area from New Jersey to Virginia. This company would later become Verizon.

As part of a rebranding of the Baby Bells in the mid-1990s, all of Bell Atlantic's operating companies assumed the holding company's name. **In 1997, Bell Atlantic expanded into New York and the New England states by merging with fellow Baby Bell NYNEX**. Although Bell Atlantic was the surviving company name, the merged company moved its headquarters from Philadelphia to NYNEX's old headquarters in New York City. **In 2000, Bell Atlantic acquired GTE,** which operated telecommunications companies across most of the rest of the country that was not already in Bell Atlantic's footprint. **Bell Atlantic, the surviving entity, changed its name to "Verizon"**, a portmanteau of *veritas* (Latin for "truth") and *horizon*.

In 2015, Verizon expanded into content ownership by acquiring AOL, and two years later it acquired Yahoo!. AOL and Yahoo were amalgamated into a new division named Oath Inc. (currently known as ‚Verizon Media™).

As of 2016, Verizon is one of three remaining companies that had their roots in the former Baby Bells. The other two, like Verizon, exist as a result of mergers among fellow former Baby Bell members. SBC Communications bought out the Bells' former parent, AT&T Corporation, and assumed the AT&T name. CenturyLink™ was formed initially in 2011 by the acquisition of Qwest (formerly named US West).

Bell Atlantic[163] (Bell Atlantic Mobile Systems – BAMS)

Bell Atlantic Corporation was created as one of the original Regional Bell Operating Companies (RBOCs) in 1984, during the breakup of the Bell System. Bell Atlantic's original roster of operating companies included:

The Bell Telephone Company of Pennsylvania

New Jersey Bell

Diamond State Telephone

C&P Telephone (itself comprising four subsidiaries)

Bell Atlantic originally operated in the states of New Jersey, Pennsylvania, Delaware, Maryland, West Virginia, and Virginia, as well as Washington, DC.

In 1996, CEO and Chairman Raymond W. Smith orchestrated Bell Atlantic's merger with NYNEX. When it merged, it moved its corporate headquarters from Philadelphia to New York City. NYNEX was consolidated into this name by 1997.

Merger of equals (2000–2002)

Bell Atlantic changed its name to Verizon Communications in June 2000 when the Federal Communications Commission approved the US$64.7 billion merger with telephone company GTE, nearly two years after the deal was proposed in July 1998. The approval came with 25 stipulations to preserve competition between local phone carriers, including investing in new markets and broadband technologies. The new entity was headed by co-CEOs Charles Lee, formerly the CEO of GTE, and Bell Atlantic CEO Ivan Seidenberg.

Verizon became the largest local telephone company in the United States, operating 63 million telephone lines in 40 states. The company also inherited 25 million mobile phone customers. Additionally,

---

[163] https://en.wikipedia.org/wiki/Verizon_Communications

Verizon offered internet services and long-distance calling in New York, before expanding long-distance operations to other states.

The name Verizon derives from the combination of the words *veritas*, Latin for truth, and horizon. The name was chosen from 8,500 candidates and the company spent $300 million on marketing the new brand.

Two months before the FCC gave final approval on the formation of Verizon Communications™, Bell Atlantic formed Verizon Wireless™ in a joint venture with the British telecommunications company Vodafone in April 2000. The companies established Verizon Wireless as its own business operated by Bell Atlantic, which owned 55% of the venture. Vodafone retained 45% of the company. The deal was valued at approximately $70 billion and created a mobile carrier with 23 million customers. Verizon Wireless merged Bell Atlantic's wireless network, Vodafone's AirTouch and PrimeCo holdings, and the wireless division of GTE. Due to its size, Verizon Wireless was able to offer national coverage at competitive rates, giving it an advantage over regional providers typical of the time.

During its first operational year, Verizon Wireless released Mobile Web®, an Internet service that allowed customers to access partner sites such as E*Trade™, ABC News™, ESPN™, Amazon.com™, Ticketmaster™ and MSN™. as well as the "New Every Two" program, which gave customers a free phone with every two-year service contract. In another partnership with MSN in 2002, Verizon Wireless launched the mobile content service "VZW with MSN" and a phone that utilized the Microsoft Windows® operating system.

In August 2000, approximately 85,000 Verizon workers went on an 18-day labor strike after their union contracts expired. The strike affected quarterly revenues, resulting in Verizon Wireless' postponement of the company's IPO (the IPO was ultimately cancelled in 2003, because the company no longer needed to raise revenue for Verizon Wireless due to increased profits), and created a backlog of repairs. This strike did not involve all company employees as strikers were mostly line technicians and user technicians of the company who are unionized.

Verizon launched 3G service in 2002, which doubled the Internet speeds of the time to 144kb a second. In August 2002, Verizon began offering local, long-distance, and mobile calling, as well as Internet service, in a bundle. It was initially only available to customers in New York and Massachusetts.

2003–2005

In June 2003, Verizon Wireless backed an FCC-issued portability requirement that permitted consumers to take their phone numbers with them across carriers. The company gained 1.5 million new subscribers the following quarter, partially due to the rule change. The following year, in April 2004, the Dow Jones Industrial Average added Verizon Communications to its stock market index. Verizon replaced telecom competitor AT&T, which had been a part of the index since the Great Depression.

On December 22, 2004, mail servers at Verizon.net were configured not to accept connections from Europe, by default, in an attempt to reduce spam email that was originating from the region. Individual domains would only be unblocked upon request.

In 2004, Verizon launched its Fios™ Internet service, which transmits data over fiber optic cables, in Keller, Texas. The company launched Fios TV in September 2005, also in Keller, Texas. Twenty percent of qualified homes signed up by the end of the year. By January 2006, Fios offered over 350 channels in eight states, including 20 high-definition television channels as well as video on demand.

MCI acquisition

Verizon began negotiations to purchase long distance carrier MCI™ in 2005. MCI accepted the company's initial $6.75 billion offer in February 2005, but then received a higher offer from Qwest Communications™. Verizon increased its bid to $7.6 billion (or $23.50 a share), which MCI accepted on March 29, 2005. The acquisition gave the company access to MCI's one million corporate clients and international holdings, expanding Verizon's presence into global markets. As a result, Verizon Business™ was established as a new division to serve the company's business and government customers. The FCC approved the deal on November 5, 2005, valuing it at $8.5 billion. Verizon's 2006 revenues rose by as much as 20% following the purchase.

2006–2010

In May 2006, *USA Today* reported that Verizon, as well as AT&T and BellSouth, had given the National Security Agency landline phone records following the September 11 attacks. That same month, a $50 billion lawsuit was filed by two lawyers on behalf of all Verizon subscribers for privacy violations and to prevent the company from releasing additional records without consent or warrant. Protesters staged the National Day of Out(R)age due in part to the controversy. Verizon stated in 2007 that the company fulfilled only "lawful demands" for information, though also acknowledged surrendering customer information to government agencies without court orders or warrants 720 times between 2005 and 2007.

Verizon won a lawsuit against Vonage™ in March 2007 for patent infringement. The three patents named were filed by Bell Atlantic in 1997 and relate to the conversion of IP addresses into phone numbers, a key technology of Vonage's business. The company was awarded US$58 million in damages and future royalties. Vonage later lost an appeal and was ordered to pay Verizon $120 million.

In May 2007, Verizon acquired Cybertrust™, a privately held provider of global information security services

Verizon Wireless reversed a controversial decision in September 2007 to deny NARAL (National Association for Repeal of Abortion Laws) Pro-Choice America a short code through which the organization could text consumers who had signed up for messaging from the group. They had initially refused the group access to a code by reserving the right to block "controversial or unsavory" messages.

In November 2007, Verizon opened its networks for the first time to third party apps and devices, a decision that allowed it to participate in the FCC's 2008 700MHz auction of "open access" spectrum. During that auction, the company bid $9.4 billion and won the bulk of national and local licenses for airwaves reaching approximately 469 million people. Verizon utilized the increased spectrum for its 4G service.

Verizon Wireless purchased wireless carrier Alltel™ for $28.1 billion in June 2008. The acquisition included 13 million customers, which allowed Verizon Wireless to surpass AT&T in number of customers and reach new markets in rural areas.

In October 2010, Verizon Wireless paid $77.8 million in refunds and FCC penalties for overcharging 15 million customers for data services. The company stated the overcharges were accidental and only amounted to a few dollars per customer.

On February 4, 2010, 4chan.org™ started receiving reports from Verizon Wireless customers that they were having difficulties accessing the site's image boards. 4chan administrators found that only traffic on port 80 to the boards.4chan.org domain was affected, leading them to believe that the block was intentional. On February 7, 2010, Verizon Wireless confirmed that 4chan.org was "explicitly blocked" after Verizon's security and external experts detected sweep attacks coming from an IP address associated with the 4chan network. Traffic was restored several days later.

In August 2010, the chairmen of Verizon and Google agreed that network neutrality should be defined and limited.

Verizon introduced its 4G LTE network in 38 markets in December 2010, as well as in airports in seven additional cities. The company planned on a three-year continuous expansion of the 4G service.

Selling wirelines (2005–2010 & 2015)

Between 2005 and 2010, Verizon divested wireline operations in several states to Frontier in order to focus on its wireless, Fios internet and Fios TV businesses. It sold 700,000 lines in Hawaii in 2005, and spun off lines in Maine, New Hampshire and Vermont in January 2007 that were then purchased by FairPoint Communications™ for $2.72 billion. Verizon also shed its telephone directory business in 2006.

In May 2009, the company spun off wirelines in Arizona, Idaho, Illinois, Indiana, Michigan, Nevada, North Carolina, Ohio, Oregon, South Carolina, Washington, West Virginia, and Wisconsin into a company that then merged with Frontier Communications™ in a deal valued at $8.6 billion. In 2016, Verizon sold its wireline operations in Texas, Florida, and California to Frontier.

2011–present

On January 27, 2011, Verizon acquired Terremark™, an information technology services company for $1.4 billion.

Ivan Seidenberg retired as Verizon's CEO on August 1, 2011. Lowell McAdam succeeded him.

In December 2011, the non-partisan organization Public Campaign criticized Verizon for its tax avoidance procedures after it spent $52.34 million on lobbying while collecting $951 million in tax rebates between 2008 and 2010 and making a profit of $32.5 billion. The same report also criticized Verizon for increasing executive pay by 167% in 2010 for its top five executives while laying off 21,308 workers between 2008 and 2010. However, in its Form 10-K filed with the SEC on February 24, 2012, Verizon reported having paid more than $11.1 billion in taxes (including income, employment and property taxes) from 2009 to 2011. In addition, the company reported in the 10-K that most of the drop in employment since 2008 was due to a voluntary retirement offer.

In June 2012, as part of its strategy to expand into new growth areas in its wireless business, Verizon purchased Hughes Telematics™—a company that produces wireless features for automobiles—for $612 million. Also in June 2012, Verizon's E-911 service failed in the aftermath of the June 2012 Derecho storm[164] in several northern Virginia suburbs of Washington, D.C., with some problems lasting several days. The FCC conducted an investigation and, in January 2013, released a report detailing the problems that led to the failure. Verizon reported that it had already addressed or was addressing a number of the issues related to the FCC report, including the causes of generator failures, conducting audits of backup systems and making its monitoring systems less centralized, although the FCC indicated that Verizon still needed to make additional improvements.

In July 2012, the FCC ruled that Verizon must stop charging users an added fee for using 4G smartphones and tablets as Wi-Fi hotspots (known as "tethering"). Verizon had been charging its customers, even those with "unlimited" plans, $20 per month for tethering. As part of the settlement, Verizon made a voluntary payment of $1.25 million to the U.S. Treasury.

In August 2012, the Department of Justice approved Verizon's purchase of Advanced Wireless Services (AWS) spectrum from a consortium of cable companies, including Comcast™, Time Warner Cable™ and Bright House Networks™, for $3.9 billion. Verizon began expanding its LTE network utilizing these extra airwaves in October 2013.

On June 5, 2013, *The Guardian* reported it had obtained an order by the Federal Bureau of Investigation (FBI) and approved by the United States Foreign Intelligence Surveillance Court that required Verizon to provide the NSA with telephone metadata for all calls originating in the U.S. Verizon Wireless was not part of the NSA data collection for wireless accounts due to foreign ownership issues.

In September 2013, Verizon purchased the 45% stake in Verizon Wireless owned by Vodafone for $130 billion. The deal closed on February 21, 2014, becoming the third largest corporate deal ever signed, giving Verizon Communications sole ownership of Verizon Wireless.

On January 14, 2014, the DC Circuit Court of Appeals struck down the FCC's net neutrality rules after Verizon filed suit against them in January 2010. In June 2016, in a 184-page ruling, the United States Court of Appeals for the District of Columbia Circuit upheld, by a 2–1 vote, the FCC's net neutrality rules and the FCC's determination that broadband access is a public utility, rather than a luxury. AT&T and the telecom industry said they would seek to appeal the decision to the Supreme Court.

---

[164]https://www.google.com/search?rlz=1C1CHZL_enUS725US725&sxsrf=ALeKk01tV87EQ3cGQy4l5yI09LKUD-deAdQ%3A1586210298408&ei=qWLXq3CGM6w0PEP9OuOuAM&q=Derecho+storm&oq=Derecho+storm&gs_lcp=CgZwc3ktYWIQAzICCAAyAggAMgIIADIC-CAAyAggAMgIIADICCAAyAggAMgIIADICCAA6BAgAEEc6BAgjECc6BQgAEJECOgUIABCDATOECAAQQzoECAAQCjoHCAAQRhD_AUotCBcSKTBnMTQwZzE2OG-cxMjVnOTZnMTA4ZzEwM2cxMTdnMTI3Zzk3ZzkwZzI4ShsIGBIXMGcxZzFnMWcxZzFnMWc0ZzFQv4YWWPOaFmDOnRZoAHA-BeACAAZsBiAH9CZIBAzkuNJgBAKABAaoBB2d3cy13aXo&sclient=psy-ab&ved=0ahUKEwitp4Dr5dToAhVOGDQIHfS1AzcQ4dUDCAw&uact=5

A **derecho** (/dəˈreɪtʃoʊ/, from Spanish: **derecho** [deˈretʃo], "straight") is a widespread, long-lived, straight-line wind **storm** that is associated with a fast-moving group of severe thunderstorms known as a mesoscale convective system. Derechos can cause hurricane-force winds, tornadoes, heavy rains, and flash floods.

On January 22, 2014, *The Wall Street Journal* reported that Verizon received more than 1,000 requests for information about its subscribers on national security grounds *via* National Security Letters. In total, Verizon received 321,545 requests from federal, state and local law enforcement for U.S. customer information. In May 2015, Verizon agreed to pay $90 million "to settle federal and state investigations into allegations mobile customers were improperly billed for premium text messages."

In late October 2014, Verizon Wireless launched *SugarString*®, a technology news website. The publication attracted controversy after it was reported that its writers were forbidden from publishing articles related to net neutrality or domestic surveillance. Although Verizon denied that this was the case, the site (described as being a pilot project) was shuttered in December.

In August 2015, Verizon launched Hum®, a service and device offering vehicle diagnostic and monitoring tools for vehicles. On August 1, 2016, Verizon announced its acquisition of Fleetmatics™, a fleet telematics system company in Dublin, Ireland, for $2.4 billion, to build products that it offers to enterprises for logistics and mobile workforces. On September 12, 2016, Verizon announced its acquisition of Sensity™, a startup for LED sensors, in an effort to bolster its IoT (Internet of Things) portfolio.

In October 2016, Verizon was accused by Communications Workers of America of deliberately refusing to maintain its copper telephone service. The organization released internal memos and other documents stating that Verizon workers in Pennsylvania were being instructed to, in areas with network problems, migrate voice-only customers to VoiceLink®—a system that delivers telephone service over the Verizon Wireless network, and not to repair the copper lines. VoiceLink has limitations, including incompatibility with services or devices that require the transmission of data over the telephone line, and a dependency on a battery backup in case of power failure. The memo warned that technicians who do not follow this procedure would be subject to "disciplinary action up to and including dismissal." A Verizon spokesperson responded to the allegations, stating that the company's top priority was to restore service to customers as quickly as possible, and that VoiceLink was a means of doing so in the event that larger repairs have to be done to the infrastructure. The spokesperson stated that it was "hard to argue with disciplining someone who intentionally leaves a customer without service."

In November 2016, Verizon acquired mapping startup SocialRadar™; its technology will be integrated with MapQuest™.

On January 26, 2017, *The Washington Post* reported that Verizon was in talks to merge with Charter Communications™.

In 2017, Verizon partnered with Alley™ to develop a number of co-working spaces under the name "Alley powered by Verizon."

On March 13, 2017, Verizon was sued by New York City for violating its cable franchise agreement, which required the provider to pass a fiber optic network to all households in the city by June 30, 2014. Verizon disputed the claims, citing landlords not granting permission to install the equipment on their properties, and an understanding with the government that the fiber network would follow the same routes as its copper lines, and did not necessarily mean it would have to pass the lines in front of every property.

On April 27, 2017, Verizon invested $10 million in Renovo Auto™, a Campbell, California-based autonomous vehicle company.

Verizon Connect™ was created in 2018, combining the individual units Telematics, Fleetmatics, and Telogis.

On Jan 17, 2019, Verizon announced that it would offer anti-spam and robo-calling features free of charge to all its customers from March.

Verizon began rolling out its 5G mobile network in April 2019 and by year's end, it was active in 30 cities. Unlike other U.S. carriers, Verizon only uses millimeter-wave (mmWave) spectrum for its 5G network. While capable of very high speeds, mmWave has limited range and poor building penetration.

Acquisition of AOL and Yahoo

On May 12, 2015, Verizon announced they would acquire AOL at $50 per share, for a deal valued around $4.4 billion. The following year, Verizon announced it would acquire the core internet business of Yahoo for $4.83

billion. Following the completion of the acquisitions, Verizon created a new division called Oath®, which includes the AOL and Yahoo brands. The sale did not include Yahoo's stakes in Alibaba Group™ and Yahoo! Japan.

On March 16, 2017, Verizon announced that it would discontinue the e-mail services provided for its internet subscribers, and migrate them to AOL Mail®.

On May 23, 2017, Verizon CEO, Lowell McAdam, confirmed the company's plan to launch a streaming TV service. The integrated AOL-Yahoo operation, housed under the newly created Oath division, will be organized around key content-based pillars.

On June 13, 2017, Verizon completed its acquisition of Yahoo for $4.48 billion.

On December 10, 2018, Verizon announced that 10,400 managers had agreed to leave the company as part of a "voluntary separation program" that was offered to 44,000 employees, resulting in a cut to around 7% of its workforce. At the same time, the company announced a $4.6 billion write-off on its media division, citing "increased competitive and market pressures throughout 2018 that have resulted in lower-than-expected revenues and earnings."

McCaw Cellular Communications

Cellular One

Cingular

AT&T Wireless

McCaw Cellular

AT&T Wireless began in 1987 as **McCaw Cellular Communications**, a cellular telephone pioneer in the United States. Savvy licensing of cellular spectrum in the early 1980s put McCaw Cellular in an extremely strong position, quickly outpacing the growth of the "Baby Bells" in the emerging market. The company purchased MCI Communications' mobile businesses in 1986, followed by LIN Broadcasting™ in 1989, giving them widespread access in all of the major US markets. Partnering with AT&T as a technology provider, McCaw introduced their **"Cellular One®"** service in 1990, **the first truly national cellular system**. AT&T purchased 33% of the company in 1992, and arranged a merger in 1994 that made Craig McCaw one of AT&T's largest shareholders. In 2002, the company was spun off from AT&T to become AT&T Wireless Services™.

In 1966, J. Elroy McCaw sold one of his cable television holdings in Centralia, Washington to his three sons, including Craig who was 16 years old at the time. Craig took an increasingly central role in the development of McCaw Communications™, and by the early 1980s had grown the company from 2,000 subscribers to about $5 million in annual revenue.

In 1981, McCaw came across an AT&T document about the future of cellular telephony, which predicted that, by the start of the 21st century, there would be 900,000 cellular subscribers in the United States. Intrigued, McCaw found that the licenses for cellular spectrum were being sold at $4.50 per "pop", meaning he could build a base for future subscribers for very low cost. By 1983, McCaw Communications had purchased licenses in six of the 30 largest US markets. McCaw then succeeded in using the licenses and collateral, based on the AT&T projections, using that collateral to take out loans and buy more licenses, and eventually buying billions of dollars of spectrum. In 1987 he sold the cable business for $755 million, and used this new capital to buy even more cellular licenses.

It was around this time that the first wave of analog cellular telephones was starting to enter the consumer consciousness. The Baby Bells started the process of buying their own licenses, only to find that McCaw owned enough of most of the major markets to lock them out unless they purchased spare licenses from him, at a huge profit. His network of licenses in the major markets was used as a lever to buy, sell or trade licenses in other markets that were not considered profitable, at a considerable discount. In 1986 the company purchased MCI's wireless operations, cellular and paging, for $122 million, and changed their name to "McCaw Cellular Communications"™. In 1989, the company outbid BellSouth for control of LIN Broadcasting, which owned licenses in Houston, Dallas, Los Angeles, and New York, paying $3.5 billion, a price that represented $350 per license.

Cellular One

At this point McCaw's focus turned from dealing licenses to servicing the network, signing up customers in what was now a maturing technology on the cusp of explosive growth. In order to handle the customer side of the business, McCaw turned to AT&T for technology.

In 1990, McCaw Cellular introduced SS7 signaling across their network. Prior to this, each cell tower in the network connected to local signaling, billing and sets of land-lines. Since only the towers in the area local to the customer's home had access to dialing and routing information, when they traveled to another area, calls could not reach them. With the introduction of SS7 signaling, the dialing and routing information could now be switched across the entire network (known technically as Non-Facility Associated Signaling), tying it together into a single national network. They called the new system "Cellular One"™, and introduced the concept of roaming charges. That year, Craig McCaw personally earned $54 million, making him America's highest-paid chief executive.

The partnership grew in November 1992, when AT&T purchased 1/3 of the company for $3.8 billion. At the time, the company was generating $1.75 billion in annual revenue, and had two million Cellular One subscribers - far more customers than AT&T's earlier projections for all cellular use in the US, at a point almost ten years earlier.

Purchase by AT&T Corp.

In 1994 the merger of the two companies was completed when AT&T purchased the rest of McCaw Cellular for $11.5 billion, at that time the second largest merger in US history, second only to the RJR Nabisco take-over documented in *Barbarians at the Gate*®. The merger was completed in late 1994, creating AT&T Wireless Group™, which was, at that time, the largest cellular carrier in the US. AT&T kick-started their cellular division with 2 million subscribers. As a result of the merger, Craig McCaw became one of AT&T's largest shareholders, but he refused to sit on the Board of Directors because he couldn't stand long meetings. McCaw left daily operations to focus on Teledesic™, passing control of AT&T Wireless to James Barksdale, and then Steve Hooper when Barksdale left for Netscape.

Hooper, a long time McCaw Cellular executive, was tapped by AT&T to be the CEO of the newly acquired division. Under his direction, AT&T Wireless grew to be the nation's largest cellular provider by the end of 1997, at which point Hooper and many of the remaining McCaw era executives departed. By 1999 and 2000 the cellular industry began to consolidate and Verizon Wireless™ and Cingular Wireless™ became the first and second largest national carriers.

The year 1999 also brought John D. Zeglis as chief executive in October, followed a few months later by Dan Hesse's departure, who had been head of the division since 1997. Over the next year and a half, all six McCaw regional presidents left the declining company.

Spinoff

In April 2000, AT&T Wireless became a separately traded entity with the world's largest initial public offering at that time. Just over a year later in July 2001, AT&T Wireless™ became a separate company rather than a division of AT&T Corp.

In 2003, AT&T Wireless was granted several mobile licenses for Caribbean countries including Barbados, Grenada, Saint Lucia, and Saint Vincent and the Grenadines. AT&T Wireless's decline climaxed in 2003 with the FCC mandating the allowance of porting numbers to other carriers. AT&T Wireless experienced a mass exodus of many customers who were fed up with years of degrading service and poor coverage. By the end of 2003, AT&T Wireless faced a public relations nightmare when a new system for adding subscribers and porting numbers in/out was implemented and botched. Realizing that it faced an impossible situation, AT&T Wireless Services, Inc. began accepting bids in early 2004 to be acquired.

As of January 1, 2004, the largest single shareholder of AT&T Wireless was Japan's NTT DoCoMo™, which was one of the first to place a bid to buy the company.

In the middle of 2004, much of the Caribbean operations and Bermuda were agreed to be sold to Digicel Group.

Acquisition by Cingular

On February 13, 2004, AT&T Wireless accepted bids for acquisition of the wireless company. The two top bidders were British carrier Vodafone™ and American competitor Cingular™. Cingular was owned by two Baby Bells; 40% by BellSouth and 60% by SBC Communications. Vodafone owned 45% of Verizon Wireless and had it succeeded in the bid, their share of Verizon Wireless would then have been sold to parent company Verizon Communications. Cingular emerged victorious February 17 by agreeing to pay more than $41 billion, more than twice the company's recent trading value, to acquire AT&T Wireless. Some analysts have said that although Vodafone, the world's largest mobile operator, was unsuccessful in acquiring the company, it was nonetheless successful in forcing a competitor to overpay for the acquisition of AT&T Wireless.

The sale received US government approval and closed on October 26. Companies that originally comprised Cingular from its inception, such as BellSouth Mobility, were absorbed into the AT&T Wireless Services corporate structure. The AT&T Wireless brand was retired by Cingular on April 26, 2005, six months after the close of the merger. This was per a pre spin-off agreement with AT&T Corp. stating that, if AT&T Wireless was to be bought by a competitor, the rights to the name AT&T Wireless and the use of the AT&T name in wireless phone service would revert to AT&T Corp.

AT&T Wireless's prepaid services, Go Phone®, was adopted by Cingular Wireless after the merger closed, and is still in use today by the current AT&T Mobility™.

Partnerships

Rogers AT&T Wireless was a publicly traded partnership between Rogers and AT&T. It operated a mobile network in Canada until Rogers bought out AT&T's stake in 2004 and took the company private. *See Rogers Wireless.*

SunCom Wireless™ was a brand name used by three separate companies: Telecorp PCS, Tritel PCS, and Triton PCS (based in Arlington, VA, Jackson, MS, and Berwyn, PA, respectively). All three used the same SunCom logo, but operated as completely independent companies, though all were affiliates of AT&T Wireless, which owned 23% of each company. Telecorp™ operated primarily in Wisconsin, Iowa, Louisiana, Tennessee, Arkansas, and Puerto Rico. Tritel™ operated primarily in Mississippi, Kentucky, Alabama, and Tennessee. Triton™ operated primarily in North and South Carolina and Virginia. In 2002, Telecorp™ and Tritel completed a merger, while Triton remained independent. In 2003, AT&T Wireless acquired Telecorp/Tritel, and closed the Telecorp headquarters in Arlington, VA.

Cincinnati Bell Wireless™ started as a joint venture between Cincinnati Bell and AT&T Wireless, in which AT&T Wireless owned 20%. When AT&T Wireless was purchased by Cingular, control of the 20% passed to Cingular as well. On February 17, 2006, Cincinnati Bell took full control of Cincinnati Bell Wireless by purchasing Cingular's 20% ownership for $80 million.

AT&T brand returns to wireless

The AT&T brand in wireless ended in 2004, but it would be brought back a few years later. On November 18, 2005, SBC Communications completed a merger with AT&T Corp., and took on the name AT&T and created a new modern globe logo. After the merger, rumors surfaced of a revival of AT&T's brand in wireless *via* a rebranding of Cingular; however, Cingular, Bellsouth, and the new AT&T maintained that the Cingular brand would remain for the time being.

Then, the new AT&T announced on March 5, 2006, that it would be acquiring BellSouth's telephone operations and its stake in Cingular Wireless. On December 29, 2006, the FCC gave its final approval to the AT&T and BellSouth merger. With both parent companies merged into one, Cingular Wireless officially became AT&T Mobility™ in 2007. The rebranding phase was a gradual process but, by mid-2007, the Cingular Wireless brand (not the company) was officially discontinued for the AT&T name.

Thus, AT&T as a wireless brand is alive and well; however, the old AT&T Wireless Services company remains defunct. Today, AT&T stores sell all AT&T products and services: Wireless, Landline, Internet, U-Verse, DIRECTV and more. AT&T currently markets all services under one brand, even though the wireless division is commonly referred to as "AT&T Mobility" both internally and externally.

Sprint PCS

Sprint's history goes back more than a century.[165]

1899: Railroad roots

The mobile service company we now know as Sprint has its origins in two companies that operated in the early 19th century.

One was the Southern Pacific Railroad, which operated thousands of miles of telegraph wire on poles along its tracks so dispatchers could monitor trains and relay track conditions to locomotive engineers. Later, the same wires could be used for voice communications. The railroad operated its telephone system as an independent company, called the Southern Pacific Communications Corporation™.

The other was Brown Telephone Company™ of Abilene, Kansas, founded in 1899. That company's history was a rollercoaster. It declared bankruptcy in the early 1930s in the aftermath of the Great Depression, and only six out of 85 subsidiary companies continued to operate. However, after its reorganization, the former Brown Telephone Company managed to get back on track under a new name: United Utilities™.

In 1972, United Utilities™ changed its name to United Telecommunications™ and started operating its own long-distance telephone service.

1972: The name Sprint is born

By the late 1950s, the Southern Pacific and other railroads started to use radio systems, and wire lines were no longer economically viable. Instead of getting rid of the wires, in the mid-1970s Southern Pacific began selling time on its extensive microwave communications system to private customers. In 1972, the company named its long-distance phone operation: **Sprint**™, which stood for **Southern Pacific Railroad Internal Networking Telephony.**

1982: Southern Pacific Railroad sells Sprint to GTE

According to a 1982 New York Times article, the Southern Pacific Railroad had cash-flow problems related to a $1.4 billion loan. So the railroad decided to sell its communication networks, including Sprint, to General Telephone & Electronics Corporation.

1986: Emergence of Sprint Corporation

In 1986, GTE merged with United Telecom as both companies were expanding their networks of fiber cables, a groundbreaking technology in communications.

At that time, Sprint was the nation's third-largest long-distance service, and United Telecom™ was the fourth. Three years later, United Telecom purchased a controlling interest in Sprint, and had completed its acquisition by 1991. The company was renamed the Sprint Corporation™.

1990s: Going wireless

Sprint entered the market of wireless communications in 1993 by purchasing Chicago-based Centel™, the 10th largest cellular company in the U.S., with operations in 22 states.

In 1996, Sprint forged a partnership with Radio Shack™ that allowed Sprint to sell its services and phones inside Radio Shack outlets.

---

[165] kcur.org/post/timeline-sprints-120-years-kansas-city#stream/0

Almost 20 years later, in 2015, Radio Shack filed for bankruptcy and shortly co-branded around 1,400 of its remaining stores with Sprint. Later, Radio Shack filed a lawsuit, claiming that Sprint took advantage of the partnership by using confidential data to pinpoint the best locations for its own retail stores.

1998: New headquarters in Overland Park

In the late 1990s, Sprint built its new headquarters in Overland Park, KS. The a 3.9 million square-foot campus consisted of 17 buildings, parking structures, hiking and biking trails, and an amphitheater for 3,000 people. The campus has a capacity for 14,500 employees.

2004: Sprint Corporation and Nextel Communications™

In 2004, Sprint Corporation and Nextel Communications™ merged to become the Sprint Nextel Corporation.

Sprint aimed to boost its number of subscribers from 20.1 million to 40 million in the deal with Nextel. But what looked like a win-win turned out to cost $37 billion in losses and millions of customers fleeing, according to Bloomberg Businessweek™. The companies were using incompatible technologies.

In the end, Sprint had to support separate networks and sell different types of phones that worked with each. Sprint's CEO, Dan Hesse, halted Nextel's network and put the remaining resources towards rebuilding Sprint's network.

2013: SoftBank Corporation™ comes to the rescue

Tokyo-based mobile phone company Softbank Corp.™ reached a deal to acquire 70 percent of Sprint Nextel for $20 billion in 2013. SoftBank™ planned to merge Sprint with T-Mobile to generate $30 billion or more in cost savings between the two companies. However, U.S. anti-trust regulators halted the proposal, preventing the two companies from bidding jointly on wireless spectrum. After the deal failed, the company's CEO Dan Hesse was replaced by Marcelo Claure.

2014-18: Rounds of layoffs

After its failure to merge with T-Mobile, Sprint slashed $1.5 billion and 2,000 total employees in 2014. The next year, it fell to last place among national carriers. In 2016, Sprint Corp. fired another 800 employees as a part of the company's $2.5 billion plan to cut operating costs. Finally, the company announced it would lose 500 jobs from its Overland Park headquarters in 2018.

April 29, 2018: T-Mobile again

On April 29, T-Mobile and Sprint announced another attempt to merge, creating a company with 126 million customers. It would bring it closer to its rivals: AT&T with 141 million subscribers, and Verizon with 150 million.

On July 16, 2020, T-Mobile announced that the Sprint brand will be officially discontinued on August 2, 2020. On this date all retail, customer service, and all other company branding will switch to the T-Mobile brand.[166]

MCI (Microwave Communications, Inc.) – Jack Goeken[167]

MCI was founded as **Microwave Communications, Inc.** on October 3, 1963, with John (Jack) D. Goeken being named the company's first president. The initial business plan was for the company to build a series of Microwave radio relay stations between Chicago, Illinois, and St. Louis, Missouri. The relay stations would then be used to interface with limited-range two-way radios used by truckers along U.S. Route 66 or by barges on the Illinois Waterway. The long-distance communication service would then be marketed to shipping companies that were too small to build their own private relay systems. In addition to the radio relay services, MCI soon made plans to offer voice, computer information, and data communication services for business customers unable to afford AT&T's TELPAK® service.

---

[166] https://en.wikipedia.org/wiki/Merger_of_Sprint_Corporation_and_T-Mobile_US#:~:text=Sprint%20Corporation%20and%20T%2DMobile%20US%20merged%20in%202020%20in,emerging%20as%20the%20surviving%20brand.
[167] https://en.wikipedia.org/wiki/MCI_Communications

Hearings on the company's initial license application between February 13, 1967, and April 19, 1967, resulted in a recommendation of approval by the FCC.

On June 26, 1968, the FCC ruled in the Carterfone case that AT&T's rules prohibiting private two-way radio connections to a telephone network were illegal. AT&T quickly sought a reversal of the ruling, and when the FCC denied the request, AT&T brought suit against the FCC in the United States courts of appeals. The FCC's decision was upheld, thus creating a new industry: privately (non-Bell) manufactured devices could be connected to the telephone network as long as the manufacturer met interface standards.

In 1968, William G. McGowan, an investor from New York with experience in raising venture capital, made an investment into the company large enough to pay all outstanding debts and create a cash reserve. McGowan received a seat on the board of directors. **Microwave Communications of America, Inc** (MICOM) was incorporated on August 8, 1968 as an umbrella corporation to help build a nationwide microwave relay system.

Licensing and build-out

On October 28, 1968, Hyrum Rex Lee became an FCC Commissioner and MCI began a series of submissions including a proposal for a low-cost educational television network designed to show MCI as being more flexible to public needs than AT&T. While MCI was performing this lobbying, the President's Task Force on Communication Policy issued a report recommending that specialized common carriers be allowed free access into the private line business.

On 14 August 1969, the FCC issued a final ruling on Docket 16509, MCI's licensing request to begin building microwave relay stations between Chicago and St. Louis. By a decision of 4-to-3 MCI was licensed for operation. This ruling was quickly appealed by AT&T, and after a denial of the appeal by the commission, AT&T filed a civil suit with the United States courts of appeals to have the ruling overturned.

MCI™ then began to form subsidiary corporations and file applications with the FCC to create microwave relays between other city pairs. Between September 1969 and February 1971, 15 new regional carriers were created, allowing for interconnection between several major cities in the United States.

In July 1969, MICOM™ purchased stock in Interdata™, an independent regional carrier that was applying to build a microwave relay chain between New York City and Washington, D.C.

MCI began selling data transmission services to paying customers on January 1, 1972.

To pay for the microwave transmission and relay equipment needed for build-out, MICOM™ began a series of private stock offerings in May 1971. In July 1971, MICOM™ was restructured into **MCI Communications™**, and the company began the process of absorbing the regional carriers into a single corporation.

MCI became a public company *via* an initial public offering on June 22, 1972.

In early 1971, MCI™ and Lockheed Missiles and Space Company™ created a joint venture which was the first company to request FCC authorization as a Specialized Common Carrier using satellite-based communications; satellite service would save the company from building thousands of miles of terrestrial network facilities. A year later, Comsat Corp.™ entered the venture which was renamed CML Satellite Corp.™ In need of cash, MCI sold its share of the venture to IBM in 1974. Lockheed also subsequently sold its share to IBM. IBM and Comsat brought in Aetna™ as a third partner and renamed the company Satellite Business Systems™ (SBS). IBM later acquired the remainder of the company and sold it back to MCI in March 1986 for $376 million in MCI stock.

Illinois Bell refused to interconnect an MCI long haul interstate circuit and, in January 1974, MCI filed an antitrust lawsuit against AT&T. On June 13, 1980, a jury in Chicago awarded MCI $1.8 billion in damages to be paid by AT&T, reduced to $113 million in 1985 on appeal. The suit, coupled with the Department of Justice antitrust suit also brought against AT&T, eventually led to the voluntary breakup of the Bell System. (emphasis author's)

In 1975, as a result of the Carterfone decision, MCI began offering switched voice telecommunications in direct competition with AT&T, using a combination of its own microwave circuits and leased circuits from AT&T. By 1977, the company operated several switches manufactured by Danray™ (later part of Nortel).

In 1982, MCI worked with Ally & Gargano™ to create what *Entertainment Weekly* referred to in 1997 as one of the 50 best commercials of all time. MCI hired the same actors used in an AT&T commercial in 1981. In the AT&T version, the son calls his mother and, when asked why, replied "just 'cuz I love you," which was not a common reason to make an expensive long-distance call, causing the mother to cry. In the MCI version, when the husband asked the wife why she was crying, she replied "I just received my phone bill"... after which an announcer's voice stated: "You're not talking too much, you're just paying too much. MCI: The Nation's New Long Distance Telephone Company."

In 1982, MCI acquired Western Union International™, the cable systems properties and the right-of-way rights of Western Union's telegraph lines from Xerox for $185 million. Xerox had acquired it for $279 million in 1979. It was renamed MCI International™ and its headquarters were moved from New York City to Westchester County, New York.

On September 27, 1983, an MCI division led by Vint Cerf, one of the developers of the TCP/IP protocol, launched MCI Mail®, one of the first email services, and a data network using the CCITT[168] X.25 packet switching protocol.

In 1983, Michael Milken and Drexel Burnham Lambert raised a $1.1 billion hybrid security, at the time the largest debt financing in history, for the company.

In 1984, MCI became the first company to deploy single-mode optical fiber (the standard had been multi-mode optical fiber), which was manufactured by Siecor™, a joint venture between Siemens Telecom™ and Corning Glass Company™. Referred to as MAFOS® (Mid-Atlantic Fiber Optic System), the fiber cable ran between New York City and Washington D.C. Eventually, single-mode fiber became the standard for US telecommunications carriers.

In 1987, MCI acquired RCA Global™ from General Electric.

In 1987, MCI partnered with IBM and Merit Network (a network run by a triad of universities in Michigan) to respond to a National Science Foundation proposal to develop a high-speed telecommunications network called National Science Foundation Network (NSFNET). This network used the TCP/IP protocol that had been developed by the United States Department of Defense ARPANet[169] and was the immediate forerunner to the Internet. In 1988, Vint Cerf was working at CNRI and obtained support from MCI and permission from the Federal Networking Council to interconnect MCI Mail with the NSFNET. In 1989, it was the first commercial e-mail service to do so. Immediately, most of the other commercial e-mail providers also received permission to interconnect to the Internet, leading to their interconnection with each other. In 1994, NSF announced that it would terminate the NSFNET operation and support the development of Network Access Point operation to link the networks that had been interconnected by NSFNET. NSF also proposed that an academic research network be built called the Very high-speed Backbone Network Service (vBNS) and MCI responded. MCI also built a separate commercial Internet service, MCI.net®, which was an integral part of the global Internet backbone. It was sold to Cable & Wireless plc™ as part of the merger of MCI with Worldcom™[170] in 1998.

In 1990, the company acquired Telecom*USA™ and became the second-largest telecommunications company in the U.S., with a fiber-optic network spanning more than 46,000 miles. The company offered more than 50 services in more than 150 countries that included voice, data, and telex transmissions, MCI Mail and MCI Fax.

---

[168] https://www.sigidwiki.com/wiki/CCITT **CCITT** is a 15 tone selcall system for VHF/UHF radios. CCITT stands for Consultative Committee for International Telephony and Telegraphy, which has now become the ITU-T. Selcall (selective calling) is a type of squelch protocol used in radio communications systems, in which transmissions include a brief burst of sequential audio tones. Receivers that are set to respond to the transmitted tone sequence will open their squelch, while others will remain muted.
CCITT has 100 ms tone duration per tone. Each tone corresponds with either a number or letter. CCITT has 15 tones to choose from, but only sends a burst of up to 5 tones. The bursts transmit preceding a radio transmission.
[169] https://www.livescience.com/20727-internet-history.html The precursor to the Internet was jump started in the early days of computing history, in 1969 with the U.S. Defense Department's Advanced Research Projects Agency Network (ARPANET). ARPA-funded researchers developed many of the protocols used for Internet communication today.
[170] https://en.wikipedia.org/wiki/MCI_Inc. On November 4, 1997, WorldCom and MCI Communications announced a $37 billion merger to form MCI WorldCom, making it the largest corporate merger in U.S. history. On September 15, 1998, the merger was consummated, forming **MCI WorldCom**. MCI divested itself of its "internetMCI" business to gain approval from the U.S. United States Department of Justice

In March 1991, the company introduced the *Friends & Family*® plan, whereby customers received a reduced rate when calling numbers they had included in their "calling circle," which could contain up to 20 MCI customers.

In 1993, the company introduced a collect call service called "1-800-COLLECT"™. Actors Phil Hartman, Chris Rock, and Arsenio Hall starred in some of its commercials, but the most commonly used spokesperson was the fictional Eva Save-a-lot, played by actress Alyssa Milano. The service was sold to viiz™[171] in 2016.

In 1995, the company partnered with News Corporation™ on a television venture. It intended to broadcast from two satellites at the 110 degree orbital slot; but the venture never started broadcasting. The orbital slot and an uplink center were sold to EchoStar™ in 1999; the planned satellites Tempo 1® and Tempo 2® were sold to PrimeStar™, whose assets were sold to DirecTV™ in 1999.

In October 1994, BT Group™ acquired 20% of the company for $4.3 billion.

In November 1995, MCI introduced 1-800-MUSIC-NOW®, a short-lived telephone-based and online music store.

Purchase by WorldCom

BT made an offer to purchase the rest of the company in November 1996 for $22 billion. In October 1997, GTE, now a part of Verizon, made a bid to purchase MCI for $28 billion in cash. WorldCom offered $34.7 billion in stock, higher than either the BT or GTE offers, which was accepted by MCI on November 10, 1997. On September 15, 1998 the transaction was consummated and the merged company renamed MCI WorldCom™. Two years later, the "MCI" part was dropped.

Following a major accounting scandal, WorldCom filed for bankruptcy in 2002 and the company was renamed MCI Inc. upon its exit from bankruptcy in 2003. Before then, however, many executive posts were taken over by holdovers from the old MCI. After the name change, one of those executives said, "We're taking our company back."

---

[171] viiz Communications provides IT services. The Company offers outsourced, on-premise, cloud, and hybrid solutions to telecommunication industry. viiz Communications also develops software for enterprise market. viiz Communications serves customers in Canada

Chapter Twenty -- What Is PCS?[172] (aka: PCN – Personal Communications Networks)

At the most basic level, **Personal Communications Service** (**PCS**) describes a set of communications capabilities which allows some combination of terminal device mobility, personal mobility, and service profile management. More specifically, PCS refers to any of several types of wireless voice or wireless data communi-cations systems, typically incorporating digital technology, providing services similar to advanced cellular mobile or paging services. In addition, PCS can also be used to provide other wireless communications services, including services which allow people to place and receive communications while away from their home or office, as well as wireless communications to homes, office buildings and other fixed locations. **Described in more commercial terms, PCS is a generation of wireless-phone technology that combines a range of features and services surpassing those available in analog- and digital -cellular phone systems, providing a user with an all-in-one wireless phone, paging, messaging, and data service.**

The International Telecommunication Union describes Personal Communications Services as a component of the IMT-2000 (3G) standard. PCS and the IMT-2000 standard of which PCS is a part do not specify a particular air interface and channel access method. Wireless service providers may deploy equipment using any of several air interface and channel access methods, as long as the network meets the service description characteristics described in the standard.[173]

Identifying spectrum assignment as a function of its application to specific services was not a new idea. As we have seen in previous pages, the pre-cellular world of radio required licenses for specific channels which were pre-designated by the FCC for specific applications, *e.g.*, Business and Education, Special Industrial, Manufacturing, Public Safety, Emergency Medical Services, and others. However, spectrum allocation for PCS originally specified frequencies from 1.8GHz-2.2GHz – technically and by virtue of legacy commercial identity, these are microwave frequencies, many of which were licensed to deliver point-to-point (Line of Sight [LOS]) connectivity. It was a problem because to license a new user on the same microwave frequencies as existing licensees was courting catastrophic consequences. A new term was invented (coined) by the FCC to address this issue: "re-farming." Effectively, it meant existing license holders of these microwave channels were forced to sell or otherwise bargain with new PCS/PCN licensees for relieving the traffic to allow new traffic. It became a nightmare of new licensees paying enough for legacy license holders to move to higher spectrum. This was an expensive and difficult solution but it ultimately prevailed. This allowed the FCC to auction bands of spectrum – 10MHz, 20MHz and 30MHz on a nationwide basis.

In Canada, Mexico and the United States, PCS is provided in the "1900 MHz band" (specifically 1850–1990MHz). This frequency band was designated by the United States FCC and Industry Canada to be used for new wireless services to alleviate capacity caps inherent in the original AMPS and D-AMPS cellular networks in the "850 MHz band" (specifically 800–894MHz). These frequency bands are particular to North America and other frequency bands may be designated in other regions.

The "cellular" concept established in the 900MHz band in effect at the time the FCC introduced its intention to allocate spectrum in the 1.8-2.2GHz bands, was a foregone conclusion to be the platform for PCS services. Propagation properties attendant to the higher frequencies demanded new topological considerations, not the least of which demanded a ratio of 5:1—meaning 1.8-2.2GHz infrastructure would effectively require five PCS cell sites for every one legacy cellular network cell sites.

In addition to the technical issues this represented, from a practical point of view, finding and securing five times as many fixed points for installing antennas was a daunting consideration. The NIMBY (not in my back yard) syndrome had already taken its toll on the cellular operators budgets and considering its impact on increasing costs associated with five times as many real estate holders was a major leap for any licensee considering deployment of PCS.

---

[172] https://en.wikipedia.org/wiki/Personal_Communications_Service
[173] Ibid

Undaunted, yet another unsung hero whose heroics in the early stages of cellular adoption re-appeared on the scene to demonstrate the efficacy of a PCS/PCN network. Wayne Schelle, the non-wireline pioneer who launched the first cellular network in the Washington, DC/Baltimore market accepted the challenge.

WAYNE SCHELLE[174]

By Reily Gregson; DECEMBER 18, 1995; Archived Articles, Carriers, Towers; **RCR Wireless News**

"It's the morning after."

"The reporter arrives at 10: 15 a.m. at the historic Willard Hotel in Washington, D.C., (conveniently across 14th Street from the National Press Building) to interview the co-recipient of RCR's 1995 Person of the Year: American Personal Communications Chairman, Wayne Schelle.

Schelle, 61, greets the reporter at the door. He's clean shaven, in shirt and tie, looking tired and moving stiffly, with a bit of a limp. He has a painfully cheerful disposition, and despite his hoarseness, begins with unabated excitement to recount the big bash the night before that celebrated the launch of Sprint Spectrum personal communications services in Washington, D.C., and America.

Elaine, his wife of 37 years, marvels to this day about how her husband rolls out of bed every morning in a good mood, ready to take on the world and explore new frontiers like cellular, in the early 1980s, and now, PCS."

"A happy warrior is he."

"I always had a lot of fun," said Schelle, who early in his career worked with AT&T Corp. before taking over a friend's family-owned paging and mobile telephone company in the early 1980s called American Radio Telephone Services initially and later American TeleServices.

Now APC is a family affair. Son Scott, 34, is chief executive officer of the company. His newlywed wife of six months, Anne, is vice president in charge of corporate communications. And Wayne's wife Elaine, is his closest business partner.

Back to the party. Schelle, still beaming from the night before, leaves not a detail out. The wisecracking of TV talkmeister Larry King. Parrothead dancing to the live music of Jimmy Buffet and the Coral Reefer Band-Key West partying on Pennsylvania Avenue..

John Kasich, R-Ohio, chairman of the House Budget Committee, arrived in blue jeans ready to go. And there were all the hugs and other congratulatory gestures that engulfed Schelle throughout the night of Nov. 30.

The party was, in fact, a celebration of Wayne Schelle, the man and his pioneering achievements in the wireless telecom industry. The man who built one of the two experimental cellular systems; his in the Baltimore-Washington market. The man who ran the first commercial nonwireline cellular system in the nation's capital, Cellular One, setting the standard for all future cellular networks.

The man, who after cashing out of the cellular industry in the late 1980s, decided there was a better mousetrap to be built, and built it-PCS, a full spectrum of voice and data digital wireless services squeezed into a lightweight palm-sized device. He was back in his element.

The inaugural PCS call was made by Vice President Al Gore-information superhighway poster child-from the White House to Baltimore Mayor Kurt Schmoke on Nov. 15.

Forget the policymakers and telephone company lobbyists who forced APC to cough up more than $100 million for a license originally awarded for free in recognition of the spunky firm's spectrum-sharing breakthrough. Forget the early battles with the cellular industry over turf. Forget the persnickety local government officials with oversight of antenna tower siting. Forget all the headaches and heartache since 1989, when APC received the first U.S. PCS experimental license. APC, embodying the entrepreneurial spirit and staying power of its chairman, partied this night with the same energy that the small firm put into all the long days during the last six years. The Bethesda, Md., firm of 275 employees had crossed the finish line. First. Now, it was time for a little fun.

---

[174] https://www.rcrwireless.com/19951218/carriers/wayne-schelle

PCS was real at last. APC is the 49.5 percent owner of the Sprint Spectrum franchise in Baltimore-Washington. The Sprint Telecommunications Venture (Sprint Corp. and cable TV giants Tele-Communications Inc., Comcast Corp. and Cox Communications) holds a 49 percent stake and The Washington Post Co. owns 1.5 percent.

"We were looking for a national brand name and I didn't think `Wayne's PCS World' was going to make it against the big guys (like AT&T Corp. and the Baby Bells)," quipped the good-natured Schelle.

It's not that the hard part is over. Schelle knows Sprint Spectrum must produce changes in attitudes to attract enough consumers away from one cent cellular telephones to pay for the nearly half-billion dollar capital and license expenditures and make a profit one day five or so years from now.

Financing, marketing and strong management are key to success, according to Schelle. "You've got to be able to stand there and take a big whipping financially for four or five years until you stabilize yourself," he said.

That's not all. AT&T Corp. will be in town soon to compete with Sprint Spectrum, followed by the winner of C-block PCS auction that is scheduled to begin today. "I think we'll fare very well against cellular," said Schelle. "They (cellular) will do all they can to re-outfit what they have to offer and they'll be tough competitors because they have a lot of money."

Not to mention a 10-year head start. Another possible snag is technology. APC uses Global System for Mobile communications technology, which is embraced in Europe and other parts of the world, while its partner, STV, and other major PCS players have adopted the Code Division Multiple Access standard developed by Qualcomm Inc.

Schelle's got it covered. Sprint Spectrum has roaming agreements with current PCS licensees and some in Europe that have chosen GSM technology and feels confident the C-block auction will produce more. In addition, Sprint Spectrum plans to spend another $100 million to overlay CDMA technology on top of existing systems.

Besides, "I think technology is a back-seat item," said Schelle. "The wars will be won and lost in advertising and distribution," said Schelle. "I think the fast food people have proven that Wendy's, Burger King, McDonalds, Hardee's and Roy Rogers can all coexist on the same street corner."

Schelle is not discouraged; there's a clever grand plan in play. The idea is to compete against, rather than with, the two cellular carriers in the Baltimore-Washington market

It means differentiating PCS-a wireless phone, pager, answering machine and more-from cellular.

How? Try better quality; lower service charges; free airtime; privacy; no annual service contracts; no early termination penalty fees; no dropped calls and no cross-talk. Just pick up a colorful shrink-wrapped Sprint Spectrum boxed phone, get activated, and start yakking away.

Schelle also points to the 30 percent churn rate in the cellular industry, which now claims 30 million subscribers.

Seeing the limitations of cellular technology and ready for a new challenge, Schelle said he became intrigued about a new wireless development in the United Kingdom during the late 1980s called personal communications networks, or PCN.

Schelle went to his lawyer, Jonathan Blake, and said he wanted to apply to the Federal Communications Commission for an experimental license. The two men approached then-chief FCC engineer Thomas Stanley, who encouraged them to go forward but with the caveat that then-FCC Chairman Alfred Sikes wanted the new service to be American-made.

Simple enough. Schelle and his wife the next day formed a new corporation, American Personal Communications. And instead of PCN, as the Brits called it, Schelle referred to this brave new world of wireless as personal communications services, or PCS.

Today, Schelle is looking beyond the coming wireless wars to something potentially bigger. He realized just how big recently after finishing a conversation with his son, Scott, from his PCS phone at home. Elaine, his wife, asked him why he didn't use the regular landline phone. "I said, `You know, Elaine, in three to five years there won't be that regular phone.' It was an interesting phenomenon.

So is Wayne Schelle."

Related Posts

Wayne Schelle: Pioneer in cellular, PCS

Editor's Note: RCR Wireless News announces that Wayne Schelle has been inducted into the Wireless Hall of Fame for 2005, now in its sixth year. The Hall of Fame recognizes the efforts of those people who have made significant contributions to advance wireless telecommunications."[175]

SPRINT PURCHASES REMAINING SHARES OF APC

KANSAS CITY, Mo.-Sprint Spectrum L.P. said it completed its purchase of the remaining shares in its partnership with American Personal Communications to make the venture wholly owned by Sprint Spectrum.[176]

In the United States, Sprint PCS was the first company to build and operate a PCS network, launching service in November 1995 under the *Sprint Spectrum* brand in the Baltimore-Washington metropolitan area. Sprint originally built out the network using GSM radio interface equipment. Sprint PCS later selected CDMA as the radio interface for its nationwide network and built out a parallel CDMA network in the Baltimore-Washington area, launching service in 1997. Sprint operated the two networks in parallel until finishing a migration of its area customers to the CDMA network. After completing the customer migration, Sprint PCS sold the GSM radio interface network equipment to Omnipoint Communications™ in January 2000. Omnipoint™ was later purchased by VoiceStream Wireless™ which subsequently became T-Mobile USA™[177]

---

[175] Ibid
[176] Ibid
[177] Ibid

Chapter Twenty-One -- History of Numbering[178]

United States

Telephone numbers were first used in 1879 in Lowell, Massachusetts, when they replaced the request for subscriber names by callers connecting to the switchboard operator. Over the course of telephone history, telephone numbers had various lengths and formats, and even included most letters of the alphabet in leading positions when telephone exchange names were in common use until the 1960s.

Telephone numbers are often dialed in conjunction with other signaling code sequences, such as vertical service codes, to invoke special telephone service features.

In the late 1870s, the Bell interests started utilizing their patent with a rental scheme, in which they would rent their instruments to individual users who would contract with other suppliers to connect them; for example from home to office to factory. Western Union and the Bell Company both soon realized that a subscription service would be more profitable, with the invention of the telephone switchboard or central office. Such an office was staffed by an operator who connected the calls by personal names. Some have argued that use of the telephone altered the physical layout of American cities.

The latter part of 1879 and the early part of 1880 saw the first use of telephone numbers at Lowell, Massachusetts. During an epidemic of measles, the physician, Dr. Moses Greeley Parker, feared that Lowell's four telephone operators might all succumb to sickness and bring about paralysis of telephone service. He recommended the use of numbers for calling Lowell's more than 200 subscribers so that substitute operators might be more easily trained in such an emergency. Parker, convinced of the telephone's potential, began buying stock and, by 1883, he was one of the largest individual stockholders in both the American Telephone Company and the New England Telephone and Telegraph Company.

Even after the assignment of numbers, operators still connected most calls into the early 20th century: "Hello, Central. Get me Underwood-342." Connecting through operators or "Central" was the norm until mechanical direct-dialing of numbers became more common in the 1920s.

In rural areas with magneto crank telephones connected to party lines, the local phone number consisted of the line number plus the ringing pattern of the subscriber. To dial a number such as "3R122" meant making a request to the operator the third party line (if making a call off your own local one), followed by turning the telephone's crank once, a short pause, then twice and twice again. Also common was a code of long and short rings, so one party's call might be signaled by two longs and another's by two longs followed by a short. It was not uncommon to have over a dozen ring cadences (and subscribers) on one "party" line.

From the 1920s through the sixties, in most areas of North America, telephone numbers in metropolitan communities consisted of a combination of digits and letters. Letters were translated to dialed digits, a mapping that was displayed directly on the telephone dial. Each of the digits 2 to 9, and sometimes 0, corresponded to a group of typically three letters. The leading two or three letters of a telephone number indicated the exchange name, for example, *ED*gewood and *IV*anhoe, and were followed by 5 or 4 digits. The limitations that these systems presented in terms of usable names that were easy to distinguish and spell, and the need for a comprehensive numbering plan that enabled direct-distance dialing, led to the introduction of all-number dialing in the 1960s.

The use of numbers starting in 555- (**KL**ondike-5) to represent fictional numbers in U.S. movies, television, and literature originated in this period. The "555" prefix was reserved for telephone company use and was only consistently used for directory assistance (information), being "555–1212" for the local area. An attempt to dial a 555 number from a movie in the real world will always result in an error message when dialed from a phone in the United States. This reduces the likelihood of nuisance calls. **QU**incy(5–5555) was also used, be-

---

[178] https://en.wikipedia.org/wiki/Telephone_number

cause there was no Q available. Phone numbers were traditionally tied down to a single location; because exchanges were "hard-wired," the first three digits of any number were tied to the geographic location of the exchange.

Alphanumeric telephone numbers

The North American Numbering Plan of 1947 prescribed a format of telephone numbers that included two leading letters of the name of the central office to which each telephone was connected. This continued the practice already in place by many telephone companies for decades. Traditionally, these names were often the names of towns, villages, or were other locally significant names. Communities that required more than one central office may have used other names for each central office, such as *Main*, *East*, *West*, *Central*, or the names of local districts. Names were convenient to use and reduced errors when telephone numbers were exchanged verbally between subscribers and operators. When subscribers could dial themselves, the initial letters of the names were converted to digits as displayed on the rotary dial. Thus, telephone numbers contained one, two, or even three letters followed by up to five numerals. Such numbering plans are called 2L-4N, or simply 2-4, for example, as shown in the photo of a telephone dial of 1939. In this example, **LA**kewood 2697 indicates that a subscriber dialed the letters *L* and *A*, then the digits *2*, *6*, *9*, and *7* to reach this telephone in Lakewood, NJ (USA). The leading letters were typically bolded in print.

In December 1930, New York City became the first city in the United States to adopt the two-letter and five-number format (2L-5N), which became the standard after World War II, when the Bell System administration designed the North American Numbering Plan to prepare the United States and Canada for Direct Distance Dialing (DDD), and began to convert all central offices to this format. This process was complete by the early 1960s, when a new numbering plan, often called *all number calling* (ANC) became the standard in North America.

United Kingdom

In the UK, letters were assigned to numbers in a similar fashion to North America, except that the letter O was allocated to the digit 0 (zero); digit 6 had only M and N. The letter Q was later added to the zero position on British dials, in anticipation of direct international dialing to Paris, which commenced in 1963. This was necessary because French dials already had Q on the zero position, and there were exchange names in the Paris region which contained the letter Q.

Most of the United Kingdom had no lettered telephone dials until the introduction of *Subscriber Trunk Dialing* (STD) in 1958. Until then, only the director areas (Birmingham, Edinburgh, Glasgow, Liverpool, London and Manchester) and the adjacent non-director areas had the lettered dials; the director exchanges used the three-letter, four-number format. With the introduction of trunk dialing, the need for all callers to be able to dial numbers with letters in them led to the much more widespread use of lettered dials. The need for dials with letters ceased with the conversion to all-digit numbering in 1968.

The dialing plan in some areas permits dialing numbers in the local calling area without using area code or city code prefixes. For example, **a telephone number in North America consists of a three-digit area code, a three-digit central office code, and four digits for the line number**. If the area has no area code overlays or if the provider allows it, seven-digit dialing may be permissible for calls within the area, but some areas have implemented mandatory ten-digit dialing.

Other special phone numbers are used for high-capacity numbers with several telephone circuits, typically a request line to a radio station where dozens or even hundreds of callers may be trying to call in at once, such as for a contest. For each large metro area, all of these lines will share the same prefix (such as 404-741-*xxxx* in Atlanta and 305-550-*xxxx* in Miami), the last digits typically corresponding to the station's frequency, call sign, or moniker.

In the international telephone network, the format of telephone numbers is standardized *by ITU-T recommendation E.164*. This code specifies that the entire number should be 15 digits or shorter, and begin with a country prefix. For most countries, this is followed by an area code or city code and the subscriber number, which might consist of the code for a particular telephone exchange. ITU-T recommendation E.123 describes how to represent an international telephone number in writing or print, starting with a plus sign ("+") and the country code. When calling an international number from a landline phone, the + must be replaced with the international call prefix chosen by the country the call is being made from. Many mobile phones allow the + to be entered directly, by pressing and holding the "0" for GSM phones, or sometimes "*" for CDMA phones.

The format and allocation of local phone numbers are controlled by each nation's respective government, either directly or by sponsored organizations (such as NANPA [North American Numbering Plan Administrator] in the US or CNAC in Canada). In the United States, each state's public service commission regulates numbering, as does the Federal Communications Commission. In Canada, which shares the same country code with the U.S. (due to Bell Canada's previous ownership by the U.S.-based Bell System), regulation is mainly through the Canadian Radio-television and Telecommunications Commission.

Local number portability (LNP) allows a subscriber to request moving an existing telephone number to another telephone service provider. Number portability usually has geographic limitations, such as an existing local phone company only being able to port to a competitor within the same rate center. Mobile carriers may have much larger market areas, and can assign or accept numbers from any area within the region. In many telephone administrations, cell phone telephone numbers are in organized prefix ranges distinct from land line service, which simplifies mobile number portability, even between carriers.

Intercepted Number

In the middle 20th century in North America when a call could not be completed, for example because the phone number was not assigned, had been disconnected, or was experiencing technical difficulties, the call was routed to an intercept operator who informed the caller. In the 1970s this service was converted to Automatic Intercept Systems which automatically choose and present an appropriate intercept message. Disconnected numbers are reassigned to new users after the rate of calls to them declines.

Outside of North America operator intercept was rare, and in most cases calls to unassigned or disconnected numbers would result in a recorded message or number-unobtainable tone being returned to the caller.

Chapter Twenty-Two -- Circuit Switching and Packet Switching

From earlier references, you will recall the earliest commercial telephone service required one end-to-end uninterrupted circuit for each conversation. It was relatively easy for the phone company to run a timer on each circuit allowing them to bill the customer for the exact amount of time the conversation captured the circuit; thus, when a long distance call demanded an end-to-end dedicated circuit, the costs were much higher than a local call simply because several circuits were required and associated costs were settled between the various phone companies required to provide each circuit. Fundamentally, circuit switching allowed time-based tariffing. This is a key concept to understand as we move into the data universe where, due to packet switching technology, packets of data do not require a dedicated circuit to route them to their designated destinations.

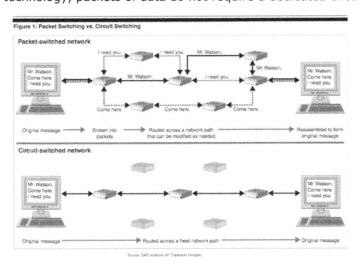

However, before packet switching technologies were incorporated into common carrier wireless networks, packets of data were transmitted over circuit switched networks. Akin to railroad flat cars on which automobiles were secured for delivery to a destination, the cars represent packets carried on an end-to-end circuit with no opportunity to be diverted until they arrive at the destination of the train.

An article, *Dealing With Data*, by this author was published in Cellular Business™ (1990) describing the state of circuit switched data over cellular at that time.

Dealing with Data

By Lee Horsman

Data transmission has somewhat mystified and baffled most of the cellular industry. However, many capabilities exist today that allow far more efficient transmission than we might think possible.

Dateline: Los Angeles. This was the city. My partner and I were on a stakeout. The suspect was entering the crack house. We were armed with a digital camera, laptop, high-speed modem and a cellular telephone. We snapped a picture, pressed F8 and waited for the response to our request for a search warrant.

We knew that, in less than two minutes, the picture would be received by our central office and scanned for mug shot verification and identification Ten minutes later, our portable printer began to type the warrant. Twenty minutes later, two suspects were in custody and all pertinent information was in process.

Although the stakeout described above was only performed as a simulation, it need not be long before this scenario becomes a reality. Reliable transmission of large, accurate files is now available at speeds ranging from 3,000 to 14,000bps [bits per second] across cellular channels.

Demonstrations using several different cellular phones attached to select laptop computers and high-speed modems have proved that these speeds and reliability factors can be achieved.

Although many of these presentations have employed image files to demonstrate the real-time data capture of files large enough to satisfy even the most dubious critic, image transfer was not the focus of this stakeout simulation. For this exercise, a GRiD™ model 1535 laptop was used. It contained special software from Picture-Ware™, an image file data base company equipped with an extension module to accommodate Telebit's™ Trailblazer® modem card (a full sized PC card) as well as a video graphics adapter (VGA) card. This configuration was then connected to a Tandy cellular phone via Telular's™ Celljack™ interface device. A digital camera from Canon™ provided the live data capture of a full-color photograph which was stored on disk in the laptop.

Next, the photograph was sent via cellular through the public switched telephone network (PSTN) to a POTS (plain old telephone service) line business extension. This was linked to a Telebit™ Trailblazer® modem, and the modem was connected to a standard desktop PC with a VGA monitor.

From the time the SEND button was pushed to the time the photograph appeared in full VGA color on the desktop monitor, one minute and forty-five seconds had elapsed.

This real-life demonstration took place in California without the involvement of the carrier handling the call. In fact, this particular demonstration was held in a board room about three miles from the nearest cell site and the room was shielded from the cell by the building.

Test equipment displayed an exceptionally high signal-to-noise ratio. Grainger compression connecting the cell site to the mobile telephone switching office (MTSO) effectively reduced available bandwidth by 50%. Actual throughput was calculated to be about 3700bps.

A second demonstration of this system occurred two weeks later in Chicago. Conditions were substantially improved and, in this demonstration, the cell site was less than two blocks away. The signal-noise ratio was significantly better and the cell site did not use microwave when transferring to the MTSO. Data speed for this demonstration was calculated to be about 6800bps.

Pulling it Together

The necessary components for achieving these results are available today. Considerable knowledge and effort are required to pull it all together, but it is being done.

Why should any carrier or dealer get excited about cellular data? How can transmission speed be a critical issue when 1200 baud error correction hasn't produced the promised rush?

Spectrum Cellular™ has pioneered the applications arena and it is primarily due to this company's efforts that the opening scenario of this article is even a contemplation.

Spectrum's demonstrated commitment to the cellular industry is unequalled. All other modem manufacturers remain considerably less committed to the cellular industry, choosing to produce instant revenues and merely tiptoe gingerly into the shallows to test the theories.

Having noted the comparative differences between Spectrum Cellular and its competitors, I still must compliment those other modem manufacturers that are now recognizing the viability of cellular data as a marketing opportunity. Unfortunately, these vendors are beginning to invest in cellular versions of traditional wireline products and these are simply not robust enough to address the hostilities presented by cellular RF channels. Only two major modem manufacturers have now recognized the importance of addressing cellular's unique characteristics.

Furthermore, too few of the manufacturers recognize the evolutionary dynamics of today's systems, and too few take the time to voluntarily test their assumptions. Typically, non-cellular data theorists ignore the multiple handoff routines fundamental to cellular network service. Plus, they neglect the problems created by power attenuation, multipath congestion, signal fade, random RF noise disturbances and the reduced bandwidth resulting from compression techniques being used to produce efficient information transfer between the MTSO and is cell sites. In short, the traditional data expert is simply not prepared to deal with the techniques required as minimums for cellular system data issues.

If we then have the temerity to introduce additional issues related to mobile data, such as the interface problems associated with different phones and the myriads of peripheral devices, we overwhelm the salesperson as well as the customers. In this regard, it is encouraging to report there are knowledgeable people producing several different solutions to most of these nagging problems.

Issues

Data speed in cellular is a reliability and performance dictator more than it is a traditional information transfer issue. Cellular channel conditions demand maximum data transfer during those times when RF channels are at their peak performance levels.

Until TDMA and the potential for 9600bps or more are commonly available, system network architecture/ synchronous data link control applications will not be viable considerations. High speeds, even those of 19.2 and above, will encounter elements in the cellular environment that will effectively reduce their actual throughput. Therefore, the astute carrier, dealer or customer will carefully analyze all the ramifications before investing in cellular as a data transport medium.

Privately licensed 800MHz systems, trunking systems, SMR networks and, in many cases, traditional 2-way systems are inherently superior to cellular for mobile and/or remote data applications. These cellular alternatives feature higher power mobile and fixed stations, no call set-up delays, service without handoff routines and higher base station antennas for more robust opportunities.

Today, we have the technology necessary to eliminate severe data stream interruptions and error producing elements common to cellular. However, there are still marketing related and political issues surrounding these problems. Many companies have the potential for practical, reliable cellular robust protocols. With adequate funding, any one, or all, of them could produce a mobile modem firmware package that most of the data devices on today's market could incorporate. It would then be possible for the carriers to accommodate the protocols at the cellular switch; and, it is easy to imagine a front-end identifier for protocol recognition and routing.

Nationwide mobile data is promised to come first from existing public data networks. Incorporating cellular robust protocols in local public data network nodes would then be an enhanced service bringing in additional revenues. Assume a licensable high-speed technology incorporated into a wide variety of data devices (including cellular telephones) with compatible fixed equipment at the public data network nodes in 500 cities. Assume a revenue sharing agreement between the public data network and any cellular carrier that encourages reduced local data rates.

Is there a marketing opportunity for Fortune 500 account penetration? Allow me to suggest that fleet management automation alone will justify the required investment.

This article's Dragnet-style introduction is intended to dramatically illustrate that high speed, 100% reliable data transfer is immediately possible using existing analog cellular channels and their support systems. Although image transmission can be put to work effectively by such users as insurance adjusters, law enforcement agencies and mobile X-ray technicians, the imaging illustration was included simply to make a point. It emphasizes the importance of data speed and shows how directly speed affects the end-user's perception of the medium's reliability.

The market will decide which applications lead the parade. Engineers will decide how technologies can be put to work to provide marketing opportunities.

In this regard, system integrators play a key role in determining how quickly cellular will reach its potential.

Many different philosophies currently surround systems integration efforts. Off-the-shelf briefcase products contain everything from fully complemented cellular to computers with error-correcting modems, printers, bar code readers, fax machines, integrated power supplies, batteries and other supporting items. In addition to these briefcases, there are self-contained packages that incorporate all the items listed above in a variety of configurations, with price tags that should not surprise anyone.

There are also cellular platforms featuring flexibilities otherwise unavailable. The platform approach offers obsolescence protection, a lower initial investment and a modular concept that allows for detaching the phone from associated data devices quickly and conveniently; thus, the phone or laptop may become standalone equipment.

In addition to the packages already described, hosts of ancillary devices such as credit card readers, bar code scanners, automatic vehicle location and fleet management systems, alarm devices and others being promoted as mobile data products. Cellular Solutions™ in Boulder, CO, distributes a catalog offering many of these products.

Who will be first to put it all together? This task will require executive vision supported by executive commitment. It will demand courage and imagination to identify potential markets and to develop successful marketing.

Is there a carrier ready to approach a public data network with a proposal for sharing the costs as well as the revenues from a joint project with cellular data? Is there a public data network that recognizes the impact mobile data will have? Does an organization exist that has the personnel equipped to manage the wide range of disciplines being contemplated?

What will it take for a carrier to solicit the participation of IBM or DEC? These companies could work with a switch manufacturer to produce a data-friendly cellular plant. Is it inconceivable that a channel dedication scheme could be seized for multiple data users? They could use simultaneously a single channel or a set of channels that would dump unnecessary overhead, accommodate higher speeds and provide increased bandwidth. It is only prudent to consider the potential benefits of an alliance with the giants of the data communications arena; after all, they could provide the expertise necessary to develop these possibilities. As a matter of fact, there are companies currently involved in just such an arrangement that have already corroborated each others' design criteria.

How exciting it is to consider an opportunity to reduce the voice tariffs to two-thirds and still maintain existing revenues! Add to this the excitement that would come from increasing the number of heavy business users (in contrast to "carrier-consuming" retail targets) and the effort required to pursue these projects becomes negligible.

The system architecture being contemplated promises to reduce, if not eliminate, set-up time for data calls. It also promises to establish a transmission rate of 10kbps regardless of cell site to switch compression. Also, there is at least one relatively inexpensive off-the-shelf product that is anticipated to provide reliable management and administration features so the switch and other existing support systems are relieved of additional loads.

Does off-peak system loading with telemetry applications appeal to anyone?

Does the above described effort encourage anyone to consider the possibility of system network architecture applications? Do Hillsdale, IL, nightmares stimulate interest for cellular back-up systems?

Will opportunities related to FCC Docket 87-390 become serious revenue producers if the contemplated system architecture can be proved?

Many of these questions have immediate answers while others await a carrier with the vision and resources to address them properly.

END ARTICLE

Two distinctly different switching technologies, circuit switching and packet switching, determined to a great degree the evolution of data over cellular.

Following its landline predecessor, cellular channels required a dedicated full duplex circuit for human conversations to be marketed. Circuit switching prompted the phone companies, and subsequently the cellular network operators, to bill the customers as a function of time. As referenced earlier, it is relatively simple to precisely measure the amount of time in seconds-minutes-hours a full circuit is in service; thus, tariffs and pricing as a function of time prevailed in early cellular networks.

The advent of packet switching for data (ultimately voice converted to packets of data much later), prompted the carriers to establish pricing based on the amount of data any given customer used in a session.

The article, *Dealing With Data*, addresses only circuit switched data applications – time based system usage. Dedicating channels for voice or data was a simple issue for the wireless carriers to accept. A circuit dedicated to a voice conversation for a few minutes was no different than dedicating a circuit to packets of data for the same amount of time. Billing a customer for time, regardless of the application was no problem.

19.2kps, the fastest data delivery speed ever implemented in a circuit switched application, was too slow for the carriers to get excited about when the investment required exceeded the profit ratios to which they had become accustomed for voice. They had no reason to accept or reject application developers imposing packets of data on their circuit switched channels simply because the time used was billed at the same rate as voice. To the carrier, time was time regardless of the cargo being transferred.

For cellular/PCS (and subsequent other spectrum designations), a packet switched network independently operating in concert with the circuit switched network was a minimum requirement if the carriers were to be motivated to invest in data over cellular.

At this time, very few contemplated the technological advances in store that would packetize all the traffic—voice and data—utilizing as much as 1.25MHz of bandwidth to facilitate cellular/PCS and subsequent traffic.

Packet Switching History

> *We will soon be living in an era in which we cannot guarantee survivability of any single point. However, we can still design systems in which system destruction requires the enemy to pay the price of destroying n of n stations. If n is made sufficiently large, it can be shown that highly survivable system structures can be built.*
>
> - Paul Baran, On Distributed Communications, Volume I, 1964.

Who invented packet switching? Like the development of *hypertext*, *packet switching* seems to have been an idea that wanted to be discovered. The packet switching concept was first invented by *Paul Baran* in the early 1960's, and then independently a few years later by *Donald Davies*. *Leonard Kleinrock* conducted early research in the related field of digital message switching, and helped build the *ARPANET*, the world's first packet switching network.

Baran invented the concept of packet switching while a young electrical engineer at RAND when he was asked to perform an investigation into survivable communications networks for the US Air Force, building on one of the first wide area computer networks created for the *SAGE* radar defense system. His results were first presented to the Air Force in the summer of 1961 as *Briefing B-265*, then as paper *P-2626*, and then in 1964 as a series of eleven amazingly thorough, comprehensive papers titled *On Distributed Communications*.

Baran's 1964 papers go well beyond documenting the breakthrough concept of packet switching and describe a detailed architecture for a large-scale, distributed, survivable communications network designed to withstand almost any degree of destruction to individual components without loss of end-to-end communications. Baran also assumed that any link of the network could fail at any time, and so the network was designed with no central control or administration.

Baran's groundbreaking work helped to convince the US Military that wide area digital computer networks were a promising technology. Baran also talked to Bob Taylor and *J.C.R. Licklider* at the *IPTO* about the concept since they were also working to build a wide area communications network. Baran's papers then influenced *Roberts* and *Kleinrock* to adopt the technology when they joined the IPTO for development of the *ARPANET*, laying the groundwork that led to its incorporation into the *TCP/IP* network protocol used on the *Internet* today.

In one of many interesting such synchronicities in the history of science, Baran's packet switching work was strikingly similar to the work performed independently a few years later by Donald Davies at the *National Physical Laboratory*, including common details like a packet size of 1024 bits. The term "packet switching" itself was taken from Davies work, since Baran had called the concept "distributed adaptive message block switching."

At the time, in the early 1960's, existing communication networks were made from dedicated analog circuits mainly used for voice telephone connections which were always on a steady stream of DC electricity interrupted by dialing or tones preceding a voice conversation once activated. Packet switching completely changed this perspective by viewing networks as discontinuous digital systems that transmit data in small packets only when required. At first glance this looks like it introduces two compromises in design:

Discontinuity. It gives up the advantage of an always-on, continuous connection.

Conversions. Analog communications, like voice, have to undergo analog-to-digital encoding to get onto the network and then digital-to-analog decoding at the destination to be read - extra work.

However, as always, the details make the difference, and it turns out that packet switching introduces four practical advantages that far outweigh any hypothetical disadvantages:

Digital. It makes communications *digital*, which means they can be made error free. It also means that communications from digital computers have no conversion overhead or transformation error.

Processing. It moves the computer into the network by placing software systems at each node, which can then be upgraded and improved to enable the network to continually get better.

Redundancy. It eliminates dependence on any one communication link, enabling the network to survive considerable damage.

Efficiency. It enables more than one communication to share a given link at the same time, greatly increasing the number of total communications the network can support at any one time.

The legacy communications establishment -- primarily telecommunications companies -- was skeptical about the idea at first, but it was quickly shown that a packet switching network typically worked better, faster, and cheaper than a dedicated circuit network. Since the network shared all of the available bandwidth on a packetized basis, many communications could occur simultaneously. This was a major discovery, and the key concept that made wide-area communication networks and the Internet itself cost-effective and possible.

Interestingly, the development of packet switching came only a few decades after the development of quantum mechanics in physics, which began when Albert Einstein showed that waves of light could also be described as streams of individual photons. Despite this background, Baran says that his direct inspiration was Claude Shannon's machine in which he trained a mechanical mouse to find its way through a maze as an existence proof. This led Baran to build on the idea and hypothesize that a message could be broken up into individual packets of information that could then find their own way to the destination through the network.[179]

As you might expect for a technology so expansive and ever-changing, it is impossible to credit the invention of the Internet to a single person. The Internet was the work of dozens of pioneering scientists, programmers and engineers who each developed new features and technologies that eventually merged to become the "information superhighway" we know today.

Long before the technology existed to actually build the Internet, many scientists had already anticipated the existence of worldwide networks of information. Nikola Tesla toyed with the idea of a "world wireless system"

---

[179] https://www.livinginternet.com/i/iw_packet_inv.htm

in the early 1900s, and visionary thinkers like Paul Otlet and Vannevar Bush conceived of mechanized, searchable storage systems of books and media in the 1930s and 1940s. Still, the first practical schematics for the Internet would not arrive until the early 1960s, when MIT's J.C.R. Licklider popularized the idea of an "Intergalactic Network" of computers. Shortly thereafter, computer scientists [Paul Baran] developed the concept of "packet switching," a method for effectively transmitting electronic data that would later become one of the major building blocks of the Internet.

The first workable prototype of the Internet came in the late 1960s with the creation of ARPANET, or the Advanced Research Projects Agency Network. Originally funded by the U.S. Department of Defense, ARPANET used packet switching to allow multiple computers to communicate on a single network. The technology continued to grow in the 1970s after scientists, Robert Kahn and Vinton Cerf, developed Transmission Control Protocol and Internet Protocol, or TCP/IP, a communications model that set standards for how data could be transmitted between multiple networks.

ARPANET adopted TCP/IP on January 1, 1983, and from there researchers began to assemble the "network of networks" that became the modern Internet. The online world then took on a more recognizable form in 1990, when computer scientist, Tim Berners-Lee, invented the World Wide Web. While it's often confused with the Internet itself, the web is actually just the most common means of accessing data online in the form of websites and hyperlinks. The web helped popularize the Internet among the public, and served as a crucial step in developing the vast trove of information that most of us now access on a daily basis.[180]

In the cellular telephony world, packet switching to facilitate data applications was delayed by the wireline carriers whose insistence on "voice will always be king" prevented adoption of early packet switching technologies. Until McCaw deployed CDPD™, the risk aversion syndrome paralyzing virtually all legacy wireline carriers prevailed.

In the first decade of cellular, several notable attempts were made by modem companies to penetrate the mental fog of visionless risk averse carrier executives. Three companies, Spectrum Cellular™, Telebit™ and Telular™ delivered packet data over circuit switched cellular voice channels (see article: *Dealing With Data* in previous pages). Attempting to convince the carriers of the efficacy of data as a source of revenues augmenting voice, these companies funded the development of data applications and fielded sales people trained to

demonstrate "data over cellular" to wirelessly facilitate credit card transactions from flea markets, restaurants and sports venues. An early application that captured a great deal of attention was using a three watt bag phone to send fax messages from laptops. Accessing data bases such as insurance company files for field adjusters, IRS field agents, and state and local law enforcement captured a great deal of public interest but these efforts were never supported by the carriers at any significant level.

CDPD® enjoyed moderate success; however, it was a stop-gap technology with limited shelf-life. It survived (mostly in secondary and rural markets) until around 2005. There are likely a few still in service for some public safety applications in small markets but access to the internet and myriad applications readily available within the base networks now dominate packet switched data delivery over cellular/PCS and advanced 4G-5G networks.

CDPD's data rate of 19.2kbps wasn't fast enough for texting or lengthy email messages. However for SMS (Short Message Service) it was adequate. As a "bursty" data delivery system, it was too expensive. Credit card processing, Electronic Benefits Transactions and the like were desirable but finding application developers and large corporate sponsors such as Visa, MasterCard, NABANCO

---

[180] https://www.history.com/news/who-invented-the-internet

and banks to support them were never fully realized. For small file transfers such as police reports from the field, insurance adjusters, and the like, it was adequate.

Basically, CDPD employed channel sniffing to locate and select idle time on a voice channel it could divert into its packet switched delivery network. As long as it did not capture the channel or otherwise impede voice traffic, the carriers found no reason to reject this early packet switched network. It utilized empty voice channel bandwidth to deliver additional revenues. CDPD was the first and only packet switched network to gain any significant purchase in the cellular carrier universe before digital networks replaced analog.

In this discussion, a small footnote in history is appropriate.

Unfortunately, simply because the "winners write the history books," you will never read or otherwise hear about the first truly commercial grade cellular data packet switched network anywhere else.

Recognizing the value of ubiquitous service delivered by cellular networks, in 1989, a start-up company called Cellular Data, Inc., led by Miklos Korodi, a Hungarian naturalized US citizen, inventor, patent holder and former president of Railway Express and ADT, funded by several Silicon Valley venture capital companies plus a significant investment by GTE Mobilnet in both cash investment as well as equipment testing resources, developed a technology theorized and patented by Stanford University Professor Lusignian, officially recognized by the US Patent Office for utilizing 3kHz channels dedicated to packet switched data delivery over cellular. In-

serting a 3kHz channel dedicated to packet-switched data between the voice channels resulted in the patent referring to "interstitial" as an official identifier. By inserting a 3kHz channel, this technology effectively expanded the licensed available spectrum by thirty percent and provided a windfall revenue stream without adversely affecting voice service.

The company's business strategy anticipated "revenue sharing" and the entrenched cellular carriers balked at this invasion of their income stream. This was very short-sighted and ignored the potential upside that would have catapulted them into the packet data arena almost ten years before packet data services, following the predictable rise and fall of CDPD, became a legitimate revenue source for them. E-mail, texting, cameras and credit card applications could have become popular a full ten years before they actually came about if the carriers had adopted CDI's "interstitial" technology.

A precedent set by Bellsouth with its commitment to Mobitex™ infrastructure dedicated to Blackberry messaging was all the carriers should have needed to recognize the benefits in a thirty percent network capacity expansion to support a spate of data services neither CDPD nor Mobitex were capable of delivering.

Myopia, the disease of early cellular network executives, killed CDI as a company and unnecessarily delayed the packet data over cellular market for ten years.

CDI's 3Khz channel delivered 2400kbps which was effective for "bursty" telemetry applications, e.g., remote monitoring and controlling vending ma-

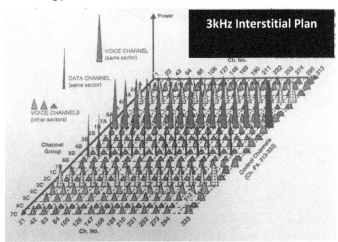

chines, pipelines and oil wells, *etc.* Also, the first fully serviced wireless credit card processing application using packet switching over cellular was demonstrated on the Commnet 2000 cellular network in Pueblo, Colorado, using CDI's technology in 1991. Participants in the demonstration included representatives (engineers) from VISA™, Verifone™, NABANCO™, BT TYMNET™, CDI™ and Commnet 2000™. The entire process, including bank settlement, was accomplished in three seconds. Today (2020) we take for granted the availability and popularity of this level of credit card processing directly from our restaurant dining table as well as many other venues using this technology but it languished unnecessarily in the darkness of carrier executive myopia for ten years.

This is the first commercially viable cellular packet switched base station. In 1991, it was installed in the Bacculite Mesa cell site in Pueblo, CO, and demonstrated the viability of cellular delivery of credit card processing and remote vending machine monitoring.

These photos of the Remote Terminal Units designed and manufactured by Cincinnati Microwave, were equipped with RJ45 I/O ports to facilitate easy connectivity with credit card processing machines and telemetry devices featuring A/D conversion.

At the Commnet office, a beverage machine was connected to the RTU allowing the beverage company to eliminate visits to the machine to determine status of compressor, bottle inventory, coin collection and need for replenishment.

Chapter Twenty-Three -- Cellular Fundamentals

- **Cellular Network Fundamentals**
- **Who decides what and how much spectrum is allocated to cellular?**
- **Who decides to whom the spectrum will be licensed?**
- **Who decides what standards equipment manufacturers must meet to maintain system integrity?**
- **How does the FCC ensure unbiased best performance criteria for network operations and management?**
- **What are FCC "Dockets?"**

It all begins with the FCC.

We are now delving into an area very few engineering students ever approach. However, engineers who know the function and processes of the FCC as their activities and decisions dictate the technical aspects of wireless communications have a leg up on competition in the job market and for higher executive positions in the licensed network operator universe. This is especially true in today's advanced cellular/PCS networks that have evolved to 5G.

Despite the historical facts related to theories and concepts of a "cellular" topology for ubiquitous wireless services, until the FCC recognized the market demand and opportunity to exponentially increase the amount of traffic limited bandwidth, by virtue of system design was capable of delivering, "cellular" labored in the shadows in the US while Japan and Europe built early cellular networks.

It is all too easy to be critical about this and, to some degree the critics have a few salient points; however, deeper understanding of the political, as well as technical, issues requiring resolution requires any objective observer to credit the FCC for what, in hindsight, appears almost miraculous.

Frequency allocation was the basic issue. Until the FCC declared what spectrum and how much of it would be dedicated to cellular, they had to deal with issues of fairness as well as technology efficiencies. This was accomplished by utilizing the legacy methods of **FCC Notices** clearly defining the intent and circumstances under which spectrum allocations would be granted and inviting responses from qualified interested parties to submit verification of qualification, technological alternatives, suggestions for FCC consideration, *etc.*

Among others, the FCC uses the following as primary pre-allocation instruments:

Notice of Inquiry

Notice of Proposed Rulemaking

When these instruments are created and published, they are identified by "Docket" numbers. This allows the primary/initial document(s) to evolve gracefully as each subsequent document, whether it is an additional amendment or otherwise by the FCC, or a response document by interested parties, is assigned a Docket Number.

The following excerpts from FCC dockets are intended to provide insight into the issues the FCC considers and with which makes rules to govern and manage the process of efficient spectrum utility.

We will limit our study to FCC instruments related only to cellular/PCS wireless network issues.

Docket No. 79-318 is not the earliest nor the most important of FCC documents spawning cellular networks. However, we will note a few excerpts from earlier instruments as we attempt to understand the role FCC decisions play in the process.

The officially recognized first FCC docket referring to what would become known as "cellular" was FCC Notice of Inquiry and Notice of Proposed Rulemaking (Docket No. 18262), 14 FCC 2d 311 at paragraph eight: "The avowed purpose of these docketed proceedings, which hereinafter will be referred to as the cellular proceedings, has been to foster the development of a "truly efficient high capacity domestic public land mobile radio service."

Recall the first commercial cellular network offered service in 1983. It does not require genius to conclude there had to be considerable work and investment by the FCC as well as possible network operators and equipment manufacturers before this docket was published.

In a time-honored process, the FCC issues experimental licenses to prove or disprove theories associated with bandwidth, legal power limits (maximum and minimum), equipment specifications, network operator qualification standards, and myriad others without which full service commercial network operation would be chaotic.

In 1970, the FCC granted experimental licenses to Ameritech (Chicago wireline) and American Radio Telephone Service (ARTS non-wireline) in Washington, DC. As you can imagine, the technical specifications for network equipment as well as mobiles at that time were very experimental; thus, granting manufacturers an early opportunity to meet what later became very tight (as compared to legacy mobile phones) specifications required a leap of faith the experimental specifications would closely match the FCC's final specifications.

In 1974, Docket No. 18262; 46 FCC 2d 752 Second Report and Order:

"Only two companies, AT&T and Motorola, have developmental systems authorized. The Commission has described these systems as having "identical" basic system concepts."

"As with any developmental grant, licensees of developmental alternative systems are given no assurance that the service will be established on a permanent basis."

It is no small historical note to acknowledge that Japan, more notably Nippon Electric Company (NEC), Oki and a few others, had taken the initiative with cellular theory and moved forward with producing the equipment as well as computer technologies to deploy and manage cellular networks.

In NEC's response to Docket 79-318, 22 April, 1980, they affirm: "One of the areas to which NEC has devoted particular attention is the development of linked computer and communications (C&C) systems. This commitment to C&C systems reflects the company's belief that the integration and interaction of telecommunications functions with computer intelligence will be the locus of technological development in the coming decade. NEC's basic position is that only through the full and successful integration of these two important technologies can the ultimate usefulness of telecommunications and information processing be realized. NEC's overriding goal as a company has long been to offer significant contributions to this integration process."[181]

"NEC's participation in the design, manufacture and installation of mobile telephone systems has included involvement in the development of systems of cellular design. NEC has played a leading role in supplying equipment and software to the Nippon Telegraph and Telephone Public Corporation (NIT) for the large-scale, 800MHz, high-capacity cellular mobile telephone system which started commercial operation in Japan in 1979. NEC also has developed smaller systems of a cellular design for installation in Sidney and Melbourne, Australia, under the auspices of the Australian Telecommunications Commission. An NEC cellular type system also is under development in Mexico City, Mexico, under the auspices of Telefonics de Mexico."[182]

"During the period in which NEC has participated in the design, installation and operation of systems of cellular design throughout the world, NEC has remained attentive to the concurrent development of such systems in the United States. NEC has participated as an observer member in the work of the Electronic Industries Association (EIA) Ad Hoc Cellular Committee (TR-8) which was formed to devise and recommend to the FCC technical standards to govern cellular systems."[183]

The following excerpts from the full text of NEC's response are presented to give you, an aspiring engineer, insight into the level of expertise and articulation of Mr. Art Peters, PE. By presenting the following, this author

---

[181] Comments of NEC America, Inc; Response to FCC Docket No. 79-318: An Inquiry into the use of the bands 825-845MHz and 870-890MHz for cellular communications systems; and Amendment of Parts 2 and 22 of the Commission's Rules Relative to cellular communications systems.
[182] Ibid
[183] Ibid

is attempting to inspire you to the highest levels of professional engineering as exemplified by Mr. Peters. Allow yourself to mull over and concentrate on all the issues with which Mr. Peters needed to have at his immediate command to compose a document of this extraordinary effectiveness.

08 January, 1980

FCC 79-774

CC **Docket No. 79-318**

RM-3200

BEFORE THE FEDERAL COMMUNICATIONS COMMISSION Washington, D.C. 20554

In the matter of An Inquiry Into the Use of the Bands 825-845 MHz and 870-890 MHz for Cellular Communications Systems; and Amendment of Parts 2 and 22 of the Commission's Rules Relative to Cellular Communications Systems.

Notice of Inquiry and Notice of Proposed Rulemaking (Adopted: November 29, 1979; Released: January 8, 1980) By the Commission: Chairman Ferris issuing a separate statement; Commissioner Fogarty issuing a separate statement in which commissioners Quello and Jones join.

Notice is hereby given of an Inquiry and Proposed Rulemaking looking toward the amendment of Parts 2 and 22 of the Commission's Rules, 47 C.F.R. §§2 and 22, concerning policies, standards, and procedures for licensing and implementation of cellular communications systems in the frequency bands 825-845 and 870-890 MHz.

A. Introduction

On March 19, 1975, the Commission adopted its Memorandum Opinion and Order in Docket No. 18262, Land Mobile Radio Service, 51 FCC 2d 945 (1975), terminating a long proceeding to provide spectrum relief for the land mobile radio services. In that proceeding, **the Commission allocated 40 MHz to the Domestic Public Land Mobile Radio Service for the development of a nationwide, "cellular" mobile radio communication system.** Cellular mobile systems are generally described as mobile radio systems with a high capacity to serve subscriber units due to the coordinated reuse of a group of radio channels. During the past year, the Commission and its staff have had the opportunity to review data from the operation of an AT&T developmental cellular system and to see the system in operation, and have discussed cellular technology and its future with many members of the telecommunications industry and potentially interested parties. In sum, **there seems to be little doubt that cellular communications offers the best means for meeting the demands of the mobile communications market through the end of this century. The time has arrived, therefore, for the Commission to establish rules and policies for the commercial operation of cellular mobile radio systems.**

B. Background. Docket No. 18262

We (FCC) initiated Docket No. 18262 in 1968 with a Notice of Inquiry and Notice of Proposed Rulemaking, 14 FCC 2d 311 (1968), as a first step in our effort to provide spectrum relief for land mobile radio users for the foreseeable future. **The Commission proposed to reallocate frequencies in the 806-960 MHz band to make available enough spectrum to accommodate the public need for both private and common carrier land mobile communications. Between 1968 and 1974, we examined how best to use these frequencies in the public interest.**

By 1974, however, policies were refined and sharpened, and we issued our Second Report and Order, 46 FCC 2d 753 (1974). The frequency allocation plan changed considerably. For example, **we reduced the band allocated for high capacity common carrier systems from 75 MHz to 40 MHz and specifically set aside** this allocation for cellular systems. **Reserve bands totaling 20 MHz were strategically placed adjacent to the cellular allocation so that additional spectrum would be available if the growth rate of cellular systems was unexpectedly rapid. We concluded that a cellular system using the full 40 MHz (with channel spacing of 40 kHz) could serve the projected urban mobile telephone market through 1990.**

During twelve years of FCC deliberations prior to 1980, particularly emphasized in Docket 79-318 and Docket 18262, the commission has stressed its objective of fostering the pursuit and development of alternative approaches and system designs.

1970 – First Report and Order and Second Notice of Inquiry (Docket 18262), the Commission reallocated frequencies 806-947MHz for increasing land mobile spectrum. Herein, and additional allocation of 75MHz for common carrier domestic high capacity public mobile system is anticipated. In this publication, the Commission stated: "In our view, it is essential in the public interest that every encouragement be given to the development of new techniques in the efficient use of these bands."

The FCC traditionally applied its power to foster competition. Here is what it stated in Docket 18262:

"The Commission is hopeful that AT&T, as well as others (Motorola, Oki, GE and 'others'), will undertake a comprehensive study of market potentials, optimum system configuration and equipment design looking toward the development and implementation of an effective high capacity common carrier service in the band 806-881MHz."

Later in this same instrument, the Commission re-emphasizes its commitment to foster competition:

"We wish to clarify our intention to encourage the development of new technology which can meet all common carrier needs in a more efficient and effective manner." This clarification included deleting an earlier restriction stating only wireline telephone companies could develop cellular systems. This change was made because, in the Commission's view, the limitation had discouraged broad participation in the developmental process. Citing the failure of parties other than Bell Laboratories to develop equipment, the Commission noted:

"Such a situation, obviously will not provide the flexibility or choices the Commission had hoped for in making the final determinations regarding the service allocations and the use to be made of the spectrum."

Author's note: Are you beginning to get the big picture of how significant the FCC is in the processes associated with delivering ubiquitous wireless services?

In granting Illinois Bell Telephone (Ameritech) an experimental license, the Commission stated:

"We do not wish to preclude consideration of alternative technological approaches. We urge the Bell System and other parties to explore other alternatives thoroughly in parallel with future cellular developments in order that the evolving nationwide radiotelephone service will continually reflect the most modern, cost-effective technology available. To ensure that this remains the basic objective, that long term system designs are not prematurely and inflexibly frozen, we believe it imperative that any developmental cellular system authorized at this time should be limited as to possible market foreclosure."

The Commission also extended the time limit for the adoption of rules and technical standards for cellular systems. In doing this, they continued to emphasize their interest in fostering new approaches, to wit:

"We still encourage the submission of new developmental proposals from the telecommunications industry. The experience gained from even a short period of developmental operation of a new system may be of more value in designing a framework of rules for future systems than an entire year of pleadings and comments. Accordingly, we are willing to entertain additional developmental proposals which would contribute significantly to our understanding of the cellular concept."

It is also in this docket the Commission advocates licensing competitive cellular systems in a single market:

"Direct competition in a market can result in different technological approaches and diversity of service options. Moreover, direct competition may provide some degree of price competition that otherwise would not be present. Two alternatives in the development and implementation of cellular systems can have meaningful competitive consequences in a given market if the two entities in that market approach cellular technology differently."

One of the most dramatic issues during the several years of deliberation was the perceived amount of spectrum cellular systems required to meet anticipated demand.

Prior to 1968, a minimum of 75MHz utilizing 30kHz channels was required to deliver quality service. By 1974, Bell Labs reduced that number to 64MHz with 40kHz channels. The FCC rejected this spectrum request and proposed 40MHz with 30kHz channels. AT&T countered by proposing two carriers per market each with 30MHz of spectrum using 30kHz channels.

A brief summary:

In the past, the Commission advocated a single cellular system per market. This gave way to a decision to license two **or more** networks per market.

The Commission's early restrictions preventing licensed cellular operators and/or their affiliates for manufacturing equipment is proposed to be relaxed – now seeking comments.

The Commission's inclination toward wireline companies being the only potential candidates due to their resources has now changed to a "two or more" position.

In its attempt to protect legacy two-way radio systems (fleet call, dispatch and the like), the Commission had adopted a hands off these services for cellular. They are now advocating revisiting that protective effort. [Author's Note: Today we take for granted the features of GPS utilized as a daily convenience with cellular telephones that owe their popularity to maritime direction assistance that became long-haul trucking management tools that produced electronic "fences" allowing management to track and receive reports on delivery vehicles locations, speed, routes, *etc.*]

To further enhance your appreciation for the challenges facing those making decisions for the future of cellular, consider a comment made by Motorola's executive, Jim Caile, published as a direct quote in *Telocator Magazine*, February, 1980: "Motorola projects that the typical planning interval for the implementation of a single cellular system is at least one or two years and, that as a consequence, the cellular industry will not grow to 'adulthood' until the 1990s."[184]

In its response to the FCC Inquiry Docket 79-318, 1980, NEC wrote the following to the Commission:

"Now, what if the system designs and concepts which are emerging at this time do not prove to be economically or technically viable? The Commission simply cannot wait to find out that the current technology has failed to gain acceptance in the marketplace. The risk of failure demands that the Commission, to the extent practicable, seek to encourage the continued development of alternatives."[185]

For you, the student, these historical records documenting the process preceding implementation of cellular service in the US, are intended to assist you in appreciating the level of detail as well as the extraordinary efforts of the FCC and those responding to the FCC to assure maximum spectrum efficiency as well as fairness in the marketplace for companies committed to investing the resources necessary to successfully deliver services anticipated by their potential customers.

In their response, Mr. Peters, representing NEC, went on to submit:

"There are other important considerations which support the NEC America proposal. First, the spectrum allocation plan does not, in any way, forestall the early implementation of cellular service. The thrust of the proposal is to earmark spectrum for continued development of cellular concepts while, at the same time, permitting existing concepts to be implemented and tested in commercial operation. The purpose of the proposal is to supplement, not to supplant, existing technology by allowing new systems to continue to emerge. Second, the proposal contains built-in incentives for progress. Proponents of 'original' cellular systems will want to implement them on as broad a scale as possible in the near term in order to be in the best posture to secure additional allocations from the 10MHz in the special developmental cellular pool at the end of the specified five-year term. Similarly, proponents of alternative systems will be induced to implement their systems as soon as practicable in order to develop the information necessary to support a permanent allocation at the end of the

---

[184] Cf. Caile, Cellular: The Motorola System, Telocator Magazine, February, 1980
[185] Ibid

developmental period. This process incorporates a desirable element of competition into the spectrum allocation process."[186]

In great part, because men like Mr. Peters, and companies like NEC, recognized the importance of open competition and were willing to share their concepts in pursuit of the greater good, we enjoy the wireless telecom services taken for granted today.

---

[186] Ibid

Chapter Twenty-Four -- CELLULAR/PCS: AMPS-5G

Original FCC Topology Assumptions:
- ✓ Any system must exhibit a bona fide cellular configuration, as...
- ✓ Base station transmitters radiate no more power than is necessary to adequately cover one cell.
- ✓ The transmitters in separate cells are connected together through a common switching and control system.
- ✓ The radio frequency channels employed within each cell are trunked together.
- ✓ The system may be fully interconnected with the landline telephone network.
- ✓ The system allows for:
- ✓ Frequency re-use over relatively short distances.
- ✓ Cell splitting to increase re-use capabilities.
- ✓ Hand-off of traffic between cells.

Cellular Radio Systems

Malcolm Appleby MA, Fred Harrison, BSc, CEng, MIEE, in *Telecommunications Engineer's Reference Book, 1993*

47.4.1 AMPS[187]

AMPS stands for Advanced Mobile Phone System and was developed in the USA primarily by Bell Laboratories as a successor for the heavily congested IMTS (Improved Mobile Telephone System). Being designed for the North American market, AMPS uses the 800MHz band allocated to mobile services in ITU Region 2 (the Americas), with 30kHz channel spacing in common with established PMR practice.

AMPS uses analog FM for speech transmission but with a wider frequency deviation (12kHz) than is the norm for a 30kHz channeling system. By adopting the wide deviation, the dynamic range of the speech channel is extended and protection against co-channel interference is increased. This, together with the use of speech compression/expansion (companders), yields a high quality voice circuit with the capability to maintain performance in a high capacity (poor interference ratio) configuration.

Signaling between mobile and base station is at 10kbit/s, with Manchester encoding applied taking the bit rate to 20kbit/s. The data is modulated onto the radio carrier by direct frequency shift keying (FSK). Error control is achieved by multiple repetition (5 or 11 times) of each signaling word, with majority voting applied at the receiver to correct errors. A BCH block code is also applied to detect any uncorrected errors.

While a call is in progress, the base station transmits a low level supervisory audio tone (SAT) in the region of 6kHz. Three different SAT frequencies are used by the network, and are allocated to the base stations so that the nearest co-channel base stations (*i.e.* those most likely to cause interference) have a different SAT from the target base station. The mobile continuously monitors the received SAT and also transponds the signal back to the base station. If the mobile (or the base station) detects a difference between the received SAT and that expected, the audio path is muted to prevent the interfering signal from being overheard. If the condition persists, the call is aborted.

AMPS underwent a long development period, and an extended trial (technical and commercial) which not only fixed the system parameters but also contributed to the basic planning rules which hold true for all cellular systems. The system design was comprehensively described in 1979 (Bell, 1979), but it was not until 1983 that operating licenses were issued and true commercial exploitation of the system commenced.

Reinaldo Perez, in *Wireless Communications Design Handbook*, 1998[188]

5.18 Using MOM (Methods Of Moments) for Designing Cylindrical Arrays for PCS

---

[187] https://www.sciencedirect.com/topics/engineering/advanced-mobile-phone-system
[188] Ibid

In the fast-growing areas of advanced mobile phone systems (AMPS) and personal communications services (PCS), section antennas on multiple beams have been used lately instead of omni-directional antennas. There is a persistent interest in acquiring better base-station antennas for cellular communications, due to constant increases in system capacity and the high cost of acquiring property for the installation of cellular station antennas. The improvements sought in base-station antennas would increase gain, diminish side lobes, and lower interference. An illustration of AMPS is shown in Figure 5.46. Many stations have this form of prototype.

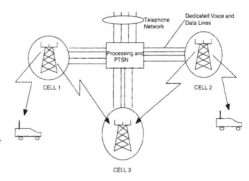

Figure 5.46. The AMPS PCS configuration.

The construction of an earth station as shown in Figure 5.47, demands a substantial capital investment in equipment and property values. Wireless service typically divides coverage around a cell site into three 120° sectors. Each sector has at least one or two transmitting antennas and a greater number of receiving antennas. Spatial diversity schemes are often implemented in which two antennas are used to receive the same signal with different fading envelopes. In the process of combining two or more fading envelopes, the overall fading is reduced, providing improved system performance.

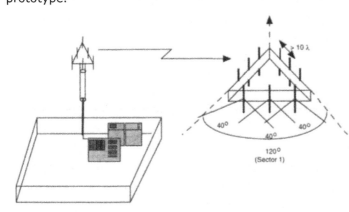

Figure 5.47. Typical earth station for an AMPS PCS system.

The antennas that cover a section are usually mounted on one of the faces of a triangular platform structure at the top of a tower, as shown in Figure 5.47. At the ends of such a face, two or more antennas are mounted, usually separated by at least 10 wavelengths.

Sector antennas typically have 60°, 90°, and 120° beam widths and are used for spatial diversity. Such directional antennas have a high gain, but have the disadvantage that, in mobiles, they must hand over coverage to another sector antenna as the mobile moves out of the coverage area of one beam and into the coverage area of another beam. The sectored antenna concept can cover the 360° azimuth, but the task of tracking mobiles becomes somewhat more complicated as mobiles move in and out of multiple beam patterns. For example, as shown in Figure 5.47, above the 9-antenna dipole configuration, each of them providing 40 beams, can cover the entire 360° azimuth plane. Although the 9-beam (or the more widely used 12-beam, with 4 dipole antennas per sector) design can provide distinct benefits, it also suffers from scan loss, which is inherent in planar arrays. In order to diminish scan loss and to provide an aesthetic look for ground mobile towers, cylindrical array antennas have been proposed [4]. Such an array configuration is shown in Figure 5.48.

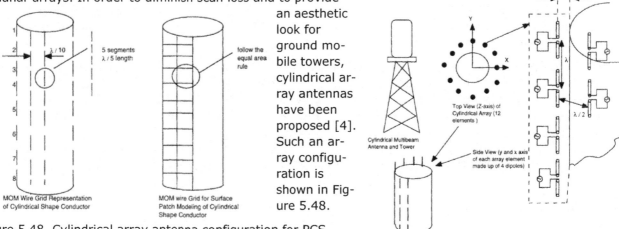

Figure 5.48. Cylindrical array antenna configuration for PCS.

The cylindrical array is composed of 12 cylindrically symmetric array elements of half-wave dipoles placed λ/4 above a cylindrical shape conductor.

In Figure 5.49, a schematic representation of the cylindrical array is shown. The array possesses four horizontal rows of dipole elements with λ spacing between rows; the columns are circumferentially spaced λ/2 apart. Each beam is generated by four adjacent columns of elements, with the inner two columns delayed by 90° relative to the outer two columns. This spatial realization yields a beam with its axis centered relative to the columns. A *method of moments* code can be used to fine-tune the design based on this concept. In the MOM model, the Green function used does not need to account for the dielectric. The dipoles are oriented vertically. The ground reflector can be represented either by cylindrically arranged vertical wires or by a surface-patch model. The wires are spaced approximately λ/10 apart and have a segmentation of λ/5. Figure 5.50 displays far-field plots of one beam of the antenna generated by the MOM model.

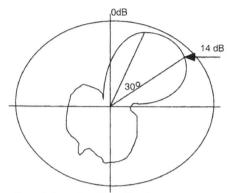

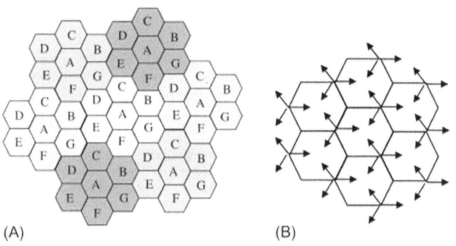

(A)   (B)

Figure 5.49. MOM wire grid model for representing the cylindrical array.

Figure 5.50. Far-field plots of antenna beam generated using MOM in the cylindrical array antenna.

Introduction to digital transmission

S. Weinstein, in Academic Press Library in Mobile and Wireless Communications, 2016[189]

1.6.1 Cellular Mobile: 1G to 4G

The first generation (1G) of cellular mobile communication systems, called Advanced Mobile Phone System (AMPS) in North America, used analog FM in 30 kHz channels and accommodated multiple users through frequency division multiple access in the 800–900MHz band allocated by the 1976 World Allocation Radio Conference (WARC) [41]. The critical cellular structure (Fig. 1.33A) came into commercial practice with the 1979 NTT deployment in Japan, followed by the 1981 Nordic mobile telephone service and the 1983 AT&T AMPS (Advanced Mobile Phone Service) in the United States. The cellular structure made possible multiple reuse of frequencies in different (separated) cells in contrast with earlier mobile systems that often had one antenna for an entire city and a very limited number of simultaneous channels. The separation between cells with the same carrier set is sufficient to attenuate signals to a noninterfering level. Additional frequency reuse within a single cell is possible with directive antennas at the vertices, a system that is called *sectorization*, with directional antennas represented by arrows in Fig. 1.33B.

Fig. 1.33. (A) Cellular structure based on a reused seven-cell pattern. Each letter represents a different set of carrier frequencies. (B) Sectorization, increasing frequency reuse with directional antennas.

Source: Adapted from G. Stuber, *Principles of Mobile Communication*, second ed., Kluwer Academic Publishers, 2001.

---

[189] Ibid

Wireless *digital* transmission came with 2G, the second-generation cellular mobile systems deployed in the early 1990s exemplified by the North American IS-54 and IS-136 standards using TDMA, the European Group Speciale Mobile (GSM) standard that also used TDMA, and the North American IS-95 code-division multiple access (CDMA) standard. By use of digital voice compression, the TDMA standards supported three times as many voice channels in the same bandwidth as the old analog systems. In GSM, the first deployed of the TDMA standards, carriers separated by 200 kHz each carried "frames" of eight time slots each, with a time slot illustrated in Fig. 1.34. This provided just under 198 kbps for traffic data, mainly multiple compressed digital voice streams but also including data from the 9.6 kbps voiceband data modems of that time and from ISDN. The upstream and downstream signals were conveyed full duplex on entirely separate carrier frequencies. IS-54, in contrast, kept the 30 kHz spacing of carrier frequencies and implemented a 40ms frame containing three slots. Both systems implemented several compressive voice coders with data rates ranging from about 7 to 13 kb/s.

Fig. 1.34. GSM time slot is carried in an eight-slot frame on one of the carrier frequencies spaced at 200 kHz.

Source: Adapted from G. Stuber, *Principles of Mobile Communication*, second ed., Kluwer Academic Publishers, 2001.

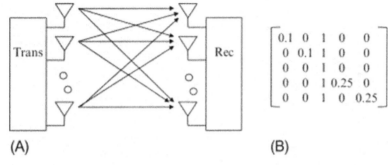

In the alternative IS-95 CDMA system [42] the user information stream (primarily compressed voice), at 9.6 kb/s, was spread over a much wider transmission bandwidth by multiplying it with a pseudo-noise (PN) bit sequence with a clock, or chip, rate 128 times faster, or 2.2288 Mchips/s. The PN sequences of different users were mutually orthogonal, making detection possible by multiplication with the correct, synchronized PN sequence. With a very large number of available orthogonal PN sequences, increasing numbers of simultaneous users were possible, with conversations already in progress experiencing a little more background noise each time a new user was added. This accommodation of more users led to forecasts of huge gains in spectral efficiency. In practice, for comparable quality, IS-95 showed gains of 6–10 times over 1G AMPS compared to IS-54's factor of 3. There are additional levels of coding beyond the scope of this brief overview and additional measures were required to regulate signal levels to overcome the near-far effect in which mobile units close to a base station overpower the signals from mobile units farther away and to meet other special needs of CDMA. As an historical note, CDMA appears to have been described in the 1930s by a Russian researcher, Dmitri Ageev.

The channel between a transmitter and a receiver is typically not the ideal unobstructed LOS, but rather a complex set of paths due to scattering, resulting in frequency-dependent fading. Fig. 1.35 illustrates nonisotropic scattering in a city street between tall buildings. The phase differences between multipath components arriving at the receiver may, due to small variations in the path delays, result in a constructive or destructive combination. Addressing the fading wireless channel is a major challenge.

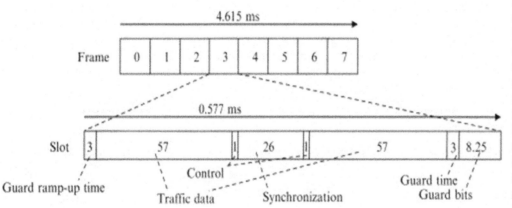

Fig. 1.35. Multipath propagation between rows of buildings [41].

The motivation for 3G cellular mobile was to move beyond the heavily voice-oriented architecture of 2G to provide at least equal emphasis on delivering data and media (audio and video) content. The IMT-2000 concept, with spectral allocations assigned by the 1992 WARC, had specific goals for transmission rates, including 144 kb/s in vehicles, 384 kb/s for pedestrians, and (asymmetric) 2 Mb/s downstream indoors. A second phase defined data rates as high as 20 Mb/s, although in practice this was left to 4G systems.

There are two major 3G standards: Universal Mobile Telecommunications System (UMTS), a successor to the 2G GSM promulgated by the 3GPP industry consortium, and CDMA2000 system, promoted by the 3GPP2 industry consortium, which is largely a successor to the IS-95 CDMA standard. Both of these standards operate in frequency bands from 1850 to 2200 MHz and utilize CDMA, but in different configurations. UMTS employs wideband CDMA (W-CDMA), with carrier spacing starting at 5 MHz and asynchronous operation of base stations, while CDMA2000 has carrier spacing starting at 1.25 MHz, the same as IS-95, and operates base stations synchronously. W-CDMA has implemented several upgrades with increasing speeds, notably High Speed Packet Access (HSPA) with 14.4 Mb/s downstream rate. CDMA2000 has evolved to similar rates.

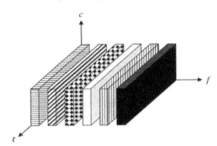

Fourth-generation (4G) cellular mobile employs a range of techniques to realize a large increase in capacity, with the goal of full accommodation of Internet applications migrating from computers to personal handsets. Peak data rate can reach 3 Gbps in the downlink and 1.5 Gbps in the uplink. Carriers have acquired or reassigned additional bandwidth for 4G services in segments between 700 and 2700 MHz. This is still within the familiar frequency range so that propagation conditions are similar to those for the previous generations of cellular mobile systems.

The characteristics of 4G cellular mobile, defined in 3GPP's Long Term Evolution-Advanced (LTE-A) specifications, include use of OFDM with its resilience against multipath delay and pulse dispersion; carrier aggregation through use of multiple frequency channels for one communication session; multiple antennas in multiple antennas out (MIMO) spatial multiplexing, a way to profit from relatively uncorrelated multipath propagation [44]; and coordinated multipoint, the collaboration of multiple base stations in communicating with a mobile unit that is near a cell boundary [45]. Relay nodes, essentially microcells embedded in ordinary cells near their boundaries to improve performance, are also supported. Either FDD or time-division duplex operation can be used.

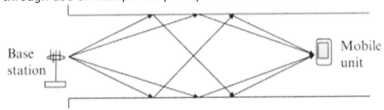

Carrier aggregation groups up to five component carriers, each with a bandwidth up to 20 MHz for a maximum of 100 MHz. The component carriers may come from different overlapping service cells offering different frequency channel sets, not the same as the spatially disjoint cells in the basic cellular mobile concept.

MIMO, a major enhancer of high speed digital wireless communication, provides the physical environment for spatial coding. For each transmitter-receiver pair, a transmitter uses multiple transmitting antennas to send appropriately designed signals to multiple receiving antennas, as illustrated in Fig. 1.36. This figure also shows a possible channel variance matrix when the matrix channel contains two very small scatterers, two larger ones, and one large scattering cluster. LTE-A supports up to 8×8 MIMO in the downlink and 4×4 MIMO in the uplink. A range of available transmission modes supports a variety of different user equipment.

Fig. 1.36. (A) MIMO with multiple antennas at transmitter and at the receiver. (B) A possible channel variance matrix for a 5×5 MIMO system [46].

Although 4G is still early in its deployed lifecycle, the relentless demand for greater bandwidth and flexibility drives efforts to devise technologies and techniques for reliable wireless access in much higher frequency bands, as described in the next section.

Richard Watson, in *Fixed/Mobile Convergence and Beyond*, 2009[190]

6.1.1 Cellular Telephony

Following the path of its circuit-switched predecessor, cellular telephony began life as an analog service: Advanced Mobile Phone Systems (AMPS). It was the wireless peer to the services provided by the PSTN, and a whole new industry was born around this technology that became pervasive in most industrialized countries. As popularity of wireless telephony grew, a trend began to emerge: The young and mobile in the societies tended to prefer to use wireless telephone services exclusively, sparking the ongoing rivalry between wired (fixed) and wireless (mobile) telephony vendors. Gateways were installed so that a fixed phone could call a mobile phone, and *vice versa*, but the fact remained: A fixed phone was fixed and a mobile phone was mobile. The two had different features and were supported by completely different industry vendors.

Analog wireless was eventually to be replaced by digital wireless technologies (Digital AMPS, GSM, and CDMA), resulting in a more reliable service with better voice quality experience for the mobile user. For the most part, digital wireless services have all but replaced analog wireless, but there remained a great technological gulf between the fixed telephone and the mobile phone.

Regarding the media on both analog and digital wireless telephony, it would travel from phone to base station to central network and finally to destination phone as a temporal circuit managed by the network. Roaming decisions between base stations were the responsibility of the "network," which assisted in managing congestion problems. Audio-encoding schemes and error-handling techniques were developed to improve voice quality and reliability, but the underlying media architecture remained basically the same.

Ali Grami, in *Introduction to Digital Communications*, 2016[191]

11.3.1 Frequency-Division Multiple Access

Frequency-division multiple access is the oldest of all multiple access schemes, and was used in the first demand assignment system for satellites (*i.e.*, single channel per carrier (SCPC)) and the first-generation of cellular mobile systems (*i.e.*, the advanced mobile phone system (AMPS)). In *frequency-division multiple access* (FDMA), the available channel bandwidth is divided into many non-overlapping frequency bands, where each band is dynamically assigned to a specific user to transmit data. In an FDMA system, signals, while occupying their assigned frequency bands, can be transmitted simultaneously and continuously without interfering with each other. In FDMA, there is a central controller that allocates the frequency band to users, solely based on their needs. This is usually done during the call set up. Once a band is allocated to a user, it then belongs to the user exclusively for the continuous flow of information during the call. To prevent interference, the allocated bands are separated from one another by small guard bands. In other words, FDMA allows the users to transmit simultaneously, but over disjoint frequency bands, a user exploits a fixed portion of the band all the time, as shown in Figure 11.4a. FDMA is best suited for connection-oriented applications; it is, however, inefficient in terms of utilization of power and bandwidth. If an FDMA channel is not in use by the user, then it sits idle and cannot be used by other users. It has poor spectral efficiency, since guard bands must be employed to avoid overlapping of the adjacent channels, and this in turn reduces the channel capacity.

Figure 11.4. Multiple access: (a) frequency-division multiple access, (b) time-division multiple access, and (c) code-division multiple access.

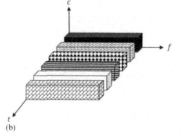

Bandpass filters are used to confine the transmitted energy within the assigned band and tight RF filtering is required to minimize adjacent channel interference. Duplexers must be employed since both the transmitter and receiver operate at the same time. FDMA is a low-cost technology to implement, and has low transmission overhead. Synchronization in FDMA is simple, once it is established during the call set up, it can be easily maintained, as transmission occurs continuously. At the hub or base station, due to the significant susceptibility to nonlinear effects of power amplifiers, such as signal spreading and intermodulation, either each FDMA channel must employ its own amplifier or a highly-linear amplifier with a significant back-off

---

[190] Ibid
[191] Ibid

power is required for the transmission of the composite signal. FDMA is generally used in combination with other multiple access schemes, where the spectrum is divided into large sub-bands. Each sub-band serves a large group of users, where within a group, another multiple access method can be employed. Examples include employing FDMA/TDMA in the GSM cellular mobile systems or in satellite systems offering VSAT applications.

John Polson, Bruce A. Fette, in *Cognitive Radio Technology* (Second Edition), 2009[192]

8.7 Example of Cellular Phone 911 Geolocation for First Responders

The productivity of ubiquitous cellular phone and handheld communications devices such as pagers or BlackBerry-type devices have dramatically increased. Additional problems, however, have been introduced. For example, with wired telephones emergency calls were traditionally easily located to the phone where the call was placed and the location was very reliable. At the time of the initial deployment of cellular telephones, a call placed to an emergency response center did not come with a location attached for the emergency operator. The problem prompted the Federal Communications Commission (FCC), in 1996, to mandate geolocation services in the cellular network infrastructure. The FCC mandate was for 125m accuracy in 67 percent of all measurements by October 31, 2001.

Multiple cellular telephone interfaces exist including Advanced Mobile Phone System (AMPS), code division multiple access (CDMA) EIA/TIA IS-95, time division multiple access (TDMA) EIA/TIA IS-136, the older TDMA IS-54, and the Global System for Mobile Communications (GSM). The common characteristic of these systems is a set of base stations that communicate directly with mobile stations or handsets. The frequencies, bandwidths, modulations, and protocols vary from standard to standard.

The two broad categories of geolocation techniques for cellular telephones are (1) network- or infrastructure-based approaches, and (2) handset-based approaches. The advantage of the network-based approach is there are no requirements placed on the owners of the cell phones. The advantage of the handset-based approach is the precision available.

Infrastructure-based approaches include ToA (Time of Arrival), TDoA (Time & Direction of Arrival), and AoA (Angle of Arrival). The geolocation application executes on cooperating base stations, measures one or more of the essential physical properties, exchanges information, and processes the signals to produce a location estimate.

The best example of a handset-based approach is putting a GPS receiver into the handset and interrogating the handset for its location when an emergency call is placed.

Ali Zaidi, ... Xiaoming Chen, in *5G Physical Layer*, 2018[193]

1.1 Evolution of Mobile Communication

In 1946, the US federal communications commission (FCC) approved a first mobile telephony service to be operated by AT&T in 1947. At this time, the equipment was bulky and had to be installed in a vehicle due to the weight and its excessive power consumption. From this point on, more than three decades of cellular communication technology evolution has led to a shift from analog to digital formats of communication, going from what was mainly voice to high-speed data communication.

Leading up from the mid-1980s, the first generation (1G) of cellular communication, which mainly carried voice, grew up using formats such as advanced mobile phone system (AMPS) in the USA and Nordic mobile telephone (NMT) in Scandinavia. These analog formats were later replaced moving towards 2G with the first digital communication schemes around the mid to late-1990s—Global System for Mobile communications (GSM) in Europe and digital-AMPS for the USA. At this point, the short message service (SMS) was introduced, being one of the first widely used non-voice applications for cellular communication. Enhancement for 2.5G using enhanced data rates for GSM evolution (EDGE), general packet radio service (GPRS) and code division multiple access (CDMA) sparked the use of mobile data communication and early cellular internet connectivity

---

[192] Ibid
[193] Ibid

in the early-2000s. This was an early enabler, which did, however, require a specific protocol, known as wireless application protocol (WAP).

Moving forward from 2G into 3G, in order to meet the increasing demand for cellular access data rates, Universal Mobile Telecommunications System (UMTS) based on wideband CDMA (WCDMA) technology was introduced by third generation partnership project (3GPP) just around 2000. With advances in mobile user equipment technology, this enabled the user to not only communicate *via* Multimedia Message Service (MMS), but also stream video content. Transitioning to 4G, Long Term Evolution (LTE) was introduced, which does not only impose major changes on the air interface, but was moving from code division multiplexing to Orthogonal Frequency Division Multiplexing (OFDM) and Time Division Duplex (TDD) or Frequency Division Duplex (FDD).

Entering the era of 4G, there were mainly two competing technologies at an early stage. These were Worldwide Interoperability for Microwave Access (WiMAX), based on IEEE 802.16m, and LTE Advanced, which is an extension of LTE. LTE-A introduced technology components such as carrier aggregation and improved support for Coordinated Multipoint (CoMP) transmission and Heterogeneous Network (HetNet) deployments for improving Quality of Service (QoS) in hot-spots and coverage for cell-edge users. LTE-A prevailed as the dominant cellular access technology today and has served as the basis of the transition to 5G mobile communications. The transition from 4G to 5G is inspired by new human-centric and machine-centric services across multiple industries.[194]

What is Radio Cognition or "Cognitive Radio Technology?"

"**C**ognitive **R**adio (CR) is an adaptive, intelligent radio and network technology that can automatically detect available channels in a wireless spectrum and change transmission parameters enabling more communications to run concurrently and also improve radio operating behavior."[195]

"Cognitive radio uses a number of technologies including Adaptive Radio (where the communications system monitors and modifies its own performance) and Software Defined Radio (SDR) where traditional hardware components including mixers, modulators and amplifiers have been replaced with intelligent software."[196]

Joseph Mitola III, in *Cognitive Radio Technology* (Second Edition), 2009[197]

14.6.7 When Should a Radio Transition Toward Cognition?

If a wireless device accesses only a single-RF band and mode, then it is not a very good starting point for CR—it's just too simple. Even as complexity increases, as long as the user's needs are met by wireless devices managed by the network(s), then embedding computational intelligence in the device has limited benefits. In 1999, Mitsubishi and AT&T announced the first "four-mode handset." The T250 operated in time division multiple access (TDMA) mode on 850 or 1900MHz, in first-generation Advanced Mobile Phone System (AMPS) mode on 850MHz, and in cellular digital packet data (CDPD) mode on 1900MHz. This illustrates the early development of multiband, multimode, multimedia (M3) wireless. These radios enhanced the service provider's ability to offer national roaming, but the complexity was not apparent to the user because the network managed the radio resources of the handset.

Even as device complexity increases in ways that the network does not manage, there may be no need for cognition. There are several examples of capabilities embedded in electronics that are not heavily used. For example, how many people use their laptop's speech-recognition system? What about its Infrared Data Association (IrDA) port? The typical users in 2004 didn't use either capability of their Windows XP laptop all that much. So complexity can increase without putting a burden on the user to manage that complexity if the capability isn't central to the way in which the user employs the system.

For the radio, as the number of bands and modes increases, the SDR (Software Defined Radio) becomes a better candidate for the insertion of cognition technology. But it is not until the radio or the wireless part of the PDA has the capacity to access multiple RF bands that cognition technology begins to pay off. With the liberalization of RF spectrum use rules, the early evolution of CR may be driven by RF spectrum-use etiquette

---

[194] Ibid
[195] https://www.webopedia.com/TERM/C/cognitive_radio.html
[196] Ibid
[197] Ibid

for *ad hoc* bands such as the FCC use case. In the not-too-distant future, SDR PDAs could access satellite mobile services, cordless telephone, WLAN, GSM, and 3G bands. An ideal SDR device with these capabilities might affordably access three octave bands, from 0.4 to 0.96GHz (skipping the air navigation and GPS band from 0.96 to 1.2GHz), from 1.3 to 2.5GHz, and from 2.5 to 5.9GHz (Figure 14.23). Not counting satellite mobile and radio navigation bands, such radios would have access to more than 30 mobile sub-bands in 1463MHz of potentially sharable outdoor mobile spectrum. The upper band provides another 1.07GHz of sharable indoor and RF-LAN spectrum.[198]

Help Key: 3G, 4G, HSPA+, LTE, WiMax – What Do They Mean To You?

Devin Coldewey@techcrunch, November 3, 2010[199]

Comment

Note the date of this articleAs the big carriers continue to upgrade their network infrastructure, we're being subjected to a torrent of confusing new terms, some of them misleading, some of them only a letter or number off from another, and so on. What's a consumer to do when confronted with such a frightening array of acronyms and jargon? A little straight talk seems to be in order. Let's get some basic facts down first, then we'll talk about what matters.

This is by no means a complete or definitive listing of terms, networks, and protocols; it is only a look at the ones most likely to be encountered by consumers today and in the near future. We'll go through these in basic chronological order, which also happens to be more or less in order of speed, from slowest to fastest, with some exceptions.

The dates I provide are general guides for popularization and common usage, not establishment or approval of the tech. A basic speed gauge to keep in mind: 800Kbps = 100KB/s. 100KB is the size of the image at the top of this post, so an 800Kbps connection would take one second to load it, an 80Kbps connection would take 10 seconds, an 8000Kbps would take a tenth of a second, *etc.*

2G: Second Generation. This is what your old flip-phone used to download games like Bejeweled™. It was the original way of transferring data over digital cellular networks. Its speed isn't easily measurable because of the way it sends and receives data, but believe me, it's not very fast.

2.5G: Improved hardware and infrastructure led to better data speeds; though no one actually ever referred to these as "2.5G," they're essentially that, since they're slower than 3G. There are two major varieties of 2.5G connections:

–**GPRS**: General Packet Radio Service. At around 30-40Kbps, it's barely suitable for retrieving a text email. You'll see a little "G" by your bars.

–**EDGE**: Enhanced Data for GSM Evolution. About three times faster than GPRS, using similar technology, so ~100-120Kbps. Occasionally called 2.75G to distinguish from GPRS. Signified by an "E."

3G: Third Generation. Networks were upgraded for the most part between 2004 and 2007 to allow for much more data traffic. Your 3G data may be traveling under CDMA, WCDMA, GSM, UMTS, or a number of other terms and frequencies, but all you need to know is that your carrier either has or does not have 3G coverage in the area where you're going to be living or working. The technical details you can look up for yourself, but "vanilla" 3G basically provides data rates at up to or around 2Mbps (that's 2000Kbps).

3.5G: Although some new networks should properly fall under this heading, everyone is opting for "4G" branding instead, mostly because it's sexier.

4G: Fourth Generation. This term is (like the others) essentially a marketing term when employed by carriers. As the different carriers and telecoms roll out faster data networks, some thought they would own the "4G" term by applying it to their network, though the name has little to do with the actual capabilities. While the actual term "4G" has been standardized to mean something none of them offer yet, what you'll likely be sold on is one of the following:

–**HSDPA, HSUPA, HSPA, HSPA+**: High Speed Download/Upload Packet Access (+ designates the "Evolved"

---

[198] Ibid
[199] https://techcrunch.com/2010/11/03/help-key-3g-4g-hspa-lte-wimax-what-do-they-mean-to-you/

newer spec). This is a major upgrade to existing 3G networks that allows for (but does not currently actually show) speeds up to 21Mbps at the moment. T-Mobile is using this, and the G2 is currently the only phone using the network, though the MyTouch 4G will as well when it hits the streets. I found my speeds maxed out at about 8Mbps here in central Seattle, which is about as fast as the average broadband connection, and a huge improvement over 3G. The HSPA+ spec does allow for much higher bandwidths, but 21 appears to be the limit for the short- to medium-term.

–**LTE**: Long-Term Evolution. This is intended to replace 3G networks altogether, and provides a major speed boost and improvements on the way different types of data are transmitted. Verizon's LTE-based test networks are currently showing 10-15Mbps, though the technology theoretically supports more than ten times that amount of bandwidth. AT&T is planning an LTE network as well, which they're planning on launching in 2011, but at the moment they've activated HSPA+ at a good number of sites around the country.

–**WiMax**: Originally rolled out as a wireless home broadband service *(i.e.* Clearwire), but now being improved to allow for access by mobile phones. The current revision allows for up to 40Mbps, and future revisions promise 1Gbps. (Author note: Sprint bought Clearwire and T-Mobile bought Sprint.)

5G 5G is the 5th generation mobile network. It is a new global wireless standard after 1G, 2G, 3G, and 4G networks. 5G enables a new kind of network that is designed to connect virtually everyone and everything together including machines, objects, and devices.

5G wireless technology is meant to deliver higher multi-Gbps peak data speeds, ultra low latency, more reliability, massive network capacity, increased availability, and a more uniform user experience to more users. Higher performance and improved efficiency empower new user experiences and connects new industries.

[200]**5G** is the fifth generation technology standard for cellular networks, which cellular phone companies began deploying worldwide in 2019, the planned successor to the 4G networks which provides connectivity to most current cellphones. Like its predecessors, 5G networks are cellular networks in which the service area is divided into small geographical areas called *cells*. All 5G wireless devices in a cell are connected to the Internet and telephone network by radio waves through a local antenna in the cell. The main advantage of the new networks is that they will have greater bandwidth, giving higher download speeds, eventually up to 10 gigabits per second (Gbit/s). Due to the increased bandwidth, it is expected that the new networks will not just serve cellphones like existing cellular networks, but also be used as general internet service providers for laptops and desktop computers, competing with existing ISPs such as cable internet, and also will make possible new applications in internet of things (IoT) and machine to machine areas. Current 4G cellphones will not be able to use the new network, which will require new 5G enabled wireless devices.

The increased speed is achieved partly by using higher-frequency radio waves than current cellular networks. However, higher-frequency radio waves have a shorter range than the frequencies used by previous cell phone towers, requiring smaller cells. To ensure wide service, 5G networks operate on up to three frequency bands, low, medium, and high. A 5G network will be composed of networks of up to 3 different types of cells, each requiring different antennas, each type giving a different tradeoff of download speed vs. distance and service area. 5G cellphones and wireless devices will connect to the network through the highest speed antenna within range at their location:

Low-band 5G uses a similar frequency range to current 4G cellphones, 600-700 MHz, giving download speeds a little higher than 4G: 30-250 megabits per second (Mbit/s). Low-band cell towers will have a similar range and coverage area to current 4G towers. Mid-band 5G uses microwaves of 2.5-3.7GHz, currently allowing speeds of 100-900 Mbit/s, with each cell tower providing service up to several miles in radius. This level of service is the most widely deployed, and should be available in most metropolitan areas in 2020. Some countries are not implementing low-band, making this the minimum service level. High-band 5G currently uses frequencies of 25-39GHz, near the bottom of the millimeter wave band, although higher frequencies may be used in the future. It often achieves download speeds of a gigabit per second (Gbit/s), comparable to cable internet. However, millimeter waves (mmWave or mmW) have a more limited range, requiring many small cells. They have trouble passing through some types of walls and windows. Due to their higher costs, current

---

[200] https://en.wikipedia.org/wiki/5G

plans are to deploy these cells only in dense urban environments and areas where crowds of people congregate such as sports stadiums and convention centers. The above speeds are those achieved in actual tests in 2020, and speeds are expected to increase during rollout.

So?

So. Those are the terms. Very informative, aren't they? —No?

In fact, no, they're still a jumble of in-progress improvements, rolling out to some regions but not others, and likely to see improvements and setbacks over the next year or two 9or more) that we have no way of foreseeing. And of course, what you're interested in is whether any of these acronyms represent a VISE — a visible improvement to speed and experience.

The truth is that even the applications and services that use the highest amounts of bandwidth — HD streaming video is probably the most popular — come nowhere near the limitations on these networks. An HD video is transmitted at around 3-4Mbps, and with lost packets, redundancy, and so on, you're probably looking at 5-6Mbps maximum. And that's for a home theater or desktop system. Mobile apps use *far less* data. You're being sold on capability above and beyond what is actually in use, or what will likely be used in the next couple years — which are the only years that matter, since you're not signing a lifetime contract.

If, in a few years, it turns out that, not only is LTE coming through with those high speeds they promised, but also you need a huge amount more bandwidth for your mobile torrent seedbox (or, more likely, your "mobile" connection will be your only data connection), then you can skip out on T-Mo and join up. But these hypotheticals are extremely low priority considering the much more salient issues of availability, price, signal, and handsets.

What matters?

What matters is what's available and how fast it is, *where you are*. When you go to the carrier store to check out their selection, don't listen to the garbage talk about how you can stream ten movies at once. And don't give any weight to shrill claims of the largest or fastest network, since those claims are both irrelevant for most users and short-lived, as the balance of power seems to shift on a monthly basis.

The new networks are *all* fast as hell, much faster than your 3G phone. What you need to find out is whether you can even get at those speeds where you live, work, and hang out. Ask a representative about local coverage, plans to expand to other parts of the city, what average speeds are in the area, and so on. T-Mobile might have super high-speed HSPA+ coverage downtown, but not in the suburbs until 2012. Verizon might not have LTE coming out in your area at all. WiMax might have a line-of-sight issue with your neighborhood. Here is some recent coverage info on T-Mobile, Verizon, and Sprint. Look for stuff like that.

Your current phone likely maxes out at 1.5-2Mbps if you're lucky, but as I'm sure you know, that only matters if you can get a signal — something AT&T notoriously failed on with their 3G network in New York. Even something like HSPA, which is actually an improvement to 3G networks and not a new one *per se*, needs to be rolled out area by area, and coverage will be as spotty as other services.

Try to ignore the marketing fluff surrounding the term "4G," and get practical. One of these new networks may be best for you, but in order to not get conned, it's something you have to investigate personally. Ask the carrier representatives, ask your friends, and of course, ask us.[201]

Since this article was written, much progress has been made with data speeds and eliminating much of the jargon confusion to which this article alludes; however, this information is provided to alert you, the student, to what went before advanced 4G and now (2020) 5G.

Femtocells

---

[201] Ibid

The following presentation of "femtocell" technology, a subset of advanced digital cellular networks, is intended to alert you, the student, to the complexities of networks enabling the wireless voice and data services we take for granted when we enjoy the benefits of using a cellular telephone, iPAD, *etc*. While the complexities and jargon presented in the following discussion may be intimidating, you are encouraged to wade through all the acronyms and unfamiliar verbiage to recognize how significant a career in wireless engineering awaits those willing to devote the time and energy to understanding it.

With "femtocells," we go from the macro-coverage to the indoor and difficult to serve areas such as low signal perimeter areas, shielded bunkers, basements and the like. Unlike cellular boosters or extension devices fixed in place mimicking mobiles, femtocells are legitimate network components when approved and registered with the carrier. They do not appear to the network as mobiles. They are very low power transceivers designed to connect cell phones/devices in low signal areas by connecting the wireless portable device to the local network switch via the internet router assumed to be available to the end user.

The critical issue in this regard is network **balance**. Where unregistered maverick cell boosters [extenders] potentially create severe system imbalances by impersonating mobiles, femtocells are invisible to the greater network and do not create imbalances within the network topology.

In telecommunications, a **femtocell** is a small, low-power cellular base station, typically designed for use in a home or small business. A broader term which is more widespread in the industry is small cell, with femtocell as a subset. It is also called femto AccessPoint (AP). It connects to the service provider's network *via* broadband (such as DSL or cable); current designs typically support four to eight simultaneously active mobile phones in a residential setting depending on version number and femtocell hardware, and eight to sixteen mobile phones in enterprise settings. A femtocell allows service providers to extend service coverage indoors or at the cell edge, especially where access would otherwise be limited or unavailable. Although much attention is focused on WCDMA, the concept is applicable to all standards, including GSM, CDMA2000, TD SCDMA, WiMAX and LTE solutions.

The use of femtocells allows network coverage in places where the signal to the main network cells might be too weak. Furthermore, femtocells lower contention on the main network cells by forming a connection from the end user, through an internet connection, to the operator's private network infrastructure elsewhere. The lowering of contention to the main cells plays a part in traffic management where connections are off-loaded based on physical distance to cell towers.

Consumers and small businesses benefit from greatly improved coverage and signal strength since they have a *de facto* base station inside their premises. As a result of being relatively close to the femtocell, the mobile phone (user equipment) expends significantly less power for communication with it, thus increasing battery life. They may also get better voice quality (via HD voice) depending on a number of factors such as operator/network support, customer contract/price plan, phone and operating system support. Some carriers may also offer more attractive tariffs, for example discounted calls from home.

Femtocells are an alternative way to deliver the benefits of fixed–mobile convergence (FMC). The distinction is that most FMC architectures require a new dual-mode handset which works with existing unlicensed spectrum home/enterprise wireless access points, while a femtocell-based deployment will work with existing handsets but requires the installation of a new access point that uses licensed spectrum.

Many operators worldwide offer a femtocell service, mainly targeted at businesses but also offered to individual customers (often for a one-off fee) when they complain to the operator regarding a poor or non-existent signal at their location. Operators who have launched a femtocell service include SFR, AT&T, C Spire, Sprint Nextel, Verizon, Zain, Mobile TeleSystems, T-Mobile US, Orange, Vodafone, EE, O2, Three, and others.

In 3GPP terminology, a Home NodeB (HNB) is a 3G femtocell. A Home eNodeB (HeNB) is an LTE 4G femtocell.

Theoretically the range of a standard base station may be up to 35 kilometres (22 mi), and in practice could be 5–10 km (3–6 mi), a microcell is less than two kilometers wide, a picocell is 200 meters or less, and a femtocell is in the order of 10 meters, although AT&T calls its product, with a range of 40 feet (12m), a "microcell". AT&T uses "AT&T 3G MicroCell™" as a trademark and not necessarily the "microcell" technology, however.

Overview and Benefits

Operating mode

Femtocells are sold or loaned by a mobile network operator (MNO) to its residential or enterprise customers. A femtocell is typically the size of a residential gateway or smaller, and connects to the user's broadband line. Integrated femtocells (which include both a DSL router and femtocell) also exist. Once plugged in, the femtocell connects to the MNO's mobile network, and provides extra coverage. From a user's perspective, it is plug and play, there is no specific installation or technical knowledge required—anyone can install a femtocell at home.

In most cases, the user must then declare which mobile phone numbers are allowed to connect to their femtocell, usually *via* a web interface provided by the MNO. This needs to be done only once. When these mobile phones arrive under coverage of the femtocell, they switch over from the macrocell (outdoor) to the femtocell automatically. Most MNOs provide a way for the user to know this has happened, for example by having a different network name appear on the mobile phone. All communications will then automatically go through the femtocell. When the user leaves the femtocell coverage (whether in a call or not) area, their phone hands over seamlessly to the macro network. Femtocells require specific hardware, so existing WiFi or DSL routers cannot be upgraded to a femtocell.

Once installed in a specific location, most femtocells have protection mechanisms so that a location change will be reported to the MNO. Whether the MNO allows femtocells to operate in a different location depends on the MNO's policy. International location change of a femtocell is not permitted because the femtocell transmits licensed frequencies which belong to different network operators in different countries.

Benefits for Users

The main benefits for an end user include the following:

- "5 bar" coverage when there is no existing signal or poor coverage
- Higher mobile data capacity, which is important if the end-user makes use of mobile data on his or her mobile phone (may not be relevant to a large number of subscribers who instead use WiFi where femtocell is located)
- Depending on the pricing policy of the MNO, special tariffs at home can be applied for calls placed under femtocell coverage
- For enterprise users, having femtos instead of DECT ("cordless" home) phones enables them to have a single phone, so a single contact list, *etc.*
- Improved battery life for mobile devices due to reduced transmitter–receiver distance
- The battery draining issue of mobile operators can be eliminated by means of energy efficiency of the networks resulting in prolongation of the battery life of handsets
- New applications and services can be created to enhance user experience or provide additional features:
- In connected car case the use of femtocells has been proposed as a safety feature (c.f. patent application EP2647257B1 by Valentin A. Alexeev)
- Femtocells can be used to give coverage in rural areas.

The standards bodies have published formal specifications for femtocells for the most popular technologies, namely WCDMA, CDMA2000, LTE and WiMAX. These all broadly conform to an architecture with three major elements:

The femtocell access points themselves, which embody greater network functionality than found in macrocell base stations, such as the radio resource control functions. This allows much greater autonomy within the femtocell, enabling self-configuration and self-optimization. Femtocells are connected using broadband IP, such as DSL or cable modems, to the network operator's core switching centers.

The femtocell gateway, comprising a security gateway that terminates large numbers of encrypted IP data connections from hundreds of thousands of femtocells, and a signaling gateway which aggregates and validates the signaling traffic, authenticates each femtocell and interfaces with the mobile network core switches using standard protocols.

The management and operational system which allows software updates and diagnostic checks to be administered. These typically use the same TR-069 management protocol published by the Broadband Forum and also used for administration of residential modems.

The key interface in these architectures is that between the femtocell access points and the femtocell gateway. Standardization enables a wider choice of femtocell products to be used with any gateway, increasing competitive pressure and driving costs down. For the common WCDMA femtocells, this is defined as the **Iuh** interface. In the Iuh architecture, the femtocell gateway sits between the femtocell and the core network and performs the necessary translations to ensure the femtocells appear as a radio network controller to existing mobile switching centers (MSCs). Each femtocell talks to the femtocell gateway and femtocell gateways talk to the Core Network Elements (CNE) (MSC for circuit-switched calls, SGSN for packet-switched calls). This model was proposed by 3GPP and the Femto Forum. New protocols (HNBAP [Home Node B Application Part] and RUA RANAP User Adaptation]) have been derived; HNBAP is used for the control signaling between the HNB and HNB-GW while RUA is a lightweight mechanism to replace the SCCP and M3UA protocols in the RNC; its primary function is transparent transfer of RANAP messages.

In March 2010, the Femto Forum and ETSI conducted the first Plugfest to promote interoperability of the **Iuh** standard.

The CDMA2000 standard released in March 2010 differs slightly by adopting the Session Initiation Protocol (SIP) to set up a connection between the femtocell and a femtocell convergence server (FCS). Voice calls are routed through the FCS which emulates an MSC. SIP is not required or used by the mobile device itself. In the SIP architecture, the femtocell connects to a core network of the mobile operator that is based on the SIP/IMS architecture. This is achieved by having the femtocells behave toward the SIP/IMS network like a SIP/IMS client by converting the circuit-switched 3G signaling to SIP/IMS signaling, and by transporting the voice traffic over RTP as defined in the IETF standards.

Air Interfaces

Although much of the commercial focus seems to have been on the Universal Mobile Telecommunications System (UMTS), the concept is equally applicable to all air-interfaces. Indeed, the first commercial deployment was the CDMA2000 Airave in 2007 by Sprint.

Femtocells are also under development or commercially available for GSM, TD-SCDMA, WiMAX and LTE.

The H(e)NB functionality and interfaces are basically the same as for regular High Speed Packet Access (HSPA) or LTE base stations except for a few additional functions. The differences are mostly to support differences in access control to support closed access for residential deployment or open access for enterprise deployment, as well as handover functionality for active subscribers and cell selection procedures for idle subscribers. For LTE additional functionality was added in 3GPP Release 9.

Issues

Interference

The placement of a femtocell has a critical effect on the performance of the wider network, and this is the key issue to be addressed for successful deployment. Because femtocells can use the same frequency bands as the conventional cellular network, there has been the worry that, rather than improving the situation, they could potentially cause problems.

Femtocells incorporate interference mitigation techniques—detecting macrocells, adjusting power and scrambling codes accordingly. Ralph de la Vega, AT&T President, reported in June 2011 they recommended against using femtocells where signal strength was middle or strong because of interference problems they discovered after wide scale deployment. This differs from previous opinions expressed earlier by AT&T and others.

A good example are the comments made by Gordon Mansfield, Executive Director of RAN Delivery, AT&T, speaking at the Femtozone at CTIA March 2010:

"We have deployed femtocells co-carrier with both the hopping channels for GSM macrocells and with UMTS macrocells. Interference isn't a problem. We have tested femtocells extensively in real customer deployments of many thousands of femtocells, and we find that the mitigation techniques implemented successfully minimize and avoid interference. The more femtocells you deploy, the more uplink interference is reduced."

The Femto Forum has some extensive reports on this subject, which have been produced together with 3GPP and 3GPP2.

[202]To quote from the *Summary Paper — Summary of Findings*:

The simulations performed in the Femto Forum WG2 and 3GPP RAN4 encompass a wide spectrum of possible deployment scenarios including shared channel and dedicated channel deployments. In addition, the studies looked at the impact in different morphologies, as well as in closed versus open access. The following are broad conclusions from the studies:

1. When femtocells are used in areas of poor or no coverage, macro/femto interference is unlikely to be a problem.

2. If the femto network is sharing the channel (co-channel) with the macro network, interference can occur. However, if the interference management techniques advocated by the Femto Forum are adopted, the resulting interference can be mitigated in most cases.

3. A femtocell network deployed on an adjacent dedicated channel is unlikely to create interference to a macro network. Additionally, the impact of a macro network on the performance of a femtocell on an adjacent channel is limited to isolated cases. If the interference mitigation techniques advocated by the Femto Forum are used, the impact is further marginalized.

4. Closed access represents the worst-case scenario for creation of interference. Open access reduces the chances of User Equipment (mobile phone handsets, 3G data dongles, *etc.*) on the macro network interfering with a proximate femtocell.

5. The same conclusions were reached for both the 850 MHz (3GPP Band 17) and 2100 MHz (3GPP Band 1) deployments that were studied.

The conclusions are common to the 850 MHz and 2100 MHz bands that were simulated in the studies, and can be extrapolated to other mobile bands. With interference mitigation techniques successfully implemented, simulations show that femtocell deployments can enable very high capacity networks by providing between a 10 and 100 times increase in capacity with minimal dead zone impact and acceptable noise rise.

Femtocells can also create a much better user experience by enabling substantially higher data rates than can be obtained with a macro network and net throughputs that will be ultimately limited by backhaul in most cases (over 20 Mbps in 5 MHz).

Lawful Interception

Access point base stations, in common with all other public communications systems, are, in most countries, required to comply with lawful interception requirements.

Equipment Location

Other regulatory issues relate to the requirement in most countries for the operator of a network to be able to show exactly where each base station is located, and for E911 requirements to provide the registered location of the equipment to the emergency services. There are issues in this regard for access point base stations sold to consumers for home installation, for example. Further, a consumer might try to carry his base station with him to a country where it is not licensed. Some manufacturers are using GPS within the equipment to lock the femtocell when it is moved to a different country; this approach is disputed, as GPS is often unable to obtain position indoors because of weak signal.

Emergency Calls

---

[202] https://www.sciencedirect.com/topics/engineering/femtocells

Access Point Base Stations are also required, since carrying voice calls, to provide a 911 (or 999, 112, *etc.*) emergency service, as is the case for VoIP phone providers in some jurisdictions. This service must meet the same requirements for availability as current wired telephone systems. Simply put—the phones must work if the AC main grid is blacked out. There are several ways to achieve this, such as alternative power sources or fall back to existing telephone infrastructure.

Quality of Service

When using an Ethernet or ADSL home backhaul connection, an Access Point Base Station must either share the backhaul bandwidth with other services, such as Internet browsing, gaming consoles, set-top boxes and triple-play equipment in general, or alternatively directly replace these functions within an integrated unit. In shared-bandwidth approaches, which are the majority of designs currently being developed, the effect on quality of service may be an issue.

The uptake of femtocell services will depend on the reliability and quality of both the cellular operator's network and the third-party broadband connection, and the broadband connection's subscriber understanding the concept of bandwidth utilization by different applications a subscriber may use. When things go wrong, subscribers will turn to cellular operators for support even if the root cause of the problem lies with the broadband connection to the home or workplace. Hence, the effects of any third-party ISP broadband network iss-ues or traffic management policies need to be very closely monitored and the ramifications quickly communicated to subscribers.

A key issue recently identified is active traffic shaping by many ISPs on the underlying transport protocol IP-Sec.

Spectrum Accuracy

To meet Federal Communications Commission (FCC) /Ofcom spectrum mask requirements, femtocells must generate the radio frequency signal with a high degree of precision. To do this over a long period of time is a major technical challenge. The solution to this problem is to use an external, accurate signal to constantly calibrate the oscillator to ensure it maintains its accuracy. This is not simple (broadband backhaul introduces issues of network jitter/wander and recovered clock accuracy), but technologies such as the IEEE 1588 time synchronization standard may address the issue. Also, Network Time Protocol (NTP) is being pursued by some developers as a possible solution to provide frequency stability. Conventional (macrocell) base stations often use GPS timing for synchronization and this could be used, although there are concerns on cost and the difficulty of ensuring good GPS coverage.

Standards bodies have recognized the challenge of this and the implications on device cost. For example, 3GPP has relaxed the 50ppb (parts per billion) precision to 100ppb for indoor base stations in Release 6 and a further loosening to 250ppb for Home Node B in Release 8.

Security

At the 2013 Black Hat hacker conference in Las Vegas, NV, a trio of security researchers detailed their ability to use a Verizon femtocell to secretly intercept the voice calls, data, and SMS text messages of any handset that connects to the device.

During a demonstration of their exploit, they showed how they could begin recording audio from a cell phone even before the call began. The recording included both sides of the conversation. They also demonstrated how it could trick Apple's iMessage–which encrypts texts sent over its network using SSL to render them unreadable to snoopers, to SMS—allowing the femtocell to intercept the messages.

They also demonstrated it was possible to "clone" a cell phone that runs on a CDMA network by remotely collecting its device ID number through the femtocell, in spite of added security measures to prevent against cloning of CDMA phones.

Controversy on Consumer Proposition

The impact of a femtocell is most often to improve cellular coverage, without the cellular carrier needing to improve their infrastructure (cell towers, *etc.*). This is net gain for the cellular carrier. However, the user must provide and pay for an internet connection to route the femtocell traffic, and then (usually) pay an additional one-off or monthly fee to the cellular carrier. Some have objected to the idea that consumers are being asked to pay to help relieve network shortcomings. On the other hand, residential femtocells normally provide a 'personal cell' which provides benefits only to the owner's family and friends.

The difference is also that, while mobile coverage is provided through subscriptions from an operator with one business model, a fixed fiber or cable may work with a completely different business model. For example, mobile operators may apply restrictions on services which an operator on a fixed may not. Also, WiFi connects to a local network such as home servers and media players. This network should possibly not be within reach of the mobile operator.

Deployment

According to market research firm Informa and the Femto Forum, as of December 2010, 18 operators have launched commercial femtocell services, with a total of 30 committed to deployment.

At the end of 2011, femtocell shipments had reached roughly 2 million units deployed annually, and the market is expected to grow rapidly with distinct segments for consumer, enterprise, and carrier-grade femtocell deployments. Femtocell shipments are estimated to have reached almost 2 million at the end of 2010. Research firm, Berg Insight, estimates the shipments will grow to 12 million units worldwide in 2014.

Within the United States, Cellcom (Wisconsin), was the first CDMA carrier in the U.S. to be a member of the non-profit organization founded in 2007 to promote worldwide femtocell deployment. In 2009, Cellcom received the first Femtocell Industry Award for significant progress or commercial launch by a small carrier at the Femtocells World Summit in London. Additional significant deployments within the United States were by Sprint Nextel, Verizon Wireless and AT&T Wireless. Sprint started in the third quarter of 2007 as a limited rollout (Denver and Indianapolis) of a home-based femtocell built by Samsung Electronics called the Sprint Airave that works with any Sprint handset. From 17 August 2008, the Airave was rolled out on a nationwide basis. Other operators in the United States have followed suit. In January 2009, Verizon rolled out its Wireless Network Extender, based on the same design as the Sprint/Samsung system. In late March 2010, AT&T announced nationwide roll-out of its 3G MicroCell, which commenced in April. The equipment is made by Cisco Systems and ip.access, and was the first 3G femtocell in the US, supporting both voice and data HSPA. Both Sprint and Verizon upgraded to 3G CDMA femtocells during 2010, with capacity for more concurrent calls and much higher data rates. In November 2015, T-Mobile US began deployment of 4G LTE femtocells manufactured by Alcatel Lucent.

In Asia, several service providers have rolled out femtocell networks. In Japan, SoftBank launched its residential 3G femtocell service in January 2009 with devices provided by Ubiquisys. In the same year, the operator launched a project to deploy femtocells to deliver outdoor services in rural environments where existing coverage is limited. In May 2010, SoftBank Mobile launched the first free femtocell offer, providing open access femtocells free of charge to its residential and business customers. In Singapore, Starhub rolled out its first nationwide commercial 3G femtocell services with devices provided by Huawei Technologies, though the uptake is low, while Singtel's offering is targeted at small medium enterprises. In 2009, China Unicom announced its own femtocell network. NTT DoCoMo in Japan launched their own femtocell service on 10 November 2009.

In July 2009, Vodafone released the first femtocell network in Europe, the Vodafone Access Gateway provided by Alcatel-Lucent. This was rebranded as SureSignal in January 2010, after which Vodafone also launched service in Spain, Greece, New Zealand, Italy, Ireland, Hungary and The Netherlands. Other operators in Europe have followed since then.[203]

---

[203] https://www.sciencedirect.com/topics/engineering/femtocells

Chapter Twenty-Five -- Iridium

From Femto to Global – Ubiquity: Anyone, Anywhere, Anytime = Iridium

Iridium® (first generation) replaced in 2017 by Iridium "Next"®

As you read this, ships at sea, anywhere on the sea or lakes or oceans, in the jungles – anywhere in the jungles of the Amazon, Africa or Asia, at the poles – North and South, in the deserts – Gobi, Sahara, Empty Quarter, Mojave, Patagonian, Atacama, in the mountains – Himalayas, Zagros, Atlas, Caucasus, Rockies, anywhere on Planet Earth, wireless telephone calls and streams of data processed by the Iridium satellite network are connecting people to people, people to machines and machines to machines.

(Author's opinion)The achievement of Iridium is the most significant advanced technological event to occur since Fessenden invented CW (continuous wave), Bell invented the telephone, and the internet became a household utility.

What is Iridium Next™?

In the world of wireless telecommunications, as opposed to a basic element identified on the Periodic Chart of Elements as number 66, Iridium is a constellation of 66 active (9 in reserve) satellites in polar orbit around the earth establishing reliable telephone service to handsets anywhere on the surface of the earth.

The wealth and richness of the Iridium and Iridium "Next" networks presented in various forums on the internet so far exceeds any attempt to describe it within this text that this author chooses to refer you to those web sites for further review. However, two books: 1) *Creating Iridium©*, authored by one of the founding team members of the original Iridium team, Durrell Hillis, and 2) *Eccentric Orbits – The Iridium Story©*, by John Bloom, are must reads for anyone contemplating a career in wireless telecommunications.

We will look at a few basic elements of the Iridium constellations; however, your interest level will determine how thoroughly you research the incredibly complex technical, political and commercial aspects of this miraculously successful enterprise.

"The Iridium constellation consists of 75 satellites (66 operational and 9 in-orbit spares) that are cross-linked in space just 780 kilometers (485 miles) above Earth. Because Iridium is the largest constellation, and orbits closer to earth than other networks, Iridium users enjoy worldwide access to voice, text, or data services with shorter network registration times and low communications latency. The large number of cross-linked Iridium satellites also makes it easier to maintain a connection while walking-and-talking on your satellite phone, while a variety of external antenna and docking stations can be used to extend the utility of Iridium devices for use in a building, vehicle, aircraft or on a vessel."[204]

"With a constellation consisting of 66 low-earth orbiting (LEO) satellites, cross-linked to operate as a fully meshed network, several overlapping satellites ensure coverage over the entire globe."[205]

"With Iridium there are no coverage gaps and an independent study found that Iridium satellite phone call quality and call completion rates are superior to its competition. This is one of the reasons the US Military uses the Iridium communications network."[206]

"Operating the largest constellation of any satellite network, the Iridium constellation consists of a fully meshed network of 66 low-earth orbiting (LEO) cross-linked satellites, and 9 in-orbit spares, that ensure coverage over the entire globe in a constellation of six polar planes. Each plane has 11 mission satellites performing as nodes in the telephony network. The 9 additional satellites orbit as spares ready to replace any unserviceable satellite. This constellation ensures that every region on the globe is covered by at least one satellite

---

[204] https://www.roadpost.com/iridium-satellite-network
[205] Ibid
[206] Ibid

at-all-times. The satellites are in a near-polar orbit at an altitude of 485 miles (780 km). They circle the earth once every 100 minutes travelling at a rate of 16,832 miles per hour. Each satellite is cross-linked to four other satellites; two satellites in the same orbital plane and two in an adjacent plane. These links create a dynamic network in space - calls are routed among Iridium satellites without touching the ground, creating a highly secure and reliable connection. Cross-links make the Iridium network particularly impervious to natural disasters - such as hurricanes, tsunamis and earthquakes - that can damage ground-based wireless towers."[207]

"The ground network is comprised of the System Control Segment and gateways to the terrestrial networks. The System Control Segment is what commands and controls the satellites for the Iridium system. It provides global operational support and control services for the satellite constellation. It also delivers satellite tracking data to the gateways. It consists of three main components: four Telemetry Tracking and Control sites, the Operational Support Network, and the Satellite Network Operation Center. The primary linkage between the System Control Segment, the satellites and the gateways is through a satellite to satellite communications system called K-Band feeder links and cross-links throughout the satellite constellation."[208]

"From man's first step on the moon to the International Space Station, space expeditions have always captivated our imaginations. And while the technology has evolved over the years, what remains alive today is humanity's bold desire to push the boundaries of where we can go and what we can do.

Iridium NEXT is an example of this drive to redefine what is possible. The launch of Iridium's second generation global satellite constellation is one of the most significant commercial space ventures ever achieved."[209]

"Iridium Certus® is an advanced multi-service platform enabled by the upgraded Iridium® constellation. Offering the highest L-Band data throughput, Iridium Certus® redefines the capabilities of mobile satellite communications across maritime, IoT, aviation, land mobile, and government applications. Iridium Certus® is ideal for supporting critical connectivity demands regardless of location, terrain, and weather events – all in a single platform."[210]

"Iridium Certus® services are provided through Iridium Connected® equipment to support broadband and, midband voice and data capabilities for ships, vehicles, aircraft, and IoT devices. One terminal can deliver a range of services from multiple high-quality voice lines to the highest throughput L-Band data speeds available, allowing simultaneous operations for business efficiency.

- Services include:
- Background IP Data
- Streaming IP Data
- High Quality Voice
- Messaging
- Prepaid Voice & Data
- Safety Services
- Secondary Data Flows
- Global Maritime Distress Safety System (GMDSS)
- Aeronautical Mobile Satellite Route Service (AMSRS)"[211]

"With speed capabilities ranging from 22 Kbps to 1408 Kbps, Iridium Certus® offers the highest speed L-Band connectivity and only truly global mobile satellite service on the market. With speeds up to 704 Kbps, Iridium Certus® was designed as a flexible platform for growth and will continue to evolve, providing both higher and lower data speeds to address customer needs."[212]

---

[207] Ibid
[208] Ibid
[209] https://www.iridiumnext.com/
[210] https://www.iridium.com/services/iridium-certus/
[211] Ibid
[212] Ibid

"For years, the maritime industry has been forced into long-term contracts and expensive service plans due to limited options for satellite connectivity. Now, with Iridium Certus®, mariners can realize the truly global advantages of the Iridium network for business operations, safety services, connected ship/IoT applications, and crew welfare. For the first time within the mobile satellite communications market, superior connectivity is available to the maritime community anywhere on the planet."[213]

"Iridium Certus® extends the reach of terrestrial and cellular infrastructure like never before with truly mobile communications capabilities ideal for critical connectivity needs anywhere on the planet. With a range of data speeds available, and even more on the way, Iridium Certus® provides a reliable connection for voice and data services, including telephony, satellite internet, Land Mobile Radio (LMR), and location-based applications. With Iridium Certus®, customers can control costs by eliminating the need to deploy expensive, ground-based infrastructure or large, directional terminals that rely on geostationary satellites."[214]

"Iridium Certus® for aviation will deliver high-performance services from the cockpit to the cabin. Through small-form-factor, low-profile antennas, Iridium Certus® will be ideal for aircraft operators looking to keep crew and passengers connected – supporting email, internet, voice and data communications, everywhere on the planet."[215]

"Global businesses need access to global data. Iridium powers new innovation and opportunity in IoT (Internet of Things) through a unique combination of global network connectivity, industry-leading core technology, and an ecosystem of value-added partners. With new Iridium Certus® for IoT solutions, Iridium Certus® will provide reliable, high-speed data communications to maximize efficiencies and enable accessibility anywhere on the planet."[216]

"The Iridium network provides unmatched secure communications anywhere on the planet, including the polar regions. Iridium Certus® enables voice and data services, including remote communications, personnel tracking, and over-the-horizon, beyond line-of-sight, and on-the-move communications at a range of speeds at your command. U.S. government and military customers can rely on the secure, low-latency connectivity of Iridium Certus® through the dedicated U.S. Government Gateway and secure infrastructure."[217]

Iridium, true and total wireless telecommunications ubiquity.

It has been a long, circuitous exploration. From Marconi, Tesla, Fessenden, Edison, Bell and so many others to the Iridium team, nothing is more obvious than the opportunities lying in wait for future engineers, scientists, inventers and entrepreneurs who will take communications to another level.

Will you be one of these?

---

[213] Ibid
[214] Ibid
[215] Ibid
[216] Ibid
[217] Ibid

APPENDIX A

The **Pacific Railroad Acts** were a series of acts of Congress that promoted the construction of a "transcontinental railroad" (the Pacific Railroad) in the United States through authorizing the issuance of government bonds and the grants of land to railroad companies. Although the War Department under then Secretary of War, Jefferson Davis, was authorized by the Congress in 1853 to conduct surveys of five different potential transcontinental routes from the Mississippi ranging from north to south and submitted a massive twelve volume report to Congress with the results in early 1855, no route or bill could be agreed upon and passed authorizing the Government's financial support and land grants until the secession of the southern states removed their opposition to a central route. The Pacific Railroad Act of 1862 (12 Stat. 489) was the original act. Some of its provisions were subsequently modified, expanded, or repealed by four additional amending Acts: The Pacific Railroad Act of 1863 (12 Stat. 807), Pacific Railroad Act of 1864 (13 Stat. 356), Pacific Railroad Act of 1865 (13 Stat. 504), and Pacific Railroad Act of 1866 (14 Stat. 66).

The Pacific Railroad Act of 1862 began federal government grant of lands directly to corporations; before that act, the land grants were made to the states, for the benefit of corporations.

1862 Act

The original Act's long title was:

"An Act to aid in the construction of a railroad and telegraph line from the Missouri river to the Pacific Ocean, and to secure to the government the use of the same for postal, military, and other purposes."

It was based largely on a proposed bill originally reported six years earlier on August 16, 1856, to the 34th Congress by the Select Committee on the Pacific Railroad and Telegraph. Signed into law by President Abraham Lincoln on July 1, 1862, the 1862 Act authorized extensive land grants in the Western United States and the issuance of 30-year government bonds (at 6 percent) to the Union Pacific Railroad and Central Pacific Railroad (later the Southern Pacific Railroad) companies in order to construct a continuous transcontinental railroad between the eastern side of the Missouri River at Council Bluffs, Iowa (opposite from Omaha, Nebraska) and the navigable waters of the Sacramento River in Sacramento, California. Section 2 of the Act granted each Company contiguous rights of way for their rail lines as well as all public lands within 200 feet (61 m) on either side of the track.

Section 3 granted an additional 10 square miles (26 km²) of public land for every mile of grade except where railroads ran through cities or crossed rivers. The method of apportioning these additional land grants was specified in the Act as being in the form of "five alternate sections per mile on each side of said railroad, on the line thereof, and within the limits of ten miles on each side" which thus provided the companies with a total of 6,400 acres (2,600 ha) for each mile of their railroad. (The interspersed non-granted area remained as public lands under the custody and control of the U.S. General Land Office.) The U.S. Government Pacific Railroad Bonds were authorized by Section 5 to be issued to the companies at the rate of $16,000 per mile of tracked grade completed west of the designated base of the Sierra Nevadas and east of the designated base of the Rocky Mountains (UPRR). Section 11 of the Act provided that the issuance of bonds "shall be treble the number per mile" (to $48,000) for tracked grade completed over and within the two mountain ranges (but limited to a total of 300 miles (480 km) at this rate), and doubled (to $32,000) per mile of completed grade laid between the two mountain ranges

The 30-year U.S. government bonds authorized by the act would be issued and backed by

the U.S. government, which would then provide the capital raised to the railroad companies upon completion of sections of the railroads in exchange for a lien on that section. The liens covered the railroads and all their fixtures, and all the loans were repaid in full (and with interest) by the companies as and when they became due. Section 10 of the 1864 amending Act (13 Statutes at Large, 356) additionally authorized the two companies to issue their own "First Mortgage Bonds" in total amounts up to (but not exceeding) that of the bonds issued by the United States, and that such company issued securities would have priority over the original Government Bonds.

From 1850 to 1871, the railroads received more than 175 million acres (71 million) of public land – an area more than one tenth of the whole United States and larger in area than Texas.

Railroad expansion provided new avenues of migration into the American interior. The railroads sold portions of their land to arriving settlers at a handsome profit. Lands closest to the tracks drew the highest prices, because farmers and ranchers wanted to locate near railway stations.

APPENDIX B

FCC 79-774

CC Docket No. 79-318

RM-3200

BEFORE THE FEDERAL COMMUNICATIONS COMMISSION Washington, D.C. 20554

In the matter of An Inquiry Into the Use of the Bands 825-845 MHz and 870-890 MHz for Cellular Communications Systems; and Amendment of Parts 2 and 22 of the Commission's Rules Relative to Cellular Communications Systems

Notice of Inquiry and Notice of Proposed Rulemaking (Adopted: November 29, 1979; Released: January 8, 1980) By the Commission: Chairman Ferris issuing a separate statement; Commissioner Fogarty issuing a separate statement in which commissioners Quello and Jones join.

Notice is hereby given of an Inquiry and Proposed Rulemaking looking toward the amendment of Parts 2 and 22 of the Commission's Rules, 47 C.F.R. §§2 and 22, concerning policies, standards, and procedures for licensing and implementation of cellular communications systems in the frequency bands 825-845 and 870-890MHz.

A. Introduction

On March 19, 1975, the Commission adopted its Memorandum Opinion and Order in Docket No. 18262, Land Mobile Radio Service, 51 FCC 2d 945 (1975), terminating a long proceeding to provide spectrum relief for the land mobile radio services.1 In that proceeding, the Commission, inter alia, allocated 40 MHz to the Domestic Public Land Mobile Radio Service for the development of a nationwide, "cellular" mobile radio communication system. Cellular mobile systems are generally described as mobile radio systems with a high capacity to serve subscriber units due to the coordinated reuse of a group of radio channels.2 During the past year, the Commission and its staff have had the opportunity to review data from the operation of an AT&T developmental cellular system and to see the system in operation, and have discussed cellular technology and its future with many members of the telecommunications industry and potentially interested parties. In sum, there seems to be little doubt that cellular communications offers the best means for meeting the demands of the mobile communications market through the end of this century. The time has arrived, therefore, for the Commission to establish rules and policies for the commercial operation of cellular mobile radio systems.

B. Background 3. Docket No. 18262

We initiated Docket No. 18262 in 1968 with a Notice of Inquiry and Notice of Proposed Rulemaking, 14 FCC 2d 311 (1968), as a first step in our effort to provide spectrum relief for land mobile radio users for the foreseeable future.3 The Commission proposed to reallocate frequencies in the 806-960 MHz band to make available enough spectrum to accommodate the public need for both private and common carrier land mobile communications. Between 1968 and 1974, we examined how best to use these frequencies in the public interest[4].

By 1974, however, policies were refined and sharpened, and we issued our Second Report and Order, 46 FCC 2d 753 (1974).5 The frequency allocation plan changed considerably. For example, we reduced the band allocated for high capacity common carrier systems from 75 MHz to 40 MHz and specifically set aside this allocation for cellular systems. Reserve bands totaling 20 MHz were strategically placed adjacent to the cellular allocation so that additional spectrum would be available if the growth rate of cellular systems was unexpectedly rapid. We concluded that a cellular system using the full 40 MHz (with channel spacing of 40 kHz) could serve the projected urban mobile telephone market through 1990.6

We also reached certain conclusions on a number of critical policies. We decided that only wireline telephone companies would be permitted to operate cellular systems. 46 FCC 2d at 760. In addition, a one system to a market policy was adopted in the belief that competing cellular systems would not be feasible because of the technical complexity and expense involved and because of the large amount of spectrum needed to make such a system viable economically. Id.

Because of concerns voiced by many parties about the potential for improper cross-subsidization and other anticompetitive acts by wireline telephone companies operating cellular systems, we stated that we would place certain restrictions on the wireline carriers to deter anticompetitive practices. Specifically, they would be required to establish fully separated subsidiary corporations for offering cellular service; they would not be permitted to manufacture, provide, or maintain mobile equipment; they would not be permitted to manufacture base station equipment; they would be required to submit to the Commission all contracts between the parent and subsidiary corporations and to report on all dealings between them; and they would be required to offer interconnection services to the public on the same basis as to their mobile telephone subsidiaries. 46 FCC 2d at 760-61.

Many parties concerned with the anticompetitive effects of cross-subsidies focused on the wireline carriers' intent to enter the dispatch service market. We decided, however, that the public should not be denied the benefits of lower-cost dispatch service if cellular systems were capable of providing it. We believed that the restrictions we imposed on the wireline carriers, as discussed above, would be sufficient to prevent anticompetitive practices. We did, however, prohibit the provision of fleet call dispatch service7 because it was considered spectrally inefficient. 46 FCC 2d at 761.

Finally, we decided that only developmental systems would be authorized at the time. This was done to provide enough time for optimal development of cellular system technology before the adoption of rules for commercial operation. The guidelines for cellular developmental applications were set forth in Appendix C of the Second Report.8

A year later, in response to petitions for reconsideration of our Second Report and Order, we made additional modifications. Memorandum Opinion and Order, 51 FCC 2d 945 (1975).9 Two changes were particularly significant.

First, we decided to permit the telephone companies to supply and maintain mobile equipment because such a prohibition could "be a limiting factor, particularly during the beginning period of system operation." Id. at 952. However, we retained our restriction against the cellular system licensees manufacturing mobile equipment.

Second, we decided that any qualified entity— not just wireline carriers— would be eligible to apply for a cellular authorization. Id. at 953. We recognized that if the wireline carriers were indeed the only entities with such resources and expertise, then the restriction was unnecessary. Id. at 953. In opening entry to entities other than wireline carriers, however, we emphasized that we were not relaxing our requirement that these frequencies be used only for the development of cellular common carrier mobile service.10 In sum, because cellular systems would only be licensed on a developmental basis, we left to a future rulemaking final decision on the policies and technical require- ments to be followed in processing applications for commercial cellular service. We recognized that we might need to revisit our earlier conclusions, including our one-to-a-market policy, in light of new developments and experience. See id. at 954.

The NARUC Decision. The Court of Appeals, in NARUC v. FCC, supra, note 1, upheld our allocation of 40 MHz for cellular systems as a reasonable exercise of the Commission's administrative discretion. In affirming the Commission's action, however, the Court did express doubts as to the effect on competition should AT&T become dominant in the provision of cellular service. 525 F. 2d at 636. This concern arose from an apprehension that AT&T would ultimately "operate most, if not all, of the cellular systems eventually put into operation."11 Such a "virtual monopoly" in the hands of AT&T, the Court noted, would seemingly give it dominance over (or at least significant market power in) the fields of radio telephone service and dispatch communication— two fields presently characterized, the Court observed, by healthy competition. In this regard the Court noted: our affirmance of the 40 MHz allocation for the development of a cellular common carrier system is with the implicit recognition that it may be subject to successful challenges at some future date . . . We do not hold that the projected effects considered above would not constitute a breach of the antitrust component of the public convenience, interest and necessity standard, were they more immediate in time or more susceptible of precise assessment. Nor do we make any comment with regard to the particular applicability of antitrust statutes, which issue is not presently before us.

The Court also expressed concern that the restrictions placed on AT&T to prevent anticompetitive effects would not be particularly effective. The Court reminded the Commission, therefore, of its obligation to supervise developmental systems with an eye to preventing anticompetitive effects, 525 F. 2d at 638.

The Developmental Systems. To date the Commission has authorized two developmental cellular systems: one is operated by the Illinois Bell Telephone Company (IBT); the other by American Radio Telephone Service, Inc. (ARTS). IBT's system covers the Chicago, Illinois, metropolitan area, while ARTS has designed its system to cover the area from Washington, D.C., and its suburbs through Baltimore, Maryland. Both systems were authorized in 1977.[12] In authorizing the IBT system we required that it be scaled down substantially from the original proposal in order to avoid an undue impact on competition; we also required IBT to submit a detailed economic and financial report at the end of its market service test, before the second phase of the developmental system would be authorized.[13]

We had originally stated that developmental authorizations would last only through January 1, 1979, as we expected to have adopted rules for commercial operation by that time. 51 FCC 2d at 955. We later extended that time by one year and invited further developmental applications. Cellular Mobile Systems, 70 FCC 2d 1639 (1978). At this time we have received eleven quarterly developmental reports from IBT and eight from ARTS. These reports are intended to yield data which will be used in this proceeding.   C. Discussion

In Docket 18262, we concluded that spectrum relief for the land mobile radio services could be achieved by the development of a nationwide compatible "cellular" mobile radio communications system. It is not the intent of this proceeding to question the merits of cellular technology or whether the demand for mobile services is likely to be satisfied without it. Rather, we are concerned here with, among other things, policies relating to the provision of mobile equipment and system facilities, their potential uses, and the market structure under which cellular mobile services will be provided. Finalization of policies and rules concerning the wide-scale commercial offering of cellular mobile services has been contingent on the results of developmental operations and regulatory experience. The purpose of this proceeding, therefore, is to address those issues essential to the policies and rules so that commercial operation of cellular mobile communications services may begin as soon as possible. To the extent it is feasible and consistent with due process requirements of the Administrative Procedure Act, it is our intent to make the necessary policy determinations and to adopt appropriate rules in this notice and comment proceeding without initiating further notice procedures.
Market Definition

In attempting to establish policies and regulations appropriate for determining entry, eligibility, and the market structure for cellular systems, we first need to consider the influence of such systems on other services.[14] In this regard, consideration must be given to the relationship of cellular mobile technology and the uses to which it may be put vis-a-vis other communications technologies and services. Related to this is the extent to which cellular mobile services may be used by the consumer as a complement or supplement to other communications services. To a large extent this involves a question of market definition. Perception of the relevant market for cellular mobile services is necessary for formulating appropriate regulatory policies relative to the provision of these services. Depending on what the relevant market is, different regulatory considerations may arise. For example, if cellular radio technology were to affect, either in its present or in its foreseeable state of development, conventional wireline local exchange service, a different set of regulatory concerns would surface than if there were no actual or prospective competitive relationship between the two.[15] The importance of the market definition, then, is to determine the public interest ramifications of cellular mobile development and utilization in light of other communications services which are, or may be, cross-elastic with, substitutable for, or complementary to cellular mobile services.

For purposes of analysis and comment we suggest that consideration be given to a) common carrier two-way mobile and b) conventional wireline telephone exchange as markets which cellular mobile systems may potentially affect. If two-way mobile service is the relevant market, because of a high cross-elasticity between the demand for cellular and non-cellular two-way service, then we need to examine the impact of cellular operation on that market, recognizing cellular service, conventional common carrier two-way mobile tele phone service, and private dispatch service as possible submarkets of the two-way market.

19. Cellular systems, however, may affect significantly an even broader market. While the uses of interconnected two-way mobile service may, perhaps, presently be perceived as separate and distinct from other services, part of this perception may relate to the generally lower quality achievable today on mobile versus landline systems. We anticipate that cellular systems, when they become operational, will be comparable in quality to landline message telephone service, and will be so perceived by consumers, especially in the portable mode. Nevertheless we do not expect, for reasons of price and use, that cellular service will easily substitute for all message telephone service. However, even if cellular systems do not offer the potential for being competitive with conventional wireline systems, cellular technology represents an evolutionary development which could be critical to further convergence of radio and copper wire. As such, ownership and control of cellular systems could have material effect upon the pace and direction of radio technology. The Commission's obligations to future consumers may, therefore, counsel limiting the role of wireline carriers in the distribution of cellular service. (See, paras. 27-29, infra). We invite comment, therefore, on cellular's potential as a competitor of conventional two-way mobile service as well as a potential competitor of the wireline carrier's local exchange telephone service. We also seek comment on the appropriate regulatory constraints, if any, and public interest factors which should be considered with respect to a given market determination.

Competitive Systems Within a Market

At the conclusion of Docket 18262, we planned to authorize, on a regular basis, only a single system to serve a given market or area. Land Mobile Service, 51 FCC 2d at 954. There are now reasons, however, why we should re-examine that approach. For instance, in the past several years we have witnessed dramatic changes in regulatory policies: changes that have made possible the introduction of competitive goods and services in markets that had long remained closed to effective competition. The terminal equipment and the private line service markets are just two examples of where competition has benefited the consumer by making available to him a variety of new options to serve his communications needs. In this environment, we deem it appropriate to reconsider our previous intention to license only one cellular operation per market.

21. In the case of cellular systems, the system design plan severely limits the number of facility-based competitors that can enter a given local market and thus reduces the reliance we can place on marketplace forces. Cellular technology requires a relatively large allocation to enable the system (and ultimately the users) to realize the cost savings that make cellular systems attractive. This large allocation is necessary because each system requires its own switching equipment and base stations, and because each cell requires some minimum amount of spectrum at any one time. It is clear that within the 40 MHz allocation, the unit costs of a given cellular system fall as additional spectrum is utilized by that system. We believe, however, that most of the economies can be realized at allocations significantly less than the full 40MHz. Balanced against this spectrum-cost tradeoff are competitive considerations, i.e., the potential costs to society resulting from above-competitive prices, and the loss of technological innovation and dynamism caused by insulation from competition. Weighing the benefits of economies of scale against the benefits of competition, we propose that within the 40 MHz allocation, up to two carriers be licensed to provide cellular service in appropriate markets, consistent with the radio licensing provisions of the Act. Allocating 20 MHz to each of two carriers appears to provide much of the cost savings from cellular technology as well as creates a competitive environment.[16]

While we recognize that our proposal to allow two firms to enter a market may not provide the most competitive market structure, we do feel there are competitive advantages to dividing the spectrum allocation between two entities. Direct competition in a market can result in different technological approaches and diversity of service options. Moreover, direct competition may provide some degree of price competition that otherwise would not be present. Two alternatives in the development and implementation of cellular systems can have meaningful competitive consequences in a given market, if the two entities in that market approach cellular technology differently and therefore differ in their incentives to exploit the efficiencies of cellular design.

23. In addition to the above proposal, we recognize that there are other possible approaches to accommodate potential entrants into this market.[17] Because cellular technology has not been implemented commercially and because only two firms so far have been developing- cellular systems, we are uncertain as to the feasibility and market implications associated with dividing the spectrum allocation among multiple entrants in a given

market. At this time we are not confident that we have before us the requisite information to enable us to make a public interest determination concerning how many firms should be allowed to compete in a local market and what the cost penalties associated with multiple entry might be. Before coming to any definitive conclusion, we believe other alternatives should be explored.

One such alternative would be to allow the marketplace to determine the number of firms that can efficiently provide cellular service in a local market. We believe that inquiry is appropriate as to whether we should consider dividing the 40 MHz allocation in a given market equally among all applicants meeting whatever minimum requirements we set, and rely on the marketplace to determine how many of these cellular systems are viable over time. Under this scheme, one would expect that as competition evolves among the cellular systems in a market, inefficient operations would have to exit from the marketplace; and the number 6f competitors would shrink to the maximum efficient number. This assumes that firms will be able to readily exit from the market place if they are unable to compete effectively. Moreover, it is conceivable that the spectrum assigned to any firm leaving a market could enter a pool that would be available to any new applicants willing to enter the market or, alternatively, be split equally among the surviving competitors.

Not only would this proposal allow the marketplace to deter mine market structure, but it also offers the potential for avoiding comparative hearings. Concern must be had for the potential for the comparative process to delay the actual implementation of cellular systems for years into the future. By assigning all qualified applicants frequencies and letting the marketplace determine how many will survive, we would not be forced to attempt to choose the "best" few applicants. An unlimited entry scheme offers the potential for the marketplace to determine the best service providers in terms of consumer acceptance and economic viability.

26. Accordingly, we invite comment on the following issues: whether unlimited entry is an economically viable concept, how such a program might be implemented, what minimum requirements all applicants in a given market should meet, how soon an applicant should be required to establish an operating system after being assigned frequencies before it would have to forfeit these frequencies, whether applicants would be required to share a single group of setup channels in order to make this proposal feasible. In addition, we seek comment on any other matters that may be relevant to this unlimited entry scheme.

Eligibility

We believe as a general principle that consumers are best served when all firms are permitted to compete freely rather than when some are restricted or excluded from service offerings altogether. Inevitably, there are exceptions, but we have made it a constant goal to hold these to a minimum. However, the potential for extension of a carrier's market power presently held in one market is a factor which should be considered. Therefore, we believe that in establishing eligibility requirements, consideration should be given to the role wireline telephone companies should play in the provision of cellular mobile service within the same service areas in which they offer wireline telephone service.

Complicating any determination of appropriate regulatory arrangements for new technologies is the assessment of potential impact. A given new technology in its initial configurations may not pose any material competitive threat to an existing technology, but it might possess the potential to evolve into a formidable challenge to the embedded technology. In this context, we question whether some potential entrants may have an incentive to restrict the supply of cellular service, or otherwise limit its potential, as a means of maintaining their investment in their other services or equipment. This could result in an artificial increase in the price that consumers pay for communications services or in the carrier's failure to allow the cellular system to grow and evolve fully (both technologically and in service applications). Our obligation is not to disadvantage today's consumers or tomorrow's by licensing cellular systems to entities with incentives to refrain from fully exploiting the technology or by surrounding cellular licenses with regulatory requirements which will prevent the technology from being fully exploited. Moreover, the importance of maintaining the proper incentives for the dynamic evolution of communications technologies may warrant the payment of a premium by today's consumer for tomorrows. Yet, one of the most difficult of our decisions is the extent to which we should inhibit entry or impose structural limitations in order to preserve or enhance the possibility that the new technology will be fully developed at some indeterminate. future time, because either alternative carries the risk of adding costs to today's consumers.[19] Nonetheless, we seek comment on the role wireline carriers should play in the provision of cellular mobile services within their service areas, or those of affiliated entities.[20] In so doing we are not unmindful of our previous findings with respect to the technical expertise, access to capital and nationwide compatibility which would attend participation by wireline carriers. However, ever increasing competition in the telecommunications industry, and specifically the potential for competition in the provision of cellular mobile service combined with greater appreciation for the potential technological evolution of mobile cellular technology suggest that adequate consideration be given to the cost/benefit tradeoffs associated with differing degrees of wireline carrier participation where the potential may exist for the extension of monopoly power.

Our desire to promote different approaches to cellular development may still be largely thwarted, despite our proposal to assign two firms to a market, if only a very small number of firms are allowed to obtain the preponderance of these assignments nationwide. In the extreme, if the same two firms are granted the two cellular assignments in every city, we would have only two entities developing and implementing this technology. Therefore, we inquire as to whether there should be any limitation on the number of licenses nationwide that any one entity may obtain in order to allow for the greatest possible diversity in technological development. In a similar vein, we also inquire as to whether there should be any separate restriction on the number of licenses a single entity might hold in the largest metropolitan areas if in fact only these markets will support full cellular development. In addition to providing for greater alternatives in technological concept and design, restricting the number of licenses held by any single entity might increase regulatory effectiveness in other ways. If the number of entities operating cellular systems throughout the country were increased, regulatory agencies would have more "yardsticks" on which to base comparison of the performance of cellular operators under their jurisdiction. Such yard-stick competition could provide benchmarks for comparing system costs and prices of regulated services. Indeed, given the potential limits on direct competition in each market due to the spectrum-cost tradeoffs discussed above, yardstick competition might yield important regulatory information that may be utilized to ensure reasonable prices for cellular services.

Equipment and Service

30. We have previously taken the position that cellular system licenses and their affiliates may not manufacture mobile equipment for use in their cellular systems except in the developmental phase. In our Memorandum Opinion, we reversed our determination, however, that carriers not be allowed to supply and maintain mobile equipment. This decision was based upon the conclusion "that supply and maintenance of equipment may be a limiting factor, particularly during the beginning period of system operation."

We are no longer persuaded that supply and maintenance of mobile units would be a significant limiting factor. We feel a number of equipment vendors stand ready to serve this market and that more will enter as commercial cellular operations are commenced. We therefore seek comment on whether we should continue our policy of permitting carriers to supply and maintain mobile units for their systems, or whether we should limit carrier involvement in this area. We also seek comment on whether, if we continue to permit carriers to supply and maintain mobile units, carriers should be required to offer such equipment on a non-tariffed basis. We believe that the provision and maintenance of mobile equipment for cellular systems could be and should be a competitive business. This Commission does not regulate the supply and maintenance of equipment provided by non-common carrier vendors. As a general proposition we see no compelling need to regulate the supply or maintenance of mobile equipment. It would appear that by requiring carriers to unbundle the mobile unit from the transmission service and to de-tariff such equipment, we would (1) reduce the possibility of undetected cross-subsidization, (2) further competition, and (3) augment consumer choice, in the provision of mobile equipment. However, we also seek comment on whether carriers should be given the option of offering such equipment on either a tariffed or non-tariffed basis.

Since the final order in Docket No. 18262, which included a proscription against manufacture of mobile units and base station equipment by cellular system licensees or their affiliates, we have had considerable experience with the furtherance of competition in the terminal equipment market. This leads us to inquire whether this proscription against manufacturing such equipment is still warranted. We seek comment on whether removal of this proscription would be consonant with our belief, as stated in the preceding paragraph, that the mobile equipment market should be competitive. We also seek comment on whether this proscription should be removed to allow the manufacture of both mobile units and base station equipment.

Finally, we are also considering whether to require, as a condition of license, that licensees or their affiliates which also design, develop or manufacture cellular system components sell their technology at reasonable fees. We are concerned that such design, development or manufacture by rate base regulated firms may have been financed by the monopoly ratepayer. We are also cognizant of the important relationship between risk and reward in business decision making. The merits of this suggestion are that it may accelerate the implementation of cellular systems and enable system developers to realize appropriate returns on their investments.

Resale of Cellular Service

We are also seeking comment on whether we should reverse our determination set forth in the Second Report, id. at 761, that cellular system licensees not provide fleet call dispatch service. "Fleet call dispatch," whereby a single dispatcher can automatically call several vehicles simultaneously, was thought spectrally inefficient. We now seek comment on whether there have been technological developments which tend to lessen the degree of spectrum inefficiency that might result if licensees were allowed to provide fleet call dispatch service.

Important in assessing the potential structures under which cellular services may evolve is an understanding of the viability of various marketing alternatives in light of their potential impact on the consumer. Consideration must be given to the competitive development of these services weighing, of course, technical and cost-related factors. In this regard, questions arise as to whether cellular system licensees should directly market services to the consumer, whether cellular services should be offered on a resale basis, and whether direct marketing and resale can co-exist within the same system. Whether resale is feasible and whether direct marketing and resale can co-exist appear dependent upon whether there is anything to "resell" to the consumer if the system licensee directly markets cellular services. It is unclear at this time whether resale of cellular mobile service is an economically viable option because it is not clear that services available to the consumer under a resale structure would be different from those obtainable from the system licensee acting as an underlying carrier.

However, we recognize that proscriptions against resale necessarily limit options available to consumers. Consequently, it is our intent not to allow restrictions on the resale of cellular services if an entity wishes to engage in resale. Rather than make a premature determination regarding resale of cellular systems, we would prefer to let the marketplace decide whether resale is economically viable. Yet, for purposes of formulating policies relative to entry, eligibility, and industry structure, consideration must be given to the various marketing alternatives by which these services can be provided. We recognize that if a resale structure is feasible, it may afford consumers additional choices in equipment and service options and afford entrepreneurs an opportunity to engage in various aspects of cellular mobile service. Accordingly, it is important that parties advocating resale as a viable option clearly set forth their perception of what exactly would be marketed and available to the consumer under a resale structure and to what extent the service could differ from that obtainable from the underlying carrier. Moreover, if resale is perceived as a competitive alternative of marketing cellular mobile services, we inquire as to the nature and degree of regulation, if any, which we should exercise over those entities which may seek to offer such services on a resale basis. In addition, we invite comment on the implications of any resale structure relative to the corporate structure under which wireline carriers must provide cellular radio services.[25] In this regard, we also seek comment on the nature and degree of separation which should exist where separate subsidiary requirements are imposed.

Federal – State - Jurisdiction

In Docket No. 18262, we concluded that cellular service should be designed to achieve nationwide compatibility. We have no reason to doubt the benefits of pursuing that policy today. Common carrier mobile telephone and dispatch services have an important role to play in our national telecommunications policy planning and we are particularly concerned that a cellular subscriber traveling outside of his local carrier's service area should be able to communicate over a cellular system in another city. The need for cellular nationwide compatibility is not solely to benefit the user of a car telephone, however. Its importance applies equally to the potential use of portable telephones carried from city to city.

Compatibility is also desirable because of its implications for mobile equipment supply and cost. Low user cost is a likely consequence of mass production of mobile units. Additional manufacturers would be likely to enter the mobile equipment market if the signaling complement, necessary for inter-system roaming, were standardized. An increase in the number of equipment suppliers is likely to be conducive to price and product competition.

Many expect that the availability of cellular service[26] will increase the demand for mobile telephone service and foster a competitive environment. If state and local entry policies conflict with our intent to stimulate the growth of a nationwide mobile communication service, these expectations may be frustrated.

40. Each cellular carrier will serve at one time as both a provider of local service and as an entry point into the nationwide cellular system and the public switched telephone network. Thus, the cellular mobile service will be somewhat different in purpose from the traditional mobile services offered by common carriers. Those offerings, in the Domestic Public Land Mobile Radio Service, have generally been characterized as primarily "local" in nature, regardless of whether they are interconnected to the wireline network. Cellular systems, however, will serve both local and national purposes in providing to the consumer the ability to place a mobile radio call regardless of geographic location.

Our plan for the growth of a competitive nationwide industry to serve the communications needs of a highly mobile society could be frustrated by conflicting state regulation. If a state were to decide, for example, that it would franchise only one cellular system per market,28 the frequencies reserved by us for competitors of the franchised carrier would be unused, contrary to the spirit of 47 U.S.C. §303(g) that underlies this proceeding: to encourage the "more effective use of radio in the public interest."

Another source of potential conflict between federal and state entry requirements relating to cellular systems arises from the possibility that federal and local authorities would apply different entry and technical standards. With respect to entry, both regulatory bodies may look to similar qualifying criteria but set different threshold requirements. We are concerned that such incompatibility between federal and local standards also could frustrate our goal of a nationwide compatible cellular network.

We have committed a large block of spectrum to the development of cellular mobile telephone to meet the needs of this country for at least the remainder of the century. Our efforts to introduce cellular mobile in a competitive environment with nationwide compatibility, and without significant delay, could easily be frustrated if entry regulation and the development of technical standards were to remain, as they are now, a joint concern of the state and federal agencies. See 47 C.F.R. §22.13(f)(2). Because some degree of uniformity in entry. regulation is essential to our regulatory program, we intend to assert federal primacy with regard to certification of cellular operators. We request comments as to whether we should preempt the area of entry certification entirely, or whether instead, we should simply override inconsistent or conflicting state regulation. We have, in the past, expressed our view "that the 'licensing' or 'franchising' functions are not among those reserved to the states" pursuant to Sections 2(b) and 221(b) of the Communications Act.29 51 FCC 2d at 974. We also believe that preemption of non-federal jurisdiction over technical standards is necessary to the achievement of a nationwide compatible system.

Our authority to preempt state regulation has been upheld where it is necessary to the integrity of an interstate program. California v. FCC, 567 F. 2d 84 (D.C. Cir. 1977), cert, denied, 434 U.S. 1010 (1978) (FCC authorization of intrastate foreign exchange service overrode state restriction on use of facilities prohibiting such service). We expect that the traffic carried on cellular systems will be a mixture of interstate and intrastate calls by both local and transient callers. To carry out the broad purposes of Section 1 of the Communications Act,30 we may assert jurisdiction over facilities which are used for both interstate and intrastate communications.31 To the extent that state regulation of these cellular facilities may conflict with our policies, we believe we have the authority to preempt state regulation.32 Comments are invited in this area.

Treatment of Competing Applications

In our Memorandum Opinion in Docket 18262 we expressed concern that the process for comparative consideration of competing applications might cause significant delays in the implementation of cellular radiotelephone service. 51 FCC 2d at 954. In some markets we expected applications to be filed by several qualified entities. In those situations, we believed we would have to follow the traditional approach of designating the applications for a comparative hearing, pursuant to Ashbacker Radio Corp. v. FCC, 326 U.S. 327 (1945). Because we are now considering the possibility of authorizing two systems per market, there may in some cases be no need for comparative hearings. For the most part, however, we still expect there to be more than two applicants in some areas. Long delays in making a selection could impose substantial financial burdens on the applicants, inconvenience the public, and frustrate our goal of a nationwide compatible cellular service. It is therefore our desire to consider all alternative procedures that may be available. Some alternatives to the present comparative process — a streamlined hearing procedure, ranking of applications on an objective basis, lotteries, and auctions— are outlined in the following paragraphs for purposes of comment. It is our tentative belief that a hybrid procedure can be developed to minimize the delay associated with the present comparative process, while retaining the benefits of comparing proposals that differ substantially on matters that may affect service to the public We describe one hybrid procedure below. We invite comments on these proposals. In addition, commenters should feel free to suggest other improvements to the existing comparative process.

Before describing alternatives to the traditional comparative hearing, we shall explain a hybrid procedure that may aid in the expeditious resolution of comparative licensing cases. This hybrid proposal would retain the traditional comparative hearing approach but would eliminate the need for comparison except where there exist substantial and material differences between the applications.

We propose to examine which factors may be relevant in choosing from among mutually exclusive applicants for a cellular system. Traditionally the comparative process has focused on the nature and extent of the proposed service (including the rates, charges, maintenance, personnel, practices, classifications, regulations, and facilities), the areas and populations to be served, and the need for the proposed service in these areas. Other areas of comparison could include plans for phased growth through cell division, marketing plans and abilities, diversification or concentration of control of telecommunications media, and effect on competition. We invite suggestions as to what criteria, if any, should be used as the basis for comparative consideration.

Under the hybrid plan, mutually exclusive applicants would be designated for hearing to determine which applicant comparatively would better serve the public interest. (This assumes that all applicants were found qualified.33 If not, the qualifying issues would be resolved prior to the comparative hearing.) If the applicants failed in a post- designation pleading cycle to justify any superiority on any of the comparative criteria, or if the presiding officer found on balance several applicants equally qualified, a lottery or drawing would be held to determine the outcome of the hearing. A variation on this plan would be to require the parties to plead their comparative case prior to designation, with the applicants then being designated for hearing on only those issues for which a prima facie case had been shown. Either of these approaches, coupled with a minimum number of threshold or basic qualifications, would, in our judgment, expedite the selection of the successful applicant. We invite comments on these hybrid approaches both as to their practicality and legality.

There do, of course, exist other ways to expedite the comparative process. For example, the comparative hearing procedure could be streamlined by (1) establishment of a firm deadline for the submission of issue pleadings related to the mutually exclusive applications; (2) adherence to a strict timetable to be established at the outset by the presiding officer; (3) the use of written testimony as often as possible; and (4) the elimination of cross-examination except upon order of the presiding officer.

The comparative process also could be expedited if the Commission (or the Common Carrier Bureau acting pursuant to delegated authority) were to rank the applications in designating them for comparative hearing. Such a ranking could be done on an objective basis using such factors as may be determined in a rulemaking proceeding. The factors, and the weight given to each factor in ranking the applications, would ensure that the public interest would be adequately considered. After designation of the applications for hearing, the various applicants would have ample opportunity to take exception to the rankings. The presiding officer would decide which applicant should be granted a license; if several applicants were tied, a lottery could be used to determine the winner, or a limited comparative hearing could be conducted between the highest-ranked applicants. Commenters are requested to address the criteria which should be included as a basis for comparison and the relative weights that should be assigned to each factor.

Another alternative is simply to implement a lottery. A lottery would be used once the Commission decided that all of the applicants met the Commission's basic qualifications requirements. The use of auctions is another alternative that appears to be economically and administratively efficient. We invite comment on whether legislation is necessary to make this change in procedure.

Technical Standards

We are aware that certain areas, because of population density and other factors, will not require fully developed cellular systems. The cellular frequency allocation will be available to applicants proposing cellular systems. But we do not propose to require a greater sophistication in design and equipment than is needed to meet current and foreseeable demand. Consistent with this approach, we expect that single cell systems may be appropriate in some communities. However, systems must possess the capability of graceful growth into a fully developed configuration. We reiterate our objective of a nationwide compatible cellular service and our intent not to license systems incompatible with this objective.

In the Memorandum Opinion we described the cellular system configuration with which applicants for developmental authorization for systems utilizing the frequencies at 825-845 MHz and 870-890 MHz would need to comply.37 In setting forth this description, we intended to provide for flexibility in design within the broad constraint of our policy determination that cellular development was the most appropriate use of the assigned frequencies. We were operating in the context of system proposals which had been received in response to the First Report which indicated that a cellular service was the most practical solution to perceived demand for mobile service over the planning period. We have considered whether, in light of the passage of time and marketplace changes since the First Notice, cellular technology remains the most viable solution to the perceived demand for mobile service. Without foreclosing alternative solutions in the future, we conclude that the objective of a nationwide compatible high capacity mobile telephone service will be achieved most efficiently by licensing systems at 825-845 MHz and 870-890 MHz which exhibit characteristics of cellular design. Although we do not expect all cellular systems to be designed in conformance with a single prototype, we will consider in the licensing phrase whether the design features contemplated by applicants comply with the guidelines which we intend to adopt.

While we are maintaining a policy of "nationwide compatibility" and a level of quality "comparable to the landline network," we do not intend by imposition of these restrictions to unreasonably limit the discretion of system designers. We will focus our attention upon the network interface, so as to insure that our quality and comparability goals are not frustrated. Our concern is that failure to adopt certain technical standards may result in mobile equipment causing harmful externalities to other users.

There are three purposes to be served by technical standards for cellular systems: (1) defining "cellular mobile radio" for purposes of qualifying for cellular mobile radio operating licenses, (2) assurance of compatible operation of equipment on both local and national levels, and (3) maintenance of signal quality and other quality aspects of system performance. We intend to adopt only the minimum technical standards necessary to accomplish those purposes. Wherever possible, detailed standards will be left to industry groups or other voluntary standards making bodies. Furthermore, we intend to adopt only performance standards (not equipment design standards), and only standards that apply at the interfaces between categories of equipment controlled by separate entities.

Having tentatively concluded that multiple entry into the cellular radio market is feasible and desirable, we expect to rely heavily on market forces to reduce or eliminate the need for quality standards. We will, however, entertain suggestions for quality standards if there are areas in which we are persuaded that market forces will not produce systems capable of quality comparable to the landline telephone network. However, in order to assure truly cellular use of cellular spectrum and to assure nationwide compatibility of equipment, some standards are necessary.

The Commission has already adopted certain design concept requirements for developmental cellular authorization.40 These include the following:

(a) a bona fide cellular configuration of base station transmitters and receivers to cover the proposed service;

(b) base station transmitters radiating no more radio frequency power than required to adequately cover each cell; 51 FCC 2d at 954;

(c) base stations connected together through a common switching and control point using wirelines; id.;

(d) a radio system fully inter-connected with the public landline telephone network and capable of providing a grade of service comparable to that of the landline system; id. at 954-55;

(e) narrow band frequency modulation for all voice channels in the radio system, and each radio channel not exceeding 40 kHz of authorized bandwidth; id. at 955;

(f) radio frequency channels employed within each cell trunked for greater spectrum efficiency; id.;

(g) for systems in metropolitan areas, the potential for orderly evolution into a highly efficient small-cell configuration capable of handling a large number of subscribers within the allocated 40 MHz of spectrum; id.,- and

(h) compatibility with other cellular systems.

In item (c) we propose to eliminate the requirement that wirelines be used to connect base stations together. We see no reason to categorically exclude microwave or optical links, although we expect wireline links, to be used in most cases. We further propose to change "40 kHz of authorized bandwidth;" to ". . .30 kHz channel spacing;" (item (e)). It has been demonstrated that 30 kHz channel spacing can provide adequate service quality, so there seems to be no need for a greater channels spacing.43 Even though under some signaling conditions the occupied bandwidth may be greater than 30 kHz, careful geographic distribution of channel assignments can avoid adjacent channel interference. Except for these two modifications, we expect to adopt the above guidelines for operational cellular systems. We invite comments, however, on specific additions or modifications which may be needed.

The most important compatibility standards will be those applicable to the interface between mobile units and the cell site. We believe the interface between the cellular system itself and the wireline telephone system is addressed sufficiently by our present rules. We specifically do not propose Commission standards for the interface between the system switching logic and the cell sites. It would appear that these system components must be controlled by a single entity. That controlling entity should have the freedom to place logic and other functions in the cell base sites and switching hardware at its discretion. Such choices might vary significantly, depending on the size and other factors of the individual communities for which the system is designed.

There are a number of parameters for which technical standards at the mobile/cell site interface may be needed. For example, frequency channeling plan is probably necessary for compatibility between base stations and mobile units. We specifically request comment on the frequency location of the setup channels. A fundamental question relating to the setup channels is whether a single set of setup channels can be shared between two (or even more than two) service providers in a given area, or each service provider must have its own complement of setup channels.

In the context of nationwide compatibility, we would like comment on whether it is necessary that every mobile or portable unit be capable of using every one of the available cellular channels. The maximum spectrum we are considering — 60 MHz, including the 20 MHz of reserve— corresponds to 1,000 radio channels. We would like commenters to address both the technical and economic feasibility aspects of this question.

We recognize that there are many other parameters and protocols which must be standardized at the cell/mobile interface if full compatibility is to be achieved. We invite assistance on specific identification of those which must be adopted by the Commission.

We also seek comment regarding allocation of discrete blocks of frequencies to specific users. If, for example, we were to allow two entrants per market, we would propose to award the bands 825-835 MHz and 870-880 MHz to one applicant, and the bands 835-845 MHz and 880-890 MHz to a second applicant. Parties seeking licenses would not be permitted to request specific assignments. As an alternative we seek comment on whether discrete blocks of frequencies should be awarded for the exclusive use by wireline carries in the event there is more than one license per market.

Granting licenses in this manner is based on the belief that the propagation characteristics of frequencies in the cellular bands are sufficiently similar as not to justify claims of parties that they are entitled to particular frequencies because these frequencies would better enable them to serve the public. We also believe that the number of comparative hearings will be reduced if applicants are required to demonstrate qualifications in a single proceeding. It is desirable that hearings be minimized, consistent with the maintenance of due process procedures and that applicants not be required to make separate applications for discrete assignments.

Spectrum Allocation

In our 1974 Second Report 44 we reduced the allocation for cellular systems from 64 MHz to 40 MHz. We expressed the belief that a 40 MHz allocation was sufficient to meet the needs of cellular users for the foreseeable future. We explained that: "A 40 MHz cellular system utilizing 40 KHz channeling should have an ultimate capacity to handle about 105,000 telephone subscribers and 105,000 dispatch users (see AT&T December 1970 filing, page 40). This is sufficient capacity to handle the predicted market for mobile telephone to the year 1990 in the largest cities, plus one quarter or more of the dispatch market in those areas. There is however, considerable uncertainty involved in predicting the mobile telephone market. This uncertainty results primarily from the possibility of the service developing into a consumer item. For this reason we have also strategically placed spectrum reserves totaling 20 MHz in proximity to the cellular allocation which could be used in the event of unexpected growth. We must stress however, that the marketing studies submitted to the Commission do not indicate that such would be the case, at least in the foreseeable future."

We suspect that the market for cellular service has probably changed since 1974. For example, advances in technology have made the availability of portable service more likely in the next several years. In addition, consumer perception of cellular service may have changed. As a result, a larger allocation than originally contemplated may be appropriate. We also recognize that should we license more than one system in certain areas there may be a spectrum efficiency loss which may have to be compensated for by the allocation of certain of the reserve spectrum.

In considering whether release of the 20 MHz block of reserve spectrum would be in the public interest, we believe the following factors should be weighed in making any such determination:

Comparison of the dollar cost of mature cellular systems using a 40 MHz allocation compared with a 60 MHz allocation, based on knowledge obtained in the development up to 40 MHz, and including the costs of mobile and portable units required as well as costs of fixed plant;

Estimates of the ultimate cellular market, based on the record as of the time the first 40 MHz is nearly fully occupied;

Estimates of the time required for full utilization of the additional 20 MHz; and

Comparison of all of the above factors with other competing demands for the 20 MHz block of spectrum.46 In this regard, we invite comment from parties which might have alternative plans for use of the reserve spectrum.

We also seek comment on ways in which our rules can encourage compatibility with digital technology. As presently designed, the cellular system will employ analog circuits for voice transmission. It may be desirable to employ digital techniques in the future. Since technology and cost trends seem to be favoring digital over analog signal processing techniques, and since we see digital techniques becoming increasingly incorporated in communications networks, considerations of system architecture suggest that the public may be better served by a digital cellular system. Besides facilitating connectivity and otherwise contributing to a more compatible communications infrastructure, digital techniques employed in cellular radio may be appropriate for the purposes of increasing privacy and spectral efficiency. Thus, even if we do not mandate the use of digital techniques, we may wish to assure that our rules allow the graceful evolution of an analog cellular system to a digital one. Parties wishing to comment on the role of digital technology in the bands allocated for cellular service may do so in this proceeding.

Conclusion

Although certain aspects of this Notice are narrowly focused, parties may submit comments on all matters which they deem relevant to this proceeding. We do reiterate, however, our commitment that the bands reserved for common carrier cellular service will not be used for systems exhibiting a non-cellular design.

68. Authority for the inquiry herein is contained in 47 U.S.C. §§154(iMj), 303, 307, and 403.

All interested persons are invited to file written comments on or before April 1, 1980. Because of our interest in expediting this proceeding in a single notice and comment proceeding, we are at this time leaving open the date for filing reply comments. The period for filing reply comments will be announced after we have some indication of the number and complexity of the comments received. Any person wishing to file a reply to a comment before the close of the formal comment period is encouraged to do so. All relevant and timely comments and reply comments will be considered by the Commission. In reaching its decision, the Commission may take into account information and ideas not contained in the comments, provided that such information or a writing indicating the nature and source of such information is placed in the public file, and provided that the fact of the Commission's reliance on such information is noted in the Report and Order.

For further information concerning procedures to follow with respect to this proceeding, contact Michael D. Sullivan, (202) 632-6450. Members of the public should note that from the time a Notice of Proposed Rulemaking is issued until the matter is no longer subject to Commission consideration or court review, ex parte contacts made to the Commission in proceedings such as this will be disclosed in the public Docket file. An ex parte contact is a message, spoken or written, concerning the merits of a pending rulemaking made to a Commission er, a Commissioner's assistant, or other FCC decision-making staff members, other than comments officially filed at the Commission or oral presentations requested by the Commission with all parties present. The Commission's interim policy regarding ex parte contacts is set out at 68 FCC 2d 804 (1978). A summary of the Commission's procedures governing ex parte contacts in informal rulemaking is available from the Commission's Consumer Assistance Division at (202) 632-2700.

In accordance with the provisions of 47 C.F.R. § 1.419(b) an original and six copies of all comments, replies, pleadings, briefs and other documents filed in this proceeding shall be furnished to the Commission. Members of the public who wish to express their views by participating informally may do so by submitting one or more copies of their comments, without regard to form (as long as the docket number is clearly stated in the heading). Copies of all filings will be available for public inspection during regular business hours in the Commission's Docket Reference Room (Room 239) at its headquarters in Washington, D.C. (1919 M Street, N.W.).

The Secretary shall cause a copy of this Notice of Inquiry and Notice of Proposed Rulemaking to be published in the Federal Register.

Federal Communications Commission,* William J. Tricarico, Secretary. * See attached statements by Chairman Ferris, Commissioners Fogarty, Quello and Jones.

APPENDIX C

Federal Communications Commission FCC 13-157
Initial Regulatory Flexibility Analysis
I. INITIAL REGULATORY FLEXIBILITY ANALYSIS

1. As required by the Regulatory Flexibility Act of 1980, as amended (RFA),1 the Commission has prepared this Initial Regulatory Flexibility Analysis (IRFA) of the possible significant economic impact on a substantial number of small entities by the policies and rules proposed in this *Notice*. Written comments are requested on this IRFA. Comments must be identified as responses to the IRFA and must be filed by the deadlines for comments on the *Notice*. The Commission will send a copy of the *Notice*, including this IRFA, to the Chief Counsel for Advocacy of the Small Business Administration (SBA).2 In addition, the *Notice* and IRFA (or summaries thereof) will be published in the Federal Register.3

A. Need for, and Objectives of, the Proposed Rules.

2. By this *Notice*, we propose to allow airlines (or more specifically, station licensees) to provide mobile communications services on aircraft (mobile communications services on aircraft). Currently, the Commission's rules prohibit airborne use of mobile devices in the 800 MHz cellular band and restrict use in the 800 MHz SMR band, while the rules governing other commercial mobile spectrum bands are silent. Since a previous *Notice of Proposed Rulemaking* that sought to address these restrictions was terminated in 2007, more than forty jurisdictions, including the European Union and Australia, have authorized the use of mobile communications services on aircraft. To the best of our knowledge, there have been no reports of these services causing any harmful interference to terrestrial networks. We believe that it is in the public interest to bring the benefits of mobile communications services on aircraft to domestic consumers and that the proposals set forth in this *Notice* further our recent efforts to expand access to airborne broadband services.

3. We propose to allow mobile communications services on aircraft by: (1) removing existing restrictions on airborne use of mobile devices in the 800 MHz cellular and 800 MHz SMR bands; (2) harmonizing regulations governing the operation of mobile devices on airborne aircraft across all commercial mobile spectrum bands; and (3) implementing a comprehensive regulatory framework to promote airborne mobile data use using all commercial mobile spectrum bands.

4. Under our proposal, we would add the authority to provide mobile communications services on aircraft across all commercial mobile spectrum bands (as categorized below) to the existing Part 87 aircraft station licenses of domestic airlines. Alternatively, the *Notice* seeks comment on whether we should permit inflight mobile wireless service using an alternative authorization method. Alternatives could include: 1) non-exclusive licenses by which applicants, an airline or other entity, could file to provide airborne wireless services; 2) terrestrial license leases whereby an airline could provide service

through lease agreements with mobile wireless service licensees; 3) auctioned "sky licenses" covering nationwide or geographic markets that would be assigned pursuant to competitive bidding, or; 4) unlicensed use or license-by-rule whereby eligible entities would be permitted to operate without the Commission issuing individual licenses.

5. We propose to allow mobile communications services on aircraft only if managed by an Airborne Access System (Airborne Access System), which would control the emissions of onboard portable electronic devices by requiring them to remain at or near their lowest transmitting power level

1 See 5 U.S.C. § 603. The RFA, see 5 U.S.C. §§ 601-612, has been amended by the Small Business Regulatory

Enforcement Fairness Act of 1996 (SBREFA), Pub. L. No. 104-121, Title II, 110 Stat. 857 (1996).

2 See 5 U.S.C. § 603(a).

3 See id.

Federal Communications Commission FCC 13-157

36

and prevent such devices from causing harmful interference to terrestrial networks. We also propose to limit mobile communications services on aircraft to aircraft travelling at altitudes above 3,048 meters (10,000 feet).

B. Legal Basis.

6. This action is taken under Sections 1, 4(i), 11, and 303(r) and (y), 308, 309, and 332 of the Communications Act of 1934, as amended, 47 U.S.C. §§ 151, 154(i), 161, 303(r), (y), 308, 309, and 332.

C. Description and Estimate of the Number of Small Entities to Which the Proposed Rules Will Apply.

7. The RFA directs agencies to provide a description of, and where feasible, an estimate of the number of small entities that may be affected by the proposed rules, if adopted herein.4 The RFA generally defines the term "small entity" as having the same meaning as the terms "small business," "small organization," and "small governmental jurisdiction."5 In addition, the term "small business" has the same meaning as the term "small business concern" under the Small Business Act.6 A "small business concern" is one which: (1) is independently owned and operated; (2) is not dominant in its field of operation; and (3) satisfies any additional criteria established by the SBA.7

8. In addition, we have adopted criteria for defining three groups of small businesses for purposes of determining their eligibility for special provisions such as bidding credits. We have defined a small business as an entity that, together with its affiliates and controlling principals, has average gross revenues not exceeding $40 million for the preceding three years.8 A very small business is defined as an entity that, together with its affiliates and controlling principals, has average gross revenues that are not more than $15 million for the preceding three years.9 The SBA has approved these small size standards.10

9. In the following paragraphs, we further describe and estimate the number and type of

small entities that may be affected by the proposals set forth in the *Notice*. If our proposals are adopted, small airlines that choose to implement mobile communications services on aircraft could be required to modify their existing Part 87 licenses and comply with new regulatory requirements, including as to the mobile communications services on aircraft equipment.11 Such compliance would involve, to varying degrees, the services described below. Under our proposals, an airline would be permitted to negotiate commercial agreements with the entities described in the following. It is possible that an airline could

4 5 U.S.C. § 604(a)(3).

5 5 U.S.C. § 601(6).

6 5 U.S.C. § 601(3) (incorporating by reference the definition of "small business concern" in the Small Business Act,

15 U.S.C. § 632). Pursuant to 5 U.S.C. § 601(3), the statutory definition of a small business applies "unless an

agency, after consultation with the Office of Advocacy of the Small Business Administration and after opportunity

for public comment, establishes one or more definitions of such term which are appropriate to the activities of the

agency and publishes such definition(s) in the Federal Register."

7 15 U.S.C. § 632.

8 47 C.F.R. § 1.2110(f)(2)(ii).

9 47 C.F.R. § 1.2110(f)(2)(iii).

10 *See* Letter to Thomas Sugrue, Chief, Wireless Telecommunications Bureau, Federal Communications

Commission, from Aida Alvarez, Administrator, Small Business Administration, dated August 10, 1999.

11 Aircraft station licensees would be required to file for a modification of their existing aircraft station or fleet

licenses on FCC Form 605 to include the newly designated airborne mobile communications authorization. To the

extent that an aircraft operator does not have an aircraft station license, that aircraft operator would be required to

apply for an aircraft station license using Form 605 in order to operate an Airborne Access System.

Federal Communications Commission FCC 13-157

37

negotiate agreements affecting all communications services listed, or an airline may reach agreements

involving only certain categories.

10. The *Notice* also request comment on whether we should permit inflight mobile wireless

services through alternative licensing methodologies. In such cases, any eligible entity (airlines or others)

would be permitted to provide mobile wireless services onboard aircraft. In such cases, the authorized

parties could be any of the service providers listed below. In addition, any device manufacturers that

choose to manufacture devices for mobile communications services on aircraft use will have to ensure

that such devices comply with any rules adopted in this proceeding.

11. **Small Businesses, Small Organizations, and Small Governmental Jurisdictions**. The

proposals set forth in the *Notice*, may, over time, affect small entities that are not easily categorized at present. We therefore describe here, at the outset, three comprehensive, statutory small entity size standards that encompass entities that could be directly affected by the proposals under consideration. As of 2009, small businesses represented 99.9% of the 27.5 million businesses in the United States, according to the SBA. Additionally, a "small organization" is generally "any not-for-profit enterprise which is independently owned and operated and is not dominant in its field." Nationwide, as of 2007, there were approximately 1,621,315 small organizations. Finally, the term "small governmental jurisdiction" is defined generally as "governments of cities, counties, towns, townships, villages, school districts, or special districts, with a population of less than fifty thousand." Census Bureau data for 2007 indicate that there were 89,527 governmental jurisdictions in the United States. We estimate that, of this total, as many as 88,761 entities may qualify as "small governmental jurisdictions." Thus, we estimate that most governmental jurisdictions are small.

12. **Wireless Telecommunications Carriers (except Satellite)**. Since 2007, the SBA has recognized wireless firms within this new, broad, economic census category.12 Prior to that time, such firms were within the now-superseded categories of Paging and Cellular and Other Wireless Telecommunications.13 Under the present and prior categories, the SBA has deemed a wireless business to be small if it has 1,500 or fewer employees.14 For this category census data2007 show that there were 11,163 establishments that operated for the entire year.15 Of this total, 10,791 establishments had employment of 999 or fewer employees and 372 had employment of 1000 employees or more.16 Thus, under this category and the associated small business size standard, the Commission estimates that the majority of wireless telecommunications carriers (except satellite) are small entities that may be affected by our proposed action

13. Similarly, according to Commission data, 413 carriers reported that they were engaged in the provision of wireless telephony, including cellular service, Personal Communications Service (PCS), and Specialized Mobile Radio (SMR) Telephony services.17 Of these, an estimated 261 have 1,500 or

12 13 C.F.R. § 121.201, NAICS code 517210.

13 U.S. Census Bureau, 2002 NAICS Definitions, 517211 Paging;available at http://www.census.gov/cgibin/sssd/naics/naicsrch?code=517211&search=2002%20NAICS%20Search; U.S. Census Bureau, 2002 NAICS Definitions, 517212 Cellular and Other Wireless Telecommunications available at http://www.cen-sus.gov/cgibin/

sssd/naics/naicsrch?code=517212&search=2002%20NAICS%20Search. .

14 13 C.F.R. § 121.201, NAICS code 517210 (2007 NAICS). The now-superseded, pre-2007 C.F.R. citations were

13 C.F.R. § 121.201, NAICS codes 517211 and 517212 (referring to the 2002 NAICS).

15 U.S. Census Bureau, Subject Series: Information, Table 5, "Establishment and Firm Size: Employment Size of

Firms for the United States: 2007 NAICS Code 517210" (issued Nov. 2010).

16 *Id.* Available census data do not provide a more precise estimate of the number of firms that have employment of

1,500 or fewer employees; the largest category provided is for firms with "100 employees or more."

17 *Trends in Telephone Service*, at tbl. 5.3.

Federal Communications Commission FCC 13-157

38

fewer employees and 152 have more than 1,500 employees.18 Consequently, the Commission estimates that approximately half or more of these firms can be considered small. Thus, using available data, we estimate that the majority of wireless firms can be considered small.

14. **Wireless Telephony**. Wireless telephony includes cellular, personal communications

services, and specialized mobile radio telephony carriers. As noted, the SBA has developed a small business size standard for Wireless Telecommunications Carriers (except Satellite).19 Under the SBA small business size standard, a business is small if it has 1,500 or fewer employees.20 According to *Trends in Telephone Service* data, 413 carriers reported that they were engaged in wireless telephony.21 Of these, an estimated 261 have 1,500 or fewer employees and 152 have more than 1,500 employees.22 Therefore, more than half of these entities can be considered small.

15. **Cellular Licenses**. The Cellular Radiotelephone (Cellular) Service is in the 824 – 849

and 869 – 894 MHz spectrum range. The most common use of cellular spectrum is mobile voice and data services, including cell phone, text messaging, and Internet.

16. The Commission adopted initial rules governing allocation of spectrum for commercial

Cellular service, including the establishment of two channel blocks (Blocks A and B), in 1981.23 To issue cellular licenses, the FCC divided the U.S. into 734 geographic markets called Cellular Market Areas (CMAs) and divided the 40 megahertz of spectrum into two, 20 megahertz amounts referred to as channel blocks; channel block A and channel block B. A single license for the A block and the B block were made available in each market. The B block of spectrum was awarded to a local wireline carrier that provided landline telephone service in the CMA. The A block was awarded to non-wireline carriers. The wireline/non-wireline distinction for cellular licenses no longer exists.

17. The licensee of the initial license was provided a five-year period to expand coverage

within the CMA. The area timely built out during that five-year period became the licensee's initial Cellular Geographic Service Area (CGSA), while any area not built out by the five-year mark was automatically relinquished for re-licensing on a site-by-site basis by the Commission.

18. The Commission established a two phase licensing approach for areas that reverted back

to the FCC. Phase I was a one-time process that started as soon as the five-year period ended and allowed parties to file an application to operate a new cellular system or expand an existing cellular system. Phase I licensing is no longer available. **Phase** II is an on-going process that allows parties to apply for unserved areas after Phase I ended. At this point, all cellular licensing is in Phase II. On June 4, 2002, the Commission completed the auction of three cellular Rural Service Area licenses.24 Three winning bidders won a total of 3 licenses in this auction. On June 17, 2008, the Commission completed the closed auction of one unserved service area. The auction concluded with one provisionally winning bid for the unserved

18 Id.

19 13 C.F.R. § 121.201, NAICS code 517210.

20 Id.

21 FCC, Wireline Competition Bureau, Industry Analysis and Technology Division, Trends in Telephone Service at

Table 5.3, Page 5-5, available at: http://hraunfoss.fcc.gov/edocs_public/attachmatch/DOC-301823A1.pdf (Sept.

2010) (Trends in Telephone Service). This source uses data that are current as of October 13, 2008.

22 Trends in Telephone Service at Table 5.3, Page 5-5.

23 See generally An Inquiry Into the Use of the Bands 825-845 MHz and 870-890 MHz for Cellular Communications Systems; and Amendment of Parts 2 and 22 of the Commission's Rules Relative to Cellular Communications Systems, Report and Order, CC Docket No. 79-318, 86 F.C.C.2d 469 (1981).

24 See Cellular Rural Service Areas Auction Closes; Winning Bidders Announced, Public Notice, 17 FCC Rcd 10582 (2002).

Federal Communications Commission FCC 13-157

39

area totaling $25,002.25 No bidders in either auction received small business bidding credits.

19. **Broadband Personal Communications Service**. The broadband personal communications services (PCS) spectrum is divided into six frequency blocks designated A through F, and the Commission has held auctions for each block. The Commission initially defined a "small business" for C- and F-Block licenses as an entity that has average gross revenues of $40 million or less in the three previous years.26 For Block F licenses, an additional small business size standard for "very small business" was added and is defined as an entity that, together with its affiliates, has average gross revenues of not more than $15 million for the preceding three years.27 These small business size standards, in the context of broadband PCS auctions, have been approved by the SBA.28 No small businesses within the SBA-approved small business size standards bid successfully for licenses in Blocks A and B. There were 90 winning bidders that claimed small business status in the first two C Block auctions.29 A total of 93 bidders that claimed "small" and "very small" business status won licenses in the first auction of the D, E, and F Blocks.30 In 1999, the Commission completed a subsequent auction of C, D, E, and F Block licenses.31 Of the 57 winning bidders in that auction, 48 claimed small business status and won 277 licenses. 32

20. In 2001, the Commission completed the auction of 422 C and F Block Broadband PCS licenses (Auction 35). Of the 35 winning bidders in that auction, 29 claimed small or very small businesses status.33 Subsequent events concerning that Auction, including judicial and agency determinations, resulted in only a portion of those C and F Block licenses being available for grant. The

245

Commission completed an auction of 188 C Block licenses and 21 F Block licenses in 2005. Of the 24 winning bidders in that auction, 16 claimed small business status and won 156 licenses. 34 In 2007, the Commission completed an auction of licenses in the A, C, and F Blocks.35 Of the 12 winning bidders in that auction, five claimed small business status and won 18 licenses.36 Most recently, in 2008, the

25 See Auction Of Cellular Unserved Service Area License Closes; Winning Bidder Announced for Auction 77, *Public Notice*, 23 FCC Rcd 9501 (2008).

26 See Amendment of Parts 20 and 24 of the Commission's Rules – Broadband PCS Competitive Bidding and the

Commercial Mobile Radio Service Spectrum Cap et al., WT Docket No. 96-59, *Report and Order*, 11 FCC Rcd 7824, 7850–52 ¶¶ 57–60 (1996) (*PCS Report and Order*); *see also* 47 C.F.R. § 24.720(b).

27 See *PCS Report and Order*, 11 FCC Rcd at 7852 ¶ 60.

28 See *Alvarez Letter 1998*.

29 See Entrepreneurs' C Block Auction Closes, *Public Notice*, DA 96-716 (1996); Entrepreneurs C Block Reauction

Closes, *Public Notice*, 11 FCC Rcd 8183 (1996).

30 See Broadband PCS, D, E and F Block Auction Closes, *Public Notice*, Doc. No. 89838 (rel. Jan. 14, 1997).

31 See C, D, E, and F Block Broadband PCS Auction Closes, *Public Notice*, 14 FCC Rcd 6688 (1999). Before Auction No. 22, the Commission established a very small standard for the C Block to match the standard used for F

Block. Amendment of the Commission's Rules Regarding Installment Payment Financing for Personal Communications Services (PCS) Licensees, WT Docket No. 97-82, *Fourth Report and Order*, 13 FCC Rcd 15,743,

15,768 ¶ 46 (1998).

32 See C, D, E, and F Block Broadband PCS Auction Closes, *Public Notice*, 14 FCC Rcd 6688 (1999).

33 See C and F Block Broadband PCS Auction Closes; Winning Bidders Announced, *Public Notice*, 16 FCC Rcd 2339 (2001).

34 See Broadband PCS Spectrum Auction Closes; Winning Bidders Announced for Auction No. 58, *Public Notice*,

20 FCC Rcd 3703 (2005).

35 See Auction of Broadband PCS Spectrum Licenses Closes; Winning Bidders Announced for Auction No. 71, *Public Notice*, 22 FCC Rcd 9247 (2007) (*Auction No. 71 Public Notice*).

36 *Auction No. 71 Public Notice*, 22 FCC Rcd 9247.

Federal Communications Commission FCC 13-157

40

Commission completed the auction of C, D, E, and F Block Broadband PCS licenses.37 Of the eight winning bidders for Broadband PCS licenses in that auction, six claimed small business status and won 14 licenses.38

21. **Advanced Wireless Services**. In 2006, the Commission conducted its first auction of

Advanced Wireless Services licenses in the 1710-1755 MHz and 2110-2155 MHz bands (AWS-1), designated as Auction 66.39 For the AWS-1 bands, the Commission has defined a "small business" as an entity with average annual gross revenues for the preceding three years not exceeding $40 million, and a "very small business" as an entity with average annual gross revenues for the preceding three years not exceeding $15 million.40 In Auction 66, 31 winning bidders identified themselves as very small businesses and won 142 licenses.41 Twenty-six of the winning bidders identified themselves as small businesses and won 73 licenses.42 In a subsequent 2008 auction, the Commission offered 35 AWS-1 licenses.43 Four winning bidders identifying themselves as very small businesses won 17 licenses, and three winning bidders identifying themselves as a small business won five AWS-1 licenses. 44

22. **Lower 700 MHz Band Licenses**. The Commission previously adopted criteria for defining three groups of small businesses for purposes of determining their eligibility for special provisions such as bidding credits.45 The Commission defined a "small business" as an entity that, together with its affiliates and controlling principals, has average gross revenues not exceeding $40 million for the preceding three years.46 A "very small business" is defined as an entity that, together with its affiliates and controlling principals, has average gross revenues that are not more than $15 million for the preceding three years.47 Additionally, the Lower 700 MHz Service had a third category of small business status for Metropolitan/Rural Service Area (MSA/RSA) licenses —"entrepreneur"— which is defined as an entity that, together with its affiliates and controlling principals, has average gross revenues that are not more than $3 million for the preceding three years.48 The SBA approved these small size

37 See Auction of AWS-1 and Broadband PCS Licenses Closes; Winning Bidders Announced for Auction 78, AU Docket No. 08-46, *Public Notice*, 23 FCC Rcd 7496 (2008) (*Auction No. 78 Public Notice*).

38 *Auction No. 78 Public Notice*, 23 FCC Rcd 7496 .

39 See Auction of Advanced Wireless Services Licenses Scheduled for June 29, 2006; Notice and Filing Requirements, Minimum Opening Bids, Upfront Payments and Other Procedures for Auction No. 66, AU Docket No. 06-30, *Public Notice*, 21 FCC Rcd 4562 (2006).

40 See Service Rules for Advanced Wireless Services in the 1.7 GHz and 2.1 GHz Bands, WT Docket No. 02-353,

Report and Order, 18 FCC Rcd 25162, App. B (2003), *modified by* Service Rules for Advanced Wireless Services

In the 1.7 GHz and 2.1 GHz Bands, *Order on Reconsideration*, 20 FCC Rcd 14058, App. C (2005).

41 See Auction of Advanced Wireless Services Licenses Closes; Winning Bidders Announced for Auction No. 66,

Public Notice, 21 FCC Rcd 10521 (2006) (*Auction No. 66 Public Notice*).

42 See *Auction No. 66 Public Notice*, 21 FCC Rcd 10521.

43 See Auction of AWS-1 and Broadband PCS Licenses Rescheduled for August 13, 2008; Notice and Filing Requirements, Minimum Opening Bids, Upfront Payments, and Other Procedures for Auction 78, AU Docket No.

08-46, *Public Notice*, 23 FCC Rcd 7496, 7499. Auction 78 also included an auction of broadband PCS licenses.

44 *See* Auction of AWS-1 and Broadband PCS Licenses Closes, Winning Bidders Announced for Auction 78, Down Payments Due September 9, 2008, FCC Forms 601 and 602 Due September 9, 2008, Final Payments Due September 23, 2008, Ten-Day Petition to Deny Period, *Public Notice*, 23 FCC Rcd 12749, 12749-65 (2008).

45 *See* Reallocation and Service Rules for the 698-746 MHz Spectrum Band (Television Channels 52-59), GN Docket No. 01-74, *Report and Order*, 17 FCC Rcd 1022 (2002) (*Channels 52-59 Report and Order*).

46 *See id.* at 1087-88 ¶ 172.

47 *See id.* at 1087-88 ¶ 172.

48 *See id.* at 1088, ¶ 173.

Federal Communications Commission FCC 13-157

standards.49

23. An auction of 740 licenses was conducted in 2002 (one license in each of the 734 MSAs/RSAs and one license in each of the six Economic Area Groupings (EAGs). Of the 740 licenses available for auction, 484 licenses were won by 102 winning bidders. Seventy-two of the winning bidders claimed small business, very small business, or entrepreneur status and won a total of 329 licenses. 50 A second auction commenced on May 28, 2003, closed on June 13, 2003, and included 256 licenses.51 Seventeen winning bidders claimed small or very small business status and won 60 licenses, and nine winning bidders claimed entrepreneur status and won 154 licenses.52 In 2005, the Commission completed an auction of 5 licenses in the lower 700 MHz band (Auction 60). All three winning bidders claimed small business status.

24. In 2007, the Commission reexamined its rules governing the 700 MHz band in the *700 MHz Second Report and Order*.53 An auction of A, B and E block licenses in the Lower 700 MHz band was held in 2008.54 Twenty winning bidders claimed small business status. Thirty three winning bidders claimed very small business status.

25. **Upper 700 MHz Band Licenses**. In the *700 MHz Second Report and Order*, the Commission revised its rules regarding Upper 700 MHz band licenses.55 In 2008, the Commission conducted Auction 73 in which C and D block licenses in the Upper 700 MHz band were available.56 Three winning bidders claimed very small business status.

26. **Specialized Mobile Radio**. The Commission adopted small business size standards for the purpose of determining eligibility for bidding credits in auctions of Specialized Mobile Radio (SMR) geographic area licenses in the 800 MHz and 900 MHz bands. The Commission defined a "small business" as an entity that, together with its affiliates and controlling principals, has average gross revenues not exceeding $15 million for the preceding three years.57 The Commission defined a "very small business" as an entity that together with its affiliates and controlling principals, has average gross revenues not exceeding $3 million for the preceding three years.58 The SBA has approved these small

49 *See* Letter from Aida Alvarez, Administrator, SBA, to Thomas Sugrue, Chief, WTB, FCC (Aug. 10, 1999)

(*Alvarez Letter 1999*).

50 *See* Lower 700 MHz Band Auction Closes, *Public Notice*, 17 FCC Rcd 17272 (2002).

51 *See* Lower 700 MHz Band Auction Closes, *Public Notice*, 18 FCC Rcd 11873 (2003).

52 *See* Lower 700 MHz Band Auction Closes, *Public Notice*, 18 FCC Rcd 11873 (2003).

53 Service Rules for the 698-746, 747-762 and 777-792 MHz Band, WT Docket No. 06-150, Revision of the

Commission's Rules to Ensure Compatibility with Enhanced 911 Emergency Calling Systems, CC Docket No. 94-

102, Section 68.4(a) of the Commission's Rules Governing Hearing Aid-Compatible Telephone, WT Docket No.

01-309, Biennial Regulatory Review – Amendment of Parts 1, 22, 24, 27, and 90 to Streamline and Harmonize

Various Rules Affecting Wireless Radio Services, WT Docket No. 03-264, Former Nextel Communications, Inc.

Upper700 MHz Guard Band Licenses and Revisions to Part 27 of the Commission's Rules, WT Docket No. 06-169,

Implementing a Nationwide, Broadband Interoperable Public Safety Network in the 700 MHz Band, PS Docket No.

06-229, Development of Operational, Technical and Spectrum Requirements for Meeting Federal, State, and Local

Public Safety Communications Requirements Through the Year 2010, WT Docket No. 96-86, *Second Report and*

Order, 22 FCC Rcd 15289 (2007) (*700 MHz Second Report and Order*).

54 *See* Auction of 700 MHz Band Licenses Closes, *Public Notice*, 23 FCC Rcd 4572 (2008) (*700 MHz Auction Public Notice*).

55 *700 MHz Second Report and Order*, 22 FCC Rcd 15289.

56 *See 700 MHz Auction Public Notice*, 23 FCC Rcd 4572.

57 47 C.F.R. §§ 90.810, 90.814(b), 90.912.

58 47 C.F.R. §§ 90.810, 90.814(b), 90.912.

Federal Communications Commission FCC 13-157

42

business size standards for both the 800 MHz and 900 MHz SMR Service.59 The first 900 MHz SMR auction was completed in 1996. Sixty bidders claiming that they qualified as small businesses under the $15 million size standard won 263 licenses in the 900 MHz SMR band. In 2004, the Commission held a second auction of 900 MHz SMR licenses and three winning bidders identifying themselves as very small businesses won 7 licenses.60 The auction of 800 MHz SMR licenses for the upper 200 channels was conducted in 1997. Ten bidders claiming that they qualified as small or very small businesses under the $15 million size standard won 38 licenses for the upper 200 channels.61 A second auction of 800 MHz SMR licenses was conducted in 2002 and included 23 BEA licenses. One bidder claiming small business status won five licenses.62

27. The auction of the 1,053 800 MHz SMR licenses for the General Category channels was conducted in 2000. Eleven bidders who won 108 licenses for the General Category channels in the 800

MHz SMR band qualified as small or very small businesses .63 In an auction completed in 2000, a total of 2,800 Economic Area licenses in the lower 80 channels of the 800 MHz SMR service were awarded.64 Of the 22 winning bidders, 19 claimed small or very small business status and won 129 licenses. Thus, combining all three auctions, 41 winning bidders for geographic licenses in the 800 MHz SMR band claimed to be small businesses.

28. In addition, there are numerous incumbent site-by-site SMR licensees and licensees with extended implementation authorizations in the 800 and 900 MHz bands. We do not know how many firms provide 800 MHz or 900 MHz geographic area SMR pursuant to extended implementation authorizations, nor how many of these providers have annual revenues not exceeding $15 million. One firm has over $15 million in revenues. In addition, we do not know how many of these firms have 1500 or fewer employees.65 We assume, for purposes of this analysis, that all of the remaining existing extended implementation authorizations are held by small entities, as that small business size standard is approved by the SBA.

29. **Wireless Communications Services**. This service can be used for fixed, mobile, radiolocation, and digital audio broadcasting satellite uses. The Commission defined "small business" for the wireless communications services (WCS) auction as an entity with average gross revenues of $40 million for each of the three preceding years, and a "very small business" as an entity with average gross revenues of $15 million for each of the three preceding years.66 The SBA approved these definitions.67

30. The Commission conducted an auction of geographic area licenses in the WCS service in 1997. In the auction, seven bidders that qualified as very small business entities won licenses, and one bidder that qualified as a small business entity won a license.

59 *See Alvarez Letter 1999*.

60 *See* 900 MHz Specialized Mobile Radio Service Spectrum Auction Closes: Winning Bidders Announced, *Public*

Notice, 19 FCC Rcd 3921 (2004).

61 *See* Correction to Public Notice DA 96-586 FCC Announces Winning Bidders in the Auction of 1020 Licenses to

Provide 900 MHz SMR in Major Trading Areas, *Public Notice*, 18 FCC Rcd 18367 (1996).

62 *See* Multi-Radio Service Auction Closes, *Public Notice*, 17 FCC Rcd 1446 (2002).

63 *See* 800 MHz Specialized Mobile Radio (SMR) Service General Category (851-854 MHz) and Upper Band (861-

865 MHz) Auction Closes; Winning Bidders Announced, *Public Notice*, 15 FCC Rcd 17162 (2000).

64 *See* 800 MHz SMR Service Lower 80 Channels Auction Closes; Winning Bidders Announced, *Public Notice*, 16

FCC Rcd 1736 (2000).

65 *See generally* 13 C.F.R. § 121.201, NAICS code 517210.

66 Amendment of the Commission's Rules to Establish Part 27, the Wireless Communications Service (WCS), GN

Docket No. 96-228, *Report and Order*, 12 FCC Rcd 10785, 10879 ¶ 194 (1997).

67 *See Alvarez Letter 1998*.

Made in the USA
Columbia, SC
29 October 2020